The Mind Doctor

A revealing portrayal of psychopharmacology corruption

A NOVEL BY
JOHN GILL

Copyright © 2019 John Gill
All rights reserved
First Edition

PAGE PUBLISHING, INC.
New York, NY

First originally published by Page Publishing, Inc. 2019

ISBN 978-1-68456-477-4 (Paperback)
ISBN 978-1-68456-478-1 (Digital)

Printed in the United States of America

Dedicated to Steven Vincent Gill

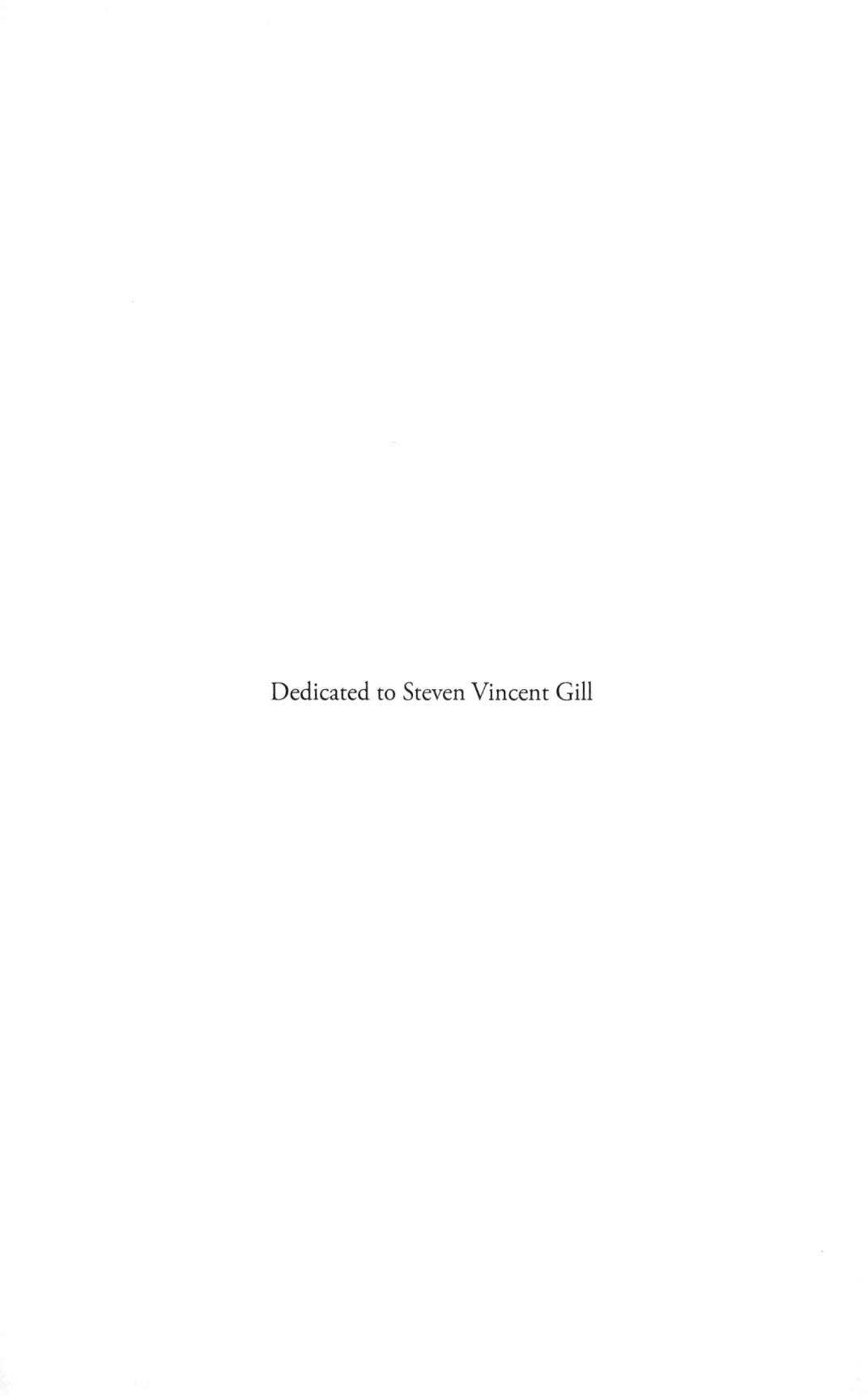

Also I will according to my ability and judgment prescribe a regimen for the health of the sick; but I will utterly reject harm and mischief.

—Part of the Hippocratic Oath to first do no harm, dating from the fifth century BCE

Contents

Introduction 11

1	Magic and Power 13
2	Invisible Hands 17
3	The Spirit Festival 24
4	The Mind Can Do Strange Things 31
5	To Counter Leftward Movement 37
6	Qualifying for Medical School 41
7	Only in Ne Win's Burma 50
8	The Dictator's Fountain of Youth 56
9	The New Rector 62
10	Constant Fear 67
11	Thein Accepts His First Bribe 71
12	Be Careful What You Promise 76
13	A Long Gauntlet 80
14	The Fixer Turns to an Old Friend 87
15	Disclosing and Negotiating 92
16	A Deal is Made 98
17	There's No Time to Pack 106
18	California At Last 112
19	The Hurdles are too High 116
20	Stealth is Required 121
21	At Last, A Psychiatric Practice 124
22	The Golden Age of Psychopharmacology 129
23	Akathisia 135
24	Gabicon has Many Uses 140
25	Reasoning Backward for Profit 144
26	A Life-Changing Accident 153

27	I Will Keep this Painting Forever	160
28	Cheerleaders Make Great Drug Reps	167
29	They Could Not Have Been More Different	172
30	Pharmacology Guesswork	176
31	Crisis Intervention Denied	183
32	Transfer Trauma	191
33	A New Onset Seizure	200
34	Hold Still	205
35	A Form for Barry to Sign	208
36	Now Look What We Have	213
37	Grief Sharing	220
38	Insidious Sepsis Takes Its Toll	224
39	The Big Golden Howled	229
40	In Pursuit of Justice	233
41	I Have the Same Motivation	239
42	The County Pays My Salary	249
43	He Sounds Well Qualified	255
44	How this Game is Played	260
45	Create a Disease for Profit	269
46	Juror Number Nine	282
47	The Judge Seeks Advice	285
48	The Twilight Zone	298
49	Neuroleptics or Antipsychotics?	303
50	The Chemical Imbalance Hypothesis	309
51	The Harold Shipman Standard of Care	319
52	Unfair Standards	327
53	The Lessons Learned Meeting	334
54	Individual Differences	343
55	Some Saw It Differently	352
56	No Say in the Matter	364
57	More Medications and New Neighbors	371
58	A Caged Tiger	377
59	A Clique Begins to Form	384
60	A Plan Begins to Form	392
61	A Hideout and Seven Outlaws	396
62	A Rube Goldberg Scheme?	401

63	This is The Place	407
64	Serious Planning by the Serious Seven	414
65	Nabbing the Prolific Prescriber	422
66	Playing Doctor	428
67	Join In	435
68	Delusions and Hallucinations	439
69	Midcourse Correction	444
70	Thein Repents	453
71	Do Not Call Me Doctor.	459
72	The Transformation	466

Acknowledgments 473

Introduction

(Thein rhymes with pain.)

Maunt Thein grew up in Burma during the turbulent years of the Ne Win dictatorship of 1962-1988. From an early age, Thein abhorred totalitarianism, and dreamed of living in democratic America.

When six years old, because of a cultural phenomenon—a spirit festival—the boy entered a recurring trance, but eventually recovered under the guidance of an insightful psychiatrist. Now Thein wanted to emulate Dr. Aung Tin, while still wanting to live in the United States.

In his desire to reduce human suffering, young Maunt Thein modeled himself after the original Buddha, Siddhārtha Gautama. But as he traveled a long, winding path toward his goal, opposing forces vied to shape Thein's character. Rumors circulated that his father, Brigadier General Maunt Saw, carried out brutal, secretive missions for Ne Win, including assassinating anyone who plotted to topple the regime. Thein agonized over whether he had inherited his father's sinister nature.

Also influencing him were the corrupt ways that medicine was taught and practiced in Ne Win's Burma as Thein struggled to become a licensed psychiatrist in his homeland. The next step would be for him to gain, by any means possible, a psychiatric practice in America.

There would be consequences when Burma's Maunt Thein became America's Dr. David Thein.

Chapter 1

Magic and Power

It is a strange desire to seek power, and to lose liberty.

—Francis Bacon
Essays (1612 edition)

A few years before installing himself as the ruler of Burma, military strongman Ne Win built a luxurious residence on the north fringe of Rangoon, the capital city. In 1962, General Ne Win deposed Prime Minister U Nu, and became both Prime Minister and President of the country. He continued to live in the same magnificent villa.

On a peninsula of Lake Inya, the spacious estate was protected by armed soldiers, tall masonry walls, and Ne Win's ownership of adjacent properties.

Designed for entertaining high-ranking military officers as well as for issuing orders to Burma's armed forces, the villa was both home and command post. Among its amenities, the residence harbored a den where the dictator met with soothsayers, and obsessed over retaining control of the country. Ne Win had not spared public funds in making the villa meet his every whim. Hidden entrances and exits enabled him to have secret meetings and, hopefully, to escape if anyone should try to topple his regime.

Ne Win cherished being able to meet with his astrologers without having to leave home and expose himself to the hazards inherent in public places. Instead, at any time of day or night, he could take refuge in a dimly lit, soundproof room attached to his office. Amid incense fumes, he made plans, smoked opium, and met with astrologers and numerologists. A golden statue of the original Buddha, Siddhārtha Guatama, oversaw the meetings. Buddha sat facing east—the direction of the rising sun—and grinned as if he knew the innermost thoughts of every person in every meeting.

Ne Win posted his most trusted guards at the door. No one entered his den without being searched even though they had been frisked before entering the villa.

Today he would meet with Min Thet Khin, an astrologer who had counseled him many times over the years. Khin was not late; he did not dare to be late. Rather, it was Ne Win's practice to enter his den early so he could acquire just the right mood to receive Khin's mystic predictions. Ne Win saluted the Buddha in a mocking way because at this stage of his life, the strong man had little respect for Buddhism. The statue's purpose was to impress visitors.

Ne Win smoked opium and relaxed. His intercom beeped.

"Who is it?"

"The honorable Min Thet Khin has arrived, Your Honor."

"Did you search him?"

"Yes, Chairman Ne Win. He carries only the charts of an astrologer."

"Send him in."

Min Thet Khin, a Burman in his seventies, bowed deeply before entering. Although Ne Win appreciated Khin's advice, both men understood it was the dictator who was to receive the greater respect.

Astrologer Khin knew the dictator would be basking in his glory while also fearing that his hold on power could be short-lived. A good astrologer pretends to know how stars and planets affect human affairs, but Khin was no mere interpreter. Years of exploiting his clients' fears had enabled him to gain the status of planetary puppeteer. Knowing how much Ne Win feared enemy plots, the old seer pulled the right strings to make the celestial bodies always address this fear.

Khin always provided a ritual—a yadayah chai—for the dictator to do to prevent tragic outcomes.

THE MIND DOCTOR

The two men sat at the table where Ne Win had smoked his opium, and the pungent smell lingered. Min Thet Khin held his own addiction at bay while he prepared to look into what the stars held in store for his powerful client.

The astrologer laid two large charts on the table. The first was the horoscope for Ne Win's birthday of July 10, 1910, and the second was the horoscope for the day of this meeting. Khin gave Ne Win time to inspect both charts, which Khin had adorned with flattering pictures of the dictator along with his favorite phrases. Ornate script proclaimed that Ne Win stands for Radiant Sun.

Although Ne Win held the titles of general, president, and prime minister, he liked "Chairman" most of all. As head of the *Burmese Way to Socialism*, Ne Win compared himself in stature to Chairman Mao Zedong, the head of China's Communist Party. Khin had stenciled "Chairman Ne Win" onto the astrological charts.

Khin spoke distinctly.

"The stars say nine is the most auspicious number for Your Honor."

"Nine is my lucky number?"

"Yes, Chairman Ne Win. You should take action on dates that contain nine."

In the years ahead, Ne Win was to make many decisions that involved the number nine. In September 1987, without warning the public, Ne Win would withdraw the country's bank notes and issue new currency in the denominations 45 and 90 because 4 and 5 add up to nine, and so do 9 and 0. His regime would provide no compensation for the currency that it was to withdraw, therefore many people would lose their savings overnight. University students who had saved for tuition would be particularly hard hit. But those events lay in the future on this meeting day in 1963.

Khin said, "The stars warn you to beware of dogs, especially dogs with crooked tails. Any dog with a tail that curls over its back is especially dangerous. Black dogs with crooked tails are the worst."

"I hate dogs."

"You are wise. Your Honor must stay away from dogs."

"I will order the army to kill all the dogs in any area before I go there."

Khin said, "The alignment of Jupiter and Saturn indicates there will be an attempt on your life within the next thirty days unless you do a yadayah chai."

Ne Win squirmed and gripped his chair's armrests. The dictator had no idea that the crafty old astrologer was playing him like a fish, and that the seer enjoyed watching the great man turn and twist. Even in the dim light, Min Thet Khin could see beads of sweat on Ne Win's forehead. Khin knew what few people did: that the country's leader was far from fearless. Ne Win suffered from paranoia, an overpowering emotion that the crafty Khin provoked at will, always netting some sort of benefit for himself—a feeling of power if nothing more tangible.

"Who wants to kill me?"

Khin had to be careful. A misstatement could cause Ne Win to order an undercover army officer known as the Fixer to kill innocent people. The astrologer chose his words carefully.

"The stars do not identify the would-be assassin. They say only that someone will come out of a crowd unless you take evasive action."

"What can I do?"

"Remember, the stars warn about black dogs with crooked tails. You must stomp on fresh dog entrails. Put a large amount in a tub. Take your shoes off, and do this in front of a full-length mirror.

"While stomping on the entrails, use your biggest revolver and shoot your image in the mirror. The gunfire, flying glass, disappearance of your image, and the blood and ooze between your toes will simulate your death. This will prevent any assassination attempt."

The planetary puppeteer wanted to give the tyrant time to calm down, so he delivered no more bad news. Eventually, Ne Win's mood mellowed enough for the two men to lie on their sides, and smoke opium.

After the astrologer left, Ne Win stepped into his office and told Sergeant Major Thu Si to order two soldiers to bring fresh dog intestines to his private lavatory, and to stand by for cleanup duty.

Chapter 2

Invisible Hands

The real rulers in Washington are invisible, and exercise power from behind the scenes.

—Felix Frankfurter
(American jurist)

In the 1800s, the British colonized a large region of Southeast Asia and named it Burma. But this region had never been a single country under one government. The British-declared borders encompassed many small, independent states that included over one hundred ethnic groups that lived primarily in the areas bordering China, Thailand, and Laos. The many different languages, customs, religions, and world views defied central governance.

During World War II, the Japanese occupied much of Burma. The British recaptured the country with the assistance of Burma's military, which at first had joined the Japanese campaign but switched sides when the British began to win.

For fourteen years beginning in January 1948—when Burma gained independence from the United Kingdom—the country had a parliamentary democracy. Although new and unsteady, this governmental system held great promise. But in March 1962, General Ne Win took over the country in a military coup, and eliminated any hint of governance by the people. He abolished the constitution, established *The Burmese Way to Socialism*, and cut off most contact with the outside world.

Ne Win consistently got what he wanted, and what he wanted was often weird, catching the populace off guard. His beliefs in astrology and numerology warped his judgment, while his greed resulted in ruinous policies for the nation. He had no idea how economics function at the national and international levels, and did not ask for advice from economic experts as did other Southeast Asian rulers.

Ne Win's policies held sway because he maintained the loyalty of virtually all his military officers by rewarding them with money and promotions. Easily corrupted, they eagerly shared in the wealth that Ne Win stole from the Burmese people by exploiting natural resources, by forcing citizens to do uncompensated labor, and by unfair taxation.

One of the officers that Ne Win rewarded the most was Brigadier General Maunt Saw, whom he called the Fixer. "Fixing" often meant assassinating Ne Win's foes. Ne Win had many soldiers and military intelligence men who would do his killing for him, but he often chose Maunt Saw for Saw's stealth. Ne Win reveled in the mysteries that resulted. He loved keeping his own henchmen in doubt as to why and how people had disappeared. The mysteries provoked fear that helped Ne Win control not only the populace but the military as well. Saw was one of very few army officers who consistently reported to the dictator in private.

Saw was married to Sang Yki, and they had a son named Maunt Thein. At an early age, Maunt Thein began to suspect what his father did for a living. He guessed his father's role in the military regime when he overheard Saw talking on the phone then giving cryptic instructions to Sang Yki. Gradually, he associated Saw's activities with disappearance of Ne Win's opponents. During these times Thein's father was absent from home for long periods, and returned exhausted, collapsing into slumber, after telling Thein that he was not to be disturbed. Saw gave his wife different instructions: to awaken him immediately if Ne Win's office called.

Ne Win's closest advisors, even the highest-ranking officers, feared Brigadier General Maunt Saw. Most military officers engaged in open conflict, for example in clashing with the many ethnic groups such as the Shan, the Karen, and the Wa, but Saw's specialty was covert operations.

No one but Ne Win and Saw knew exactly what his clandestine assignments were, although the head of military intelligence was aware of Saw's basic duties, owing to the Fixer's requests for information. Spy networks gathered information on senior members of the government and the armed forces, and informed Ne Win whether certain persons appeared to be internal threats.

When Colonel Myat Hmen Tin Oo was head of military intelligence, he alerted Ne Win to several potential coups. If the dictator agreed that someone appeared disloyal, there was no attempt to rehabilitate the individual; instead, he was "purged." The only question was what form the purging would take.

If purging were to be done by arresting the suspect for treason, or for a trumped-up charge of corruption, Brigadier General Maunt Saw would not be involved. But if the suspect was to be quickly and permanently neutralized, Ne Win selected the Fixer to handle the matter.

Saw's effectiveness depended on his being unrecognized. He usually wore nondescript civilian clothes and sometimes disguises, and used a hidden passageway when entering and exiting Ne Win's command post. Skill in the martial arts rounded out Saw's credentials.

Ne Win feared being killed during a coup or being charged by an international court for crimes against humanity. The Fixer secured his standing with the dictator by calming the tyrant's nerves. Saw assured Ne Win that, by working behind the scenes, he could not only quell fledgling insurrections, but could make it appear that it was Ne Win's subordinates—acting without his knowledge—who perpetrated any crime against humanity.

Saw had studied law at Harvard University during the 1950s and graduated with honors. During his years at Harvard, he often conversed far into the night with fellow students about systems of government. They debated the strengths and weaknesses of communism, socialism, capitalism, totalitarianism, and even anarchism.

Saw hoped to become a military advisor back home, so he made friends with students who someday might hold positions of power. To influence Burma's government, he would need politically connected allies. To ensure that he could count on a few close friends, he pledged that he would assist them in any way possible once he returned to Burma, and was established in the government.

Saw cultivated especially the friendship of twenty-three-year-old Lester Jordan, whose father was an intelligence officer for US president Dwight Eisenhower. Lester had set his sights on serving on the staff of one of the senators who were friends of his father. Lester's father often said that elected officials might not last long in Washington's treacherous political environment, but that a senior staff member could stay in place for decades, perhaps serving a succession of senators during that time. The senior staff, the elder Jordan said, could strongly influence legislation by working diligently behind the scenes.

Lester sometimes spoke of the "right of the first draft," regarding matters such as proposed legislation. His father had taught him that a staffer could be as powerful as a senator by planting ideas in his boss's head. The key was to be the person who first drafts a position paper on an important issue or a proposed statute. The concept is the same as a law clerk drafting a legal decision for a Supreme Court justice. Senators and judges routinely claim as their own the ideas conceived by their staff. A draft document might undergo many revisions by various committees, but a staff member's original core ideas often survived.

Some of Saw's fellow law students at Harvard were married and lived off campus; some had held career positions and had returned to school to bolster their credentials. Others, mostly the younger ones like Saw and Lester, lived in dormitories. Some of Saw's classmates had taken other courses together, and knew each other well. Cliques formed, and five or six of Saw's classmates often met for coffee if examinations were imminent or for beer if the exams were behind them.

The most common place to get together and discuss the law was the lounge on the ground floor of the dorm where Saw and Lester lived. The discussions usually were intense because these aspiring attorneys were rehearsing roles they hoped to play in future careers. One cold February evening in 1956, five students gathered in the lounge.

Ralph Matell, a tall, thin man thirty years old, sank into a stuffed chair.

"What's our topic this evening? I'm ready for a good argument."

"So am I," said a man called Brit because he always defended the United Kingdom's past behavior as the world's foremost colonizer.

Pop, a man of forty-five with gray hair and glasses, said, "I know the perfect topic in view of that awful murder in Baltimore that's in the news. Let's talk about mental illness and the law. In this case, the suspect plans to plead not guilty by reason of insanity."

Sullivan, a big Irish fellow said, "It's a real shame that not guilty by reason of insanity fails so often as a defense in court.

"Juries simply don't appreciate how insidious mental illnesses can be. They can sneak up on an unsuspecting person. The public is poorly informed and apathetic. Most jurors like simple answers to the question of why people kill, and evil is the simplest answer. Well, sometimes it's the wrong answer."

Getting carried away by the discussion, Saw surprised himself when he said, "I disagree, Sullivan. Mental illness should never succeed as a legal defense.

"Being crazy should not be considered a mitigating factor. In fact, insanity should be considered an aggravating factor, same as robbery is held to be a worse crime if the perpetrator is armed. Mental illness should weigh against the accused. A killer might very well be insane, but insanity doesn't result from a brain injury which is no fault of the suspect. That's myth.

"The wrongdoer is deranged because he is evil, because of wrongful things he did in a past life. Spirits are punishing him. They've made him insane, so insanity is actually proof that the accused is evil. He should be summarily executed as soon as a court-appointed psychiatrist declares him insane. There's no need for a trial."

The group fell silent. Was Saw joking about spirits causing mental illness and that this justifies execution without a trial? He seemed serious. Moreover, he had never told a joke in the classroom or in any of these extracurricular discussions.

Saw realized he had screwed up, but he knew how to rescue himself.

"Just kidding. I thought I'd bring levity to a gloomy subject."

The retraction brought laughter, and the group went on to discuss mental illness and the law.

Saw had a hidden agenda every time students got together. More than wanting to learn from the discussions, he wanted future contacts, persons he could call on for help with political problems. He worked hard to make sure the most likely to succeed of his classmates would remember him if he contacted them years later from far away Burma.

However, Saw knew it would be futile to ask someone like Lester Jordan for help unless the two kept in touch after graduation from law school. In future years, Saw wrote or phoned Lester every few months. The two corresponded and exchanged snapshots of their families. Both found government positions, which they described in glowing terms. But both disguised exactly who they worked for and their specific duties as well. Saw did not tell Lester that he worked directly for the dictator of Burma, and Lester did not tell Saw that he had secured employment with the US Central Intelligence Agency.

When back home in Burma, Saw desperately wanted to believe that his years at Harvard Law School had made him especially effective at achieving objectives. He never practiced law, and no one in Burma could take Ne Win to court anyway. But his legal training gave him a frame of reference for viewing his relationship with the dictator. Saw fancied himself as Ne Win's lawyer, a special kind of lawyer which worked entirely behind the scenes, and which the tyrant particularly needed. This frame of reference enabled Saw to rationalize that his gruesome duties were justified. Harvard had taught him that the law is elastic, dependent on interpretations of powerful persons like law enforcement officials, lawyers, and judges. Saw now viewed himself as one of those powerful persons, entitled to take advantage of the law's elasticity. His unique interpretation stretched to whole new dimensions the doctrine that even the guilty deserve legal representation. In his eyes, Ne Win could do no wrong, and Saw was his protector, his Fixer.

An early example of the Fixer's handiwork was his success in fooling the international news media into believing that Ne Win's March 1962 takeover of the government was "a bloodless coup," words that the media repeated many times in print and over the air. This misleading catch phrase took root because of Saw's skill in working secretly through Burma's propagandists. One of Ne Win's opponents, Sao Mye Thaik, was shot dead and another, Sao Kya Seng, disappeared after being stopped at a checkpoint near Taungyi.

As early as 1962, Ne Win showed his predilection to rule through violence and fear. On July 7, students at the University of Rangoon protested against the new, autocratic government. The Fourth Burmese Rifles Battalion, led by Sein Lwin, the commander for the university region, suppressed the demonstrations by shooting dead 130 students. The next day, army troops dynamited the Students Union Building. These troops also were led by Sein Lwin who forever after was known as the Butcher of Rangoon.

Chapter 3

The Spirit Festival

The nat cult has many features that resemble shamanism. In the Burmese nat cult, the preietesses, as well as the priests, fall into a trance, during which they act as oracles or healers to the community that commissioned the ritual.

—Jukka O. Miettinen
Asian Traditional Theater

It was 1970. Maunt Thein was five years old. His father was reviewing their options as he prepared to enroll Thein in school. Despite his loyalty to the head of state, Saw was upset over what the tyrant had done to the educational system. Ne Win had slashed the education budget and decimated the opportunities for young people. At least Saw was among the military elite so that his choices of a school for his son were far better than the choices available to poor families.

For the poor, schooling at the lower grades had traditionally taken place at Buddhist monasteries, whereas secondary and tertiary education had occurred at government schools. Also, in the early years after Burma gained independence in 1948, the country had an extensive network of missionary schools that employed foreign teachers who recognized the importance of the English language for its worldwide usage. But Ne Win decreed that since English was the language of Burma's former colonizers, it no longer would be taught in the nation's schools.

Being fluent in English, Saw felt strongly that his son must master this widely used language, which he and his wife spoke at home, along with Burmese. Saw resented Ne Win having ordered the military to deport foreign teachers, and was concerned that isolationism could impair his son's education.

Because of the government's lack of investment in education under Ne Win, schools charged unofficial fees, which mainly went to the teachers to offset their unrealistically low salaries. Many families, particularly those in poorer rural areas, could not afford the fees, and withdrew their children from school.

But elite and well-connected parents—which usually meant military officers—still could send their children to the private schools which had been less deprived by Ne Win. This is where Thein began school for he was among the privileged few.

Although highly educated, Saw believed in spirits. Having grown up in Burma, he had heard many stories about spirits affecting people in both good and bad ways. Called nats, almost all these spirits once were humans who had died violently, and could not escape their lamentable fates. They were in limbo between their past lives and the present one.

Nats had fascinating biographies. Min Maha Giri, Lord of the Great Mountain, was a popular and handsome blacksmith who was burned to death in the ancient city of Tagaung by a king who feared the young man would contend for his throne. Min's wife, Shwe N'bay, also became a nat, half serpent half human, for she died of heartbreak after her husband was killed.

Belief in nats was widespread, and Saw had learned about them from his father. In turn, he was teaching his son, Thein, which nats to ask for favors and which to be wary of.

It was 1971. Thein entered his sixth year. Saw decided it was time for the boy to see firsthand how spirits and people interact. He took his wife and son to the biggest spirit festival in Burma, held annually at the village of Taungbyone, fourteen kilometers north of

THE SPIRIT FESTIVAL

Mandalay. Each year the festival ran for a week during the August full moon. Similar to a huge county fair in America, the celebration attracted thousands of visitors from far and near.

Lodging was not available in Taungbyone, so Saw rented a hotel room in Mandalay. The room was clean and the service adequate because he paid a premium price.

The family commuted by cab between Mandalay and the village. Most people attending the spirit festival, called a nat pwe, crowded onto buses so overloaded that many sat on the rooftops. Others rode motorcycles and bicycles. Thousands walked, despite dust and sweltering heat. Saw chose a taxi because, of the limited transportation options, this was the safest and least uncomfortable. Even so, the trip was slow and grueling, owing to the throng that jammed the road.

Again, Saw paid extra, this time to persuade the driver to refuse additional riders. Saw's family traveled in style compared to the masses who were inching their way along the narrow, dusty road toward the village of spirits.

The Fixer normally avoided crowds but there was no other way to expose his son to the special ceremonies that Taungbyone was famous for. Saw's martial arts skills and concealed Glock pistol made him feel he could handle any problem that might arise.

During the sweltering cab ride, Saw tried to ease the discomfort by entertaining his wife and son with stories of the nats they would connect with at the festival. Besides seeing statues of nats, they would witness people falling into trances as spirits entered their bodies.

Saw said, "This festival is the main gathering place in Burma for spirit mediums. According to legend, two Indian brothers, Byat Wi and Byat Ta, gained extraordinary powers after eating a dead alchemist they found.

"The older brother, Byat Wi, lost his supernatural power after he walked under a clothesline on which women's skirts were hanging."

The cab driver could not resist helping to tell the legend.

"Because of his cannibalism, Byat Wi was captured and severely punished. He died after his loved ones tried to revive him by giving him a quid of betel and a cup of water. Byat Ta, the younger brother, was killed by King Anawrahta's magic lance after he was late to bring flowers from Mt. Popa for the royal audience."

At first, Saw did not mind the cab driver cutting in because the man's passion was part of Thein's education about the spirit world. The taxi driver's testimony was a good example of the importance that most Burmese people attached to nats. For this family outing, the Fixer had willed himself into a more tolerant frame of mind than he usually maintained.

Saw said, "Byat Ta's wife, Popa Medaw, was so grief stricken that she also died. Fifteen years later, the two sons of Byat Ta and Popa Medaw, who had been adopted by King Anawratha, forgot to bring one brick each for construction of a shrine known as the Pagoda of Wishes. King Anawratha learned of this and gave the order to hit them a light blow with a fillet stick.

"The king's son was devious, so he defied his father's instructions and had the two young men hit hard with a bamboo stick. Both of Byat Ta's sons died."

The cab driver cut in again.

"The names of these two sons are Shwe Phyin Gyi and Shwe Phyin Ngeh, so they are called the Shwe Brothers. They are the main purpose for this big festival. Many pilgrims and mediums, which we call nat-kadaws, come once a year to Taungbyone to see the reincarnations of the two brothers."

This time the cab driver's commentary angered Saw because it usurped what he had planned to say. But he hid his displeasure.

Saw said, "Nat kadaw means spirit's wife. Statues of the two brothers, along with two bricks, were placed in the Pagoda of Wishes."

The talkative taxi driver uttered a short commercial.

"Taungbyone is the biggest nat pwe in Burma. Dancing, singing, drinking booze, merchants selling goods, people milling about—all this goes on day and night."

The cab finally arrived at the nat pwe. The Maunt Saw family was happy to exit the cramped, sweltering taxi, but felt overwhelmed by the immense crowd and the loud music.

Statues of nats were everywhere. Both the spirit mediums and the crowd were offering the statues food, drink, and cigarettes.

THE SPIRIT FESTIVAL

Some gave bottles of Jack Daniels and Johnny Walker. Alcohol was not offered to any nat who had shunned the tonic while a human. Coconuts and bananas were piled at the feet of the statues.

Food for sale included steamed rice, fried rice, noodles, bananas, coconuts, roasted chicken, dried fish, betel nuts, prawns, mangos, papayas, shrimp, scallops, and squid. A Ferris wheel fascinated Thein for it was powered entirely by boys. Those on the ground pushed and pulled on the cars while others caused the wheel to accelerate by climbing the frame and jumping into the descending cars. Thein had never seen anything like the conglomeration of food, carnival rides, colorful clothes, loud music, dancing, singing, and play acting.

Most of the booths were the same stalls found at carnivals in other countries, and the crowd mingled with the barkers and entertainers. There also were larger, partially enclosed areas where the nat kadaws performed alongside percussion orchestras. In such areas, the foot traffic was more regulated. Some of the larger enclosures had stages for the performers and seating for spectators wealthy enough to pay the cover charge.

Saw guided his wife and son to a large enclosure which had a stage and appeared to offer one of the better-organized performances. For good seats, Saw paid more kyat than most of the revelers earned in a week.

A nat kadaw with long hair and a microphone was describing the next spirit that "she" would call forth from another world. The spectator sitting next to Saw was telling his companions colorful facts about the on-stage entertainer. Although "she" claimed to be the wife of the soon-to-appear nat, the performer actually was a male crossdresser.

As a boy of six, Thein was overwhelmed not only by the crowd but also by the information he was hearing. He had never heard of a man pretending to be a woman.

The nat kadaw's stage name was Thiri Sanda and "she" wore a long, flowing robe of red, yellow, and green to which paper money was pinned in many places.

Sanda said she would call forth Shwe Phyin Gyi, the older of the two Shwe Brothers. She began to sing and dance. An interpreter provided background information.

"Once upon a time during the reign of King Anawrahta of Bagan, there lived two mighty warriors, Byat Wi and his younger brother, Byat Ta. Byat Ta fell in love with a princess of Mt. Popa, and they had two sons, Shwe Phyin Gyi and Shwe Phyin Negh. After their father was murdered in one of the court's intrigues, King Anawrahtha took pity on the two boys and made them his favorites.

"Then King Anawrahta went to war against the Chinese to obtain the Buddha's tooth relic, and on his way back home made camp at this very village of Taungbyone. The king commanded that a wish-granting pagoda be erected at this site to mark his expedition. He also commanded his followers to contribute one brick each to the pagoda's construction.

"But the two brothers, now in their teens, were more interested in drinking toddy wine, betting on rooster fights, and having fun. Both brothers forgot the king's command, and this left two spaces vacant on the inside brick wall of the new pagoda.

"The king came to the pagoda's consecration ceremony and saw the two empty spaces in the brick wall. When told that the two brothers had ignored his command, he told his courtiers to punish them. The king wanted them caned lightly with a fillet stick, but jealous court officials had other ideas.

"They bound the two youths, and bludgeoned them to death. Because of their violent deaths, both became nats.

"The time came for the king to leave for Bagan, but his raft would not move. The two young nats appeared and told of their having been bludgeoned. The king took pity on them and commanded that they be given this region as their fiefdom. Two life-sized statues were made, and this started the custom of the Taungbyone Nat Festival every August."

Sanda was calling for Shwe Phyin Gyi to come forth from the spirit world.

THE SPIRIT FESTIVAL

"Gyi, we all love you. We are sorry that King Anawratha's disobedient helpers killed you. We cannot imagine a worse crime. Please show yourself so that we may better praise you."

The spirit's wife twirled and sang in time with the orchestra's beat. Suddenly, Sanda collapsed, but kept moving while flat on the stage floor. She twisted and spun about. Two stage hands raised the beautiful person to a standing position, but she was limp and could not stand on her own.

Sanda was moaning, but Thein understood little of what she was saying. Then he heard her say, "I am not Shwe Phyin Gyi, but he has entered my mind and body, and now I must be with him. Oh, Gyi, thank you for spending precious time with me."

Sanda was being helped off the stage and the crowd was cheering. Thien's world began to spin. He fell forward from his sitting position onto the wood shavings that covered the floor.

The next thing he knew, his father was asking, "Thein, are you all right? Can you hear me?"

Thein heard the question, but saw only a blur. Gradually his vision cleared, and his father had a distinct outline again.

Thiri Sanda had given a convincing performance. One in five in the audience momentarily blacked out. Others danced wildly, gyrating in time to the music. Sanda's dance movements had been hypnotic, and spectator reactions were contagious. Saw believed Thein would be all right because other affected people seemed to be recovering and to have enjoyed the trance experience. He helped Thein to his feet and to walk outside where the air was not as stale or the music as loud.

Thein's parents tended to believe their son was simply overcome by emotion and the power of suggestion from the performer and the crowd. However, neither Saw nor Sang Yki ruled out the possibility that Shwe Phyin Gyi had entered Thein's being.

Chapter 4

The Mind Can Do Strange Things

It's not what we don't know that gives us trouble. It's what we know that ain't so.

—Will Rogers
(American actor and humorist)

Even a day of magic must end. The Maunt Saw family returned by taxi to their Mandalay hotel room.

Thein crawled between the sheets at 9:00 p.m., but was awakened at midnight by Shwe Phyin Gyi who wore a longyi and sandals, and stank of whisky, tobacco, and betel. The scowl and deep voice scared Thein the most.

"So Daddy wanted you to learn about nats! Well, the lesson is leave us alone."

Thein said nothing.

"Don't go to spirit festivals and don't give me any coconuts. I hate coconuts. I've been given millions of the damned things."

Shwe Phyin Gyi came closer. "I'll sit on your chest so you can't breathe."

The nat disappeared, but Thein felt a great weight on his chest. He began to wheeze as if from whooping cough.

Saw and Sang Yki came to Thein's aid. Saw gave artificial respiration, and his son began to breathe normally.

"It was Shwe Phyin Gyi. He sat on my chest."

Saw began reciting ways he might appease the powerful nat. When he named a gift of coconuts, Thein said, "No, Mr. Shwe Phyin Gyi hates coconuts. He said we must leave him alone and not go to the festival."

Thein's remarks ran counter to everything Saw had ever heard about the Shwe Brothers. Nevertheless, he took his son's advice. Instead of attending the nat pwe the next day, the family returned to their Rangoon villa.

In the weeks that followed, Thein suffered sporadic night-time attacks that suppressed his breathing. Shwe Phyin Gyi appeared and said he was glad the Maunt Saw family had been leaving him alone but that he still would sit on Thein's chest now and then to make sure there was no backsliding.

As the weeks went by, and the nat continued to attack Thein, the boy spent more time alone and was losing weight. Saw sought advice from varied sources as to how he could help his son. Saw considered exorcism, a practice used in many parts of the world. The Catholic Church had a long history of exorcising spirits on thousands of occasions. But shamen and the nat kadaws in lower Burma advised Saw against exorcism, saying this ritual could further upset Shwe Phyin Gyi.

The Fixer turned next to Buddhist monks who said they rarely practiced exorcism and when they did, it was in the form of a request because they wanted the spirit to regard any exiting from a human as in the spirit's interest. The Buddhist process was more appeasement than exorcism, and Saw had already prayed to, and negotiated with, Shwe Phyin Gyi without success. During each discussion with practitioners of animism or of Buddhism, Saw explained that Shwe Phyin Gyi had told Thein to simply leave him alone because he was exhausted from too much appeasement and too many coconuts.

Saw also took his son to physicians in Rangoon, but they did not find anything physically wrong. The medical doctors advised Saw to take Thein to a psychiatrist, but there were two problems with this advice. First, the Fixer did not want to admit even to himself that anyone in his family might have a mental illness. But he eventually set this reluctance aside, realizing that his personal reservations were less important than getting Thein the medical help he needed. The second problem was more obstinate.

In Burma, doctors largely depended on government support. Ne Win had so severely cut government funding for medical specialties that many doctors had gone out of business or had left the country. Saw found only two private psychiatrists still in business in Rangoon. He interviewed both, and decided that he could not trust either to keep Thein's medical condition a secret if their files were audited by Ne Win's functionaries.

Saw was wondering where next to seek help for his son when he learned that Ne Win periodically traveled to Vienna, Austria to see a psychiatrist. The dictator obtained psychiatric treatment in a foreign country, accessing healthcare that he denied Burma's citizens.

Ne Win saw Dr. Hans Hoff, Chairman of the Psychiatric and Neurological University Hospital of Vienna and author of the 1961 book, *Contemporary European Psychiatry*. Dr. Hoff had assisted Nazi doctors with experiments during World War II. He had infected patients with malaria to see if the resulting fever would counteract mental illness caused by syphilis, learning that high body temperatures failed to kill the causative bacteria. Despite his checkered past, Hans Hoff had regained respectability, and was well established in Vienna.

Imitating his ruler, Saw decided the best way to get psychiatric care for his son was to go outside Burma. He believed that of the Southeast Asian nations, Singapore was the most advanced in healthcare.

Like Burma, Singapore was ruled by a long-term autocrat, but his policies differed greatly from Ne Win's. Burma was a large country with vast natural resources which suffered economically because of mismanagement. Singapore was a small island nation with few resources, but was prospering because its dictator, Lee Kuan Yew, knew how to manage a nation's economy. Although he often denied people participation in their government, and jailed many unjustly, Lee made his country into an international financial center and manufacturer of finished products.

Saw found a good psychiatrist in Singapore. He had not looked for a renowned expert, but for a doctor who could relate to his son. Dr. Aung Tin, who had left Burma to work in Singapore, spoke not only English but Burmese as well.

One day in October, following the nat pwe of August 1971, a small aircraft carrying Saw and Thein landed at Singapore's Changi Airport. They took a taxi to Dr. Aung Tin's office which was near the Woodbridge Mental Hospital on Yio Chu Kang Road. Saw talked with the psychiatrist then waited in the outer office while Thein and his doctor considered the boy's problem with one of Burma's legendary nats.

Dr. Tin said, "Thein, would you like to have a chocolate bar?"

Thein said nothing.

"I always eat a chocolate bar at this time of day. So please excuse me while I have one."

Dr. Tin unwrapped the treat while looking as happy as he could.

"Don't you want one? I have plenty. I keep a big stock."

Thein said, "OK, I would like one."

The psychiatrist and the patient sat there eating chocolate in silence. Finally, Dr. Tin spoke.

"Your dad said you sometimes have trouble breathing at night. Would you like to tell me what happens?"

"A big nat named Shwe Phyin Gyi comes into my bedroom and wakes me up. Then he says bad things and sits on my chest so I cannot breathe."

"Did Mr. Gyi say why he does this?"

"He said it is because Father, Mother, and I insulted him by giving him coconuts at the Taungbyone nat pwe."

"Why does Mr. Gyi torment you instead of your dad or mom?"

"I do not know."

"Have you ever wondered why you?"

"Maybe it is because I am the littlest, the youngest."

"I think you're right. It's easier for him to bully you than your mom or dad. What did you think of the spirit festival? What was the biggest impression it made on you?"

Thein hesitated.

"Don't worry. I won't tell your dad. What did you feel while the nat kadaw was performing?"

"I was scared. I did not know what was going on. The music was so loud, and so many things happened all at the same time."

"We're getting somewhere, Thein. Can I tell you what I think happened?"

"Yes."

"This will surprise you, but I don't believe in nats. There's a term that I want you to learn. It is 'the power of suggestion.'"

Dr. Tin asked Thein to say the phrase aloud and then to repeat it. Thein did so.

"There are many ways to suggest that someone do what I want. The most common way is to just say it. Your mom might say, 'Thein, I suggest you wear a raincoat to school today because it's the start of the monsoon season.' But your mom might make the same suggestion by putting on her own raincoat before going outdoors. This will make it more likely that you will put on your coat as well."

"What does this have to do with the big nat sitting on my chest?"

"A spirit festival is a performance by actors, not a real calling forth of spirits, even if the crowd thinks that's what is happening. The whole atmosphere, the music, the dancing, and singing all suggest that spirits are real and that they may invade your body and mind. And when the spirit wife and some of the crowd act like or even believe they are invaded—well, the suggestion becomes very strong, especially for a young, impressionable person."

"You think I imagined that Mr. Shwe Phyin Gyi came into my room and sat on my chest? But I saw him and heard him talk."

"The brain is a physical organ, and the mind is its workings, the thoughts we have. The mind can do strange things and make unreal things seem real. As an intelligent, impressionable boy, you were overwhelmed by the acting and the crowd.

"The next time that coconut-hating Shwe Phyin Gyi shows up, tell him that Dr. Aung Tin said for him to take a hike. My doctor's orders are for you to tell that creep that you like coconuts. And tell him that if he tries to sit on your chest, you'll sit on his."

Thein laughed. Dr. Tin's advice brought him immediate relief. The answer lay within himself, how he looked at his problem. There would be no more giving in to a spirit that his doctor said does not exist.

"But what will Father say? He believes in nats."

"You can respect your dad's beliefs. You just don't have to believe in nats yourself. Just tell your dad that your doctor told you how to deal with the nat and that you'll take it from here. He will appreciate your new take-charge attitude. So you can respect your dad while telling the imaginary nat to jump in the lake."

Thein thought that he would like to be a psychiatrist when he grew up.

Chapter 5

To Counter Leftward Movement

It is easier for a tyrant to act than to think.

—Yugoslav proverb

Ne Win was hanging out in his den at his Inya Lake villa. His astrologer, Min Thet Khin, was due to arrive within an hour. There was time to smoke opium. Soon, the dictator's paranoia subsided, and he felt that he was history's greatest military strategist. The astrologer arrived.

Once again, Khin bowed and showed respect. Once again, Ne Win would ask questions and receive advice.

"Many of my subjects and even some of my officers are moving to the left politically. I don't like it."

"I appreciate your concern, Chairman Ne Win."

The dictator said, "I expect an attack from the left."

This was a variation of a familiar theme. Once again, the wizard was dealing with Ne Win's fear of losing power. Khin lowered his eyes to show sympathy and respect.

"How do I stop this leftward movement, and ward off an attack?"

Khin had never been asked how to counter a movement to the political left. The astrologer did not know enough about government to advise Ne Win to negotiate with those he felt were a threat, or to consult his cabinet members, or to hold a referendum. Besides, such advice was too mundane. The astrologer wanted to propose a dramatic plan.

"Allow me to consult your astrology chart, Chairman Ne Win. It will indicate a course of action."

The wizard pretended to study planetary positions.

"The reason for the leftward movement is that people are driving on the left side of the road. When thousands of people do that day after day, they naturally become left-leaning and drag others along with them in their beliefs."

"This makes sense."

"Chairman Ne Win should decree that people must drive on the right-hand side of the road."

"This too makes sense."

Khin said, "Just as movement of stars affects the affairs of man, movement of thousands of cars affect the thoughts of your officers and subjects."

The next day, Ne Win issued a decree: beginning in seven months, all vehicles were to drive on the right-hand side of all highways, roads, and streets. From May to December was ample time for people to get used to the idea. Traffic signs would have to be changed, but Ne Win did not foresee any other problems. He did not require there to be lefthand drive cars to accompany his new rightside road rule.

Farmer Than Thaw Tun owned two hectares forty kilometers north of Rangoon where he had raised poultry and vegetables for the last twenty years. Ne Win's policies required Tun to give chickens and vegetables to the army when it camped in the area, making life harder for him and his family. Tun was nearing fifty, and none of his extended family had ever lived past fifty-five. He wished the government would leave him alone to live out his last years without having to give away much of what he eked from the land. In recent years he had raised chickens and Chinese cabbage, using the chicken manure to fertilize the cabbage plants. It was a hard life, but he managed to feed his family and to sell a small surplus at the village market three kilometers west of his farm. He never hauled the chickens and the cabbage in his ox cart at the same time. In one trip he hauled chickens only, and after cleaning the cart, hauled cabbage only in the next trip.

Than Thaw Tun traveled a country road in taking his cabbage or chickens to the village market. Tun could not read, and had not heard of the rule that changed which side of the road he was to use. When he noticed oncoming cars on his side of the road he did not make much of it. He had always used the left side and continued to do so.

Tun owned two bullocks, one four years old and the other five. He had reared them, having owned the mother ox. Tun had trained both bullocks and named them Sam and Samson. Tun kept the oxcart, the yoke, and reins in good repair, but he lavished even greater care on his bullocks. People at the village market often said how robust and sleek Sam and Samson were, causing Tun's chest to swell with pride.

One morning, Tun was on his way to market, allowing Sam and Samson to find the way as they had done many times. Tun, Sam, Samson, and the cart full of cabbage were moving along the left side of the country road as they approached a curve ahead.

Saw was teaching ten-year-old Thein how to drive. He owned three cars, and was training his son to drive the Mazda instead of the more expensive Toyota or Mercedes. A seat cushion was all it took to enable Thein to see over the steering wheel, but the foot pedals had to be lengthened for him to reach them.

Accustomed to doing things his way, the Fixer saw no reason to postpone the driver training until Thein was old enough to qualify for a learner's permit, but he saw a great need to get permission from the nat known as God of the Road. Most drivers in Burma would not start their engines without first asking Shwe Nyaung Bin to bless their vehicle and their journey.

"Thein, we have checked the water and oil. But before we leave, we must do one more thing."

Saw began to chant.

"Good morning, Shwe Nyaung Bin. Good morning to you, God of the Road. We ask your blessing for our safety today. Please keep our car running smoothly and ourselves safe from accidents."

Saw had always asked for the blessing of Shwe Nyaung Bin, but until this morning had never said the words aloud for Thein to hear.

Saw tied a red and white ribbon to the hood ornament. Without looking at his son or saying anything further, he settled in the front passenger seat.

This was Thein's third driving lesson, and his control of the vehicle had improved enough that Saw was relaxed as they left their Inya Lake villa.

Saw had carefully selected the places where Thein would learn to drive. At first, the boy had driven only on pavement. Saw decided that today his son was ready to drive on a country dirt road. It was time for Thein to get the feel of how a dirt road with patches of gravel affected a car's steering and braking.

They drove north from Rangoon, and as time passed, Saw began to gaze at the countryside. Rounding a brush-lined bend that curved hard right, they came face-to-face with a man and two oxen. Thein stomped the brake pedal. The car skidded and turned sideways in the road. Gravel and dirt flew through the air, landing on Tun, Sam, Samson, and the cabbage.

In an instant, Saw was out of the car, scolding Tun in Burmese. Thein sat behind the steering wheel, trembling.

"Dirt farmer, don't you know the rules of the road? Prime Minister Ne Win ordered cars to drive on the right side of the road."

"Kind sir, I'm not driving a car."

"Cars and oxcarts are the same under traffic law."

"No one told me to travel on the right. I'm sorry, kind sir. I'll do that from now on."

Tun spent the next hour picking gravel and dirt out of the cabbage. Sam and Samson had remained calm.

Saw told Thein to pull the Mazda ahead to a safe distance from the blind curve. They sat in the stationary car for a few minutes before continuing the trip.

"Son, you handled that badly. You should've veered left instead of stomping the brakes. Cars skid in the gravel. If a car was coming, we could've been killed."

Thein took the scolding without defending himself.

Saw said, "Thank you, O God of the Road for keeping us safe today."

Chapter 6

Qualifying for Medical School

Consistency is contrary to nature, contrary to life. The only completely consistent people are the dead.

—Aldous Huxley
Do What You Will (1929)

It was 1982. Thein was about to graduate from high school. Ne Win's flawed educational policies limited Thein's choices of universities if he were to remain in the country. Many of his friends relocated to other countries to pursue career goals. The dictator closed most universities for months at a time because university students were prone to lead civil uprisings. Military academies along with a few engineering and medical schools were allowed to remain open.

Ne Win never considered the most fundamental way to prevent student-led rebellions, which would have been to govern more inclusively. But the regime was correct in identifying university students and Buddhist monks as the groups most likely to organize uprisings. All three of the rebellions during colonial times against the British in 1920, 1936, and 1938 had been led by Rangoon University students. The student-protest tradition at the university continued in the post-Colonial era with rebellions in 1962 and 1974. Ne Win feared that more uprisings could come at anytime, so he took the preemptive measure of periodically closing universities.

QUALIFYING FOR MEDICAL SCHOOL

When Ne Win allowed institutions of higher learning to resume teaching, he permitted only a few four-year schools to operate, and favored community colleges in which the students had less time to build alliances and organize demonstrations. Students would attend a community college for the first two years and then a finishing university for the third and fourth years. The dictator also required new schools to locate on the outskirts of cities so that students were distant from political centers.

Saw urged Thein to become a lawyer, to learn how to interpret the law in his favor. Such interpretations had guided Saw in handling problems that Ne Win continually caused, and they helped him to justify in his mind the gruesome jobs he did for the ruler. Thein would prosper if he acquired a lawyer's ability to rationalize.

But Thein wanted to reduce human suffering. He believed suffering was caused not only by tragic circumstances, but also by people's thoughts. Some people are unflappable in a crisis while others suffer panic attacks. The way problems are viewed can make big differences in people's lives. If people could be taught to think in more constructive ways they would suffer less.

Thein often recalled how Dr. Aung Tin years earlier had helped him understand that his impaired breathing was caused not by an evil spirit, but by his own thoughts. Changing the way Thein viewed the problem had so greatly relieved his anxiety that now he wanted to teach others to rely on psychiatric analysis instead of falling prey to superstition. Thein held steadfast to his decision to pursue psychiatry as a profession.

Uncharacteristically, Saw gave in and decided to support his son's decision. He rationalized that Thein might still become associated with the law by testifying in court regarding mental illness. Also, Saw came to believe that it was important for the lad to pursue higher education in any field as soon as possible so as to not develop the notion that he could get by without doing advanced studies. For Thein to maintain momentum in learning was now more important to Saw than whether the youth would become a lawyer or a doctor.

THE MIND DOCTOR

Thein was relieved that his father now agreed with his choice of careers, but another, far more serious problem remained. This problem lay in Thein's own mental makeup, the factors that combined to make him a complex individual.

This problem had persisted since Thein was eight years old. He possessed a high IQ as in intelligent quotient. But another IQ boded ill for him. His inconsistency quotient showed itself at the worst of times.

Thein usually excelled when taking written or practical exams. He studied hard, and usually was rewarded for the effort. But three or four times a year—when his performance mattered the most—Thein was immobilized by a force of unknown origin, which seemed to be a form of performance anxiety, akin to stage fright or maybe writer's block. Even when he knew the answer to a test question, he could not utter the words or write them down. Was he subconsciously punishing himself for his father's crimes? The Fixer harmed or even killed people who opposed Ne Win. This repulsed Thein, but also created conflicted feelings because he wanted to admire his father. He tried to suppress his feelings, to smother them. But deep down Thein felt he had inherited Saw's evil nature. At a subconscious level he lacked self-worth. At crucial times when he was being tested, was it feelings of guilt or something else entirely that caused him to sabotage himself? To Thein, any low test score proved he was an unworthy person.

Inconsistency quotient was not a diagnosis made by a doctor, but was a term coined by Thein himself. At first he did not want to attach a label to the condition because he believed in self-fulfilling prophecy. Naming the problem might turn it into a permanent part of his mental makeup.

However, over the years, correlated with the importance of whatever exam he was taking, the problem had manifested no matter how much he tried to deny its existence. In arguing with himself, Thein considered other labels that could stand for IQ, shorthand for the strange condition that plagued him. He considered "ignorance quotient" and, because he felt great shame, "ignominious quotient." Finally, he assigned the label of inconsistency quotient. He needed to identify the existence of the problem without giving it a sterner name that might—by way of self-fulfilling prophecy—make it worse. He hoped inconsistency quotient was a benign-enough label to not agitate any nats who just might be involved. But why was he allowing nats to enter his thinking? Dr. Aung Tin had said Thein should not believe in evil spirits. Was his father's belief system creeping into Thein's mind after all?

Thein had wanted for years to talk with someone about his inconsistency quotient. He ruled out talking with his father because Saw would see the problem as a grave weakness in his son.

Thein considered seeking his mother's counsel. He trusted her to keep their discussion confidential, and to advise him wisely, but he believed it would be unfair to Sang Yki to ask her to keep their discussions from her husband. Also, Thein thought his mother might blame herself for his mental block.

At last, Thein made an appointment with Kyaw Zeya, a high school counsellor. Thein was not acquainted with him but knew that other students respected him. Thein stayed after school one day to get advice on how to cope with his long-standing problem.

"Hello, Thein. Your records show that you are a senior. You will soon be gone from this institution, and will experience the world in whole new ways. How can I help you?"

"I have a problem that is hard to describe. It lowers my grades."

"Is this problem limited to the school environment?"

Thein said, "It often knocks me off the honor roll. And I do not think I am just imagining it."

"Many things outside of school can affect how well we do in school. You can talk to me about anything that may be troubling you. What's bothering you?"

"I study hard and most of the time do well on my tests. But sometimes I seem spellbound. I cannot write down the answer to a test question even though I know it."

"Do you realize the correct answer just as soon as you hand in the examination paper?"

"No. That is not the problem. Many times I have recalled the correct answer after leaving the class room. That seems to be normal forgetfulness or perhaps the stress of taking the test. This problem is different. It is weird.

"When it happens, I know the answer. I am certain of it. I just cannot write it down. I leave the item blank. If it is an oral test, I cannot say the answer. It is like I am punishing myself."

"How often does this happen?"

"Nine or ten times a year. But this has been going on since I was about eight. The worst part is that it happens on the most important tests when it is vital that I get a good grade. Like when I pass from one standard to the next. In fact, it happens only on the most important exams. I am afraid it will happen on the matriculation tests that are coming up. I want to qualify for medical school."

The counselor said, "This problem seems psychological. You should seek the advice of either a psychologist or a psychiatrist. That's what I'd do."

"Is there anything else I can do?"

"Read as much as you can of the research literature to find out if there are any clinical cases like yours. You might find something. There are some corrective steps you can take on your own which might solve the problem, and should not make it worse."

"I have tried giving myself a good talking-to."

The counselor said, "Work on the content of what you tell yourself. I would say things like 'I know this answer and I'm writing it down right now.'

"Another message to yourself might be 'There will be no blank spaces on my test papers.' Try any self-talk that causes you to act. Create catchy phrases, maybe a rhyme that's easy to remember or fun to repeat."

"Thank you."

"One last suggestion. Don't let your imagination make this problem worse than it is. Don't imagine that some evil spirit is at work. Keep it simple. You seem to be punishing yourself through your own special version of self-loathing. Just stop it. Right or wrong, write down an answer to every question. Be compulsive about it. If there's a blank, fill it in. Just fill it in. You'll feel better."

QUALIFYING FOR MEDICAL SCHOOL

University matriculation exams were required before high school students graduated, and Thein's strange affliction had asserted itself. He had scored too low to qualify for any of Burma's medical schools. This upset Saw, especially in light of news stories that Ne Win's daughter, Sanda Win, had obtained the highest matriculation scores of all the students in the nation.

Thein decided to compensate for his failure to pass Burma's exam by studying hard and passing America's entrance test. He reasoned that it did not matter that he had failed Burma's exam because he wanted to live in America anyway. He took the test at the USA embassy in Rangoon. The university admittance exam was difficult because America was very selective as to who entered its medical schools. Thein awaited the results which eventually came in the mail.

"Father, I failed America's tests. I did not meet their standards."

"Thein, there are other countries and other universities."

"But I might fail their tests too."

The Fixer fell into his usual mode of thinking that there was some "unofficial way" to solve this problem. It would have been good if his son had passed America's entrance exams, but Saw could fix it so that Thein would be accepted into a medical school in Burma and eventually into a medical residency. Saw schemed how to persuade university officials to not only accept his son but even guarantee his academic success.

The Fixer was confident that he could get Thein accepted into Institute of Medicine 1, Rangoon. He knew when to bribe someone and when to threaten him instead. He decided to go to a head decision maker, a person in authority, who could accept his son into medical school.

"Thein, I can arrange for you to retake Burma's matriculation test. If you pass, you could go to a university right here in Rangoon. The Institute of Medicine Number 1 has a psychiatric curriculum, and Rangoon Psychiatric Hospital is where you would get your supervised work experience."

"But Burma has a rotten attitude toward higher education. You never know when a university will close or for how long. Maybe I can pass Singapore's matriculation test."

"Give it a try. Find out if you can take Singapore's test at its embassy here in Rangoon."

Thein took Singapore's matriculation exam, and the results came by mail. The answer was the same as America's—thanks for taking the test, but you did not score high enough to qualify for medical school.

Saw said, "I'll pull strings so you can retake Burma's matriculation exam."

Although Thein now wanted to leave Burma, he believed his father's intervention was the only chance for him to become a psychiatrist.

The Fixer's first step was to find out who was in charge of entrance requirements for the Rangoon medical institute and whether there was anything in that person's past that could be used to make him see things Saw's way.

Saw did not want anyone to know he was fixing things for a family member. This was the first time such was necessary. Always before he had acted on behalf of Ne Win.

The Fixer went to the head of military intelligence, who was now Brigadier General Aye Myat, and asked who chaired the university acceptance committee. He let the general believe he was representing Ne Win. He didn't say so, he just let Aye Myat draw his own conclusions.

The Fixer said, "It's necessary for a certain student to be accepted into the main Rangoon medical school. I don't want to leave anything to chance. The student didn't pass the state-wide entrance exams.

"I want to deal directly with the main decision maker who can ensure that this young man is accepted into the Institute of Medicine Number 1. I want continued cooperation up through the time he serves his year of supervised patient care at the Rangoon Psychiatric Hospital."

This was a mundane undertaking compared to other problems that the two generals had worked out in the past. Usually those problems had centered on who the Fixer needed to expunge. So Brigadier General Aye Myat was at ease when he responded to Saw's request for information.

"If I were you, I'd go directly to the rector of the university, Dr. Aung Panna. His decision would be final, and he could make sure that his staff is creative in handling the paperwork involved."

"Good. Do you know anything I can use against the rector to make him see the wisdom of accepting this pupil?"

The intelligence chief said, "Dr. Panna has been cautious during his years in academia so I don't know of any black marks against him, but I bet there are some. There always are."

"Can you think of anything that I can use?"

General Aye Myat said, "Something comes to mind. Even though Chairman Ne Win has Chinese ancestry, he hates Chinese people. He made that clear by promoting strife between the Burmese and Chinese over a rice shortage. Ne Win did this so he himself would not be blamed for the shortage. Dr. Panna is part Chinese despite his Burmese name, and he would not like that fact pointed out to our leader."

It pleased Saw that even the head of military intelligence did not know that he was the one who had engineered the scheme for deflecting the blame for the rice shortage from Ne Win's policies onto the Chinese rice merchants.

"I need something stronger," Saw said.

"I'll ask one of my investigators how Dr. Panna has reacted to past student demonstrations. If he was sympathetic to any rioting students, Chairman Ne Win would see red. A threat to pass such information to our leader would make the rector most cooperative."

"Good idea," Saw said.

"Wait while I check with my investigator. I won't refer to you or Chairman Ne Win. I'll just ask if my spy knows anything bad about Dr. Panna."

After fifteen minutes, the head spy returned, wearing a grin.

"It's rumored that Dr. Panna had relations with male students who were brought before him for disciplinary reasons over the years. It's said that he absolved young men in exchange for sexual favors. If you drop the names of a few of those students, the rector will see to it that your student is accepted into medical school."

THE MIND DOCTOR

Burma's head of military intelligence handed a sheet of paper to the Fixer. It was a list of student names and disciplinary decisions made by Dr. Aung Panna, the rector of the Institute of Medicine Number 1, Rangoon.

Chapter 7

Only in Ne Win's Burma

Suffering is a pervasive, unwanted, and distressing experience that fundamentally alters one's sense of self, others, and the world.

—Sarah Elizabeth Adler
Burmese Buddhist Understandings of Suffering
PhD thesis (2008)

It was the autumn of 1982. Thein entered a six-year medical program offered by the Institute of Medicine 1, Rangoon. The curriculum specified that the final year would consist of supervised work experience at the Rangoon Psychiatric Hospital.

After completing registration, three hundred thirty-one students were assembled at the Lanmadaw campus for orientation by university professors and administrators. The students aspired to be surgeons, cancer doctors, trauma specialists, psychiatrists, neurologists, and heart specialists. Some were enrolled for training in traditional medicine, which included aspects of Buddhism, animism, astrology, and palm reading.

Thein sat in the front row. Next to him sat a man three years his senior who, over time, had changed his field of study from zoology to civil engineering to psychiatry. Than Aung Foy's father, a general in Burma's Air Force, had the money and connections necessary to ensure that Foy got a quality education.

The two young men talked while waiting for the keynote orientation lecture. The auditorium was noisy with chatter because the other assembled students also were getting to know their future classmates.

Foy said, "I'm from a military family, and I grew up near Mandalay. What's your background?"

"I grew up in the Inya Lake area, and went to school in Rangoon."

"How did you decide that you want to be a psychiatrist?"

Thein said, "I want to reduce suffering as did Siddhārtha Guatama, the original Buddha, and I think people with mental illnesses suffer more than most."

"If you want to reduce suffering, you picked a good career field. But I hear that being in psychiatry can mess up your own head because of all the misery you confront. That worries me. Have you thought about that?"

"I can handle it."

The auditorium fell silent. A gray-haired man walked onto the stage, sporting a surgical gown and a stethoscope, symbols of the medical professions that the would-be doctors yearned to enter.

Dr. Aung Panna, the rector of the medical university, would have little future contact with the students, but he liked to take center stage at student orientations. He considered himself the university's best speaker and the face that politicians and military elite associated with the Institute of Medicine.

For two minutes, Rector Panna stood at the podium, saying nothing. Finally, he spoke.

"Your teachers and I expect many things of you during your time at this majestic institution. We expect you to learn about diseases and injuries and proper treatment against the maladies that humans suffer. We expect you to develop good relationships with your patients and to do no harm when treating them."

Again, the rector was silent for a long time.

"But most of all, we expect you to adhere to the vision that the state has for the future of medicine. You must follow the blueprint designed by Prime Minister Ne Win and the Burma Socialist Programme Party.

"When you become doctors, you must influence your patients to obey our leaders. As doctors you will have many opportunities to influence what people think. If people obey the state, they will suffer less mental anguish, and this will be a success for you as a healer. It is that simple and that profound.

"In 1962 and 1974, students led demonstrations against the state. Those wrongful acts might not have happened if the professors at Rangoon University and Mandalay University had taken responsibility for their students' conduct. Every teacher, every doctor, and every official of any kind has a responsibility to make sure their pupils, patients, and patrons obey the wishes of the state."

Thein looked at Foy for his reaction, but his new acquaintance was a statue.

Aung Panna concluded his indoctrination speech with a final directive.

"Now as students and later as doctors, you young people owe allegiance to the state, and must report any misconduct by your associates."

The rector left the stage.

The audience was breaking up, and the commotion muffled Foy's words.

"Thein, we'll hear that drumbeat again and again in the years ahead. Because of our government's misplaced priorities, our job will be to become good doctors in spite of our teachers."

During Ne Win's years as Burma's ruler, the country spent five times as much money annually on the military as on education and health care combined. This crippled every school from kindergarten through university, and the Institute of Medicine 1, Rangoon was no exception.

Lack of funds weakened the medical training that Thein and Foy obtained. Thein had expected an austere educational program, but the skimping was worse than he had imagined.

The curriculum called for the psychiatry students to dissect cadavers, and Thein recognized this was an important method of learning the anatomy of the brain and body. But he was repulsed by having to dissect several cadavers every month.

Foy explained to Thein why the medical program required psychiatry students to do so many dissections.

"It's the austere budget. The psychiatry department has little money to spend, but still wants us to get hands-on experience. And because of the tragic way this country is governed, there are many dead bodies available for just picking them up and refrigerating some for a while. This provides the psychiatric department with low-cost educational material.

"And when we are done cutting into the bodies, the regime makes further use of most of them. Soldiers place corpses in parts of the city that they want civilians to avoid. Or they put the bodies where they will scare people and keep them obedient."

Thein said, "But the bodies have to be disposed of sooner or later."

"That's right. But disposal doesn't cost much when Burma has so many soldiers on the payroll anyway. Most bodies are dumped into mass graves that bulldozers cover with dirt. Some are buried in a Potter's Field. Others are dumped in the Rangoon River to be carried downstream."

Thein had often heard male professors say that women should not try to gain the status of doctors. But the nine women in Thein's medical cohort were trying hard to do just that.

Sang Soe was an attractive young woman who had passed the matriculation test with high marks, and was excelling in the early months of medical school. Thein never imagined that one day in December 1982 would be the last time he would ever see her.

Thein's dissection table was between the one used by Foy, his best friend, and the one used by Sang Soe, someone he wanted to know better. A cadaver lay on each table, face up and covered with a bedsheet. A forty-year-old male professor was giving instructions.

"Your assignment today is to do a frontal lobotomy. You practice on a dead person so you will be skilled when you do the procedure on a live one. Cutting away all the white matter that connects the two frontal lobes to the rest of the brain will eliminate seizures and reduce depression. Also, the patient will be docile and easier to care for, whether at home or in a hospital.

"Remember, there are two ways to do a frontal lobotomy, depending on how you want to gain access to this part of the brain. The original way is to drill two holes in the side of the head. A way that was developed a few years later is to gain access through the eye sockets. Today, you are to do your lobotomy the original way, and next week when you have a fresh specimen you will take the ocular route.

"Before you remove the bedsheet, understand that these humans died for all sorts of reasons. No one knows all the reasons. Some had cancer, some had heart attacks, and some had tuberculosis.

"Your first job is to identify the cadaver's sex and approximate age. Try to figure out the person's occupation. For example, people who work in rice paddies have short, rounded, widespread toes, and their feet and lower legs are discolored.

"Make careful observations, and write them down. Autopsy notes are important records that help the government figure out statistically where to focus life-saving programs. Make your initial notes before you begin cutting.

"OK, get started."

Thein had just pulled back the sheet on the cadaver assigned him when he heard Sang Soe scream. The students, the instructor, and the assistant instructor looked at Soe to see what was wrong. She was trying to contain her emotions to prove that she could handle any situation. But she could not handle this one. The person on the dissection table was her mother.

"Mom was healthy two days ago when I saw her."

The instructor led Sang Soe away while the lab assistant reestablished control over the bewildered students.

"This is a tragedy for the young lady, but for the rest of you it can be a learning experience. Sang Soe's assigned cadaver turned out to be her mother. But you must understand that these things often happen to doctors. You have to be tough enough to handle tragedies which often come as a surprise.

"We instructors don't have time to check out all the possible relationships between the cadavers that we obtain and you students who take this practical, realistic program. You just have to be tough, and continue to do your job. So get back to your assignment, to the business at hand."

After class, Foy said to Thein, "Only in Ne Win's Burma will you see that kind of colossal screw up."

Chapter 8

The Dictator's Fountain of Youth

Every man desires to live long, but no man would be old.

—Jonathan Swift
Thoughts on Various Subjects (1706)

Ne Win told astrologer Min Thet Khin that he wanted to live past ninety. The wizard said this would be assured if Ne Win bathed in dolphin blood, and added that this practice also would benefit Burma because the longer Ne Win lived the longer he would provide great leadership. This remark caused the dictator to realize that he must keep this key to a long life a secret from his enemies lest they extend their own lives.

Only one officer was stealthy enough to set up procedures for the ruler to regularly take these baths without alerting his enemies. Ne Win summoned Brigadier General Maunt Saw to the dictator's command post.

"I need you to handle a top secret mission, which includes setting up procedures for a recurring event."

"Yes sir."

"The wizard Khin said I will live to be more than ninety years old if I bathe in dolphin blood three times a year."

"That's the best news I've ever heard."

"I need you to set up procedures so that every four months dolphin blood is delivered to my private lavatory. I'm worried because dolphin numbers are going down. I need to be assured a supply that will not run out. This is top secret. My enemies must not learn how to extend their own lives."

Saw said, "You can count on me. How many liters of blood will be required for each bath?"

"I don't know. I'll leave those details for you to figure out. But I have a big bathtub. Take a look at it. Measure the volume of water needed to fill it."

"How soon do you wish to take your first bath, Chairman Ne Win?"

"Three days from now, in the evening."

"Is there anything else I need to know before I get started?"

"The blood has to be fresh, drained from the dolphins in the last six hours and kept on ice."

Saw determined the volume of blood necessary to fill Ne Win's bathtub by having an assistant sit in the tub while Saw poured in water one liter at a time. Sixty liters were needed.

Saw did not know how much blood is in a dolphin, and decided this was something he could establish once he found a supply of the animals. Finding dolphins on a regular basis was the biggest challenge. Saw knew that commercial fishermen occasionally caught dolphins accidentally while trawling in the Andaman Sea.

He planned to start his search along the Andaman waterfront when he remembered that his wife had a cousin who subsisted by fishing in the Irrawaddy River. San San Than lived in a village called Hopmung one hundred-fifty kilometers northwest of Rangoon.

At home that evening, Saw said to Sang Yki, "I need to bring a few dolphins to Chairman Ne Win. An astrologer said he will live much longer if he bathes in dolphin blood."

She did not comment.

Saw continued. "Do you think San San will help me get dolphins for our leader?"

"San San will help you because he is my cousin."

Saw said, "But he and I scarcely know each other. It's been years since we talked, and then I saw him only twice. You and Thein visited San San and his wife now and then over the years, but I wasn't with you. I have only three days to carry out this mission. I could get crosswise of Chairman Ne Win if San San refuses to help me, as I would've lost valuable time by seeking him out."

Sang Yki said, "I have pictures of San San, his wife, Thein, and me together. The photos will help you get reacquainted."

"That'll help. But I'm still worried. I don't have a rapport with your cousin to rely on."

Sang Yki said, "San San's kids played with Thein several times while growing up. My cousin always liked our son. I believe San San will help you if Thein acts as a goodwill ambassador."

Thein had just returned home from his shift at the Rangoon Psychiatric Hospital where he was still a medical student, an "almost-doctor." Saw went to his son's room and described Ne Win's latest orders.

Thein had the next day off work. For the other two days that Saw needed him, Thein phoned his supervisor who agreed he could have the time off if he arranged for another intern to fill in for him. Thein made more phone calls, and eventually told Saw that he could spend the next three days helping to get dolphin blood for Ne Win.

The Fixer worked through Sergeant Major Thu Si who ordered an army sergeant to check out a pickup truck from the motor pool, and meet two men on a specific street corner for a brief military mission. Saw told Thein to be friendly to the sergeant but to say little and to not mention Thein's real name or where he lived or worked.

Early the next morning, while it was still dark, Sergeant Mun Nyein pulled his motor pool pickup to the curb when he saw two men standing at the designated street corner. The men, one dressed in fatigues and the other in civilian clothes, matched the description Mun had been given.

Although the label on Saw's work uniform falsely identified him as a staff sergeant, Mun quickly stepped from the pickup, snapped to attention, and saluted him.

"Reporting as directed, Sir."

THE MIND DOCTOR

"Lay off the army rigmarole, son. Don't draw attention to me."

Saw peered at the things stowed in the pickup bed. There were nine large ice chests that Mun said he had filled with ice. There also were thirteen empty 5-gallon jugs and two big tubs for initial collection of the dolphin blood. Small buckets, along with ladles and funnels, also were evident. Tool boxes contained knives and saws, rounding out the inventory of equipment and suplies. The sergeant major had done a good job of anticipating project needs, and made sure that Mun had come prepared.

Saw told the sergeant their destination and that they would be on temporary duty for three days. He said little else during the trip, and Mun limited his questions to logistical matters such as which roads to travel.

There was no way to contact Sang Yki's cousin in advance of their arrival at the village because San San did not have a phone. They made good time in spite of the bad roads, and pulled into the village of Hopmung at 3:00 p.m.

Thatch huts were built on stilts to keep out the Irrawaddy which rose each monsoon season. The village was independent, having its own blacksmith, wheelwright, and carpenter. The roads were not paved, no one owned cars, so oxcarts were the only means of ground transportation.

Saw and Thein went to San San's hut. His wife was pleased to see Thein again. Her husband would be home soon. His routine was to arise early, eat a breakfast of rice, fish, and tea, and launch his boat at first light.

While waiting for San San to return home, the general and the sergeant napped, sitting upright in the pickup's cab. Thein stretched out in its bed alongside the ice chests and empty containers for the dolphin blood. Soon, San San arrived. Saw did not allow Mun to hear his conversations with the villager and Thein.

San San asked what brought his visitors so far from Rangoon.

Saw said, "An astrologer told General Ne Win that he will live to be over ninety if he takes a bath every now and then. That's always good advice, but the astrologer said the bath must be in dolphin blood, not soap and water."

San San said, "You're kidding. I never heard that before."

"Wish I was kidding. This is real. We have two days left to deliver sixty liters of dolphin blood to Ne Win. We brought coolers and ice. How many dolphins will we have to kill to get sixty liters of blood?"

"Ne Win is nuts. And you're just as nuts if you do what he wants. No one here will help you. Go back to Rangoon."

"Hold on," Saw said. "Don't go back to your hut. We used precious time in coming here because my wife—your cousin—thought you'd help us. Why do you feel so strongly about a fish? If you won't help us, at least tell us who might. We can't go back empty handed."

"Dolphins are not fish. They're warm-blooded mammals, like us. That matters to me. Some fishermen here use gill nets. All the fishermen are my friends. Related to most of them. But I hate to see anyone use gill nets. They don't mean to catch dolphins but they sometimes do. Dolphins get tangled in the nets and drown. Those deaths are by mistake. What you're talking about would be on purpose and for a crappy reason."

After a long silence, San San said, "Come with me in my boat in the morning. My helpers can take a different boat so there'll be room for you and Thein. You'll see that dolphins truly are my brothers."

"San San, we'd love to see for ourselves the ways of the dolphin, but we don't have time."

"OK, but I'm going to tell you more so that you might change your plan. Dolphins help me feed my family. When I get to where they gather, I tap on the side of my boat with a stick. This tells them I'm ready to fish.

"The dolphins drive fish toward me. I stand in the boat and cast a net like those over there piled under my hut. The net comes down on the fish. I pull it in and usually get some fish. The dolphins eat the ones that fall out of the net.

"In the old days, there were more dolphins. Every river village had its own pod."

Saw and Thein waited for San San to resume speaking.

"When a dolphin dies, I'm as sad as when my mother died. Many fishermen feel as I do. This is why I don't use gill nets. Many dolphins have died in gill nets. They get tangled and can't break free. Fish caught in gill nets also die, but the struggle is worse for dolphins. Unless a dolphin can stick its nose into the air, it can't breathe. I tell fishermen to check their nets twice a day."

"OK, San San, we understand your concern. But what can we do to protect ourselves from Ne Win's wrath?"

San San said, "Did Ne Win say that you must deliver the dolphin bodies along with their blood?"

"No."

"Well?"

On the way back to Rangoon, Saw, Sergeant Mun Nyein, and Thein stopped at a pig farm. Saw paid the farmer and his hired hand to kill and bleed seven hogs. The blood was put into containers and these were placed in the ice chests. They were several liters short of sixty, so they added water and stirred the mixture.

Mun dropped Thein off near the family's villa. The general and the sergeant then continued on to the enlisted men's barracks where Mun and some fellow soldiers unloaded the pig carcasses.

Saw said, "Enjoy your barbeque and forget you ever saw me."

Mun delivered Saw to Ne Win's villa and the dolphin blood to Sergeant Major Thu Si. He then returned the pickup to the motor pool.

Saw debriefed his commander.

"Chairman Ne Win, you said I should establish procedures to assure you of a future supply of dolphin blood. It was hard to get the blood because fishermen respect this fish. The best way to ensure you a regular supply is for me to stay personally involved to make logistical adjustments as necessary. I will cultivate a relationship with the fishermen."

Ne Win said, "Good. My desire to live a long time is not for my personal benefit, you know. I'm following the wizard's recommendation for the good of our nation."

"All Burma will benefit, Chairman Ne Win."

Ne Win died in December 2002 at age 92. To the end, he swore that he owed his long life to bathing in dolphin blood.

Chapter 9

The New Rector

Blackmail is more effective than bribery.

—John le Carré
Smiley's People (1979)

Medical school was a long slog for Thein. He did well for months, but then would not answer crucial test questions. He tried to explain his behavior to his major professor, but found the man to be less understanding than his high school counselor had been. The professor was intrigued by what might have been going on in Thein's brain, but felt that someday his subconscious mind would cause him to harm a psychiatric patient.

Thein's major professor tried to persuade Rector Aung Panna to expel the young man, but was surprised when the usually thoughtful rector rebuffed him as soon as he said Thein's name.

But Aung was moving to a new government position. There would be a new rector, a man named Win Kyaw. Thein's major professor told Win of his concerns even before the new appointee took office. Consequently, Win balked when the exiting Aung told him that as the new rector he would need to ensure that Thein received passing grades. Win said Thein did not deserve special treatment. He would kick him out of medical school for low grades, just as he would any other student.

Aung Panna realized that the Fixer would not let him off the hook just because he was leaving the rectorship for a different government position. "The Fixer" was the way the menacing man had referred to himself the first time he appeared unannounced in Aung's university office. The man had not suggested what his relationship to Thein might be. What he did was show Aung a list of male students whom the rector had absolved of misconduct charges in return for sexual favors.

Aung intended that the next time the Fixer showed up, he would tell him of the upcoming change of rectors. But Aung knew that his blackmailer would want him to ensure that the medical school's favoritism of Thein would not be disrupted. Aung asked the incoming rector to go for a walk with him on the campus grounds so they could talk without being overheard.

"Win Kyaw, you're full of yourself because you soon will be the new rector. So you say you will not exercise leniency in judging the scholarship of Maunt Thein, the student I've mentioned a couple of times."

"Yeah, I heard you both times. You want me to overlook his poor performance or even defend him against the professors who recognize you've been protecting him. I won't be corrupted."

"Win, just for a while, just this morning, right now, while we're on this walk, please listen to me. Your life might depend on understanding that Thein has a sponsor who will take extreme measures to ensure that he graduates."

"If there's a bribe, it'd have to be a big one. One I could share with his major professor. But I don't want to consider it. I won't start off that way. You know all the players. I don't. Give me a year to learn the ropes."

"We don't have a year. Thein would flunk out before a year went by."

"Big deal," Win said.

"Thein has a mysterious sponsor who will stop at nothing. I promised this man, his sponsor, three years ago that I would help Thein get into supervised training at the psychiatric hospital at the end of his regular coursework. I said I would mediate with the superintendent of the hospital to make sure Thein completes the training so he can graduate."

"This man? Who is this man?"

"I'm asking you as my replacement to keep the commitment that I made."

"It's your commitment, not mine. Patients could be harmed if we graduate an unqualified psychiatrist. New drugs are powerful, and some cause movement disorders and weird thoughts. Who is this man, this sponsor?"

"I'll level with you," Aung said. "But you better not say a word to anyone about this."

"Level as much as you want. I won't risk my career for an erratic student. I've heard about him. Who is this sponsor, as you call him?"

"He looks different every time he shows up. The first time was in my office. I don't know how he got past security and my secretary, but there he was in my office. I didn't see him come in. The next time was when I was at the cafeteria. And another time was at my house when I stepped out onto the porch."

"Does he represent Ne Win or military intelligence? Sounds like an undercover agent."

"I don't know," Aung said. "If Ne Win is involved, it seems like he'd just order the university to graduate Maunt Thein."

"If this sponsor, as you call him, is acting on his own, he must have something on you. He must be blackmailing you. Otherwise, you wouldn't back Thein like you do. You wouldn't tarnish your reputation. What's this guy got on you?"

"Nothing. He's got nothing on me."

"Then why do you go overboard to keep Thein from flunking out?"

"The Fixer—that's what he called himself—scared hell out of me. I'm not ready to die."

Win said, "The Fixer? I've heard of him. He works for Ne Win. Assassinates Ne Win's enemies, folks say. That scares me too but your man doesn't sound like what I've heard about the Fixer. He works strictly for Ne Win."

"I did my research as best I could. Had to be careful. Didn't want to get crosswise of Ne Win's office."

"What did you learn?"

"This guy operates just like the Fixer. Wears disguises. Shows up out of the blue. He told me he's the Fixer for a reason. He knew that piece of information would keep me on edge. He didn't just slip up when he dropped that name."

"If he's the Fixer, he must be working you without Ne Win's knowledge. What's he got on you?"

"Nothing. I told you he's got nothing on me. He uses fear. Sometimes I can't sleep."

"Did he threaten to kill you?"

"He did. He held a gun to my head. Two times. Wait till he chambers a round in his pistol, and puts the muzzle against your forehead."

Win blinked several times. His Adam's apple bobbed up and down.

"I don't want to be rector. The prestige is not worth it. I don't want the job. I'm turning it down."

"Don't be foolish. It's a great job. Just take good care of Thein, and the first time the Fixer shows up, tell him of our talk and that you'll do anything he wants. I bet he knows about me leaving and you coming in. I expect to see him any day now, it could be when we get back from this walk. I'll tell him that you're eager to help Thein."

"I don't know."

"When you're in your new job, just look out for Thein. Don't let some overzealous professor flunk him out. Thein will graduate in a little over two years and your problems will be over. I've already blazed the path, so you only need to stay on it and keep doing what I've done. The faculty will figure you know something they don't, that you have your reasons."

"But you said the Fixer might appear out of nowhere. At any time. I can't take that."

"You have to, if you want to be Rector of Medical Institute Number 1, Rangoon."

One day during Thein's fifth year at the medical institute, a university administrator entered the classroom to carry out what he called "an important housekeeping task."

Students who had progressed to this point were likely to complete their medical training, so the administrator was enforcing a requirement that he called "payback." The central government intended to get a return on its investment in education. The students were to sign contracts with the Burma Socialist Programme Party. Upon obtaining their medical licenses, they would work for four years in some part of Burma, probably a remote rural area, where medical services were severely lacking. The first year would be an internship and the last three years would be tenured. Meeting this requirement would make the budding psychiatrists eligible for residency in government hospitals.

All the students immediately signed the contract since they had accepted it as a requirement when they had enrolled in medical school five years earlier. At that time, the requirement did not seem so onerous, but now the pupils fully realized their career options would be severely limited for the first few years after graduating. Nevertheless, some of the public-spirited students felt good about the prospects of working in medically underserved areas. Thein had felt the same when he began medical training, but his desire to reduce human suffering was slowly being displaced by a desire for financial gain.

Thein completed his fifth year at The Institute of Medicine Number 1 at Rangoon. To graduate and be eligible to take his licensing exam, he needed only to complete one year of supervised work experience at the Rangoon Psychiatric Hospital.

Chapter 10

Constant Fear

One person I talked to compared the military intelligence to nats, always keeping you under their surveillance. He said that you have to respect, fear, and appease them, because otherwise they may show up and make life very uncomfortable for you.

—Christina Fink
Living Silence: Burma under Military Rule (2001)

Rangoon Psychiatric Hospital was a prison as much as a hospital. A high, brick wall enclosed the grounds, and brick buildings housed the patients.

The hospital was on the main road of the village Tadagalay. Construction of the original buildings was completed in 1927.

In 1945, during World War II, the Japanese occupied the hospital, and the British dropped bombs on it in response. The Burmese restored the buildings, making the hospital functional again by late 1946. The Tadagalay facility achieved the status of a specialist hospital in 1967, and a few years later became a teaching hospital for Rangoon's two medical schools.

When Thein served his year of supervised work experience, Rangoon Psychiatric Hospital had 1,200 beds and three sections: one for chronically ill male patients, a second for males with acute illnesses, and a third section which housed females with either chronic or acute illnesses. The male chronic section also housed patients classified as criminally insane. Some patients slept in dormitories; others occupied locked cells.

All 1,200 beds were continually occupied, and a varying number of about three hundred additional patients slept on the floor. Most of the additional patients were villagers accustomed to sleeping on floors, but of bamboo, not concrete.

Tadagalay treated outpatients as well as inpatients. Outpatients arrived every day of the week, including Sunday. Some were admitted as inpatients if they were very sick and if space were available. Because the facility was so crowded, it was necessary to discharge a patient before admitting a new one. There was a never-ending assessment of who was the most in need of care, although bribes had a way of altering the medical opinions of the admitting officers.

During his year of supervised work experience, Thein was paid an allowance of seven thousand kyat per month. This skimpy stipend of about seven U.S. dollars was not as much a problem for Thein as it was for many of the other aspiring doctors because he still lived with his parents, and had few expenses. But he felt that he deserved more money after all his hard work in seeking his medical degree.

Thein was proud that he now wore a doctor's white gown like the one Rector Aung Panna had sported during his orientation address to Thein's incoming class in 1982. But dampening Thein's joy was the confining environment of the psychiatric hospital and the tragic biographies of the patients. Grave injustices were integral to most case histories.

For Thein, the saddest place in the gloomy hospital was where the patients deemed criminally insane were incarcerated. Most would be hanged sooner or later.

For those accused of noncapital offenses to be released, they had to serve their sentences, and recover mentally enough to satisfy hospital psychiatrists that they were not a threat to the government. The state did not bother with return-to-sanity hearings. Instead, the chief medical officer and the superintendent of the hospital made the decision based on recommendations of senior doctors. No one notified the patient's family before the person was released. The supposedly recovered individual was sent through the main gate and ordered to not loiter in the vicinity.

Several medical crises were playing out somewhere in the hospital at all times. Now and then, there was good news as when someone's illness turned out to be less severe than first believed, or as when a suicidal patient decided life was worth living after all. But the prevailing atmosphere was impending doom.

Thein needed mentoring in this gloomy place, yet his immediate supervisor had little time for him. Fortunately, there was someone else to fill the need.

Than Aung Foy had graduated from the medical institute in the same commencement ceremony as Thein, and also was gaining work experience at Tadagalay. The two young men had spent time together in many classroom exercises, and had studied together outside of class. Each was an only child, so they developed a brotherhood during their years at the medical school. Foy fulfilled the role of older brother and mentor. The relationship that had developed at the medical school continued at the psychiatric hospital.

Thein and Foy had visited Rangoon Psychiatric Hospital many times during the years they attended the medical university because the facility was the teaching hospital for undergraduates as well as graduates. Students periodically came to the hospital to observe the doctors, nurses, and assistants at work, and to interview patients.

But the two men were now working in parts of the hospital they had not entered during undergraduate coursework assignments. There were buildings and rooms they had not imagined. And there were crowded and unsanitary conditions as well as improvised medical procedures. Worse than the sights and sounds was the stench that wafted through the hospital because the plumbing had been inadequate to begin with and had fallen into disrepair.

Thein wondered about the veracity of the information that the medical school professors had served up to him and his classmates. Did the professors know what went on behind closed doors at the hospital? Did they know that frontal lobotomies were done not to facilitate patient recovery but to make difficult patients easier to take care of?

As much as he could, Thein limited the amount of stimuli that he was exposed to each day. Knowing how much trauma he could handle, he compartmentalized his activities, concentrating only on the specific task at hand. Thein took one thing at a time and did as he was told. He stifled his curiosity as a defense against trauma. The less he knew the less he would feel a patient's pain. Thein worried—how could he reduce the suffering of others if he could not even bear to witness their agony?

Thein wondered if the hospital could achieve humane standards even if funding were increased. Could more government funding, more staffing, modern equipment, and improved procedures make the place a decent medical facility, or was it hopelessly broken? Was there anything he could do to significantly help more of the patients? It did not seem enough for Thein to treat patients one at a time when the entire healthcare system was failing them all.

Thein realized that Tadagalay plus a 200-bed ward at Mandalay General Hospital could not possibly serve the country's mental health needs when most of Burma's people lived in rural areas. A decentralized system would be much better. How many people in Burma needed psychiatric care who were not getting it?

Burma had a greater percentage of mentally ill people than neighboring Thailand and Laos. Yet both—like Burma—were ruled by military dictatorships. What was different about Burma's regime?

As time passed, Thein learned that other dictatorships in Southeast Asia, although cruel, ruled in more predictable ways. Ne Win made sudden, arbitrary decisions such as nationalizing private companies, barring almost all trade with foreign countries, switching the side of the road people were to drive on, and devaluing the currency. He positioned military tanks around the cities as a show of force, put informers in urban neighborhoods, and encouraged people to spy on each other. Ne Win was paranoid and, as head of state, was in a position to make his subjects paranoid as well.

After serving in the psychiatric hospital for several months, and listening to his patients' stories and to collaboration by their friends and families, Thein realized the Ne Win regime was driving people mad by causing them to live in constant fear.

Chapter 11

Thein Accepts His First Bribe

What man was ever content with one crime?

—Juvenal
Satires (satirical poems written between about 100 and 127 AD)

The outpatient clinic operated just outside the high wall that surrounded the Rangoon Psychiatric Hospital. To be admitted as an inpatient, a person not only had to be diagnosed with a serious mental illness, but he or someone acting for him also had to pay a bribe. To get medicine or a blanket or to use a toilet required another bribe.

Most people seeking help received only a diagnosis and aspirin before being sent away. Some were carried into the hospital on gurneys, some used wheelchairs, and some walked. All were escorted not only by medical personnel but armed soldiers as well.

Some who appeared sick actually were informers planted by the government. Two or three spies were present in the outpatient clinic most of the time, and usually were known to the medical personnel. But sometimes even the doctors were fooled because an informer would feign a mental illness, and be admitted to the hospital. The person then continued to act as a spy inside the hospital population.

The government did not ask the informers to report whether the hospital provided good care. Instead, the dictatorship wanted to

THEIN ACCEPTS HIS FIRST BRIBE

know whether any nurse, technician, doctor, or patient was doing anything that might harm the Ne Win regime, for example, stealing medications to sell on the black market. The government did not care if a doctor accepted a bribe for admitting a person to the hospital.

One month into his supervised work program, Thein was examining people in the outpatient clinic. His supervisor, Way Tun, and two nurses were on duty with him. The clinic was jammed with sick people.

Thein was in his final year of medical school but not yet a full-fledged doctor. He was authorized to refuse admittance to any prospective patient because the hospital was filled to capacity, but when it came to admitting someone, he was authorized only to make recommendations to a senior doctor like Way Tun.

Thein worried about contracting a contagious disease such as tuberculosis or syphilis. An infectious disease was not the reason an afflicted person came to the psychiatric hospital; for that one went to Rangoon General Hospital. But a new patient admitted to the psychiatric hospital because of a mental illness could have an accompanying infectious disease. Tuberculosis could be present anytime a person had been in a prolonged weakened condition, and was exposed to the tubercle bacillus. Syphilis might be present because in an advanced stage this disease could be the cause of the mental problem that had prompted admittance.

Thein was leaning toward asking for twenty-five-year-old Kyi Soe Kyi to be admitted. He suspected syphilis was beginning to ravage her brain. She had recently began suffering irritability, hallucinations, and delusions. Thein did not see any skin lesions, but he understood that the neurosyphilis form of the disease might lack such symptoms. The famous Canadian physician Sir William Osler had called syphilis "the great imitator" because of its varied presentations. Thein hoped Way Tun would approve diagnostic tests. Without a blood test or microscopic examination for spirochete bacteria, alternative diagnoses would be very difficult because Kyi's symptoms were common to several mental illnesses.

Thein suspected Kyi was a prostitute because the trade was a common occupation for young women in Rangoon, she was beautiful, and had no calluses on her hands. Also, the old man and old woman who had brought her in hesitated when Thein asked Kyi Soe Kyi's line of work.

The man said, "My niece is a secretary for a big company." But he could not name the company or its products. He looked at his sister. She nodded almost imperceptibly.

He said, "Honorable doctor, I have here a gift of 1,500 kyat for your medical services. Please understand how sick my niece is."

Thein consulted his conscience. He then thought of the ridiculously small stipend that he received from the hospital. He would not think of the old man's offer as a bribe but as a means for him to afford to continue to practice medicine.

Thein said, "I'll be right back."

When Thein reported the offered bribe, Dr. Tun did not look up from the patient he was examining.

"Tell them to make it 1,700 kyat. I'll take 750, you can take 750, and the two nurses on shift will each get 100."

Thein waited for his supervisor to say more, to ask how sick the patient was compared to other care seekers, to ask which disease signs were exhibited, or to acknowledge that ethical issues were involved. But Dr. Tun was done talking.

Thein returned to Kyi Soe Kyi's aunt and uncle, said that 1,700 kyat were required, and accepted the first bribe of his medical career.

A high percentage of Thein's patients had recently attended nat festivals, and had trance symptoms like the ones he had suffered when a boy. Taungbyone, the biggest spirit festival in Burma, continued to send spellbound citizens to the mental hospital, with the numbers reaching a peak soon after the festival opened in August. Other spirit festivals held at other locations and seasons ensured that the psychiatric hospital was always treating revelers grappling with trance symptoms.

Thein's supervisors and coworkers appreciated his skill in helping spellbound patients, and they used his talking points. His methods were like those of Dr. Aung Tin who had counselled him long ago in Singapore.

Increasingly, Thein understood that nat festivals and the underlying animistic belief system were "crazy-making." He wondered how many other customs or widely held beliefs damaged the health of Burma's citizens.

Worse than those customs, government policies seemed to cause most of the mental illness that Thein saw. Most patients would not criticize the government, but after he gained their confidence, a few opened up. They revealed their disdain for the placing of informers in neighborhoods and public places like tea shops and pagodas, criticizing the government for causing constant fear. Poor farmers spoke of fearing punishment if their fields were to not yield enough rice to meet government quotas. They also feared starving to death after having to sell produce to the army at far below market price.

Moe Aye suffered both auditory and visual hallucinations. He usually could ward off, or at least conceal, the hallucinations when other people were near, and when he was awake. But Moe's fellow patients told Thein that he often had nightmares and talked in his sleep, sometimes shouting.

While on night shift at Tadagalay, Thein sat in Moe's room after his patient fell asleep. Perhaps Moe would say something that he dared not utter while awake. Moe shared a room with five other men who gradually became accustomed to Thein's presence as he sat by Moe's bed.

It was 9:00 p.m. when Moe's nightmare became evident to Thein. Moe thrashed and turned in his bed.

"Teddy, how could you do it?"

Moe turned from lying on his left side to lying on his right then back again.

"Teddy, I trusted you. How could you tell on me?"

Much of what Moe said was unintelligible, but he seemed to refer to family members and friends. Thein could not decipher what Moe had done that he did not want the government to know about, but it was clear that he was afraid of informers.

A fistfight broke out two beds away in the crowded sleeping quarters. Thein hurried to separate two frail, old men.

One said, "Why am I always the one to sleep on the floor?"

The other said, "I paid extra for this bed and it's mine."

Thein said to the first old man, "Ye Naing, that's the hospital system. To sleep on a bed instead of the floor costs more. If you deserved a bed, you would have a ticket pinned to your bedclothes like Dai Than here. You'll have to make the best of it on the floor. I'll get you a better mat."

Ye Naing stopped objecting. When Thein returned with the reed mat, Ye Naing seemed content. But the next evening he complained loudly not only because the floor was hard and cold, but also because he felt inferior to Dai Than who slept in a bed.

A few days later, Ye Naing's bother came to visit. Ye Naing said he could not get a good night's sleep because the floor was hard and cold. His bother pledged to bring bribe money.

That evening, Ye Naing said to Thein, "Kind doctor, my brother will bring money. Who do we give it to so that I can sleep in a bed?"

"I'll ask my supervisor."

Thein described the situation to Dr. Tun who said, "Find out how much Ye Naing's brother is willing to pay. If it's a decent sum, try to find a spare bed. Maybe one is in storage and just needs to be repaired. But then you have to find a place to put it. A bed takes up more space than a floor mat.

"If you can't find a spare bed, take one away from some other patient who is paying less than Ye Naing's brother is willing to pay."

Chapter 12

Be Careful What You Promise

A promise made is a debt unpaid.

—Robert W. Service
The Cremation of Sam McKee
In *The Spell of The Yukon* (1907)

Chlorpromazine, marketed as Thorazine in the United States and Largactil in Europe, became available in the mid-1950s, and was the first widely used antipsychotic. Haloperidol, a much more potent drug marketed as Haldol, came on the market a few years later. Two French psychiatrists, Pierre Deniker and Jean Delay, named chlorpromazine and similar drugs "neuroleptics," which means to seize the nervous system. These drugs seize the nervous system and change behavior but do not cure anything. In perturbing the central nervous system, they happen to temporarily interrupt delusions and hallucinations.

Neuroleptics often seem effective against psychosis in the short term, but prolonged use causes a disabling, usually irreversible movement disorder called tardive dyskinesia. This crippling disorder is defined by involuntary movements of the tongue, lips, face, trunk, and arms and legs. The less obvious psychosis component is often undetected by psychiatrists. Frequently neither the tardive dyskinesia nor the tardive psychosis are manifested until the drug dose is lowered.

Akathisia—Greek for "without sitting"—also is caused by neuroleptics, and it too has both a movement component and a psychological component. The afflicted person not only cannot sit down and relax but paces about hurriedly, and is highly agitated. Many patients with akathisia are so filled with anxiety that they cannot describe what they feel. If they recover, they report wanting to jump out of their skin, and in fact some patients jump from heights to kill themselves. Others cut open their abdomens to release the jagged, electrical feeling inside.

In Tadagalay, common chronic diseases included alcoholism, multiple personality disorder, schizophrenia, depression, manic-depressive disorder, extreme anxiety, and various phobias, especially fear of snakes and spiders. Psychosis was common in both schizophrenia and the manic phase of manic-depressive disorder.

Most of the hospitalized patients suffering from psychosis were simply left to cope as best they could. The ones whose families could afford to pay bribes were given chlorpromazine pills or syrup, or perhaps the more powerful haloperidol. Patients whose psychosis caused them to disrupt the ward received injections of chlorpromazine or if available the long-lasting fluphenazine, marketed as Prolixin. More likely they were fitted with a straitjacket and placed out of the way of foot traffic.

Aye Sitt Nyein had been in Tadagalay for over three years when Thein came to work there as a doctor in training. Aye was suffering from psychosis as a result of schizophrenia, but he rarely disturbed anyone, so none of the doctors saw fit to administer expensive medication.

One day, Aye's brother, Zin Min, was visiting him, and Thein noticed the visitor's expensive clothes. Thein could help Aye Sitt Nyein feel better while supplementing his own skimpy stipend. He told himself that he would never act on his idea solely for money, but that what he was contemplating was really an act of kindness because he would get medication for Aye. To solicit a bribe was not immoral under these circumstances since Thein knew his supervisor would insist on a payment before approving chlorpromazine for Aye.

Thein wondered why Zin had never offered a bribe. He visited his brother regularly, and seemed to care about his wellbeing. Maybe Zin did not know that a medication existed or maybe he believed schizophrenia was untreatable.

But Thein had to be careful. What if Zin consented to a bribe but Thein's supervisor wanted a bigger bribe? This could make Zin angry, and it was possible he had political connections. Thein needed to get his boss's approval before making a proposal to Zin Min.

Thein found Dr. Way Tun in his cramped office.

"Sir, do you have a few minutes?"

"What can I do for you, Thein?"

"There is an elderly patient named Aye Sitt Nyein in the male chronic ward."

Dr. Tun said, "Yes, I know his case. Psychotic."

"Yes. He has a brother named Zin Min who visits him often."

Tun waited for Thein to speak again.

"Zin Min appears to be well off, judging by his clothes," Thein said.

"Drives a Mercedes. What do you have in mind?"

"I think that Aye Sitt Nyein might benefit from receiving chlorpromazine and that his brother might be willing to pay us a little extra for this medicine."

"That's a good idea. Work out the numbers. What does chlorpromazine cost the hospital and what would be a—shall we say a good markup? Work up the numbers and come back to me for approval before you approach Zin Min."

"Yes Sir."

"And, if the numbers look good, explain to Zin Min that the medicine is safe, but that we are looking at only incremental improvement. I don't want either Zin or Aye to expect a miracle. They could get angry if we raise their expectations but fail to deliver."

Thein said, "Will Zin Min take the bait if I do not use salesmanship in describing what chlorpromazine could do for his brother?"

"If we receive a gift for admitting someone to the hospital or for letting someone sleep in a bed instead of on the floor, well those are things we can deliver without doubt. But whether a drug will relieve symptoms is dicey. We must be careful because we don't know what powerful persons Zin Min might know."

"I see."

"The simple fact that we can offer a medication might be enough to prompt Zin to make an investment."

Thein had just learned how to solicit an "investment" while avoiding a complaint.

Chapter 13

A Long Gauntlet

A wise man will make more opportunities than he finds.

—Francis Bacon
Essays (1625 edition)

It was January 1988. Under supervision of senior doctors, Thein had provided medical care for a year at the Rangoon Psychiatric Hospital. A notice came in the mail saying he had failed the state medical licensing exam. Depression set in. It was not that Thein wanted to practice in Burma but that a medical license would be an essential step toward securing a psychiatric practice in America.

The Fixer enlisted the help of Aung Panna, the former rector of the Institute of Medicine 1, Rangoon. Aung met with an official of the state medical licensing board. He said he knew Maunt Thein's clinical skills were far higher than indicated by his examination scores. As he said this, the rector handed the official an envelop stuffed with 600,000 kyats.

Thein's depression disappeared when he received a second notice in the mail, this one saying he should disregard the first notice because an administrative error had been made, and he had passed the licensing test after all. Thein told his mother and father the good news. Sang Yki was surprised and pleased. Saw also acted surprised.

So far Thein had pursued his career entirely within Burma because no other options had been open to him. But now he could see other possibilities. In 1982 he had not qualified to enter medical school in America, but now that he had graduated from the Institute of Medicine 1, Rangoon, and held a medical license, perhaps he could be accepted in the USA as a post graduate and psychiatric resident.

But a major complication existed. His contract with the Burma Socialist Programme Party legally bound him to work four years in a medically underserved part of Burma. If he did not fulfill this commitment, he would not meet America's accreditation standards.

Thein decided to discuss his chances of practicing psychiatry in America with his best friend, Dr. Than Aung Foy, but he would not admit that he intended to renege on his contract with the Burma Socialist Programme Party.

Thein met with his friend in Foy's Rangoon apartment. He said he had passed Burma's medical licensing examination and now was assessing his career options.

Foy said, "Thein, your decision regarding where to practice psychiatry will affect the rest of your life as well as the lives of many other people. For a decision this important, you first need to make sure your criteria are sound. What are your criteria? What do you want from your career, now that you've come so far?"

"I am tired of relying on my parents for financial support. I want to be independent and to bring in enough money to compensate for the time I spent in medical school."

"That's an important criterion. We should not have to live in poverty just because we chose to be doctors."

"That is how I see it."

"There are other things to consider also," Foy said.

"Such as?"

"The things that drew you to psychiatry in the first place. When we first met, you said you wanted to reduce the suffering of people with mental illnesses. You pointed out that Buddha's main goal was to reduce suffering."

"I have not forgotten those noble sentiments, but it is time I got a return on my investment in education."

"I agree. And I understand your desire to move to another country where psychiatry is more lucrative."

Thein said, "The main place I am considering is the United States of America. Although I thought about the United Kingdom and Singapore, I really want to live in America."

"You would be an asset to any of those countries. But you could reduce suffering more by staying in Burma. We already have lost too much medical talent to other lands. You know the Burmese and English languages, the prevalent mental illnesses, and the customs of ethnic groups. And there are many mentally disturbed people here because of Ne Win's policies. This country needs you more than any other.

"Ethical principles are never absolute. They must be tempered by competing rights. Burma's population has a right to health care which is just as important as the USA's right. That's my take on the decision you're about to make."

"Foy, I appreciate your values. However I wager I can find pressing mental health needs in America and better compensation too."

"Understood," Foy said. "But I'd like to describe some of the drawbacks to practicing medicine in a foreign country like the USA."

"That is why I came to you. Enlighten me."

"I recently considered moving away, so I checked out what two other countries require of new foreign doctors."

"Wait a minute. You were considering doing the same thing that you are criticizing me for?"

"Thein, I'm not criticizing you. Just like you, I recently got my license to practice psychiatry in Burma. And we went through hell to get those licenses. It's natural to weigh our career options at this point.

"I'm just saying I looked into the prospects of practicing medicine overseas, so I know something about the move you're considering. I researched what Singapore and especially the USA requires foreign doctors to do to practice in those lands. I finally decided to stay right here in Rangoon partly because I don't want to contribute to the 'brain drain' that's damaging Burma so much."

Thein said, "Let us see if what you learned about America corresponds with what I have heard."

"OK. But for you to make a good decision about whether to relocate to America, you need a basis for comparison—an opportunity here in Burma.

"I've decided to set up a private practice here in Rangoon as soon as I fulfill my contract with the state to treat mental illness in an underserved region. My father is offering to put up funds for me to lease office space, buy medical equipment, and hire staff. It's a great opportunity for me."

"I am happy for you, Foy. Congratulations."

"I'd like you to be one of my doctors. If everything works out, I'd eventually offer you part interest in the practice.

"The state said that working in my clinic will meet residency requirements as long as I hire a senior doctor to oversee the operation, to be the attending physician. The state is cooperating with me because of the taxes that my practice will pay."

Thein began to dream of sunbathing on a beach in Southern California, surrounded by bikini-clad women.

"Foy, I cannot tell you how much your offer means to me. I will consider it very carefully."

"You're a hard worker. I'm in a position to know."

"Perhaps we should not talk any more about my possibly leaving Burma. I do not want to give the impression that I do not appreciate your offer of employment. It is the first career proposal that I ever received."

Foy said, "Oh, we need to complete this conversation about the medical accreditation requirements of other countries. I want to share with you what I've learned."

Thein began thinking about Bruce Lee and other Asians who had lived glamorous lives in America.

"I do not want you to think I am not enthused about your offer."

"Stop worrying. You came to me to discuss your next career step. And the possibility of moving to a more open society to practice psychiatry should be carefully considered."

A LONG GAUNTLET

Thein asked, "What hurdles does America place in the way of a foreign doctor becoming part of the medical establishment?"

"The US federal government sets requirements but those standards are administered by the individual states. Which state are you considering?"

"I have heard so much about California. It is my first choice."

Foy said, "In California, immigrant doctors, no matter how well trained and experienced, must run a long, costly, and confusing gauntlet before they can practice there. The process starts with an application to a private nonprofit organization that verifies medical school transcripts and diplomas. That organization will ask Rangoon's Institute of Medicine Number 1 to send a sealed transcript of your coursework. This nonprofit group may then contact some of your former professors for independent verification. The validity of your license to practice psychiatry here in Burma also will be investigated.

"Burma paid for your medical education with the belief that you'll practice medicine in this country. The USA investigations of your credentials might cause the Ne Win regime to decide that you must stay here so the state can recoup its investment in you.

"You signed a contract with the state, agreeing to work in an area underserved by doctors. Ne Win's functionaries are likely to enforce that contract if you try to go to America. Even if you get to the promised land, Burma's government can sabotage your residency application by reporting to the American medical authorities that you didn't fulfill your responsibilities here.

"You better complete the four years of service here in Burma before you try to go to the USA.

"But if you go to work for me, there will be no USA poking around in your records so our government won't be aroused. After you fulfill your contract with the Burma Socialist Programme Party, you could settle into a psychiatric career right here in Rangoon. During the four years you are honoring your contract with the state, you would be comforted by the knowledge that you had a job waiting for you."

Thein stared at his friend who had just made a strong case for staying in Burma. But his determination to practice psychiatry in

California had only grown while Foy had described the hurdles. He saw himself caressed by a tall, blonde girl while other beautiful women watched enviously. His mind was compensating for the stumbling blocks that his friend was strewing in his path to California.

Foy said, "Difficulties also will arise on the other side of the ocean. For example, there are immigration hoops to jump through. The entry into the USA of foreign-born people is governed by the US Citizenship and Immigration Services.

"At first you would not be a permanent resident of the US, so you would need to get a work visa. And the visa could require you to return to your home country after training in America. That happens all the time. The work visa may require you to return to Burma, or to go to an underserved and less desirable part of the United States.

"For several years after the 1962 military coup, the Ne Win regime was happy when any of Burma's medical professionals left the country. But today the government tries to prevent any doctor, nurse, or medical technician from leaving. Our government could retaliate against you for leaving by barring you from visiting Burma ever again."

Thein thought that would not be a problem if he was happy in the Golden State.

"You'll have to pass three separate steps that make up the US medical licensing examination. This is difficult, and many competent foreign doctors fail. The problem often is not inadequate technical knowledge, but is not knowing the art of test taking in America. Cultural nuances and shades of meaning—the phrasing of questions—can trip you up.

"If you fail any of the three steps of the licensing exam, you can't retake the test for about six months, I believe. And each time you fail any step, the medical schools will see you as less worthy of a residency even if you later pass the test.

"To be accepted into a residency, you'll need to get recommendation letters regarding your dedication and medical expertise for work done in the USA. To get those letters, you would need to work in a hospital, clinic, or research facility, and to get such a job you may have to serve as an unpaid volunteer for at least a year."

Thein's thoughts swirled in his head. Why did life have to be so complicated? Why did people always make things so complex and difficult?

Foy continued to complicate Thein's plans. Thein wondered if his father—the Fixer—could solve this problem. Was Saw's ability to get things done behind the scenes equal to this formidable task?

"The biggest challenge is that an immigrant physician must win a coveted slot in America's medical residency system," Foy said. "An internship here in Burma won't fulfill this requirement. You would still have to serve a whole new residency in the USA, and this takes at least four years. Worse yet, you may never get accepted into a residency. There are far more applicants than residencies. And native-born USA citizens will be favored over you, a native of Burma.

"Thein, here in Burma, the government paid for our education such as it was. But in the USA, the student pays for his schooling. And it's expensive. Most wannabe doctors get student loans and end up thousands of dollars in debt. This could happen to you if you have to take more courses to impress a teaching hospital enough to award you a residency.

Thein felt sick to his stomach. He wished Foy would just shut up. His impulse was to bolt from the apartment, but he did not want to offend his friend. He had asked Foy to inform him, but he had wanted a cupful of water, and his friend had turned a firehose on him.

Foy persisted. "Most foreign doctors spend years studying for their license exams. And you better do that extensive preparation because if you take the test right after getting to America, you could get low scores that would make it impossible to get a residency.

"You might pass the exams, but earn scores too low to be considered by any residency program. The whole process can consume upward of a decade—for those lucky few who make it through."

Thein thanked his friend and stepped outside. He felt that Shwe Phyin Gyi was sitting on his chest.

Chapter 14

The Fixer Turns to an Old Friend

Rules are made to be broken.

—Douglas MacArthur
(American general)

Over the years, Thein had heard people speak of the Fixer in a mythical sense. From an early age, Thein knew his father was the mysterious and feared man who gave rise to the myths.

Now he needed the Fixer to help him sidestep laws and regulations that seemed to exist for the sole purpose of preventing him from becoming a psychiatrist in California.

In a prepared speech, Thein said, "Father, I am grateful for all that you and Mother have done to help me become a psychiatrist. Now, the time has come that we have talked about many times. I hope to enter psychiatry in America."

"The accreditation requirements worry me," Saw said. "My legal training at Harvard went on forever with one requirement after another. But if you relocate to the USA, your medical school training will take almost as long because you won't be given enough credit for your training in Burma. If you stay in Burma, you'll need to be accepted as a resident and to take refresher training every few years, but the hardest part of your required training is over with.

"If you move to America, you'll have to serve a residency for at least four years, and you'll have to pass tests to get accredited. If you obey all the rules, you'll be retirement age before you ever begin to practice medicine. Look for a country where the requirements are more reasonable."

Thein said, "I agree. I want to practice in the United States, but I do not want to spend years as a low-paid medical resident."

"USA requirements are too difficult. What other countries pay their psychiatrists well? Which ones won't turn you into an indentured servant? Have you done your homework?"

To prove he had done research, Thein told Saw what he had learned from Foy, but the full list of accreditation requirements upset Saw even more.

Thein tried a different tact.

"Father, they call California the Golden State for a reason. Professional income is higher on average than most anywhere. As a California psychiatrist, it would be easier to repay Mother and you for the financial support that you have provided me."

"How much higher than other places? Give me some examples."

"I will have to do some research. The answer will depend on whether I suppose I will enter private practice or obtain a government position."

"Oh Hell, don't go to the bother," Saw said. "Are you renewing your commitment to send money back home?"

"I am. It is the least I can do after all you and Mother have done."

"I won't block your path to the Golden State, as you call it."

Saw began to see the financial merit in his son practicing psychiatry in California. If only there were a way to get around the strict immigration, accreditation, and residency requirements. He decided to look at Thein's impasse as a challenge for the Fixer. A plan began to take shape. Laws were made to be broken.

Instead of the incremental approach he had taken in Burma to advance his son's education and career, the Fixer would try in one step to bypass the USA requirements. Neither Saw nor Thein was willing to defer gratification for years. And the Fixer did not have the means to repeatedly tamper with the authorities in faraway America. He could not do the checking and rechecking that he had done with the Institute of Medicine, the Rangoon Psychiatric Hospital, and the Burma medical licensing board.

How could he help Thein bypass the regulatory barriers to a lucrative psychiatric practice in California? He thought of his old friend, Lester Jordan. He didn't know what position Lester held in America's federal government, but over the years in phone conversations his former classmate had implied that he exercised behind-the-scenes power.

Maybe Saw and Lester together could figure out how to strip away the red tape in getting Thein accepted as a psychiatrist in California. Since Lester lived in America, he would be in a better position than Saw to research the medical education systems there.

Saw did not know if Lester could help him or what he could offer his old friend in return, but he would explore the possibilities.

Unbeknown to Saw, in recent years he had become of special interest to Lester Jordan and his employer. They had monitored the Fixer's activities for several years because of his close relationship to Burma's dictator. Lester had led Saw to believe that he was on the staff of US Senator Gene Clowers. Instead, soon after Lester graduated from Harvard, his father had helped him land an entry level position with the US Central Intelligence Agency.

Although he had been hired as an entry-level political scientist, within eighteen months Lester became an apprentice undercover operative, spurred on by his long-held belief that the most powerful people are those who work behind the scenes. Lester proved a natural for foreign intelligence work, and assumed ever more responsible positions within the CIA.

Saw expected he might need to make many phone calls in order to defraud California's medical accreditation system. Lester might refer him to a number of experts. He never used his home phone to make confidential calls, suspecting that a Ne Win workman had long since tapped the line.

Saw bribed a phone company official he knew to secretly install a private line to his house. After conducting his business with the appropriate parties in America, whether it were to take days or weeks, he would then have the phone line removed.

Saw placed a call to the last number that Lester had given him. He assumed the phone he was calling was in Lester's home, but it was in an office at Langley, Virginia. Lester's phone showed the origin of incoming calls.

CIA operative Jordan let the phone ring a few times before he answered, remembering to pretend he was at home and did not know who was calling. He was delighted that Saw was phoning him because Lester's superiors had recently directed him to use their relationship to get strategic information about Ne Win.

After the exchange of greetings, Saw said, "Lester, I need help with a sensitive matter and hope you can guide me. Is this a good time to bring it up?"

"I'll help you if I can. But there will be a better opportunity for us to consider your needs if you can wait a few days. I'm coming to Rangoon on business next week. How about that?"

Saw said that waiting a few days was no problem.

Lester declined Saw's offer of a ride from the Mingaladon Airport, and said Saw could meet him at the Strand Hotel anytime after noon the next Tuesday.

Saw was having difficulty believing his good fortune. Lester's presence in Rangoon would eliminate the risk of anyone listening in on phone calls. And Saw wanted very much to see his old friend.

However, Saw could not help but wonder how it was that his need for assistance from Lester coincided with the latter's business trip to Rangoon. How could this be? To begin with, except for China, North Korea, Thailand, and a few more, Ne Win had cut off almost all commerce with businesses and governments outside of Burma. Moreover, in the twenty-nine years since they had graduated from Harvard, Lester had never come to Burma or anywhere in Asia.

Or had Lester made trips that Saw didn't know about? Saw wondered if more than coincidence was involved. Maybe he didn't know Lester Jordan so well after all.

Saw drove to the Strand Hotel. Wearing a longyi, sandals, eyeglasses, and a fake mustache, he went to the front counter and asked to see a room on the third floor. He allowed the bellhop to escort him. Saw inspected the room. After mentally filing an image of the physical layout, he tipped the bellhop, and returned to the front counter where he reserved the room for three nights, beginning Monday.

The Victorian-style Strand Hotel opened in 1901. Named for its address at 92 Strand Road, the grand structure faced south, overlooking the Rangoon River. In its early days, many guests, including royalty and nobility, regarded it as the finest hotel east of the Suez Canal.

During colonial times, the Strand's clientele were exclusively whites. The hotel underwent major renovation in 1937. In 1941, during World War II, it briefly served as quarters for Japanese troops.

In 1945, for the first time, Burmese became part of the Strand's clientele. After Burma achieved independence in 1948, the hotel was neglected by post-colonial governments. In 1988, the old hotel was in only fair condition. Lester Jordan chose to stay at the Strand because he had read Rudyard Kipling, George Orwell, and Somerset Maugham, famous writers who had stayed there.

It had been twenty-nine years since Saw and Lester had seen each other. Both still were in top physical and mental condition because of their rigorous duties, which were similar although Saw was a hitman and Lester a spy. Both of their government positions required secrecy, deception, and sometimes violence.

Lester planted eavesdropping devices in his hotel room but decided to not wear a bug or a concealed weapon. He left his Glock 23 in a dresser drawer in the bedroom.

Chapter 15

Disclosing and Negotiating

Knowledge is power.

—Francis Bacon
Meditations Sacrae (1597)

For his meeting with Lester, Saw wore slacks, a knit shirt, and a sports jacket, reminiscent of how he and Lester had dressed as law students. He rang the doorbell.

"Saw, you look like you could whip any kick-boxer in Rangoon. It's good to see you."

"And you look like John Wayne. I'd recognize you at a hundred meters anywhere in the world."

They shook hands, exchanged more compliments, and decided drinks were in order. Saw insisted that the celebrating would be in his room. Burma was the host country and Rangoon his home town. He wanted to bear the expense, so he had rented a room and made sure it was stocked with booze and snacks. And if they went out to eat, he would pay the tab.

"I want to show you that Burma is more hospitable than you may have heard."

Saw stopped just inside his room.

"Lester, I'm not wearing a wire, and my room isn't bugged. I want the same assurance from you. Are you wearing a bug?"

"Saw, relax. I'm your old buddy, Lester. I'm not wearing a bug. You said Burma is more friendly than its reputation suggests."

"Sorry. Living under a military government has made me paranoid."

"Forget it. I understand. I'm thirsty."

They had drank beer when students at Harvard. So they reverted to form except that Saw insisted Lester try Dagon beer instead of the Budweiser they had favored in the old days.

"Like most Burmese beers, Dagon is made from rice. If you find it bland, add lime juice."

Lester said, "For someone seeking a favor, you were rather aggressive a few minutes ago."

"Well, I've come to believe that you want something from me."

"You're perceptive," Lester said. "We can divulge who we each work for after we get reacquainted."

Lester and Saw drank and recalled former classmates and professors. One day long ago, Saw, Lester, and other students were sitting in a Harvard classroom waiting for a lecture to begin. The dean of the law school, as a favor to the regular instructor, was to give a rare, guest presentation.

To build suspense, the distinguished William Carter stood at the front of the class without speaking, biding his time, pretending to be lost in profound thought. Saw sat behind Lester who was seated near the entrance to the classroom. Ralph Matell sat next to Lester who was delving into a textbook, studying relentlessly as he always did.

Except for Lester, the class was paying rapt attention to the dean. Lester had his head down, reading. Noise drifted in from students passing by in the hallway.

Dean Carter lowered his eyes to review his lecture notes, and spoke to no one in particular.

"Please close the door."

Ralph tugged on Lester's shirt sleeve and whispered "Lester, close the door."

Without looking up from his book, Lester bellowed at his pesky classmate.

"Close the door yourself!"

Dean Carter's jaw dropped, his face turned red, his eyes bulged. He glared at Lester just as the latter looked up from his book. Their eyes met, and Lester grinned.

Dean Carter said, "See me after class."

Saw said, "Ralph Matell knew exactly how this misunderstanding came about, but he didn't stay after class to rescue you, and you know, I didn't either."

Both Saw and Lester doubled over in laughter.

Saw finished the story with a rhyme.

"That semester the lowest grade went to Lester!"

The former classmates swapped more stories including the one about Saw announcing that spirits made people mentally ill as punishment for evil deeds done in past lives, proving guilt and thus eliminating the need for a trial. An immediate execution was in order. Lester told the story, and Saw pretended he had been joking on that night in 1956.

As the night wore on and drinks were downed, the spy and the assassin grew philosophical. Saw described his attitude about the individual's place in society.

"The individual thinks the most important fact of reality is his own existence, but this is only his personal point of view, a frame of reference not shared by the rest of us.

"This self-importance lacks perspective. The brief existence of one person should be considered in the context of prehistory, history, eternity, the world population, all mankind, and the endlessness of outer space. In other words, the individual is of no importance."

They told stories and jokes, and reported what they knew of the fortunes and misfortunes of their former classmates. Neither man was as drunk as he pretended, knowing better than to let his guard down. But they agreed to sober up before attending to the business that had brought them together after twenty-nine years.

Late that afternoon, the American and the Burman met again in Saw's room. The time had come to disclose who each worked for, and what each wanted.

"I report directly to Ne Win, the man in control of all Burma."

"Saw, I know some of what you do. It would be unfair for me to sit here and feign ignorance while encouraging you to tell me more. I'm leveling with you."

"I figured that you know a lot about me. Tell me about your duties so I know about you half of what you know about me. We can go into depth later, but right now I need to know who you work for."

"I don't work for US senator Gene Clowers. I work for the CIA."

"I'm not surprised. And I can guess why you're interested in me."

"The CIA is interested in you because of your close working relationship with Ne Win, the man who rules Burma."

"I'm trying to look at this professionally, and not get mad at you personally. Even though you work for the all-mighty CIA, don't assume that I lack power."

"The CIA and I take you very seriously. We have high regard for your abilities. Here's my interpretation of our situation.

"If you and I can work together as friends we'll have a lot of control over our powerful bosses. They desperately need information, and we control that information, that knowledge. If you and I trust each other we'll fare much better than if we part company.

"If we fail to cooperate with each other, the CIA wouldn't leave you entirely alone, and I couldn't help you with your problem. You phoned me for a reason, and I'm not entitled to anything from you unless I can help you. I really do care about your need, whatever it is. If I can't help you, I'll say so straight away."

"Fair enough. But I need to think about how to deal with the CIA. Maybe I need a half-day alone before we talk further."

"Saw, I can't leave you alone with this new information. You might decide to shoot me or to break my neck. We're disclosing information and adjusting to each disclosure as we go along. I need you to stay with me till we get this thing hashed out.

"I assure you that the CIA is interested in you only as you relate to Ne Win. It's the head of Burma that my agency is concerned about. If you keep me in the picture, I'll make sure that no one messes with you. We just want information about Ne Win as to his evolving relationships with Communist China and North Korea. I'm sure none of this surprises you."

"It's true that I help Ne Win carry out his agenda. I need assurance that your government isn't interested in me as some sort of threat to your nation."

"My agency considers whatever you do as purely internal to Burma. What we care about is what Ne Win does that can affect America."

"Lester, you're saying the right things, but I'm not sure I can trust you. I was sure I covered my tracks over the years on every assignment. It's troubling to think that the CIA knew what I was doing."

"Whoa! I'm not saying that the CIA knows how you carry out your duties. I'm saying only that we have for some time been interested in the fact that you report directly to Ne Win, and that your meetings almost always include only you and him, or maybe the head of military intelligence as well."

"How did the CIA infiltrate the Ne Win high command?"

"You know how this kind of thing works. All we had to do was find disgruntled officers and pay them handsomely. Sometimes they didn't even have to be disgruntled, just greedy. We had to be patient, but usually it was as simple as leaving an envelope of cash where an officer could find it. If he took the cash, we left another envelope at the same site. After he took the cash several times, we approached the officer and pointed out that Ne Win wouldn't like what he'd been doing. We told him that if he provided us with information, we would not only keep his misconduct a secret, but would regularly pay him more cash. We had snared the officer as soon as he took the first money that he found. Most army officers can be bought in this way."

Saw said, "What you're saying scares me. How many of the officers that I serve with have you co-opted? How many of them could the CIA bring down just by letting Ne Win know they have become informers? I need a guarantee that the CIA won't take me down, and instead will protect me."

"I assure you of that at my level, and I have a lot of clout. But I'll go further if we do business. I'll get the assurance you want from the CIA director himself. We can't make headway in our negotiations until you accept my word that we're interested in you only as a potential informer."

"You sound so matter-of-fact. You want me to spy on Ne Win. If he finds out about even this meeting alone, he'll kill me. Keep in mind that I haven't said I will help you."

"I realize that. From the beginning of our reunion, there was no good way to approach this situation. Who gives information first? We only knew we both had needs."

"Yeah, well I'm concerned about staying alive. I wish I hadn't come here to meet you. It appears I've made a big mistake."

"Saw, I'm your friend. And I'll try to help you with your problem that we can't seem to get around to discussing. If you lay out your problem, and if my agency can't help you, I'll do my best to make the CIA leave you alone."

"OK, I don't have many choices, given my history, my duties, and what I want. I'll tell you what I need. It involves the career goals of my son, Maunt Thein."

"I figured as much. I know he means a lot to you."

"What you just said—since you're a CIA operative—makes me worry whether your agency will harm my son or my wife."

"Hold on, Saw. I'm not insinuating that your family is in danger. What kind of spy agency would we be if we harmed our informers or their families? I can't imagine anything more counterproductive. We don't do business that way. What I meant to convey is exactly the opposite of the way you took it. I meant only that it's natural for you to be interested in furthering your son's career.

"Thousands of times the CIA has gone to great lengths to protect its informers. We're sneaky, but we protect the people who help us accomplish our mission, even if we don't like their style. There still is such a thing as human decency even in our lines of work."

"OK, Lester, but you have to admit that the CIA knowing anything about my duties or my family is very upsetting. But to finish stating my reason for contacting you—I want you to help Thein achieve his dream of practicing psychiatry in California."

Chapter 16

A Deal is Made

It is an old maxim that every man has his price.

—Sir Robert Walpole
The Bee (1733-1734)

The CIA's interest in Saw scared him. How long had the spy agency been watching him?

Lester too was on edge. He knew more about Saw's purging of Ne Win's enemies than he had admitted. Saw was adept at killing people in a variety of ways. If it came to hand-to-hand combat there in the hotel room, Lester was no match for the Fixer.

Saw said, "I'll lay out what I want from the CIA, and I better get a good measure of help or I won't do a thing for you. For us to do business, I'd be risking my life while you guys just create official-looking documents, and help my son get a psychiatric practice—the kind of things that you do all the time."

Lester started to speak, but Saw cut him off.

"I want you to set Thein up with a practice in California. I want him to begin practicing psychiatry soon after he arrives there."

Lester said, "Now that I know what you want, let's take one thing at a time. You need to recognize there are many educational and medical requirements that Thein must meet—or appear to meet—to qualify for a psychiatric practice in America.

"Don't underestimate how demanding your goal is. And don't underestimate the difficulties involved in falsifying a work history and authentic-looking documents, especially for a doctor in America.

"Let's consider alternatives that might satisfy Thein. It would be easier to set him up with a practice in a place like Thailand or India. Half the doctors in India got their credentials from a mail-order catalog. Must Thein live and work in California? Let's have a broader discussion before we choose a specific plan."

"Thein has worked hard to get through Rangoon Institute of Medicine Number 1. He's fed up with Burma. He wants to practice in America and live there the rest of his life. No other place lures him like California does."

Lester nodded.

Saw said, "Thein has completed six years of medical school which included one year of supervised work experience at the Rangoon Psychiatric Hospital. He passed a test and got a license to practice in Burma. That's on the plus side of the ledger.

"On the minus side is that the central government made him sign a contract that he'll work at least four years in some medically underserved part of Burma. He'd rather spend those years practicing psychiatry in America.

"Also on the minus side—in America, he'd have to initially take any medical job he could get so he could get letters of recommendation for work done there. He'd have to pass licensing tests, and score highly enough that someone would take him in as a resident.

"And residencies are hard to come by in the USA, especially for foreign medical graduates. I told Thein to forget his big plans and stay here in Burma. But he's determined to practice in California."

"And you thought I could help you meet these challenges? And you thought this even before you knew that I work for the CIA?"

"I didn't know where else to turn. I thought you could do research and inform me about the medical accreditation requirements in America and maybe give me some advice."

Lester said, "But you really want much more."

A DEAL IS MADE

"Well, when you said you work for the CIA, I could see more is possible. You guys create documents like school transcripts, diplomas, and fake passports all the time.

"If you can't help Thein and me, we'll accomplish our objective some other way. Stay out of my business, or I'll tell Ne Win what you're up to, and that'll shut off your flow of information for sure."

"Now, hold on. I didn't say we can't help you. I just want you to know that what you're asking will be difficult. Ne Win doesn't want any medical personnel to leave the country. He's gone back and forth over the years in wanting doctors to stay in Burma, and wanting them to get out. But right now, he's dead set against any doctor leaving the country. We might have to smuggle Thein out of Burma.

"The CIA will have to make it look as though Thein has already served his four-year contractual obligation with the Ne Win regime. We can do that. We also can make it look like he served a residency in Burma.

"But we can't make it appear he has already served a residency in the United States. It's too easy for medical authorities to check out his history in the USA. And too many doctors know each other. Hospital administrators and medical school faculties communicate freely. It's altogether different in America than in Burma."

Saw said, "I learned that when I attended Harvard."

"The CIA can't make it look like Thein gained medical certification and served a residency in America. We can't do that."

Saw said, "What can you do?"

"We can help Thein get a physician assistant position in the Los Angeles area so he can get letters of recommendation for medical experience in America. We can place him in a residency at a school like UCLA and persuade the attending physicians to not be too demanding, but he'll have to serve that residency.

"He won't suffer the disappointment of working hard for years and then fail to get a residency. And we can place him in a practice after he completes his residency. That would take the uncertainty out of whether his efforts would bear fruit."

"Lester, we're both out in the open now. Thein is an excellent student although he has been known to freeze up when confronted with a particularly hard test question. By the way, according to the news media, the student in Burma with the highest matriculation test score is Sanda Win, the ruler's daughter."

"What a coincidence!"

"Will the CIA commit to helping Thein pass the medical licensing exams? And I don't mean that you help by tutoring him, but that you will intervene with the regulatory agency that administers the exams if necessary. Can you do that for him?"

Lester said, "The medical board in each state administers the federal licensing exams. So it would be the California Medical Board that we would have to persuade to assign Thein passing grades, I can't promise that we would succeed, only that we will try."

"Will you personally see that your agency tries hard to get the medical board to make allowances for Thein if necessary?"

"I promise I will be personally involved."

"OK," Saw said. "I'm holding you to your word."

"The main thing is that Thein is actually physically present, and literally serves as a physician assistant and then as a resident. If his attendance is excellent, and he gets along with his superiors, we'll intervene for him as needed. And we'll see what we can do to keep him from failing licensing exams. But this is a tall order, so I hope you'll reciprocate by keeping me well informed."

Saw said, "I'll summarize the whole package for Thein, and you let me know if I'm right. The CIA will create documents showing that Thein fulfilled his responsibility to work four years in an underserved part of Burma. Your agency also will create documents that show he served a residency in Burma. You'll transport him by air from Burma to California.

"In California, the CIA will place Thein in a medical position of some kind, probably a physician assistant position, so he can get medical experience in America, and this will be supported by letters of recommendation. And your agency will place him in a medical residency. You'll make sure the people in charge of the residency realize that Thein is academically qualified. And, if necessary, you'll make sure he passess the medical licensing exams. After Thein fin-

A DEAL IS MADE

ishes his residency, the CIA will ensure that he is hired into a psychiatric practice."

Lester said, "That's the entire package, but I can't guarantee success, only that we will do our best. These things would be in exchange for you doing certain things for the CIA. And you and I will have a continuing relationship. If you expire for any reason, well of course you would no longer be able to fulfill your part of the contract, and my agency would cease to help your son."

"You just gave me a good reason to live on."

"I think I can get my superiors to approve this agreement, but then actually doing these things will be very hard. Are you ready to discuss the CIA's needs?"

"You're overstating the difficulty of what I'm asking you to do in order to make me feel like I'm getting a bargain. Tell me what the CIA wants me to do for the USA."

"I'll give you an overview and then the details," Lester said. "Realize that the CIA is concerned about what might affect America, not whether there is fair play and justice throughout the world.

"The CIA doesn't care if Ne Win's drug dealing harms people. The US Drug Enforcement Administration can worry about that. The CIA actually likes to see Ne Win and the ethnic minorities in the border areas fighting over who gets the biggest share of the drug trade. That lessens Ne Win's ability to spend time cultivating relationships with Communist China and North Korea."

"Lester, your agency's involvement with the Southeast Asian drug trade exceeds your description. True, the CIA is happy enough to see Ne Win have to compete for his market share. But throughout the Cold War, the CIA used gangsters and war lords, many of them drug dealers, to fight the Chinese communists. Your agency engaged in complicity, tolerance, and willful ignorance about the trade and the harm it was causing, even to American soldiers in Viet Nam as they consumed opium and heroin.

"In fighting the communists, the CIA provided drug lords like Lo Hansing Han with transport, arms, and political protection. Your agency still provides Ne Win's troops with airplanes to move opium from Burma's northern highlands to Bangkok.

THE MIND DOCTOR

"One of the CIA's front businesses is Air America, and its planes and helicopters are still moving drugs from Burma to Thailand and other countries. And most of the drug sales benefit Ne Win and his drug king partners, Lo Hansing Han and Khun Sa, depending on which one happens to be out of prison at the time.

"As early as 1962, Ne Win cut off almost all commerce between Burma and western countries, but he makes an exception for the CIA. He's happy to see Air America planes and copters still landing and taking off in Burma."

"Thanks for the history lesson. But who are you to deliver an ethics lecture?"

Saw stood up, glaring at Lester.

"Hey, Saw, I'm just kidding. Honest. You're right on all counts. All counts. Let's get back to what the CIA wants to get out of our deal."

Saw sat down.

Lester said, "We want to know how cozy Ne Win is with Communist China. America is worried about a Sino military threat. Any alliances that China forms with other countries could become a problem to America's national security. We want the same kind of information regarding North Korea."

"That's all you want from me? Sure, it will be difficult to prepare documents for Thein, and maybe you'll have to smuggle him out of the country and create a cover story, but no one in Burma's government is going to worry about what happens to him. People in Burma disappear all the time.

"But you're asking me to commit treason, punishable by death. You're asking a lot more of me than I'm asking of you."

"But Saw, you can ease into this new role a little at a time. Just go as far as you feel comfortable. You'll report to me, and I can interpret cautiously worded reports. Most of this will be oral—we rarely would ask you to give us documents—just to give us hints and leads."

Saw began to think about what Ne Win had done to Burma and how he had damaged the education and health care systems. He began to see himself as a double agent. But the risk was too great for

A DEAL IS MADE

the rewards that Thein would reap. He would tell his son to stay in Burma. Saw rose to see Lester to the door.

Lester said, "What would it take to persuade you to work with me for at least a while?"

"First, you would set up the means of getting my wife and me out of Burma real fast if necessary. Second, you would come up with a solid plan to protect me. Your plan would have to include how I could pass information to you. How would you limit my exposure? I won't meet with anyone except you and then only rarely and never in public. You would need to make it appear the information came from someone other than me."

"I can do those things."

Saw said, "And there's a big uncertainty that could drastically change my status in Burma. People are fed up with Ne Win and his dictatorship. There's great unrest among students, Buddhist monks, farmers, and even the rank-and-file military. It's dangerous times. So far Ne Win has controlled all those factions. But pressure is building, and Ne Win is now seventy-seven. He's mortal, afterall, and could die at any time from something as matter-of-fact as a heart attack. Will the CIA still protect me if Burma suddenly has a new ruler?"

"Would a new ruler need a professional with your skills? Would he need you?"

"I don't know," Saw said. "I don't know who the next dictator will be."

"We never know the future. Have you thought about taking control of Burma? You could be the next strongman."

"I've toyed with the idea, but I'm living pretty well now. I'm more interested in persuading the next ruler that he'll need me."

"The CIA thinks you would prevail in such an effort. We're willing to bet that you will serve any subsequent regime."

"You're saying you'll need an inside man no matter what."

"That's right."

"I want you to explain to my son how to answer questions that an education accreditation authority might ask."

"We can do that. Anything else? Please don't throw in any deal-killers."

"You're asking me to risk my life, and all I've asked for are false documents, a cover story, a medical residency, maybe manipulation of some test scores, eventually a job for my son, and a means of escape for my wife and me. My list may be long, but I repeat—it's just administrative stuff that a spy agency does every day."

"I know. But these things are a lot harder to do than you might imagine. I'll have to sell this to others in the agency. Can I consider this the complete list?"

"I'll need money if things go awry. I want thirty thousand American dollars each month placed in a Swiss bank account. That's the complete list."

"I'm painfully aware that I address this question to a Harvard-trained lawyer skilled in the art of negotiation. May I now consider you, Maunt Saw, a CIA asset who will report to me?"

"If the CIA honors our agreement, I will too."

Chapter 17

There's No Time to Pack

In 1988…the people of Burma rose against their government. They were brutally put down on a scale matched only by the Chinese repression of Tiananmen.

—Bertil Lintner
Outrage (1989, 1990)

Early on, Lester told his CIA team to create false records of Thein's medical training in Burma. Counterfeit documents were made to indicate that Thein had worked four years in medically underserved villages in Burma, and that he had served a three-year residency in the mental health ward of Mandalay's biggest general hospital. Lester examined the falsified documents with an experienced eye. They appeared genuine.

Lester obtained the help of a CIA planner, Lawrence Grant, who was expert at helping informers start new lives. Mr. Grant knew how to create new identities for people, how to help them find employment, and how to live in distant communities, safe from those they had informed on. He excelled at bypassing government regulations.

Lawrence's value to the CIA was increased by the many personal relationships that he maintained. Over the years, he had met many people in positions of authority, and had done favors for many of them. Using CIA funds, Lawrence bought gifts for people for their birthdays and other special occasions. The packaging, the greeting cards, and the address labels made it appear the gifts came from Lawrence personally.

He also monitored the news media, and noticed whenever a friend of the CIA obtained a new job, promotion, or award. He always sent a congratulatory card or a gift, and stayed in contact with those likely to be of value to the agency.

Lawrence Grant met with Dr. Everett Goodwin, the senior partner of a group of physicians who owned a chain of medical clinics in Southern California. Lawrence showed Dr. Thein's employment resume to Dr. Goodwin, and described in general terms the national security need to place the Burman in a psychiatric position in California. Lawrence disclosed only that securing a position for Dr. Thein was part of an international deal to keep America safe.

Everett agreed to reserve a physician-assistant position for Dr. Thein, understanding that Thein intended to move on as soon as he secured a psychiatric residency at a teaching hospital. Everett would provide Dr. Thein letters of recommendation, praising him for excellent work at the Southern California Medical Clinics.

Mr. Grant's next task was to persuade the UCLA Medical Center to reserve a residency for Dr. Thein after he completed his year as a physician assistant.

Lawrence met with Dean Franklin Alexander, the director, and Associate Dean Arthur Young, the deputy director. The three men readily reached an agreement. In the interest of national security, the medical school would help the CIA, provided of course that Dr. David Thein had minimum qualifications. Again, Lawrence disclosed only that what the CIA was asking was in the interest of national security.

The two medical center administrators saw it their duty to assist the federal government. They were simply diverting one residency from a more likely recipient to a less likely one, and this diversion would help the CIA gain strategic information to keep America safe from a foreign threat. They persuaded themselves that Thein was at least minimally qualified for the kind of residency they had in mind. And after all, it was only one residency.

Assigning a medical residency to a young Burmese doctor was a small price to pay for America's security.

Deputy Director Young said that whenever the medical center received Dr. Thein's application, he would ensure that the relevant UCLA computer program matched him with a residency that Young would have preselected. Managing the computer program would be the easy part. The human element would be far more difficult. Young would have to persuade certain medical school department heads and staff doctors that Dr. Thein was a suitable candidate.

The applicant from Burma would have to appear before a selection committee, and be interviewed by several professors. They would not like being told to accept someone whom they were sure to find was only marginally qualified. Administrators Young and Alexander expected to have to call in loyalty debts that various professors owed them in order to persuade the committee to award Dr. Thein a residency. And they expected to also have to do administrative and political favors for certain members of the future selection committee.

Lester did a cost-benefit analysis that confirmed the worth of the actions he was causing his agency to take. The pay-off would be valuable information about Ne Win who was interacting with Communist China and North Korea in ways that could harm US interests. The mentally unstable despot could not be allowed to acquire nuclear technology. The Fixer was in a key position to obtain crucial intelligence information. An emergency could arise at any time that would make Saw's information of great value. Who knew what Burma state secrets Saw might provide in the future if the CIA indeed created career opportunities for his only son?

Ne Win and his military elite prospered by exploiting Burma's natural resources, and by depriving its citizens of a decent standard of living. To raise money quickly, the government sold logging, mining, and fishing rights to other countries, especially Thailand. The resources were extracted with no regard for sustainability, environmental impacts, or profit sharing with local villages. The government used most of the proceeds to buy arms and ammunition to use against the ethnic minorities living in the country's border regions.

The government took property from citizens by simply ordering them off the land. It also forced men, women, and children to work without compensation. They built roads, railroads, and other public works. Women used sledgehammers to break rocks into pieces small enough to serve as ballast for the roadbeds while their infants slept, crawled, or toddled nearby.

In September 1987, the military regime demonetized three of Burma's banknotes, the 25, 35, and 75 kyats. This removed about 80 percent of the money that was in circulation and left university students unable to pay tuition that was due within days.

These government policies caused 1988 to erupt into the most violent year in Burma since ancient kings ruled the land. Millions of university students, Buddhist monks, youngsters, housewives, doctors, and even rank-and-file members of the army, navy, and air force demonstrated against the regime.

On July 23, 1988, in a speech to the nation, Ne Win resigned as Prime Minister and as Chairman of the Burma Socialist Programme Party. But this was in fact a show put on to mislead the public. It later came to light that Ne Win secretly continued to exercise great power. For the next few years, the despot continued to give orders to the series of figureheads who replaced him until a senior general, Than Shwe, seized power in 1992.

In August and September 1988, a series of marches, demonstrations, protests, and riots jolted the nation. The revolt was against the one-party system, the Burma Socialist Programme Party, that remained in place after Ne Win had pretended to surrender power.

Key events occurred on August 8, 1988, giving rise to the name, *The Four Eights Uprising*. Acting on the advice of astrologers, the organizers decided the uprising's main events would begin in August on the eighth day at eight minutes past 8:00 a.m. At that moment, a general strike began. Dockworkers at the Rangoon Seaport walked off the job. Simultaneously, tens of thousands of people began marching toward the center of Rangoon. Similar marches began at the same moment in cities throughout Burma.

Although in disarray, the government violently suppressed the 1988 uprisings, with the military and the riot police killing between three thousand and ten thousand people. A government coverup prevented journalists from compiling accurate records. Bodies were immediately picked up and cremated, buried in mass graves, or dumped into rivers. Before it could dry, blood was washed from the streets.

Saw was monitoring the people's growing agitation and unprecedented level of organization. He knew what the people did not—that Ne Win was still in command and was on the verge of using the army and the riot police to violently suppress the demonstrations. Saw had taken Ne Win at his word when the tyrant issued a warning during his July 23, 1988, fake resignation speech:

"In continuing to maintain control, I want the entire nation, the people, to know that if in the future there are mob disturbances, if the army shoots, it hits—there is no firing into the air to scare."

Saw was disappointed in Thein's failure to perceive the danger that was building. His son understood how much the public hated the oppressive political system, but did not foresee the brutal measures the government would take to suppress the civil uprisings. Thein's work at the Rangoon Psychiatric Hospital had made him painfully aware of the day-to-day cruelty that the dictatorship exerted, but the notion that the police and military would kill masses of citizens had not occurred to him. Saw, on the other hand, believed the country was about to suffer violence of historic proportions.

It was August 7, 1988. At their home on that evening, Saw asked his son to come out of his room for a meeting with his parents.

"Son, the pot is about to boil over. Civil unrest is worse than at any time during Ne Win's reign. A major uprising is underway, and the military is about to kill the demonstrators. Many will die. Ne Win is about to close the borders. You better get on your way to the USA before the army closes the airports."

Thein was not ready for this. His father was telling him he had to get out of the country—now.

Saw said, "I've been talking by phone with Lester Jordan. The CIA has an Air America helicopter at Mingaladon Airport that's ready to fly you to Bangkok. You'll take commercial airliners from there to California."

The phone rang. It was Lester.

"Saw, I'm at the airport. If Thein wants to relocate to California, he better get here right now. Unless he has already packed his bags, he better leave with just the clothes on his back."

They hung up.

"Thein, you don't have time to pack. Your mother and I will drive you to the airport. Let's go."

Saw handed his son an envelope filled with American currency.

"Leave your belongings here. You can replace them when you get to the USA."

Thein said, "I will not pack a duffle bag. I will just put a few things in a satchel."

"Get in the Honda. We're leaving."

Chapter 18

California At Last

California, Here I Come

—Buddy De Silva and Joseph Meyer
Song title (1924)

Thein's father and mother drove him to Mingaladon Airport, twelve kilometers north of their Lake Inya villa. An Air America helicopter was waiting, its engine idling noisily.

Lester Jordan and a tall white man in a dark jacket were talking with two Burmese soldiers, each with a rifle slung across his back. The four men were relaxed, enjoying their conversation. Air America had transported opium and heroin in and out of Mingaladon for years in assisting Ne Win's drug dealing. And now Thein was about to benefit from the long-standing relationship. The two soldiers had just received a bribe for agreeing to let Thein board the helicopter.

Saw, Sang Yki, and Thein approached the foursome on foot but stopped a short distance away. Lester joined Saw's group.

"Things are happening fast. This is our last chance to get Thein out of the country."

Saw said, "Ne Win will turn San Lwin loose on the people, and the Butcher will live up to his name."

"At any moment these soldiers could receive new orders," Lester said. "Also, reinforcements might arrive."

Saw said, "Thein, tell your mother goodbye. You're on your way to America."

Thein hugged his mother. They said their goodbyes.

He turned to his father and stood still while Saw put both hands on his son's shoulders and established eye contact, a show of respect in Burma from an older man to a younger one.

Thein walked to the helicopter. An American marine in fatigues reached out of the craft and gave Thein a hands-on assist inside, half-lifting and half-pulling him. Sergeant Patrick McGraw closed the helicopter door while Thein fumbled with his seat belt, and the chopper took flight.

The helicopter sat down at the Don Muang Airport in Bangkok. Sergeant McGraw hustled Thein inside the terminal.

"Dr. Thein, we left Mingaladon just in time. We got word on the chopper's radio that the Butcher's soldiers arrived just as we got airborne. If we'd been a minute later, they might've shot us out of the sky."

"Are things that bad?"

"Yes. Many will be killed. The people are not standing down. Their hatred of the dictatorship can no longer be held in check."

"Your flight leaves in thirty minutes. I understand that you have some American currency on your person. I'll help you get through customs. I know the officials here. You'll have to pay a bribe, but I'll make sure it's not excessive. From then on you'll have to catch your flights unaided. Here are your tickets and itinerary."

Thein's commercial flight left on time. For the next eighteen hours, he was either in flight or waiting for a connecting plane. Eventually he arrived at the Los Angeles International Airport.

As he entered the terminal, a marine sergeant in uniform welcomed him to America.

"Am I in California?"

The sergeant said, "Indeed you are."

The sergeant helped Thein get his cash through customs, and this time he did not have to pay a bribe. Thein had arrived in the land he had heard so much about.

At first, Thein had trouble handling his emotions He missed his mother, father, and Foy. Everything had happened so fast. Everyone at this monstrous airport was in a hurry. The lights were too bright, and the public address systems too loud. Had he made a grave mistake by coming to California? Maybe Foy had been right. Maybe he should have stayed in Burma.

Thein tried to phone home but failed to get through because of damage caused to Burma's phone lines during the civil unrest. Three days passed before he mailed a letter to his parents to let them know he was safe. For his return address he used a post office box instead of the address of the apartment he had rented.

On Saw's advice, Sang Yki wrote few letters to their son. She gave each letter to Saw to read to ensure the wording was innocuous. Little correspondence got through because of the civil unrest and the government's militant reactions.

Thein tried over and over to reach Foy by phone. On his fourth day of repeated dialing, he was startled when his friend answered.

"Foy, this is Thein. Can you hear me?"

"Barely. Where are you? What happened to you? I called your phone, but no one answered."

"I am in California. Father made me leave before the army closed the borders."

"I guessed you had left like thousands of others. I'm glad you're still alive."

"How are things there? Are you injured?"

"I'm well enough, but many have died or are injured. I've been volunteering at Rangoon General Hospital. I came home to get some sleep."

"I should be there helping out just like you."

"No, Thein. Don't worry about it. People reacted in many different ways to the government violence. If you hadn't left when you did, you might never have left Burma."

"Are things that bad?"

"They're bad. You must have left things unsettled here. Are there loose ends that I can help you with?"

"How can you think of me when things there are so bad?"

THE MIND DOCTOR

"We're friends. I might never see you again, and I want you to have that long career you prepared for. Tell me if there are loose ends that I can help you tie up."

"Well, we recently completed our year of supervised medical training at the psychiatric hospital, but no one there said I had served my last day of work."

"You should contact your supervisor. Write him a letter, and try to reach him by phone. Make the letter a good one, suitable for your personnel file. Apologize for not clocking in and out for what would have been your last few days at the hospital. He'll understand that circumstances kept you from reporting for work. You got along well with him, so he should be happy to see there is no problem with attendance records. It'd help to thank him for being good to work for."

"I am afraid it would come to light that I now live in the United Sates. Someone might come after me."

"Thein, set the paranoia aside. You're a psychiatrist now. You treat people with paranoia, and must develop insight into delusional thinking. No one is coming after you. Why would they? If for no other reason, the massive disarray here in Burma rules out anyone doing more than just wondering what came of you. To establish your career there in California, you'll need to refer to your medical training in Burma. You'll need to explain that the government's violent suppression of the citizen uprising caused you to flee. You can explain that you had planned to leave anyway. No one'll blame you."

The conversation ended. Both men doubted they would ever again talk with each other.

A band of generals, acting on Ne Win's advice, staged a coup, and took control of Burma. They called themselves the State Law and Order Restoration Council.

Chapter 19

The Hurdles are too High

It is difficulties that show what men are.

—Epictetus
Discourses (lectures written down about 108 AD)

Thein served one year as a physician assistant for the Southern California Medical Clinics owned by Dr. Everett Goodwin and Associates. This step would have been unnecessary if Thein had been a graduate of a North American medical school because he would not have been at a competitive disadvantage with others vying for psychiatric residencies. But he was a graduate of Medical Institute Number 1, Rangoon, and the attending physicians and professors in the United States were wary of awarding him a coveted residency. Even with the agreement that Lawrence Grant had negotiated with the UCLA Medical Center, Thein still needed to present the best credentials he could muster.

    US medical educators questioned the quality of instruction in Burma, a place most knew only from news stories critical of the dictatorship. How modern was the Rangoon medical institute in this distant, mysterious, Southeast Asian country? What role did superstition play in teaching medicine? How much had civil unrest disrupted the academic training?

THE MIND DOCTOR

Such questions made it necessary for Thein to establish a solid medical work history in the United States. He needed US doctors to provide letters of recommendation saying he had worked for them, and had proved diligent and dependable.

So even though Thein had ostensibly achieved the title of psychiatrist in Burma, he now had to take a less prestigious, attainable position in America as a physician assistant in order to eventually achieve his dream. He took one step back in order to take a giant leap forward.

Thein desperately wanted an excellent performance appraisal from the Goodwin clinics. His coworkers and supervisor noted his sincere effort, but also saw a serious performance problem.

Intermittently, when under pressure, he fell into what seemed to be a brief trance. It usually cropped up when he was answering a staff physician's questions about diagnostic data he had gathered for the doctor. Thein might answer several questions about the medical procedures he had followed when suddenly he would clam up. After a few moments, he might or might not answer the doctor's last question. Thein always acted like nothing had happened.

Thein's supervisor reported the problem to the clinic's director.

"This momentary freezing up might not be a severe problem if this guy remained a physician assistant. But he intends to become a psychiatrist like he was in Burma. His lapse in speaking and acting might be linked to a lapse in judgment for all I know. I hate to think about him prescribing psychotropic drugs."

But Thein never missed a day of work, applied himself, and was exceptionally polite to those he worked with, so Everett Goodwin kept his promise to the CIA, and made sure that the clinic director assigned the Burman an excellent performance rating. The director also wrote a letter of recommendation for Thein that would help the UCLA Medical Center justify awarding him a psychiatric residency.

In January 1990, Thein completed his year of training as a physician assistant. He now had a record of medical performance in America.

When Thein began his four-year residency at the UCLA Medical Center, the physical and mental demands increased exponentially. He was seeing over one hundred eighty psychiatric patients each week. Most of his patients were either very young or very old. Many were in the children's hospital, and another large group was in the geriatric ward.

Thein worked at least one hundred hours a week even when there were holidays. He found the will to complete his residency because of Lester Jordan's promise of a psychiatric position.

Thein approached the end of his residency. In a few months he would take the third and last part of the United States medical licensing examination. Rumors circulated among the residents that the test would be very difficult.

Thein often studied with a small group of fellow residents. His study group had inherited sample test questions from previous study groups. Over the years residents had remembered many of the questions from their licensing exams. Eventually, a big file of possible questions had accrued. After Thein's cohort of residents took their exams they would pass the file along to the next generation of aspiring psychiatrists. When Thein's study group of seven or eight students assembled, the keeper of the file would break out the questions. Then each participant would be grilled.

Thein answered many questions orally and never stumbled. He had begun to think he would never again freeze up when it happened.

In front of the study group, a young female resident asked Thein, "According to the *Diagnostic and Statistical Manual of Mental Illnesses, Fourth Edition*, what three key elements must be present to constitute a mental disorder?"

This was an easy question. The third-step exam included much harder questions, asking how to conduct differential diagnoses or what to do in specific clinical situations. Those "how to" questions were the core of the exam. This question asked during a study session was simple. Thein knew the answer. But he said nothing. His face was blank.

"Thein, did you hear the question? Would you like me to repeat it?"

Thein was silent. The questioner was about to ask another student when Thein said, "Yes. Please repeat the question."

"According to the current *DSM*, what three key elements must be present to constitute a mental disorder?"

Thein said, "The first element consists of symptoms that involve disturbances in behavior, thoughts, or emotions. The second element consists of symptoms associated with…"

The words would not come out of his mouth. He sat in silence while the young resident asked the question of another student. Minutes later he left the study group.

Thein feared he would never pass the final licensing exam no matter how many times he tried. What could he do?

What would his father do? Thein believed the Fixer would pressure Lester Jordan to ensure that Thein received a passing grade. The agreement between Saw and Lester, as Thein understood it, was that the CIA would ensure that Thein obtained a psychiatry position as long as he had done his best to acquire the requisite medical training and experience in America. And Thein had tried with all his might to fulfill all the medical and regulatory requirements that the country had put in front of him.

After placing phone calls, leaving messages, and waiting for a return call, Thein finally heard from Lester who reached Thein by phone.

"Hello, Thein. This is Lester."

"Hello, Mr. Jordan. Have you kept current on my progress?"

"I have. You passed the first two medical licensing exams before you were matched with a residency. You'll complete your residency in about eight weeks, so you probably are preparing to take the third and final licensing exam."

"That is correct," Thein said. "But I hear that this last exam is difficult beyond belief. I have been studying with other residents, and there is no way that I will pass the test."

"Just do your best. If you fail the test, you can always take it again."

"I do not think I can pass it no matter how many times I try. I am about to give up. I am about to tell my father that I am done trying to be a psychiatrist in this country. The hurdles are too high."

"Don't give up. You've come too far and are nearing the finish line. Could I meet with you?"

Thein said, "I wish you would. Where and when?"

"In the restaurant where we last saw each other. Say at 1:00 pm three days from now. That would make it Thursday."

"I'll be there."

THE HURDLES ARE TOO HIGH

The restaurant included an Italian deli that specialized in pasta salads. When Thein arrived, Lester was seated at a corner table.

Thein said, "Thank you for taking the time to see me."

"That's OK. This is important. Can I talk you into taking the step three licensing exam? You're bright and you've studied hard. I bet you can pass the test."

"I know better than you what I am facing. I shall ask for my physician assistant job back unless you help me."

"Don't consider that any further. If you don't stay with the program and become a psychiatrist, Saw will stop providing me information."

"So Father's services are of value to the CIA?"

"Yes, they are. Senior General Than Shwe has Ne Win's old position as dictator of Burma. And Saw is working for him.

"Here's an example of the information that Saw passes to me. The Than Shwe regime is associating more and more with North Korea in the hope that Korea will develop nuclear weapons and then share the technology with Burma.

"Senior Burmese officials recently traveled to Russia and North Korea. Than Shwe considered the simple fact that there was a trip to be confidential information. Two of his staff mentioned the trip to someone, so Than Shwe ordered them hanged. This barbaric act, done so casually, shocked the entire military.

"Burma's association with North Korea and Russia threatens America's security. The intensity of the senior general's feeling on the matter makes the CIA uneasy."

Thein said, "I do not want to jeopardize your working relationship with my father. But I have heard many stories about how difficult the last step of the federal licensing exam is. I need your help. Please help me over this last hurdle."

"I'll check with a special agent to see what he thinks, and I'll get back to you. I'll look into what we can do, so don't do anything rash like quitting."

"I shall wait to hear from you."

Chapter 20

Stealth is Required

Thou shalt not steal; an empty feat,
When it's so lucrative to cheat.

—Authur Hugh Clough
From the poem, *The Latest Decalogue* (1862)

In carrying out its clandestine missions, the CIA paid many bribes. Ira Ingram had recognized this fact shortly after coming to work for the agency. Early in his career, he decided to increase his value to his employer by specializing in bribery. Ira studied the psychology of bribery, and came to believe that anyone can be bribed if the circumstances were right and the offer attractive enough. As he practiced the craft, he developed cover stories and techniques to prevent the bribees from learning of the CIA's involvement.

Each time Ira offered a bribe, he pretended to be someone else, someone not connected with the CIA. Those he dealt with often realized that Ingram was not who he said he was, but the ploy still prevented them from being certain that the CIA was responsible.

Over the years, Ingram came to think of himself as the great imposter, which in fact was what he had become. Unmarried, he became reclusive as an aid to protecting his identity.

STEALTH IS REQUIRED

Ingram was reading a George Smiley novel in his cubicle at the CIA headquarters at Langley, Virginia when he received a surprise visitor. He had seen the man once before in a hallway there at headquarters. That earlier sighting and the fact that the man was now unannounced in his office gave Ira the impression that the visitor was high in the agency's hierarchy.

"Is the bribery business a little slow these days, Ira?"

Ira closed his paperback. "George Smiley was really something. Did you ever read of his exploits?"

"*The Spy Who Came in from the Cold* should be required reading for anyone starting out in our line of work."

"I agree. How can I help you?"

"I cleared my request with your boss so you can check with him now or after I leave, but he thought you have enough slack in your work schedule to help me."

"I will if I can."

"In talking with your boss, just refer to me as Lester."

Without using Thein's name, Lester asked Ira how a certain psychiatric resident at UCLA could cheat on the final medical licensing exam.

Ira said, "Since your doctor in training is certain he'll fail this final exam, he probably would do that very thing. And even if he takes the test a second time, the questions will be different, so he might fail again. Each time he fails he will look worse to a prospective employer even if he eventually passes.

"I can make sure that your client passes this medical licensing exam. After all, bypassing administrative requirements is standard fare for the CIA."

Lester said, "Stealth will be required. The CIA's enabling legislation bars us from carrying out certain kinds of operations inside US borders."

"Don't worry, my middle name is 'Stealthy.'"

"Oh, I thought it was 'Smiley.' What should we do to guarantee that my doctor in training will pass the test?"

"The California Medical Board gives the test that your client is worried about. Give me a few weeks. I'll pretend to be a friend of someone about to take the test. I won't mention the CIA or your client. I don't know his name and don't want to. I'll find a corrupt medical board official with access to the examination questions."

Lester asked, "Will that be hard?"

"After I find an official with access to the test, I'll have to establish a rapport. That'll be the hardest part, unless the person happens to be a friendly sort. Portraying this as a victimless crime will help the official decide to accept a bribe and provide the test questions. It'll take time to negotiate the size of the bribe and how the official wants it delivered. And of course I must make the board official believe their identity will be protected—that their act won't be detected. All this takes time, but we'll succeed, human nature being what it is.

"I don't know how well you know the medical student that we're helping out, but you need stealth at your end of the transaction also. The student must be able to keep a secret and not share the test questions with anyone."

"I appreciate the reminder," Lester said. "I've done some work with my client regarding secrecy, but I'll work on him some more. He comes from a family known for secret missions. Nonetheless I'll build safeguards into our plan. You'll give the questions to me instead of handing them to our pupil. I'll have an agent ask him the questions orally, paraphrasing and that sort of thing so that my medical resident never has paper or electronic copies. As I think about it, maybe you would be the best agent to do the quizzing since you're good at assuming false identities and also want to ensure the secrecy of our undertaking."

Ira said, "I like that idea."

"Then consider that part of your assignment."

Chapter 21

At Last, A Psychiatric Practice

The disease...the man...the world go together and cannot be considered separately as things in themselves.

—Oliver Sacks
Awakenings (a 1973 memoir)

Riverside County and Riverside City, California are so named because the Santa Ana River passes through them on its westerly journey to the Pacific Ocean. Like other rivers, the Santa Ana's mood depends on the weather. For most of a typical year, the river is easy-going, standing still or oozing, with dry stretches between the pools. But rainstorms and snow melt in the San Bernardino Mountains can turn the river into a torrent.

Riverside County is mostly desert in the central and eastern portions, and is a Mediterranean climate in the western portion. Once a majestic landscape and a balanced ecosystem, much of the county is severely degraded by a large, burgeoning human population.

The exhaust from millions of motor vehicles in the Los Angeles metropolitan area is carried by prevailing winds to Riverside and San Bernardino Counties. Here, the winds stall at the base of the San Bernardino Mountains, pollution accumulates, and the result is the most unhealthy air in the United States.

THE MIND DOCTOR

Dr. David Thein knew little about the area that the chamber of commerce called The Inland Empire. He had not planned to come to this part of California, having dreamed of coastal regions with a blue ocean, pristine beaches, and bathing beauties. But the CIA's choices of professional positions for Thein were limited to where job openings existed. The agency had manipulated the California Department of Health into hiring him to fill a vacant position as a psychiatrist in the Riverside County Community Mental Health Center.

It was a Tuesday morning in June 1994. The county mental health center was holding a staff meeting, chaired by department head Dr. Richard Conway, age 61.

Participants included eleven psychiatrists, one psychologist, three sociologists, five psychiatric technicians, one secretary, and five clerks. Although the psychologist, Thomas Prescott, was called "doctor," he was not a medical doctor but held a PhD in psychology. Margret Gross, 50, was a senior psychiatrist who had worked at the clinic for twelve years. In addition to seeing patients, she served as de facto deputy to Conway. Dr. Gross hoped to become the department head if Dr. Conway were to leave the clinic before she did.

Dr. Conway stood before his staff members.

"I have good news. We have hired a replacement for Dr. Graves who suffered a heart attack a year ago. Soon after the attack, he notified the county he would not return to work.

"We are filling Dr. Graves's old position with Dr. David Thein. He was born in Burma but has been practicing in Los Angeles for the last several years. Dr. Thein's credentials are excellent."

A senior psychiatrist, Ralph Newkirk, asked, "Does this mean we psychiatrists will have a lighter workload?"

"That is our main reason for hiring Dr. Thein. This will enable you all to spend a little more time with each patient."

"How soon will he report to work?" Newkirk asked.

"Next Monday morning. I want each of you psychiatrists to look over your caseload and recommend to me six cases that are appropriate to assign to our newest team member. I can't say that all the cases will be transferred to him, but most will. Dr. Gross and I will examine the cases and decide which will go to our newest doctor."

Psychologist Prescott said, "When is the center going to hire an additional psychologist? I'm the only one on staff, so at some point I see almost every patient. Talk about being overloaded. As soon as Dr. Thein comes on board we'll have a dozen psychiatrists but only one psychologist."

Dr. Conway said, "I hear you, Dr. Prescott. Dr. Gross and I are working on a position description and a request for funding for an additional psychologist position."

"How many psychologists will you hire if the higher-ups give their approval?"

"One."

Prescott said, "The county continues to believe the answer to mental illness amounts to nothing but funneling pills down a patient's throat. Hang on. I'm going to give you my standard speech. The newest staff members haven't heard it, and anyway the point can't be made often enough.

"Mental illnesses are complex individual responses. They are less like hypothyroidism, in which you fall ill because your body doesn't secrete enough thyroid hormone, and more like metabolic syndrome, in which a collection of risk factors such as high blood pressure, fat around the waist, a sedentary life style, and smoking increase your chance of heart disease."

Conway said, "Dr. Prescott, I understand your position. I agree with the part about these disorders being complex. But the county is merely going along with the rest of the nation in moving toward more medication and less listening and counseling. That's just the way it is.

"But I assure you that Dr. Gross and I are pressing our superiors for approval to hire an additional psychologist. We recognize your valuable contribution, and assure you that psychology will always be ingrained in the therapy we provide here."

"Well, keep the pressure on for the go-ahead to hire that second psychologist to limp along with me."

"We will. The main way we extend the reach of psychology is for you to advise the psychiatrists here regarding their cases. Most have had psychology courses during their university training and they all welcome your input, I'm sure."

The department head returned to his original topic, "So Dr. David Thein will be here next Monday. Dr. Gross will bring him around to your offices so you will have a proper introduction. That will be the lead-in to your working with him as a fellow staff member."

Psychiatrist Newkirk said, "I have a complaint. Every staff meeting, our resident psychologist criticizes the use of medications to treat mental illnesses. And every staff meeting you give him the floor, and he goes on and on. It doesn't matter what the meeting agenda is—you let him expound. Dr. Crenshaw and I, along with other psychiatrists, are fed up."

Conway said, "Well, this is an important subject. The whole country is concerned about appropriate use of psychiatric medications, and Dr. Prescott is current on the issue—not the pharmacology—but the overall broad controversy.

"Besides, Dr. Prescott's participation at staff meetings is a way of infusing psychological thinking into the staff. This is what he's complaining about—that we're not paying enough attention to what psychology has to offer. He has a point, and since he is our only psychologist, it would make matters worse if I prevented him from talking during staff meetings.

"Also, I have always welcomed input from every one of you. It doesn't matter what kind of expertise you have. We will listen to you. If we don't have enough time during the staff meeting, you're welcome to see either Dr. Gross or me afterward."

Psychiatrist Charles Crenshaw said, "Yes, but the rest of us respect our coworkers' time. We don't go on and on like Prescott does. I agree with Dr. Newkirk. I've heard Prescott's standard speech a hundred times. It doesn't enhance my practice. It makes me less likely to listen to anything he says."

"Crenshaw, you're a pill pusher," Prescott said. "You might be a well-meaning pill pusher, but you're one nonetheless. And your patients get worse the longer you treat them."

Both Newkirk and Crenshaw stood up, started toward Prescott, and then stopped when the department head spoke.

"Hold on, all three of you. This has gone far enough. I'll work with the three of you to keep the right balance between pharmacological therapy and talk therapy."

Newkirk and Crenshaw sat down.

Conway said, "Everyone here has something crucial to offer our patients. Beyond the psychiatrists and the psychologist, we have sociologist case workers, an occupational therapist, psychiatric technicians, clerks, and a secretary. All of you are valuable. This program doesn't revolve around psychiatry versus psychology, which is a silly argument anyway. It isn't either-or. There's a lot of overlap.

"That's enough for now. Dr. Gross will bring Dr. Thein around to meet you next Monday. In the meantime, I want recommendations for cases to transfer to him.

"Meeting adjourned."

Chapter 22

The Golden Age of Psychopharmacology

> *The discovery of chlorpromazine, the first of the antipsychotics, brought in its wake the discovery of a host of other drugs. It led to the discovery of the antidepressants from imipramine to Prozac, which became a symbol of the 1990s, to Valium and Ritalin, which have had as great an impact on the culture of our times as on the treatment of our nervous disorders.*
>
> —David Healy
> *The Creation of Psychopharmacology* (2002)

Ralph Newkirk and Charles Crenshaw had been classmates in medical school at the University of California, Los Angeles. Newkirk was the first of the two to be hired by the Riverside County Community Mental Health Center. Six months later, his recommendation helped persuade the center to hire Crenshaw. Both Newkirk and Crenshaw had worked at the county clinic longer than Thomas Prescott. In recent months, Prescott had become the main topic of their private conversations.

In his office at the county clinic during a lunch break, Newkirk said, "It was bad enough for that guy to sneak around and pry into our prescriptions, but in the staff meeting the other day, he came right out and called you a pill pusher. Said your patients grow worse under your treatment. Of course he was also implicating me."

"He hurt our standing with our bosses and the staff. How can we shut his big mouth? What if he talks to the FDA?"

"I don't know. I'm worried."

Crenshaw said, "I'll tell you what I'd really like to know. What motivates this guy? To begin with, why is he so concerned about what medicines we prescribe?"

"Maybe he's bitter because California law bars psychologists from prescribing medications. We're physicians, and he's not. Our power to prescribe gives us a therapeutic advantage, and our salaries are higher than his."

"You're probably right," Crenshaw said. "He's probably envious and frustrated that he picked the wrong profession. Maybe he's jealous of our professional status. Still, I feel like there's something else that's tormenting him."

Thomas Prescott had a deceased brother, younger by a year, who at seventeen had been diagnosed as having schizophrenia. After six weeks of psychiatric treatment, Louis ended his life. Thomas was there the day it happened.

Louis was not rebelling against his parents, Robert and Alice, or doing anything dangerous or threatening. He had withdrawn from interactions with people, and was spending a lot of time alone in his bedroom. He was eating less and had lost interest in hobbies. He spent most of his time with Bouncy, the family's dog, and with Susie, the family's cat, stroking her and talking to her. Louis had taken to continuously wearing a baseball cap even when indoors.

Alice took Louis to see psychiatrist Byron Westlake in one of Riverside's few high rises. She expected a diagnosis of something like shyness and a prognosis such as, "He will grow out of it." After the examination, Dr. Westlake asked Louis to wait in the outer office while he talked with Alice. She was shocked at the diagnosis of schizophrenia.

"Doctor, are you sure? What I hear about schizophrenia is frightening."

"There is no doubt in my mind."

Alice said, "But Louis isn't doing anything reckless or disruptive. Until recently he played high school sports. He's polite and docile. My main concerns are that he has become withdrawn, and isn't eating enough."

Dr. Westlake said, "Schizophrenia is characterized by two kinds of symptoms. The ones that you heard about are what psychiatrists call positive symptoms, meaning overt behavior, not positive as in something good. Hallucinations and delusions are positive symptoms. Psychosis is another name for positive symptoms.

"The symptoms that you recognize in Louis are what psychiatrists call negative symptoms. They include listlessness, withdrawal, and loss of interest in things like hobbies and personal hygiene. The public hears less about the negative symptoms, but they are more entrenched than the positive ones. Louis displays classic negative symptoms."

The psychiatrist paused and then said, "Louis wore a cap during the office visit. This is a negative symptom."

"Why would that be a symptom?"

"Louis appears to be afraid that someone will read his mind or steal his thoughts. He hopes the baseball cap will stop that from happening."

"OK, Louis has negative symptoms of schizophrenia. Does this mean he doesn't have positive symptoms, and only the negative ones?"

"No. He might not have positive symptoms just yet but they could manifest at any time. Or more likely, he has positive symptoms that he's hiding from you."

"What can I do?"

"First, don't lose hope. Schizophrenia can be severe, but it can also be mild or any level in between. Louis might have only a mild or moderate case."

"OK, I'll not jump to conclusions and will maintain a good outlook."

"That's half the battle."

"What else can I do?"

THE GOLDEN AGE OF PSYCHOPHARMACOLOGY

"Well, first, you came to the right place. My associates and I are very knowledgeable regarding schizophrenia. We treat this disorder with the latest pharmacotherapy. The drug chlorpromazine was the first one discovered for treating schizophrenia. It's low cost. Maybe you know this drug by its trade name, Thorazine."

"I've never heard those names."

Dr. Westlake said, "Thorazine was followed onto the market by other drugs in the same class of chemicals, and we call them "antipsychotics.""

"Do you recommend treating Louis's condition with antipsychotic drugs?"

"Definitely. We're fortunate to live in this golden age of psychiatry and pharmacology. We can conquer mental illnesses because we've learned how the illnesses disrupt the brain's chemical messengers, and because in this modern age we have the drugs to counteract the contrary chemistry."

Alice said, "It's beginning to sound more hopeful."

"It is hopeful. You brought Louis in at an early stage in his illness. There are a few things I would like you to understand about the pharmacotherapy I will administer."

"What is that?"

"There is a space called a synapse between the end of one nerve cell or neuron and the beginning of the next neuron. Electrochemical impulses need to get across that gap and in a normal fashion. So although a synapse is a space, it nevertheless is a connection between nerve cells, precisely because impulses pass through it on the way to the next neuron. There are billions of nerves and synapses in the brain, arrayed in vast networks."

"I'm following you."

"It's important that the electrochemical discharge from one nerve cell ending get through to the dendrites or branching structures of the next nerve cell. So there are natural chemical substances in the synapses that facilitate this transmission. Those chemical substances are called neurotransmitters."

"I remember this information from my college biology course. So I'm tracking what you're saying."

"Good. Because I'm about to tell you the main reason why our pharmacology works so well.

"With the billions of nerve cells in our brains, we have vast numbers of nerve synapses containing neurotransmitters. There are different kinds. The most common neurotransmitter is glutamate."

Alice asked, "Is acetylcholine a neurotransmitter? I remember my biology teacher talking about this one."

"Yes. Acetylcholine is the first neurotransmitter that was discovered. But there are other neurotransmitters that are involved in mental illnesses. I'd like to acquaint you with two of them. Modern psychopharmacology focuses on regulating the levels of dopamine and serotonin."

"Is that what your medications do?"

"Yes. I want you to remember the names of these two key neurotransmitters—dopamine and serotonin. A person with schizophrenia has too much dopamine in his synapses. A person with depression has too little serotonin. Most of the medications that I'll prescribe for Louis will regulate imbalances in the levels of dopamine and serotonin."

"I'm glad you explained this."

"And I'm glad that you understand the chemical-imbalance hypothesis of mental illnesses."

"You used the word 'hypothesis.' How sure are the medical experts that this hypothesis should be relied on?"

"I've relied on it for years with outstanding results. Pharmaceutical companies have spent billions in developing drugs that correct chemical imbalances, and the Food and Drug Administration approves psychiatric drugs based mainly on their effect on chemical imbalances.

"To remind doctors and pharmacists to keep an open mind and to be scientific in our work, we refer to this concept as a hypothesis. But if it were up to me, I'd call this idea a well-founded theory. I have that much confidence in the thinking and research that's been done."

Alice said, "I shouldn't keep Louis waiting any longer."

"Right. I'm writing Louis's first three prescriptions. They are for Thorazine, the reliable old standard antipsychotic that I mentioned earlier; Prozac, a new antidepressant; and Cogentin, an anticholinergic. Cogentin regulates acetylcholine, which is the neurotransmitter that your biology teacher told you about. Cogentin's purpose is to prevent Louis from getting Parkinsonianism, a movement disorder that Thorazine or Prozac can cause.

"Fill these prescriptions immediately. Read the package inserts and see that Louis takes these medications according to instructions on the vial labels."

Chapter 23

Akathisia

Make no mistake about people who leap from burning windows. Their terror of falling from a great height is still just as great... the fear of falling remains a constant. The variable here is the other terror, the fire's flames: when the flames get close enough, falling to death becomes the slightly less terrible of two terrors. It's not desiring the fall; it's terror of the flames.

—David Foster Wallace
(regarding akathisia)
Infinite Jest (1996)

Louis believed he did not need Dr. Westlake's medications. Whether he would take the drugs became a daily contest between Louis and his parents. Robert and Alice usually won, being convinced they were acting in his best interest. The argument that worked best was that Louis would feel better, without reminding him that he had a diagnosis of schizophrenia.

Within eighteen hours of taking the drugs for the first time, Louis suffered nausea, grogginess, and a parched mouth. He gritted his teeth hard enough to crack four molars, but continued to grind them even while he slept.

But the drugs also blocked some of Louis's symptoms. After four weeks, the psychosis and depression subsided. He came out of his bedroom more often to talk with his parents and his brother. He quit wearing his baseball cap, and spoke of taking up photography.

Robert said to Alice, "I was losing faith in Westlake's treatment plan, but it looks like he was right after all. Louis is doing much better and even has regained his sense of humor. He was kidding around with Thomas yesterday."

"We just had to stay with the program and be patient. I'm glad we didn't give up on the medicine."

But as the weeks went by, new symptoms developed. Louis paced back and forth. He strode in and out of the house and around the neighborhood. He would sit down, but immediately get back up and resume pacing. When he sat for a few minutes, he was not at rest. He crossed and uncrossed his legs or jiggled his feet up and down. Then he rose and resumed pacing. Next, he sat again but only for moments before beginning to pace once more.

Robert phoned Dr. Westlake's office. "Louis is hurting. I think a doctor would call it severe agitation."

The receptionist said, "Hold a moment. I'll ask Dr. Westlake what we should do."

In two minutes she was back on the phone.

"Mr. Prescott, please bring Louis to our office. How long will it take for you to get here?"

"Fifteen minutes."

"Good."

Thomas went with his dad and brother. In the car, Louis shifted his feet back and forth.

The Prescott men arrived at the office building, and took an elevator to the fifteenth floor. Dr. Westlake insisted on seeing Louis alone. Robert and Thomas waited in a small room separate from the main waiting room. Comfortable chairs, pastel green walls, and a view of the city below eased their tension. Their job was to remain calm while Dr. Westlake worked his magic.

In an examination room, Dr. Westlake said, "Louis, tell me what you're feeling."

"I want to jump out of my skin. I can't stand it."

"Have you taken your medications?"

"It's your medicine that's messing with me. I'm done with your damn pills."

"You can't do that, Louis. Are you hearing voices?"

Louis rose from his chair, and began to pace.

"Sit down. I'm going to give you an injection that will make you feel better."

"The hell you are."

Louis bolted from the room and rounded a corner, startling the patients in the main waiting room.

"Dad, Tom, where are you? Come on. We're going home."

Robert and Thomas appeared, as did Dr. Westlake.

Wild-eyed, Louis tramped about the waiting room, looking for something heavy. The receptionist fled. Louis grabbed her office chair and threw it against the window. It bounced off the glass, but cracks appeared. Louis grabbed the chair again, held it chest-high in front of him, and charged the window. The chair and Louis broke through and fell fifteen stories to the sidewalk below.

The horror of that day haunted Louis's father, mother, and brother the rest of their lives. From then on, their existence was shaped by grief. Over time, the agony changed from constant and piercing to highly variable, sometimes subliminal and sometimes fresh and raw, but it never ceased.

Robert and Alice came to suspect that Dr. Westlake's medications had caused Louis's restlessness and agitation. They hired an attorney, Raymond Ferris, who obtained medical records, filed a wrongful death lawsuit, and deposed Dr. Westlake as well as the pharmaceutical companies that manufactured the medications he had prescribed.

Attorney Ferris obtained an expert witness, Dr. Michelle Stanton, who held degrees in psychiatry and neurology, and who often testified in wrongful death trials. Citizens almost never won suicide lawsuits, but Dr. Stanton's performance record was the best of all the expert witnesses that Ferris and the Prescotts considered. Compared to other expert witnesses, a greater percentage of her cases were resolved through out-of-court settlements.

Attorney Ferris asked Dr. Stanton and the Prescotts to meet with him in his office. Early in the meeting, he said that as the legal case progressed, there was to be no direct communication between Dr. Stanton and the Prescotts. They were to ask questions and provide information only to him. This would prevent the defendants from claiming that the plaintiffs had compromised the independence of Stanton's medical review. Under his supervision today, Attorney Ferris would allow Dr. Stanton to describe the basic medical issues she had identified.

Dr. Stanton said, "First, I am very sorry for what happened to Louis. From my review of the medical records, I can assure you that the suicide was not his fault. The blame goes to Dr. Byron Westlake for prescribing too much medication. The doses were too high. Also, he should have prescribed a newer antipsychotic instead of Thorazine whose side effects are notorious.

"The condition that Westlake caused has a name—akathisia. The term comes from two Greek words that together mean 'without sitting.' Because a patient's pacing and inability to sit still is terribly obvious, most psychiatrists think of akathisia as entirely a movement disorder. But its overpowering psychotic component is of far greater consequence. It is the psychosis—the hallucinations, the delusions, and the disorganized thinking—along with the extreme emotional pain that compels homicide or suicide.

"Akathisia then is a psychomotor disorder, usually caused by antipsychotic or antidepressant medications. Its dominant characteristic is overwhelming fright, making it impossible for the victim to describe the source of his agony.

"Doctors often mistake akathisia for extreme anxiety or agitated depression. If they make this misdiagnosis, they are likely to increase the dose of antipsychotic or antidepressant, the worst thing they could do."

In court, with Judge Jacob Barker presiding, Dr. Westlake and the pharmaceutical companies argued that Louis's suicide was caused entirely by his underlying mental illness and his refusal to take prescribed medications. They successfully defended against the Prescotts' claim of wrongful death. The drugmakers were represented by highly-paid lawyers who also aided the doctor's attorney. The expert witnesses who testified for the defendants also were experienced and expensive.

The jury decided that Westlake had met the medical standard of care. The jury also decided the pharmaceutical companies had provided adequate legal warning of the risks of taking their medications. The medications' package inserts listed all the adverse side effects—except akathisia—that could result. As for akathisia, the companies argued that Louis actually had depressive agitation, and that Dr. Stanton's diagnosis, made without her ever meeting Louis, was simply wrong.

After the verdict was rendered, Alice asked, "Raymond, should we appeal? Judge Barker was patently unfair."

Ferris said, "I doubt we would win. The judge was stealthy, careful to not say things that would incriminate him in the trial transcripts. He pulled off most of his misdeeds by meeting in private with the lawyers in his chambers, and by using body language, gestures, and grimaces that influenced the jury."

Robert said, "I noticed that. Judge Barker let the jurors know he disliked our case and us too by using contemptuous body language. Do you think the court reporter made note of those gestures?"

"The transcripts that have been issued so far do not mention the body language," Attorney Ferris said. "I don't think the final transcript will either although I'll check as soon as it's made available. Sometimes court reporters make entries about the gestures they see, but only if it's an attorney or a witness who misbehaves. The reporters ignore a judge's transgressions. A judge can prevent an overly observant court reporter from getting any further business in his jurisdiction."

Robert and Alice had paid over $190,000 in legal fees, and no longer trusted the court system.

A year after the Prescotts' wrongful death trial, Judge Jacob Barker was in the news for accepting bribes for rendering court decisions in favor of pharmaceutical companies. Based on this new information, Attorney Ferris filed for the Riverside County Appeals Court to consider whether Judge Barker might have accepted bribes from the defendants in Louis's case. The Appeals Court heard the case, but did not remand the matter to the lower court. There would be no new trial.

Chapter 24

Gabicon has Many Uses

Therapeutics is the pouring of a drug of which one knows little into a patient of which one knows less.

—Voltaire
(French Writer)

Ralph Newkirk had six patients waiting when he received a special person ahead of them. When Laura Nielsen of Alphatron Pharmaceuticals came to his office, he adjusted his priorities. The blonde sales representative wore black slacks, a white blouse, a maroon blazer, and a black beret.

"Hello, Dr. Newkirk. Do you have time for me?"

"Of course. Come in, Laura."

"I want to acquaint you with a new medication called Gabicon that Alphatron has developed. The FDA approved it for treating one kind of epilepsy. But researcher Norman Thurber found that Gabicon treats a range of psychiatric conditions."

Laura handed Dr. Newkirk a brochure that showed satisfied customers engaging in outdoor activities. They were smiling, and the sun was shining.

"Laura, I'm not in charge of the county's formulary or list of approved drugs. I can't assure you that the county will approve Gabicon for its doctors to use in treating mental illnesses."

"But you can make a recommendation. Riverside County never fails to add to its list the medications that its psychiatrists recommend. The county doesn't want to be behind the times. Have you ever written a prescription for a new drug that the county refused to approve?"

"No. As long as a drug is FDA approved for any condition, the county lets us prescribe it for mental illnesses."

Laura reached over and squeezed Dr. Newkirk's hand. His pulse quickened.

She said, "And the patients in your personal practice also could benefit from Gabicon."

"If it's good enough for my county patients, it's good enough for my private-practice patients."

Laura took forty minutes of Dr. Newkirk's time. By then, ten patients were waiting to see him. He had trouble concentrating until after he had seen the first three.

The staff were surprised when they met Dr. David Thein. They had expected an older man, based on the extensive education and experience that Dr. Conway had attributed to him. Newkirk and Crenshaw immediately wondered about the veracity of Dr. Thein's personnel records and work history.

Thein could hardly believe he was now a Californian. It had seemed he would remain in Burma for his entire life. But in looking back, he could see why his father and Lester Jordan had demanded that he leave at once. When conditions worsened, changes came fast. The people rose up, and just as quickly the government put them down. Riot police and soldiers clubbed, bayoneted, or shot thousands. Many of the survivors would suffer mental trauma for as long as they lived. If Than Aung Foy were to succeed in opening a psychiatric practice in Rangoon, he would have no trouble finding patients.

Thein's parents were not threatened by either the civil uprising or the government's brutal suppression tactics. Saw not only was the ultimate insider, but was adept at handling challenges of all kinds.

Thein could hardly believe that he now sat in a comfortable office in Riverside, California. True, he was not in heavenly Hollywood, but then he was not in ravaged Rangoon either.

GABICON HAS MANY USES

Dr. Thein had seen his last patient before lunch. The receptionist said over the intercom, "Two medical sales specialists are here to see you."

"Please send them in."

A young man and a young woman entered Thein's office. Dressed in black slacks, white shirts, and maroon blazers, they also wore big smiles. Thein wondered if he had ended up in Hollywood after all.

"Hi. I'm Neil Kronberger and this is Laura Nielsen. We're drug reps for Alphatron Pharmaceuticals. Welcome to the Inland Empire."

Dr. Thein rose and shook hands with both visitors.

"Let us sit at the table."

Neil said, "Laura can visit if you have the time, but I have a lunch appointment with one of your colleagues."

Thein said, "It is good to meet you, Neil."

He turned to Laura, "Yes, I have time for you, Miss Nielsen."

They sat across from each other at the small table. Spellbound, Thein stared at Laura's long, blonde hair. She handed him a brochure about Alphatron and another about Gabicon.

"I'm glad to meet you, Dr. Thein."

One of her legs happened to rub up against one of his under the table.

"I understand you've been here at the center for three days now. Have you written any prescriptions?"

"Oh, yes."

"Are you interested in hearing about Gabicon? It's Alphatron's latest drug, and an immense amount of research went into developing it."

"I am very interested."

Laura said, "The FDA approved Gabicon for treating epileptic seizures, but in the six months that it has been on the market, many doctors have found it effective for a variety of other uses."

Laura slipped her shoes off. Her right foot stroked the doctor's thigh under the table. Thein sat still, his face without expression.

He said, "I find this Gabicon very interesting."

"I thought you would. Do you have any questions?"

"No. Just continue explaining its merits."

"The FDA approved Gabicon for treating partial seizures in adults, and it's great for that purpose. But researcher Norman Thurber has found that it effectively treats mood swings, anxiety, panic attacks, schizophrenia, schizoaffective disorder, bipolar disorder, severe depression, obsessive-compulsive disorder, dissociative identity disorder, post-traumatic stress disorder, eating disorders, obesity, phobias, insomnia, borderline personality disorder, compulsive gambling, general uneasiness, and sexual dysfunction."

"As a doctor in America, I can prescribe a drug for purposes other than what the FDA approved it for. Is that what you are saying I should do with Gabicon?"

"That's what I'm saying."

Dr. Ralph Newkirk dropped by Thein's office to cultivate a friendship, and to begin turning the Burman against psychologist Prescott. Newkirk assumed the newest staff member would be in his office, and there was time for a short bull session before they had to see their afternoon patients.

Thein's office door was closed. Newkirk checked with the receptionist.

"Hi, Olivia. Is Dr. Thein in his office? I'm wondering if he held over a client who might be having a difficult time."

Olivia said, "He's in his office. He has a walk-in visitor, one of our drug reps."

"Which rep?"

"Laura Nielsen from Alphatron."

Newkirk darted to Thein's office, knocked, and simultaneously opened the door.

Thein rose from his chair.

"Is something wrong, Dr. Newkirk?"

"At this clinic, we leave our doors open when we see drug reps. I advise you to honor this custom."

"That is what I shall do from now on."

Newkirk said, "Miss Nielsen, please stop by my office. I need some information."

Chapter 25

Reasoning Backward for Profit

Reasoning "backwards" to make assumptions about disease causation based on the response of the disease to a treatment is logically problematic. The fact that aspirin cures headaches does not prove that headaches are due to low levels of aspirin in the brain.

—Jeffrey Lacasse and Jonathan Leo
Serotonin and Depression: A Disconnect between the Advertisements and the Scientific Literature (2005)

De facto Deputy Director Gross was in her office, meeting with psychologist Prescott.

"So, Margret, is this a personnel counseling session?"

"It's true that Dr. Conway asked me to speak with you, but I don't consider this a counseling session. I wouldn't dream of counseling someone as prestigious as you, Thomas."

Both laughed. They had known each other for years. Both believed medications were overprescribed at the clinic although Gross, unlike Prescott, kept her opinions to herself.

Margret said, "Dr. Conway believes the dispute between you and Dr. Newkirk lowers the morale of other staff members."

"I apologize for upsetting my bosses and coworkers. I'll try to contain myself, but most of our doctors are overmedicating most of our patients, and I'm the only one objecting. Dr. Conway is part of the problem. I've taken the issue to him, and he won't do anything about it."

"What did you ask him to do?"

"I tried to persuade him that the staff psychiatrists are in fact overprescribing powerful drugs, and that this is a serious problem for the patients," Thomas said. "Many of our patients don't recognize the dangers inherent in medications, and some trust their doctors totally. Of course, some patients don't trust anyone, but many follow doctor's orders even when the medications are harming them. The doctors always insist that any problems are caused by the diagnosed disorder and never by the medicine."

"How did Dr. Conway react to your message?"

"He said overmedication is not a problem here. Like most of the psychiatrists at the center, he's been brainwashed by pharmaceutical companies."

Dr. Gross said, "Are you including me among the brainwashed psychiatrists?"

"No. In working with patients, and reviewing their medical charts, I've seen which doctors prescribe too much medication. You prescribe the least medication of any of the psychiatrists. It looks as though your prescribing at very low levels is mostly to take advantage of a placebo effect."

"Thomas, you might be right, but please don't mention that possibility to anyone. Don't wound the person—me—who might be the only psychiatrist friend you still have. Our supervisors wouldn't like me prescribing low levels of medication while allowing my patients to think they're taking potent concentrations."

"I applaud you because you're prescribing these drugs in about the only way they are safe. You're not only fooling the patients, but you're fooling our bosses as well. To your supervisors and coworkers, you appear to be a mainstream psychiatrist, but you're in a very different class. Your low doses render the drugs harmless, and the only effect they can possibly have is that of placebo.

"It's sad that you have to resort to trickery, but you've devised a way to beat this clinic's mercenary and dangerous system of dispensing medications."

"That implies that you believe medications do have a place in treating mental illnesses. How should they be used, in your opinion?"

Thomas said, "Some of the medications are helpful when the psychiatrist acts with restraint. A safe and effective use is to do what psychiatrists call 'stabilizing the patient.' Give the medication to someone who is experiencing their first psychotic or manic episodes. Try to stop the hallucinations, delusions, and panic attacks. Then begin the talk therapy and proper regimens of nutrition and rest. Work with the whole family in helping them to understand disorders and medicine, and how to treat each other with kindness and respect. Help them develop better ways of interacting. Try music therapy, art therapy, hikes or camping trips, and anything else that might add meaning or pleasure to their lives. The short-term use of medication might calm someone down and set the stage for these therapies. But then for the sake of the patient and the family, taper the patients off the medications as soon as possible."

"But there's evidence that antidepressant drugs are like insulin for diabetes," Margaret said.

"I'm trying to decide if you believe that or if you're baiting me."

"There's a lot of support for this claim. Alphatron just put on a continuing medical education course where Dr. Norman Thurber gave a lecture on how SSRI antidepressant medications are like insulin."

"Yeah, I know," Thomas said. "And the California Medical Board approved the course, but it's dishonest to compare antidepressants to insulin."

"Why? If you're so smart, why?"

"If I've said it once, I've said it a thousand times. It's myth that that antidepressant drugs are like insulin."

"And I'm asking again, why?"

"It's a combination of circular thinking and lies. The circular thinking is stupidity. And the lies are to boost pharmaceutical sales, and to make psychiatrists appear scientific.

"I'm listening."

"Margaret, don't rush me. This takes a minute to explain. First, psychiatrists learned that some antidepressant drugs increase serotonin activity in the brain. This led them to decide that depression simply must result from too little serotonin. That was their biggest mistake or deceptive act, whichever it was. It's called postulating.

"To postulate is to assume or assert that something is true without having much evidence. That's all right if one says I'll make this assumption on a tentative basis only. I'll use this assumption as a working hypothesis only while I do experiments and gather facts. But pharmaceutical companies and psychiatrists claimed without a doubt that too little serotonin in the synaptic gaps causes depression."

"So you're saying psychiatrists and drug companies either illogically or falsely claim that depressed patients need a regular infusion of serotonin like some diabetics regularly need insulin."

"Right," Thomas said. "The notion was originally based on rudimentary studies in the 1960s, done without the benefit of placebo-controlled clinical trials. The initial claim was that the early antidepressants, iproniazid and imipramine, increased the levels of serotonin and norepinepherine in the brain's synapses. In the late 1980s, to boost the sales of its new antidepressant, Prozac, the Eli Lilly company promoted the same postulate through an advertising campaign of historic proportions. As they say, advertising pays."

"So this is what led to psychiatrists telling patients that SSRI antidepressants are like insulin?"

"Yes. Once you buy into the notion that too little serotonin is the problem, it's a small step to tell a patient that he needs to continually consume a drug that increases the serotonin level. Insulin is a hormone produced in the pancreas, which is essential for metabolizing carbohydrates and regulating blood sugar. Too little insulin results in diabetes, a chronic disease. It's great salesmanship to claim antidepressants are like insulin. The analogy resonates with the public."

Margaret said, "Many times I've told a patient that depression is caused by a chemical imbalance in the brain. That depression is like diabetes which is a chronic illness in the body. I said that if he wanted to live a more nearly normal life, he would take medicine every day for the rest of his life. Now you've debunked that misconception. You educated me but also make me feel guilty."

"Don't feel guilty," Thomas said. "You were played for a sucker like many other doctors and patients."

"You've persuaded me that depression is not like diabetes."

"And it follows that if depression is not like diabetes, well antidepressants are not like insulin, which is naturally produced in the body. Synthetic antidepressants are not produced in the body.

"When you give insulin, you give something the body lacks. Researchers have never shown that a person with a mental illness lacks something. Patients with depression don't lack serotonin. Insulin replaces what the patient is short of. So-called antidepressants don't do that. The final difference is that insulin doesn't have loads of side effects like antidepressant drugs do."

Margaret asked, "Don't you ever tire of criticizing psychiatry?"

"No. I'm on a crusade."

"A crusade? Tell me about it."

"History and statistics help us understand what is happening in the use of psychoactive medications. Medicaid records show that thousands of new cases of mental illnesses are diagnosed every year. The number of people that our government adds to the disability roles per one thousand citizens steadily increases. This wasn't true before the wide use of psychotropic drugs.

"The World Health Organization did studies in the 1970s and 1980s that indicate that diagnosed patients in poor countries have better recovery rates than patients in highly developed countries. The main reason seemed to be that patients in poor countries took far less medication than those in the wealthy countries.

"You put all this together, and most reasonable people would decide that powerful antidepressants, antipsychotics, mood stabilizers, and all the rest actually cause psychiatric illnesses."

Thomas had stood up half way through his speech. His face was red, and his fists were clenched.

Dr. Gross said, "You shouldn't be so laid back about this, Thomas."

Thomas laughed, unclenched his fists, and sat down.

THE MIND DOCTOR

Margaret said, "I'm changing the topic. Actually I'm returning to an earlier topic. Tell me more about your meetings with Dr. Conway. You met with him several times. Why do you fault him regarding the clinic's prescription practices?"

"Conway won't control the visits by drug reps. He lets them come in the clinic anytime they want. They bring so many free samples of medications that every doctor has at least one cabinet chock-full of them.

"Conway has a cabinet full himself even though he's a full-time administrator who doesn't see patients any longer."

Dr. Gross asked, "Why would Dr. Conway stock up on free samples?"

"He's getting some kind of benefit from them. I see drug reps giving him samples. In fact, he gets more medication in a week than his cabinet can hold. So he must be redistributing them. The cabinet is just temporary storage."

"I'm changing the topic again. I just now decided that I don't want to know what Richard is doing with the samples that he receives. Please tell me in general terms, without mentioning any personalities, what is the harm in free samples anyway?"

"Drug reps say free samples enable patients to try new medications to see if they are right for them without having to spend any money initially. But in a government clinic like this one, the patients are on Medicaid so they don't have to pay for their prescriptions anyway. Free samples are more likely to benefit patients at private practices."

Dr. Gross asked, "So what are the real reasons why drug reps drop off free samples at this county clinic?"

"To corrupt the psychiatrists. To make them feel obligated to prescribe the reps' products. You already know this stuff, Margret. Why are you asking me things you already know?"

"I need more insight into the free-samples issue, particularly as you see it. You show no sign of relenting in your criticism of the clinic. I'm trying to decide whether you're right, or whether Conway and Newkirk are right. I'm trying to separate the technical issue from the personality conflicts.

"Thomas, if we don't reduce the tension, you or Newkirk will have to leave the clinic. Have you considered going to work some place where the prescription practices are more in line with your way of thinking?"

"You said this isn't a personnel counseling session, but it feels like one."

"I'm sorry. I don't mean to come across as a boss. I'm interviewing you as Dr. Conway wanted. Of course I know your position on these matters, but I'm trying to get at your deep-down motives.

"Let's try this again. What specifically are the drug companies' motives for leaving free samples at this government clinic?"

"You already know the motives, but I'll be explicit. The free samples benefit the clinic's psychiatrists far more than the patients. The doctors can take the drugs themselves. And many do. Some people became psychologists or psychiatrists because they have their own mental problems, and think that by studying these fields they will be better able to handle their own issues. With that being the case, they simply consume the free samples themselves. That's the cheapest drug habit one can have."

Margret said, "Tell me right now if you know of drug abusers on staff. We'll get that person help even if he or she is a psychiatrist."

"I was speaking of statistics that I read in medical journals. But I want to be certain before reporting drug abuse by specific staff members."

"OK, go ahead and lay out the other possible reasons for drug reps to leave large quantities of free samples here."

"Well, remember, we're talking about a doctor receiving free samples that he doesn't have to account for. He could take the medications himself, or he could give them to family and friends. That saves them money on their own prescriptions, or feeds their addictions for free.

"Or the doctor could sell the drugs on the black market. He doesn't have to stand on a street corner to do this. He can simply provide them to a drug dealer, and take a percentage of the proceeds.

"If someone develops an addiction by taking free samples, he could wind up being treated by a psychiatrist, and then the pharmaceutical company can sell another drug like methadone to treat the habit they helped create. It's always a winning situation for the drug companies."

"Tell me more."

Thomas said, "Besides the ways I've described, there might be still more ways free samples can make a psychiatrist feel indebted to a pharmaceutical company."

"I can't think of any, but apparently you can. Do you ever think of anything other than the failings of this clinic?"

"The center is going down the wrong road when it comes to medications. For some patients, it could prove to be a dead-end street, with emphasis on 'dead.' Future medical experts will think of this generation's use of these psychotropic drugs the way we think of trepanning, lobotomy, and bloodletting. In their hay day, all these so-called therapies were considered magical cures for mental illness. But today medical people scoff at them.

"I was going to tell you another way that some of our doctors could use free drug samples. As you know, this clinic allows doctors to moonlight. Outside their hours here they can either have their own private practice or can work for one. For example, Newkirk has his own private practice, and Crenshaw works for him.

"Any doctor with a private practice can use free samples in large quantities to improve his clinic's bottom line. The doctor can give uninsured patients free samples so they don't have to pay for medications. This induces the patients to return to a clinic such as Newkirk's."

"Is there anything good you can say about free samples?"

"Free samples help the pharmaceutical companies sell more drugs. Free samples help drug reps earn their paychecks by handing out the samples for their employers. Incidentally, drug reps keep a lot of the samples themselves to consume, sell, or give to friends. Research surveys have proved this.

"Free samples bring enjoyment to doctors who are addicted or whose friends and relatives are addicted. Free samples help doctors make their private clinics more profitable. It's a matter of who benefits. Our county patients do not benefit from free samples."

"But you said that doctors with private practices give free samples to their patients. In that case the patients must benefit, at least in terms of the pocket book."

"Not necessarily. The samples that doctors hand out are always name-brand drugs. Never the cheaper generics. Drugmakers bring in most of their money by selling the new drugs that still have patent protection and exclusive marketing rights. The free samples encourage the patients to stay with the brand of medication given them. If later they start filling prescriptions at pharmacies, they will stay with that brand which invariably is more expensive than generic drugs.

"Psychiatrists often stop handing out free samples at some point for a variety of reasons, causing the patient to have to buy from a pharmacy. And what does he buy? The expensive name-brand drug of course. So over the long run, patients may pay out more money than if they had never received free samples. They save money only while they are receiving the samples, and not after they become wed to a name brand drug that they must pay for themselves."

Thomas paused, took a deep breath, and continued.

"Free samples are designed to corrupt the doctors and get the patients hooked. And they do those things very well. There are many other kinds of gifts—actually they're bribes—that corrupt doctors, but huge volumes of free samples is the most common."

"Thomas, you'll be happy to know that I don't accept free samples."

"I know that. It goes along with the fact that you prescribe the least medication of all the psychiatrists here."

"I will counsel you after all. Be careful that your detective work doesn't get you fired."

Chapter 26

A Life-Changing Accident

Each player must accept the cards life deals him or her: but once they are in hand, he or she alone must decide how to play the cards in order to win the game.

—Voltaire
(1694-1778)

It was 1996. For six years, soft-spoken, thirty-eight-year-old Barry Vincent had been an outpatient under the care of Dr. Margret Gross at the Riverside County Community Mental Health Center. Although shy enough that he had few acquaintances, he was respected by those who knew him best: his father, mother, older brother, two buddies he had grown up with, and Monica, a student in one of his art classes.

When Barry began seeing Dr. Gross, she diagnosed him as having schizophrenia. Under her care, his symptoms subsided dramatically within two months. She led a treatment team that included psychologist Thomas Prescott who provided counselling, and psychiatric technician Anna Wong-McDowell who instilled hope in Barry.

Dr. Gross had Barry taking very low levels of the antipsychotic Zyprexa, the antidepressant Paxil, and the anticholinergic benztropine. Also known as Cogentin, benztropine was routinely prescribed at the county clinic whenever a staff psychiatrist prescribed antipsychotics, with the intent of preventing Parkinson's-like side effects.

Dr. Gross and Dr. Prescott considered Barry one of the center's greatest successes. His hallucinations and delusions had ceased, he took medications as prescribed, and never missed an office appointment. Prescott pieced together the story of an off-road motorcycle accident that probably precipitated Barry's schizophrenia. He interviewed Barry and his parents, Jack and Joan Vincent. Thomas also learned aspects of the story from Boyd Klingman, a Riverside citizen, and an article in a back issue of the *Press Enterprise*.

Thomas learned that Barry had been a healthy young man mentally as well as physically until the motorcycle accident. He reasoned that Barry might have had genetic predisposing factors for a mental illness, but Thomas believed schizophrenia would never have manifested but for the accident.

In 1989, Barry Vincent was a happy thirty-two-year-old when he mounted his off-road motorcycle one October morning. He lived with his brother, Matt, in a small house on the north edge of Riverside and often rode in the nearby hills, as he would that day. The cool air—cleaned by a hard rain of the night before—felt good after the hot summer that had seemed without end.

Barry was riding on Big Mound, a foothill of the San Bernardino Mountains. Standing three miles north of the city, its west-facing slope was a few hundred feet to the east of north-south Riverside Drive. Having sandy and erosive soil, Big Mound was sparsely vegetated with California buckwheat, sagebrush, and cheat grass. Blue gum eucalyptus trees dotted the landscape.

He rode his bike over rough terrain, following switchback trails and continually climbing until he reached the crest of the hill. He stopped, killed the engine, and got off his bike to stroll and enjoy the view. Barry looked forward to attending classes that evening at the local community college where he was learning about painting and photography. He enjoyed the solitude during these hours outside of class.

After fifteen minutes of milling around, Barry started for home to do some reading before class. He mounted his motorcycle and started downhill on one of several trails that laced the hillside.

The new rain had cut gullies in the dirt-bike trail. Barry was moving along, did not see a new gully, and rode headlong into it. He and his motorcycle were airborne. Man and machine swapped places, with the machine landing on top of Barry, the motor still running.

He lay pinned down in one of the gullies that cut across the trail. Gas spilled out of the Suzuki, drenching his clothes.

The engine's manifold burned a hole in his coat and seared his flesh. Fumes choked him. Panicky and in shock, Barry managed to reach the ignition keys and kill the engine. He tried to get the motorcycle off his chest but could not. His right femur was broken near his hip, the jagged bone protruding through his pants leg. Most of his leg was folded under his back. He could not judge how much he was bleeding. Maybe he would die right there. Maybe there was no reason to worry. Dying would take no effort.

But surrendering was not his way. He would do his best to stay alive until help came. He told himself that someone would find him. He passed out.

Barry drifted in and out of consciousness. To surrender to the black void would be to die where he lay. He needed to stay awake to attract attention. He fought to remain conscious. The motorcycle on his chest suppressed his breathing. Cars passed by on a highway one hundred yards to the west, but no one looked in Barry's direction. The scenery where he lay was commonplace, nothing to attract anyone's attention. And Barry and his bike were scarcely visible because of the gully they lay in.

He shouted for help, but no one came. He lay there, hallucinating. He saw the older neighbor kid who used to bully him. Brit had changed. He was half human and half motorcycle. Barry saw the ancient god, Pan, who gave the world the word "panic."

"Brit, get out of here and take that goat man with you."

Boyd Klingman loved dogs. At fifty-three, he had never been without a canine companion. Except for Shep, who had contracted bone cancer, all his dogs had survived into old age because Boyd took such good care of them.

He worked the night shift as a security guard, and had time that day to take Oscar burn up energy before he would pack a lunch and leave for work. He could take Oscar to any of several places for a run, but his preference was a dirt road along the base of Big Mound.

Boyd pulled his sedan off Riverside Drive onto the narrow side road. He got out and opened the passenger door to let Oscar begin his romp. When Oscar's feet hit the ground, he made a beeline for Barry.

"Oscar, come."

Oscar was busy licking Barry's face.

Boyd drew near.

"Oh my god, are you alive?"

"Please help me."

"The fastest way is for me to stop traffic headed into Riverside. Hang on, I'll be right back."

Boyd ran to the main road, crossed it, and flagged down the first car headed toward Riverside.

"There's been an off-road motorcycle accident. Please call 911. The medics can spot this place by my green Chevy parked over there."

The driver said he would deliver the message.

Boyd worried whether the driver was reliable. Would he actually call for help? You can never tell what people will do. Boyd stopped a second car and repeated his request for help.

When he returned to Barry's side, the young man had passed out. Boyd lifted the motorcycle off Barry's chest. Barry woke up.

"Thank you."

"I'm not going to move you. Talk with me. Stay awake."

"I'll try. I'm cold."

Boyd put his coat over Barry. An ambulance-fire truck with four paramedics arrived.

The first task was to get Barry out of the gully without further injuring him. The paramedics could see the broken femur sticking through his pants leg. But there could be other injuries such as broken ribs that could puncture a lung when they moved him. Yet they had to immediately get him into a position where they could stanch the bleeding.

"We can't just lift him out of there, it's too risky," the second-in-command said.

The lead technician said, "The shovels in our rig. Get two."

Two medics dug the saturated soil from the downhill side of the gulley, immediately gaining access to Barry. Two other team members moved in to stop the loss of blood by applying pressure on Barry's right groin while simultaneously bandaging the wound. The team collapsed a gurney next to Barry, slid a heavy blanket under him, and used it to lift their patient onto the gurney.

They could not wheel the gurney on the wet, loose soil, so they lifted it into the ambulance-fire truck.

The medics realigned the broken leg only enough to keep it from dangling off the gurney. It was more pressing to ensure they had stopped the loss of blood, and to get Barry to Arrowhead hospital as soon as possible. While in transit, they removed Barry's wet clothes, and covered him with a blanket. They radioed ahead to inform the emergency department what to expect.

A nurse wearing surgical scrubs met the paramedics and Barry at the entrance of the emergency department. She led them to an operating room where a surgical team was coming together.

The team leader was Dr. Sterling Dugan, a veteran orthopedic surgeon in two respects. He was a veteran in the sense of having been an orthopedic surgeon for twenty years, and a veteran also in the sense that he spent those years as an officer in the US Army. He spoke distinctly into a microphone in order to make his instructions clear, and to create an auditory record of the standard of care decisions he was making. De. Dugan's first instructions were to the team's anesthesiologist.

"Inject the patient with a local pain killer while we take his vital signs and decide if it's safe to adminsiter general anesthesia."

Next, he spoke to a scrub nurse. "I smell gas. Give him a sponge bath and dry him off as gently as you can. Aside from the broken femur, we don't know what other injuries he might be suffering."

The vital signs were within normal ranges, so the anesthesiologist placed Barry in a medically induced coma, which would reduce the severity of the shock.

Stanching the bleeding was complicated by the need to prevent infection not only of the blood, but also of the broken bone and its marrow. Dr. Dugan sealed off blood vessels, trimmed the torn flesh, and tucked the still-broken bone back into its original place within Barry's thigh. He sterilized and bandaged the exit wound that had been made by the femur's jagged end. But now he needed access to the bone, which had broken into three pieces.

So Dugan made his first of two incisions, this one so he could access the bone and fit its pieces back together. He used a strong, fast-drying glue to cement the parts together. It set up within ten minutes, and he realigned the femur.

Even while the surgeon contemplated the second incision he would make, another problem vied for the team's attention. Barry's thigh muscle was pulling the two parts of the wound together, a natural reaction but one that if left unchecked would shorten the leg and increase the bleeding and pain. The anesthesiologist injected a local muscle relaxant, while a physical therapist set up the necessary apparatus and placed Barry's leg in traction. Traction kept the leg stretched out, and the femur aligned and stable.

Now it was time for Dr. Dugan to make his second incision and complete the effort to prevent his patient from being crippled. He could not help but think of the man who invented the simple but powerful technology that Dugan was about to use.

In 1939, a German surgeon named Gerhard Kuntscher created an ingenious device called an intramedullary nail or the Kuntscher nail. In later years in America, this device more often came to be called an intramedullary rod. It proved highly effective as both an internal splint and as a load-bearing support. In fact, many German soldiers were able to return to the front in just a few weeks. Over the years, improvements were made in the design but the basic concept remained the same. Now in 1989, Dugan's new patient, an American civilian, like many previous Americans, was about to benefit from a device invented half a century earlier to help German soldiers recover from World War II injuries.

Barry lay on his back on the operating table so that the side of his thigh was accessible to Dr. Dugan. A nurse shaved, cleaned, and disinfected the area where Barry's thigh bone articulated with the hip socket.

Dugan made an incision in the side of Barry's hip and gained access to the top of the femur. He drilled a hole in the top of the bone. Next, using a long bit, he reamed out the marrow cavity. He then used a mallet to drive a titanium rod into the cavity so that it crossed through the fracture site and down into the bottom of the bone. Dugan inserted surgical screws into the top of the femur, through the rod, and into the femoral head to secure the rod. He used two more screws to anchor the bottom end of the femur to the intramedullary rod. The screws at the top and bottom of the rod ensured that it would not turn, twist, or shift in position.

Dr. Dugan began to breathe easier, and allowed an assistant to suture and bandage his second incision.

A day later, a physical therapist urged Barry to stand and put weight on his mended leg. Barry used a walker to take his first timid steps after the near-fatal motorcycle accident.

Barry was hospitalized for three days during which he was visited by his father, Jack, his mother, Joan, and his brother, Matt. Physically, he seemed to be recovering so he was sent home to wait for the swelling to subside. After the swelling went down, physical therapy would begin.

While the doctors had expertly repaired Barry's femur, they failed to notice that he needed psychiatric help. Because he had worn a helmet, his doctors assumed there was no need to look for a traumatic brain injury. But Barry had suffered a concussion. This and the prolonged pain from the compound fracture and the surgery precipitated schizophrenia.

Upon release from the hospital, Barry returned to the little house that he shared with his brother. Jack paid Barry a visit.

"Barry, how are you doing?"

"When I was in the hospital, the doctors put my head in a vice and squeezed it real hard. I asked them to stop, but they wouldn't."

"Barry, the doctors didn't do that. Where did you get that idea?"

"You weren't there. You don't know."

Chapter 27

I Will Keep this Painting Forever

A good picture is equivalent to a good deed.

—Vincent van Gogh
(Dutch Painter)

Barry withdrew from school and family activities. His mother, Joan, persuaded him to see Dr. Stephen Lawson, a private-practice psychologist.

Dr. Lawson diagnosed Barry as having schizophrenia, and engaged him in psychotherapy for several months. But he did not think the young man was making sufficient progress, so he referred him to Dr. Simon Keener, a private-practice psychiatrist. Dr. Keener treated Barry with medications for several months before referring him to the Riverside County community mental health center.

Psychiatrist Keener pointed out that the county treated many outpatients with Barry's diagnosis, and could attend to his needs at lower cost to Barry's family. Jack and Joan had been paying Keener's going rate of one hundred twenty-five dollars per hour, but Keener said this expense could work a hardship on the family over the long run. He did not state his real reason for no longer wanting Barry as a patient.

Dr. Keener believed that persons with schizophrenia never recover. He found treating them to depress himself. He preferred to treat people he called the worried well who happened to have generous health insurance policies. Upon accepting Barry as a patient, the community mental health center assigned him to the care of Dr. Margaret Gross.

Barry had been paying half the rent for the house he shared with his brother, Matt. Now unable to hold a job, he moved in with his parents. He did not have to pay rent to his parents, and Matt could get a new housemate to help him with expenses there.

Barry helped maintain his parents' house and grounds. He worked slowly and took frequent breaks, but managed to paint the house inside and out, to tend the garden, and to walk the two dogs—Proton who belonged to his dad and mom, and Sadie who belonged to Barry. He retired at 8:00 p.m., to arise the next morning at 6:00. Dr. Gross was pleased with Barry's healthful lifestyle.

Using picks, shovels, and rakes, Jack and Barry converted their sloping back yard into two terraces to be separated by a retaining wall. Boulders were available free-of-charge from a nearby subdivision tract that had been excavated, graded, and leveled in preparation for new-home construction. The boulders' rounded and oblong shapes made a vertical, retaining wall impossible. as they did not fit together like bricks or cinder blocks. But the boulders' variety of shapes and sizes provided an opportunity for Jack and Barry to be creative in their landscaping.

Some of the rocks were as big as a washing machine or a refrigerator. But the two men were determined. They managed to bring the boulders home by using an old pickup truck, heavy planks that served as an inclined plane, log chains, and hand winches.

Instead of a conventional retaining wall, they created a steep, rock-lined slope, or ridgeline as they called it. They positioned the biggest boulders to form the lowest tier. Their great weight anchored these huge rocks firmly in place. Next, Jack and Barry placed smaller stones—the size of foot lockers and medicine balls—on top of and in the spaces between the foundational boulders. Because the stones were large, only three tiers were needed to stabilize the entire lead edge of the upper terrace. The rocks were anchored by virtue of their great weight and by being positioned to lean back against the slope. Mortar was not needed, and none was used.

Father and son planted clematis, cat's claw, and trumpet vines to fill the gaps between the rocks. They made sure that some of the stone surfaces would not be covered by the vines so that Barry could paint scenes and designs reminiscent of the rock art of ancient Indians. He painted bison, deer, and hunters with spears and bows and arrows. His muted colors simulated those that had been available to ancient Native Americans.

Jack and Barry worked on their project when the weather was good and when they felt like it. They worked a few hours at a time and might not get back to the task for days. But over the months, a rugged, original landscaping feature took shape.

The heavy lifting caused Jack to wrench his back muscles, and occasionally the pain flared up. A hot shower, a couple aspirin, and rest provided relief.

When the next-door neighbors moved away, they abandoned a calico cat, leaving her outdoors to fend for herself. De-clawed, she could not climb fences or trees to escape the dogs and coyotes that roved through the neighborhood. When Barry found the little cat, she was skinny and covered with corkscrew weed seeds. Barry took her home, named her Honey Child, and nursed her back to health.

Every morning, Honey Child awakened Barry at precisely 6:00 o'clock. She lay on her side and used her front feet to beat on Barry's bedroom door, making it jiggle back and forth until he got out of bed and came out to feed her. Honey Child brought in each new day with humor and good will.

Barry's friends now consisted only of his dad, mom, brother, and James, a participant in Dr. Gross's therapeutic discussion group. Monica had lost track of Barry because he had stopped going to art classes after the motorcycle accident. Barry's two buddies from high school days no longer dropped by or called on the phone.

Despite his reclusive ways, Barry's life was fulfilling. He read about art history, resumed his artwork, and took good care of Proton, Sadie, and Honey Child. Although Barry had little money—$850.00

of monthly Supplemental Security Income—he gave a dollar to every homeless person he met.

Barry drew insightful comic strips that he gave to people. As good as his cartoonist talent was, his talent as a painter was even greater. He painted landscapes and portraits of people and animals.

Barry emulated the art of Vincent van Gogh not only because he admired the artist's works, but also because he identified with the man. In the 1800s, van Gogh suffered from a severe mental illness which could have been any of several conditions such as epilepsy, bipolar disorder, or porphyria. Van Gogh's first name was the same as Barry's last name, and Barry felt this symbolized a spiritual bond. He respected van Gogh not only for his talent but also for the kindness that the great artist had extended to downtrodden people of his day.

Barry gave his post-impressionist paintings to Dr. Gross who displayed them in her office. She admired every picture.

"Barry, this looks like a van Gogh!"

Most of the county clinic's patients regardless of diagnosis were required to participate in group discussion sessions. It did not matter whether they were thought to have schizophrenia, bipolar disorder, chemical substance dependence, dissociative identity disorder, or a severe eating problem. MediCal paid the clinic a sum for each patient reported to have attended a discussion session, while it cost the county no more to conduct a large session than a small one.

Dr. Ralph Newkirk often said, "The more the merrier."

After listening to a discussion on suicide prevention led by psychiatrist Charles Crenshaw, a twenty-year-old man diagnosed with schizophrenia went home and overdosed on Zyprexa. The group discussion's role in the suicide attempt came to light when the young man recovered enough to answer questions from emergency room doctors.

Concerned over the patient's brush with death, Dr. Gross contacted Thomas by local area network and asked him to meet with her. A few hours later, they met in her office, just as the clinic closed to patients for the day.

"Thanks, Thomas, for meeting with me on such short notice."

"Is this another thinly veiled personnel counseling session?"

Margaret said, "It won't be thinly veiled. But it is a counseling session. Only this time, you get to do the counseling."

"You've got my attention. I sense that you're serious."

"I'm serious. I assume you haven't heard about Crenshaw's patient."

"No," Thomas said, "what happened?"

"Crenshaw held one of his Bob Newhart-style group discussion sessions. One of his patients, a young man with schizophrenia, went home and overdosed on Zyprexa. His father found him unconscious, and got him to an emergency room in time for doctors to save him.

"Based on what the patient said, and since he had just come from the group session, Crenshaw looks to be in trouble. The father is raising Cain. I think Richard will make some changes in how we run our group sessions."

"It's about time he instituted some quality control."

Margaret said, "It appears he will be forced into acting. The patient's father is politically connected and is threatening a civil suit. At the least, there will be meetings with our state office higher-ups. I want your advice on how I should weigh in regarding the proper way to run group discussion sessions. Am I running my own group sessions in appropriate ways? I won't be listened to unless I'm doing things right myself."

"Thanks for asking my advice. Maybe partly because California psychologists can't prescribe medications, we have held true to our beliefs in talk therapy.

"Why did Crenshaw act as moderator instead of having his psych tech do it as usual?"

"Helena was on sick leave that day. I imagine Crenshaw also underestimated how hard it is to steer the discussions in healthful directions."

Thomas said, "I understand your desire to be seen as a good example. Otherwise, you would have little credibility if you have to criticize Crenshaw's actions. And of course, you want to watch out for your own patients anyway.

"First, you have a good psych tech in Anna. She's qualified to run the sessions as long as you, the psychiatrist, sit in from time to time. Do you audit her work periodically?"

"Of course. You know that."

Thomas said, "I know. We're just running down a checklist of good and bad practices as I think of them."

Margaret prompted, "Crenshaw's patient has schizophrenia."

"If not carefully constructed, group therapy can be counterproductive for patients with schizophrenia. I'm always harping on the unintended consequences of prescribing medications off-label. Well, bad side effects also can happen when a group discussion session gets out of hand."

Margaret said, "A person with schizophrenia might think that others in the group are stealing his ideas or magically planting thoughts in his head. And such thinking can be aggravated by the back-and-forth that goes on in most group discussions. I get that."

"The individual doesn't want to share his innermost thoughts with anyone, least of all strangers. Of course, public debate is out of the question."

"So you can't just toss a person with schizophrenia into any old group therapy session."

"Right," Thomas said, "group therapy might help a schizophrenic patient, but the sessions must be designed with his or her symptoms in mind. A vigorous exchange of views easily overwhelms this patient."

"I apologize for cutting this short, but it's getting late, and I need to get home to fix dinner."

Thomas said, "I'll sum up. If group sessions are to benefit schizophrenic patients, structure the sessions with their symptoms in mind. Limit each groups to about six patients. Never put a patient with schizophrenia on the spot. Never require him to respond. If he responds, it must be because he feels comfortable."

One day during a small group discussion session, Barry's friend James said he admired Mohamed Ali. Barry went home and searched magazines until he found a picture of Ali in a boxing stance. He painted a large portrait of James's idol.

At the next group discussion session, Barry presented the painting to his friend.

"This looks just like him. I can tell he's about to lower the boom. Here, Barry, I'm buying this painting." James reached for his wallet in his back pocket.

"No, James, this is my gift to you. I ask only that you never get in the ring with Ali."

"Don't worry. I won't make that mistake. I'll keep this painting forever."

Barry was devastated when psychiatric technician Anna Wong-McDowell found a new job and announced she would leave the county clinic. At home, Barry painted wild geese in flight against a sunset sky and added a poem.

> Learn From the Wild Geese
>
> In a V formation,
> Geese fly south for the winter.
> The lead goose parts the wind
> For the next in line.
> When lead goose tires,
> His sister takes his place.
> The cooperation
> Aids recuperation
> And prompts harmony and peace.
> People should learn from the geese.
>
> Barry Vincent

Barry presented Anna with the picture and poem at the last group discussion that she facilitated. She made the same pledge that James had.

"I will keep this painting forever."

Chapter 28

Cheerleaders Make Great Drug Reps

At the front lines of this massive marketing campaign stands the drug company representative, or drug rep, usually a handsome young man or a shapely young woman who has been recruited more for his or her good looks and outgoing personality than for any aptitude in science or medicine.

—Shannon Brownlee
Overtreated: Why Too Much Medicine is Making Us Sicker and Poorer (2008)

Myron Mulroy had worked for Alphatron Pharmaceuticals since graduating from the University of Southern California. Before attending USC, he had been the quarterback of a football team at a small high school in Arizona. He was smart, fast, and strong, but not big enough to play football for the Trojans.

So Myron became a cheerleader. This put him close to the action on the gridiron. And cheerleaders are athletes in their own right, performing acrobatics and leading spectators in chants. They raise the morale of both the football players and the crowd, and know their role is key to winning games.

After graduating from USC, Myron sought employment as a high school biology teacher. He never dreamed that his cheerleading experience would net him a job. But pharmaceutical companies had found that cheerleaders made excellent drug reps because they were the ultimate team players, being both outgoing and politically correct. Their good looks and energy helped them relate to the doctors they called on.

While waiting to hear the results of his latest application to an Arizona school district, Myron answered a *Los Angeles Times* classified ad for a pharmaceutical sales associate. When Alphatron executives learned he had been a cheerleader, they hired him the next day.

Myron Mulroy, Neil Kronberger, and Laura Nielsen all were former cheerleaders.

Alphatron's new building in Long Beach was elaborate. The grounds were landscaped with native plants, and the huge building had an exceptional view of the harbor. The overall effect was a boost to Alphatron's corporate image.

Myron had trained new drug reps the previous week, and this morning was giving refresher training to twenty-five of his experienced staff. While waiting in the conference room for Myron to begin the training session, Laura Nielsen and Neil Kronberger visited with coworker Ernesto Sanchez.

The drug reps were dressed in black slacks, white shirts, and maroon blazers. The women wore black berets. Myron wore a tailored, gray suit.

Myron set the example for how drug reps should treat their physician clients. Tables were laden with pots of coffee, glasses of water, pastry, and for the health conscious, grapes and diced cantaloupe and watermelon. Attendants kept the platters full.

Training drug reps was a delicate business. The FDA regulates the marketing of drugs but not the practice of medicine. An off-label use of a drug occurs when it is prescribed for any purpose other than what the FDA has approved. Thus, although it is legal for doctors to prescribe drugs off-label, it is illegal for pharmaceutical companies to advocate the practice. Myron's training course had to take into account that off-label marketing was prohibited whether by advertising on television or by drug reps calling on doctors.

Despite this prohibition, after the FDA approved a drug for a specific condition, drugmakers often promoted it for other uses. Money always was the motive. The broader the market for a drug, the greater the sales and hence the profits.

But Myron knew that Alphatron had to be stealthy. He recalled that in 1993 the FDA approved Warner-Lambert's gabapentin only for treatment of seizures. But Warner then used continuing education for doctors to promote gabapentin so that it soon became widely used to treat pain, migraine, and psychiatric conditions. For a few years, the profits were great, but an employee blew the whistle and eventually Warner-Lambert paid four hundred thirty million dollars to the federal government to settle the claim.

To meet the ambitious sales quotas set by Alphatron's upper management, Myron's reps had to violate FDA rules, but he did not want them to see their actions in that light. His task today was to convince the reps that public health always benefited when they persuaded doctors to prescribe Alphatron medications off-label.

Myron wanted his drug reps to promote drugs off-label without alienating the doctors by being aggressive or by making stupid remarks during their sales presentations. If a doctor complained to the FDA, the agency could order the drugmaker to stop marketing in the illegal manner. More serious blunders by drug reps could even cause a United States Attorney to file a civil lawsuit against the offending company.

One of the worst things that could happen to a pharmaceutical company was for a drug rep to take legal action against being pressured by management to advocate off-label uses. If drug reps became whistleblowers, they could join with the federal government in filing a civil lawsuit under the federal False Claims Act. The whistleblower could be awarded up to one-third of any monetary damages collected from the pharmaceutical company.

Without saying so directly, Myron wanted to persuade his drug reps that promoting drugs off-label was lucrative enough that they did not need to take the more dicey route of complaining to the government and hoping to share civil damages that might be awarded. The vast majority of drug reps had always remained loyal to their employers and enjoyed a high income, consisting of a base salary, commissions, and bonuses.

So on this training day, Myron would coax his drug reps into doing off-label marketing without feeling they were doing anything illegal. He never used the word "off-label." To avoid directly telling the drug reps to break the law, Myron talked in code much of the time. He cleverly instructed the reps how to violate the law while appearing to be law abiding.

The group he was training consisted of old hands who already had worked out their own rationalizations for lawbreaking. So they primarily needed reminders as to how they could make their sales pitch without causing prescribers to complain to government regulators. This remedial training was needed because some of the staff had fallen short of Alphatron sales goals, and others were careless in how they urged doctors to prescribe drugs off-label. Also, sloppy field reports to Myron could become incriminating evidence in any investigation of alleged wrongdoing.

Myron leaped onto the stage. "Would you like to be rich?"

The drug reps chanted, "Yes."

"Would you like a great house in an upscale neighborhood?"

The drug reps shouted, "Yes!"

"Such rewards are what being an Alphatron representative is all about. I'll show you how to increase your sales and earn bigger commissions and bonuses."

Myron hopped off the stage and circulated among his staff.

"For the most part, it's psychiatrists you will inform of the merits of Alphatron medications. Psychiatrists are so smart that they can diagnose a patient even before the first office visit begins."

Straight man Neil Kronberger said, "That's impossible."

Myron said, "Here's how they do it. If a patient's late for the appointment, he's depressed.

"If he's early, he's suffering from anxiety.

"If he's on time—well, he's obsessive-compulsive."

The trainees laughed. Myron urged them to be assertive with their doctor clients, neither aggressive nor shy. Doctors knew more about the practice of medicine than the drug reps did, but the reps were the experts when it came to the virtues of Alphatron medications and the psychology of marketing.

Myron said, "When you buy dinner for a doctor, you want him to think of you as his friend, while you think of him as a client."

Ernesto Sanchez stood up.

"I'm troubled by whether we can ethically recommend using powerful drugs like Gabicon off-label."

Myron made a show of looking at his Rolex.

"I forgot that I have a phone call I must make. Excuse me. I'll be right back."

Myron's supervisor was in his office, and his door was open. Myron knocked on the doorframe but did not wait to be invited in. He approached Paul Warren who was seated at a massive mahogany desk.

"Sir, a drug rep named Ernesto Sanchez is asking about the ethics of off-label sales. We're in the early stages of our training, and I'm afraid he'll poison the minds of the other reps."

"Have one of your staff bring Mr. Sanchez to me. Don't do it yourself. Get the class re-focused on the training. I'll bring in someone from our office of counsel. If we terminate his contract we'll give him severance pay and have him sign a confidentially agreement so he won't run to a regulatory agency."

Myron hurried back to the conference room.

"I apologize for taking off like that. My secretary scheduled me to make a call and didn't tell me until this morning. We will have a question-and-answer session after lunch, and all questions will be welcome. For now, let me describe some of the marketing techniques that worked for me when I was a sales associate like you."

As he had promised, Myron answered questions after the lunch break. The issue of off-label promotion of drugs like Gabicon did not arise, however, as Ernesto Sanchez was elsewhere.

Chapter 29

They Could Not Have Been More Different

A big problem with medications is that they blunt the sensitivity of the doctors, allowing them to imagine they are dispassionate brain fixers instead of fellow human beings in complex relationships with their patients.

—Barbara Taylor
The Last Asylum: A Memoir of Madness in Our Time (2011)

Dr. Gross had seen her last outpatient for the day. Department Head Conway knocked on her office door.

"Come in, Richard."

"Margret, I have good news."

"Good news is always welcome."

"I received the go-ahead to establish a deputy director position and for you to fill it. This is a promotion, and you don't have to compete for it. Human Resources and our state office agreed that you've accrued enough administrative duties that you already are doing the work of a deputy director."

Dr. Gross said, "Thank you for coming up with the accrual of duties idea. Also for reminding the bean counters of our need for this new position."

"The clinic just kept taking on more patients. And our administrative chores just kept increasing. I was lucky you were willing to help me with management duties in addition to seeing your patients."

"What's our next step?"

"Your title is now deputy director. Your duties are one hundred percent administrative and supervisory. You need to transfer your patients to the other psychiatrists on staff."

"Dr. Thein arrived just in time to take some of my patients."

"Transfer some to him and some to our other doctors. Reduce your caseload to zero."

A month had passed since Barry's last appointment with Dr. Gross. He had lost Anna Wong-McDowell who gave him hope that he would fully recover from schizophrenia. He could understand her leaving for a higher-paying job. That was one thing. But for Dr. Gross to no longer see him even though she remained at the clinic was something he did not understand.

Over and over, Barry asked himself, what did I do, what is wrong with me?

He had had no say, no input as to when the office visits with Dr. Gross would end or which psychiatrist he would be transferred to. Had he offended her? Barry could hear a man and a woman speaking to each other about him. He looked about but could not see them.

The woman said, "That Barry Vincent is a dumb cluck. No social skills. No wonder Dr. Gross got rid of him."

The man said, "He never takes a bath, and his clothes aren't color coordinated. What a hick."

"Yeah, and he wears that baseball cap and those yucky sunglasses."

As his first office appointment with Dr. David Thein drew near, Barry's anxiety soared. Would his new doctor be as nice to him as Dr. Gross had been? Other outpatients said Dr. Thein was from Burma. Where was Burma? Why had he come to California?

Barry arrived ten minutes early for his 8:30 a.m. appointment. Dr. Thein called him in at 9:10 a.m. By making him wait, was Dr. Thein punishing him? What could he have done? Had Dr. Gross told Dr. Thein that he was a bad patient?

THEY COULD NOT HAVE BEEN MORE DIFFERENT

Dr. Gross had worn flowery, colorful dresses. Dr. Thein wore a black, three-piece suit. She was cheerful while he was solemn. The two psychiatrists could not have been more different.

"Hello, Mr. Vincent. Have a seat. I am your new psychiatrist, Dr. David Thein."

Barry said nothing.

Dr. Thein said, "How are you today?"

"OK."

"Must you wear that baseball cap? I shall thank you to take it off when you are in my office."

Barry removed his cap. He held it on his lap, gripping it with both hands.

Dr. Thein said, "And those dark glasses—are they prescription?"

"No. I wear them because the light hurts my eyes."

"Well, you are indoors. There is no sunlight in here. Please remove your sunglasses."

Barry removed his glasses and looked down at his lap.

"That is better. It is rude to wear a cap and dark glasses when you are indoors."

Barry said nothing.

"Your medical chart says you are schizophrenic. Are you taking your medicine?"

"Yes."

"That is good. I have a requirement. All my patients take part in group discussions. If they do not participate, I do not prescribe them medications. Do you understand that requirement?"

Barry said, "Yes."

"Good. We shall get along together just fine. Do you have any questions?"

"How many people are in your group discussions?"

"Approximately twenty-five at the beginning of a session. All my patients start their day in the group session. My nurse calls them one at a time to have their office appointment with me. After I see a patient, he or she is free to smoke outdoors, drink coffee, or watch a movie on television while I see the next patient. We do this until

I have seen all the patients. Then they get on a bus and go back to Spruce House."

"What's Spruce House?"

"It is a big house where some of my patients reside. They take medicine there that helps them manage their addictions."

"Oh."

"Is something wrong, Mr. Vincent? Is there something you do not understand?"

Barry said nothing.

The doctor said, "Drug and alcohol abuse is what I specialize in since becoming a doctor for Riverside County. Only you and two more of my patients have diagnoses other than drug abuse."

"Do the patients in the group sessions with me have the same diagnosis as me?"

"No, with two exceptions. Because Dr. Gross transferred three of her patients to me, the group sessions will include you and two others with similar diagnoses. All the rest of the discussants have addictions of one kind or another."

"Will a patient named James be in my group sessions?"

"You will find out when you come for your next appointment. Set the date with the receptionist at the front counter. Be here at 8:30 that morning and go directly into the group discussion."

Thein increased the doses of the three medications that Dr. Gross had held steady for six years. He increased Zyprexa, Paxil, and Cogentin six fold.

Thein filled out an informed consent document, listing the increased dosages. He handed the form to Barry and pointed at a blank line.

"Sign here."

Chapter 30

Pharmacology Guesswork

Most physicians do not make decisions about which drug to use on the basis of research or cost. They base their decision almost entirely on which drug is the most popular choice of their colleagues.

—Michael T. Murray
Natural Alternatives to Drugs (1998)

Each prescription that Dr. Thein wrote made him feel more powerful. Words on a prescription pad required patients—male or female, young or old—to consume powerful chemicals in the amounts he specified. His feeling of power was magnified when those same prescriptions brought him rewards from pharmaceutical companies.

He regularly told Laura Nielsen how many prescriptions he had written recently and for which drugs. He had many incentives to prescribe psychoactive medications. There were no disincentives.

In Burma, Thein had been limited in what he could prescribe. Ne Win's annual budget for medicine and education together averaged one-fifth the amount spent on the military. Most of the medications that the state purchased from other countries went to treat military officers and their families whose medical needs were met by a separate, better-funded government system than the one that served civilians.

THE MIND DOCTOR

The Ne Win government had restricted the medications available for doctors to prescribe to the populace. The supply was further reduced when drugs were stolen from medical institutions and sold on the black market. Many poor people were treated by folk remedies such as charms, potions, incantations, and tattoos instead of Western-style medications.

Things were different in America. Writing prescriptions was the main thing that psychiatrists did to earn their pay. The standard of care was for a psychiatrist to prescribe medication within minutes of meeting a patient.

Medications available for Thein to prescribe included antipsychotics, antidepressants, anticonvulsants, antianxiety pills, mood stabilizers, stimulants, pain killers, tranquillizers, appetite stimulants, appetite depressants, and sleep aids.

Dr. Thein believed there was at least one medication that would calm any mental perturbation that a patient might be experiencing. He needed only to add another medication to whatever regimen the patient was taking. If the additional medicine did not sufficiently reduce the symptoms then Thein would increase the dose. If the higher dose did not do the job then he would add yet another medication. He was satisfied if the patient became indifferent and lethargic. His goal was less to aid recovery than to produce someone who was easy to take care of.

Pharmaceutical companies were aware of Thein's track record as a heavy prescriber. The companies purchased the pharmacy records of California's doctors, and knew exactly which drugs in what quantities each prescribed. Prescription records were for sale not only from private companies but also the American Medical Association.

Laura Nielsen brought her supervisor, Myron Mulroy, to meet Dr. Thein whose name was showing up as one of three physicians who prescribed the most medications in California. Mr. Mulroy asked if Dr. Thein would like to put his name on medical journal articles written by Alphatron's technical writing staff. The answer was an enthusiastic yes.

Next, they arranged for him to attend a symposium in Honolulu in January.

Thein enjoyed life as a licensed psychiatrist in California. His bank account grew and he bought a fine house.

Laura Nielsen moved in with him.

The number of drugs that Thein felt justified in prescribing increased dramatically as a result of a discussion at home one evening.

David said, "Laura, I am tired of contending with unnecessary distinctions between disorders and symptoms. Clinical depression is a disorder. Yet depression is a symptom of disorders like schizophrenia and bipolar illness and even of many physical diseases. For example, someone who suffered a heart attack is apt to be depressed.

"Anxiety is another example. It is both a disorder and a symptom. Sometimes I give a patient a diagnosis of generalized anxiety disorder. But I might also diagnose someone else as having obsessive-compulsive disorder with a symptom of anxiety."

"What's wrong with depression being a disorder in some cases but a symptom of a disorder in other cases?"

"That classification system limits the amount of medicine I can prescribe. Conventional advice says a psychiatrist is to medicate disorders, not each separate symptom. Do-gooders say medicating each symptom results in too many drugs for the patient to cope with. If a disorder has eight symptoms, they say I should prescribe one medication for the overall disorder, and not a separate pill for each symptom. So if I follow conventional advice, I prescribe one medication instead of eight."

Laura said, "I see what you mean."

"One way to get around this constraint would be to declare all symptoms to be disorders, no matter whether the symptom appears by itself or as part of a syndrome."

"Hey, I like that. If we convert all symptoms into disorders, we'll have a lot more disorders that we can aggressively treat. That way you can prescribe more Alphatron medications."

Laura had waited to have her furniture delivered until she was sure that David would not return to his home country.

She need not have worried. He had no inclination to return even for a visit because he now was Dr. David Thein, a psychiatrist living in America with a gorgeous blonde woman. Except for not residing on the seacoast, he was living his most enduring dream. He did not waste time worrying about things in Burma.

Thein began to reflect that evening on his new identity and his new life. For years, he had suppressed thoughts about the embarrassing and debilitating condition he had called his inconsistency quotient. But this evening, as he shared his luxurious home with Laura, he realized that for the last two years he had not frozen in place on any occasion. Not once had he failed to answer a tough question. What had changed in his psyche to have freed him from the recurring trances?

The most likely reason seemed to be that he no longer had to compete academically and that mental stress had subsided. He no longer had to compete for a residency or a psychiatric practice. He no longer had to study endlessly and to cram for exams. He no longer aspired to be a psychiatrist in America because now he was one and moreover was living in the Golden State. Indeed, he had arrived and was now a recognized psychiatrist. Or perhaps the change had come about because of his relationship with Laura, the woman of his dreams.

Or perhaps the freezing up had stopped because of distance from his father, Burma's most notorious assassin. The geographic distance from Saw, and the scant communication with him, had removed the continual reminders of his father's misdeeds. Perhaps Thein no longer subconsciously feared that he might turn out to be sinister like his father, and maybe this was what freed him from the inconsistency quotient.

Laura said, "David, I like that you wear a suit while working at the county clinic. It makes you look important, which you are."

"You are leading up to something."

"And I note that you've acquired the ability to read minds."

"That is what a psychiatrist does," David said. "Get to the point."

"I've been thinking of ways to enhance your image of success.
"And?"

Laura said, "The big shots at Alphatron play golf."

"And of course you play the game also."

"Most lady drug reps at Alphatron play golf. It's a way to improve relationships with high-prescribing doctors."

David said, "I never had time for golf. I was always studying to pass some examination."

"That's the point. People who play golf are saying 'I don't have to struggle to get ahead. I'm ahead right now. Look at me. I've arrived. I'm a big deal.' David, you are now a big shot and you should act like one."

"I do not know whether to feel inflated for being a big shot or deflated for not acting like one."

"You're a big shot and it's time you acted like one beyond wearing a three-piece suit and carrying a gold watch. Myron Mulroy invited you to next month's medical convention in Honolulu. That proves you're a big shot. But you need to recognize that the other big shots will spend time on the golf course."

"There is not enough time for me to learn how to play golf by next month."

Laura said, "So you've missed your chance to get on the course this time. But six months after the Honolulu convention there will be one at Orlando. Why not arrange tutoring by a golf pro so you'll be ready for Orlando?"

"I do not want to spend my money that way."

"Remember that Alphatron thinks highly of you."

Thein phoned Alphatron's district manager, Myron Mulroy.

"This is Dr. David Thein."

"It's good to hear from you. How can I be of service?"

"Next month I will be at the Honolulu continuing education event."

"I'm glad you have accepted our invitation," Myron said.

"Do you plan to spend time on the golf course?" Thein asked.

"Yes. Would you like to play a round or two with me?"

"I have never learned how to play golf."

"Would you like lessons from a golf pro?"

"I was wondering if that were possible."

"Of course it is."

Thein said, "I would not have time to become proficient enough to play at Honolulu. But could you arrange tutoring for me so that I could join you on the course at Orlando?"

"Sounds great. Would you like to receive your instructions at the Riverside Country Club for convenience sake? That way you can write a few prescriptions, take a golf lesson, and write a few more prescriptions before calling it a day."

"I would appreciate a country club membership."

"OK, I'll arrange both membership and golf tutoring lessons for you at Riverside Country Club. At Alphatron's expense of course."

"I still regret not being able to get onto the golf course at Honolulu just to enjoy the scenery."

Myron said, "I'll line you up with preliminary lessons at Honolulu. That'll get you out on the course and give you a running start for your lessons at the Riverside country club."

"I will need golf clubs and proper apparel."

It was Barry's third office visit with Dr. Thein. The doctor had raised the dose to sixty milligrams per day at the last visit a month earlier. Medical literature said there was no known benefit for a patient to take more than twenty milligrams of Paxil per day. Graphs showed that as far as therapeutic value was concerned, Paxil had a flat dose-response line beginning at twenty milligrams. Unfortunately, while the medical effectiveness of Paxil plateaued at twenty milligrams, its toxicity continued to increase as the dosage increased.

Barry could not sit still, and he told Dr. Thein that he felt an animal was clawing to get out of his stomach.

Thein wrote in Barry's medical chart, "He is hyper. He has too much energy."

Thein decided that schizophrenia had morphed into schizoaffective disorder and that Mr. Vincent had the manic form. This accounted for his sudden increased energy level. Thein changed his patient's diagnosis to schizoaffective disorder and prescribed more Paxil. He had not read any of FDA's widely-distributed "Dear

Doctor" warning letters that linked Paxil and chemically related antidepressants to suicidality in children and young adults.

He also added Gabicon, an anticonvulsant, although the FDA had approved this medication only for treating one form of epilepsy. Thein had not read a FDA letter that warned Gabicon was likely to cause seizures in anyone who was not already taking certain kinds of anticonvulsants such as phenobarbital and carbamazine.

These two anticonvulsants and a few others produced liver enzymes that happened to make Gabicon less potent. They did this by speeding up the rate at which Gabicon was eliminated from the body. Being in the body for a shorter period made it less toxic. Barry had never suffered a seizure so he had never consumed an anticonvulsant of any kind, and had no protective enzymes.

In the clinical trials that had led to FDA's approval of Gabicon, Alphatron Pharmaceuticals had arrived at the recommended starting dose of eight milligrams of Gabicon per day by testing this compound on epileptic patients who had a reservoir of protective enzymes. No other patient groups were tested. For anyone not having these special enzymes, Alphatron's recommended starting dose was four milligrams.

Thein did not know this biochemical history for determining the drug's potency. He had overheard a fellow psychiatrist mention in passing that eight milligrams was the starting dose for epilepsy.

Thein had a gut feeling that schizoaffective disorder was twice as bad as epilepsy. He prescribed sixteen milligrams per day for Barry.

Chapter 31

Crisis Intervention Denied

Yet, change will have to come from below, which can happen when the American people realize that it will take popular action to make doctors practice medicine.

—Otis Webb Brawley
How We Do Harm (2011)

On a Friday morning in August 1996, Barry's hallucinations became evident to his parents.

Jack asked, "Barry, how are you doing?"

"I'm OK."

Minutes later, Barry assumed a boxing stance. an awkward one, unlike Muhammad Ali's in the picture that Barry had painted for his friend, James.

Barry crouched, held his fists close to his face, and squinted. He never threw a punch, but guarded against being hit. Even when hallucinating, Barry was not trying to injure his attacker. Instead, he was trying to fend off a foe that his dad could not see.

Fear showed in Barry's face.

"Joan, please take Barry to the county clinic and report this as a medical emergency."

CRISIS INTERVENTION DENIED

Joan asked Barry to go to the clinic with her and said she would drive. They arrived at the mental health center at 9:30 that Friday morning. As they drove into the parking lot, they passed a yellow bus with the name "Spruce House" on the side. Men were sitting in the bus, smoking cigarettes.

Joan and Barry entered the main building and approached the front counter. The attendant's name tag said, "Julie." Joan identified herself as Barry's mother and said that her son was Dr. Thein's patient.

"Barry is suffering a medical crisis. He's hallucinating and appears to be boxing with an attacker. He needs to see Dr. Thein right away."

"Go through that door," Julie said. "Open it when you hear the click."

Julie did not log Barry in or write down what Joan had said. Her thoughts were of the weekend ahead.

Instead of entering an examination room and being received by a nurse or doctor, Joan and Barry stepped into a big meeting room where several men and women sat around a table, and others milled about. A heavyset, middle-aged nurse was explaining the need to take medications exactly as prescribed.

Joan tried to get the nurse's attention but Dorothy continued to lecture. Joan decided to not risk offending her so she and Barry sat and waited.

After forty minutes, Joan approached Dorothy who looked away.

"Pardon me. Are you affiliated with Dr. David Thein?"

"You're interrupting a group discussion session."

"I'm sorry, but my son is suffering a psychiatric crisis. Your clinic's brochure says this is the place to come for emergency intervention. Also, Barry is Dr. Thein's patient."

"I'll tell the doctor, but it's Friday, and Barry doesn't have an appointment. The doctor is leaving at one o'clock for the weekend."

Dorothy left the conference room through a side door.

Joan returned to her chair beside Barry.

Dorothy returned. "The doctor will see your son in a few minutes."

A young man with a ponytail brought a diskette to Dorothy who inserted it in a television set. They all sat down to watch a movie.

Blood and Guts in Los Angeles portrayed The Bloods and The Crips fighting for control of a ghetto. A vile biker got punched out, fell to the pavement, and got his head kicked in by a handsome fellow wearing engineer's boots.

The man with the ponytail said, "Way to go! Kill him!"

The patients cheered. Joan expected Dorothy to turn the TV off, but she was cheering too.

Barry rose and left the room. Joan thought he was going outside to wait until Dr. Thein came to examine him.

Akathisia would not let Barry wait any longer, especially since he did not know when Dr. Thein would decide to see him.

When Barry had sat in on Dorothy's previous group discussion sessions, Thein always saw all the addicted patients first and Barry last. The addicted were Thein's present medical specialty. Barry was merely someone added to his workload because Dr. Gross had to get rid of him so she could do her new job.

For each of Barry's previous office appointments, Thein had told him to report at 8:30 a.m., but did not see him until 11:00 a.m. On this August morning, Barry realized that again he was being made to wait until after his doctor saw all the substance-abuse patients.

Home was six miles away, through city and suburb. Barry walked as fast as he could. It was 11:30 a.m., and the temperature hovered in the midnineties. Cogentin prevented him from perspiring, and Gabicon caused excitatory neurons in his brain to fire excessively.

Thein continued interviewing patients and writing prescriptions. Julie and Dorothy had said that Barry Vincent was hallucinating, but this was typical of schizophrenics. No need to change his routine. The Spruce House bus would not leave until after he had seen all the substance-abuse patients.

After Barry was gone from the conference room for fifteen minutes, Joan looked for him in the back courtyard. He was not there. A gate stood open. She reentered the conference room, and then the lobby. No sign of Barry. She looked for him in the front parking lot. No Barry.

The day was getting hotter.

Joan reentered the lobby and asked Julie to again let her enter the group therapy room and the offices beyond.

Julie said, "Your son is not with you, and you are not a patient here. I can't let you go back there."

"Dr. Thein never saw Barry. He kept us waiting and waiting. Now my son is missing. Let me into your inner sanctum so I can get the psychiatrist off his dead ass."

Julie glared at Joan but pressed the button that unlocked the door. Joan entered the group therapy room and spotted Dorothy.

"Where is Dr. Thein's office? I need to see him right now."

Dorothy started to object, but Joan cut her off.

"I brought Barry here because he's suffering a medical crisis. And now he's missing. Either take me to your doctor or get out of my way."

Dorothy walked Joan to Dr. Thein's office. He had just finished seeing his last substance-abuse patient, and was backing into the hall as he pulled his office door closed.

Joan said, "Are you Dr. Thein?"

"Yes. Who are you?"

"I'm Joan Vincent, Barry Vincent's mother. Were you told that he is having a medical crisis and that we were here to see you?"

"I was told you were here. I did not hear anything about a crisis. Barry did not have an appointment. Mrs. Vincent, you seem overwrought. You need to calm down."

"When you didn't come to examine Barry and your nurse showed a violent movie, he left. Violence of any kind makes him physically ill. I hope he's going home, but I don't know. He's on foot and we live miles away. He could overheat since he's taking your medications."

Thein said, "Well, he should have waited for me. I cannot do everything at once. I had patients to see, and your son did not have an appointment. He had to wait his turn."

THE MIND DOCTOR

"Wait his turn when he's having a medical crisis? State law says this clinic provides crisis intervention. It isn't the only place that does, but it's the logical place for us to come to because you're Barry's doctor. Please ask your mobile response team to look for my son."

"The mobile team does not know what he looks like. Find him yourself and bring him back here."

Joan said, "You must have an attendant who knows Barry. Or you could ride with the team."

"We will not look for him. Many patients hallucinate. Go find him yourself."

"Julie said that you're leaving at 1 o'clock. You won't be here to treat him."

"That is correct, but a doctor will be on standby duty. Or you can dial 911."

Joan gave up trying to get Thein to help her son. She wished she had taken him to Arrowhead Regional Hospital. She went to her car.

Thein said to Dorothy, "It is Friday. We have had a full week. And along comes a woman and her grown son, who should be able to take care of himself, and they demand to be seen out of turn. Am I correct that they do not deserve special treatment?"

"That's the way I see it. I never did like that Barry Vincent. He wears a baseball cap and dark glasses during group sessions. Claims that light hurts his eyes. Even said our medications had something to do with it."

Thein said, "He told me that too. I said he was making up an excuse so he could wear dark glasses. That made it so he could see us without us seeing his eyes. I need to see the eyes to make a proper diagnosis."

"And he didn't contribute to the group sessions. Didn't say ten words."

"By this last day of the week, I am exhausted. It is bad enough that I have to see those addicts from Spruce House without having to contend with an intruder who refuses to wait his turn."

Dorothy said, "Fridays are special. That's when we wind down. Unless there's an emergency, patients need to leave us alone until Monday morning."

CRISIS INTERVENTION DENIED

The beast raged inside Barry, clawing to escape. He got a little relief by walking, so he walked faster to get more relief. But it was awfully hot. Could he make it all the way home?

He ignored traffic when he crossed intersections, stepping in front of oncoming cars. He must get home as soon as possible so Mom and Dad would not worry about him. How could he get that wildcat out of his insides?

Joan drove the streets, looking for Barry. She drove in a criss-cross pattern, guessing which streets he might use. She thought he would head for home but could not be sure since he had been hallucinating. Joan cussed David Thein, Dorothy, Julie, and the entire Riverside County mental health center. If something bad happened to Barry, she would seek revenge against the doctor and the county. They had violated their oath to help the mentally ill.

Joan headed for home. If Barry were not there, Jack would help her search for him. If they used two cars, they could cover twice as much ground. She chose to not call the police, hoping she or Jack could find Barry sooner on their own.

Joan arrived at home.

"Jack, they wouldn't see Barry at the clinic. They stuck us in a group discussion session. Showed a violent movie. Kept us waiting until he got frustrated and went outside. When I looked for him, he was gone. Being medicated, it's too hot for him to walk all the way home."

"We'll use both cars. I'll head for the clinic and start my search from there. I'll work my way back here. How about starting your search from here and working toward the clinic?"

Just as Jack took his car keys from a desk drawer, Barry walked through the front door, his face flushed.

Joan said, "Barry, I looked for you."

"Mom, I walked as fast as I could."

Barry had survived walking six miles in the heat. Maybe things would be all right.

Jack said, "Barry, sit down and rest in here where it's cool."

THE MIND DOCTOR

Joan fixed Barry a lemonade. He tried to stay indoors, but the beast within would not let him rest. He couldn't describe the terror to his parents.

Barry opened a sliding, glass door and walked out onto the back patio. He stood in the shade, sipping his drink, trying to calm down.

Jack and Joan watched their son through a window.

Barry fell forward. His right shoulder struck a patio pillar on his way down, spinning him around so that he landed on his back.

Joan rushed to Barry's side to make sure he was breathing while Jack called 911. Paramedics arrived within minutes.

One of the medics broke open a capsule of smelling salts and held it under Barry's nose. Barry awoke with a start, shaking his head. He tried to stand, but the medic held him down.

"Don't try to get up yet. Stay down and relax."

But the beast would not let him lie there. Again, Barry tried to get up. This time, the medic stood back, prepared to catch him if he fell again.

"Barry, what's your last name?"

"Vincent."

The emergency workers placed Barry on a gurney and wheeled him to an ambulance.

Joan explained to the paramedics what Barry had been through that day. He was afflicted by schizophrenia and was heavily medicated. He might be suffering a psychotic relapse because he might have stopped taking some medications within the last few days.

Joan said, "Please take him to Arrowhead Regional Medical Center. They have a behavioral health unit."

The lead paramedic said, "We have to contact our dispatcher for instructions, but I'll recommend Arrowhead."

Joan said, "Tell the dispatcher that Barry has schizophrenia and this needs to be taken into account."

The paramedic walked to the ambulance-fire engine where he contacted his dispatcher by two-way radio. He returned to where Joan waited.

"My dispatcher said we have to take your son to Saint Rita's."

"Did he or she say why?"

"No, he didn't. But the decision usually is based on a number of factors."

"Like what?"

"One of the biggest factors usually is which hospital emergency department might be tied up with other emergencies at the moment."

"Your dispatcher is overlooking the most important factor—which hospital can cope with mental illnesses. Please ask him to reconsider."

"Sorry. I won't do that. I relayed your request, and I got my orders."

Joan rode in the ambulance with her son.

Chapter 32

Transfer Trauma

Patients may experience the news of the upcoming end of treatment as abandonment and loss; a mourning process may follow, and treatment outcomes may be negatively affected.

—David Mischoulon, et al.
*Transfer to a New Psychopharmacologist:
Its Effect on Patients* (2000)

At lunch in the clinic's cafeteria, Thomas sat at a table with Thein, Dr. Shelia Marsh, and two other psychiatrists. A rumor was circulating that Dr. Marsh was dating Alphatron's Neil Kronberger. Thomas wondered if this relationship was another case of the pharmaceutical company corrupting a doctor's prescribing practices. If money, ghost-written medical reports, and symposia in Honolulu did not corrupt Dr. Marsh, maybe romance would.

Shelia said, "Dr. Thein, one of my patients is from Burma. May I ask you for advice as to how I might provide him better health care?"

"I will share my knowledge."

"Thanks. I appreciate the chance to pick your brain."

"Dr. Marsh, I will discuss Burma, but you are not picking my brain! Nobody picks my brain!"

"Wait, that's just an idiom in America. It just means to get ideas from someone."

"Oh."

The conversation got back on track, and Dr. Thein gave Dr. Marsh tips on understanding patients from Southeast Asia.

"It is important for a medical doctor to understand the cultures that exist in Southeast Asia. Let us assume a doctor is examining a patient from Burma who has high blood pressure. An American doctor might ask, 'Do you add salt to your meals?' and the patient would say 'No.' Well, if the doctor did not know enough about Burmese culture to ask a follow-up question, he would have an erroneous impression and probably would make a wrong diagnosis.

"On the other hand, a doctor who grew up in Burma would ask, 'Are you eating dried fish paste?' and the patient would say, 'Of course. That is part of my daily diet.' Since fish paste is laden with salt, the Burmese doctor would know that the patient was consuming a large quantity of sodium on a regular basis."

Dr. Marsh said, "Your example illustrates exactly why I want to learn about the native culture of any patient that I have from any part of the world. We have many different nationalities here in Southern California, much like Burma does.

"Let me tell you about the problem that my patient from Mandalay is having. He has become obsessed with America's legal system. He was thrilled when he learned he has legal rights. Now, however, he's going overboard in filing frivolous lawsuits. His latest legal misadventure is to sue his landlord for intentional infliction of emotional distress although the landlord merely asked him to turn down his radio. I understand the landlord did use some vulgar language, but this was after Sidney kept turning up the volume even though neighbors were complaining.

"Sidney is obsessed with his latest lawsuit, but I pointed out that he doesn't have a leg to stand on."

Thein said, "Do not overlook the loss of his legs as a possible cause of Sidney's deranged thinking."

"Thank you, Dr. Thein, for sharing your knowledge with me."

At first, Thomas thought that Thein was simply unintentionally showing his ignorance of American idioms. But he knew Thein had been a physician assistant in Southern California, and had completed a UCLA psychiatric residency. Both undertakings would have required him to learn common American customs as well as pecularities of the English language. Then how was it that Thein hadn't recognized any of the common idioms that Shelia had just now mentioned? Thomas began to wonder if Thein was mocking his colleagues by acting uninformed, and testing whether they would catch on.

Thomas had not seen Barry for several weeks. He worried that Barry's improved mental health would suffer a setback now that he had been transferred to Thein who was prescribing his patients a complex mix of drugs.

California law did not permit Thomas, a psychologist, to prescribe medications. But because he advised the clinic's psychiatrists regarding psychosocial therapies, he was authorized to see the medical charts of every patient at the Riverside clinic. He made it a practice to know which medications the patients were prescribed. He looked for correlations between which drug reps the psychiatrists were cozy with and which drugs they prescribed.

Thomas photocopied six months of the clinic's sign-in/sign-out sheets which the security police maintained and which the drug reps were required to sign. And he photocopied medical charts of patients whose health seemed to be worsening.

At night and on weekends at his home, Thomas tabulated and graphed the data he had pulled together. The pattern was clear, the correlation strong, especially for Newkirk, Crenshaw, and Thein. The drugs they prescribed were overwhelmingly the drugs made by the companies whose drug reps the psychiatrists saw most often. Those drugs were still under patent protection and were the most expensive on the market.

Thomas was alarmed when he reviewed in depth the prescription record that Thein had established during his time at the clinic. Thein was prescribing more drugs than Thomas had ever imagined.

Thomas was concerned about the three patients diagnosed with schizophrenia that Thein was treating. He was especially concerned about Barry because of the latter's recent absence from the clinic. Thein had dramatically increased the dosages of the three drugs that Dr. Gross had prescribed Barry. That was during the first office visit.

During the second visit, Thein added Abilify while continuing to prescribe Zyprexa. He had written on Barry's medical chart that he intended to replace Zyprexa with Abilify because the former was known to cause obesity. But Thein had not tapered down Zyprexa while gradually ramping up Abilify. Instead he prescribed a high dose of Abilify from the beginning. For weeks he kept Barry taking high levels of Zyprexa and Abilify although later he would testify that he had cross tapered the two drugs. In addition, during that second office visit, he had increased the dose of Paxil to sixty milligrams per day.

During the third office visit, Thein changed Barry's diagnosis from schizophrenia to schizoaffective disorder, prescribed Gabicon, and once again increased the dose of Paxil. Thein's notes for the fourth office visit continued the drama: he abruptly stopped prescribing Zyprexa, cutting the dose to zero in one step.

Thomas knocked on Gross's office door.
"Thanks for seeing me now that you are a VIP."
"I'm never too busy to see you. How can I help you?"
"Has Dr. Thein reported to you as to how Barry Vincent is doing?"
"No, I didn't ask any of the psychiatrists for progress reports on the patients that I transferred to them."
"You should have."
"Why?"
Thomas said, "Because you fell short of the standard of care when you abruptly transferred your patients."
"What's your basis for this ill-founded opinion?"
"Medical literature tells of bad outcomes, including suicide, for many patients carelessly transferred between psychotherapists."
Margret said, "I'm not a psychologist so that piece of lore doesn't apply to me."

"It doesn't matter whether the therapist is a psychologist or a psychiatrist. The point is that patients form an attachment to any caregiver who has treated them for a long time. Why do you think the problem would be less just because the transfers were between psychiatrists?"

"Well, psychiatrists mostly prescribe medications," Margaret said. "They don't spend near as much time talking with and listening to patients. It isn't the same relationship."

"Are you saying that after you provided years of excellent care, Barry didn't form an attachment to you and your immediate staff? Are you saying that he didn't respect you and your psych tech, Anna? What about the van Gogh-style paintings that he gave you and that you displayed in your office? What about the wild geese painting that he gave to Anna as a going-away present? Barry's attachment to you and your psych tech was as strong as any attachment he could have developed with a talk therapist."

"OK, OK, OK. How should I have transferred my patients, in your high-minded opinion?"

"Reports in medical journals recommend certain steps that ensure the safety of the patients. First, the patient needs to be given a few weeks warning that a transfer is being considered so he can get used to the idea. The switch needs to be gradual, done in small steps. The patient has to feel that he or she has some control over the transfer. The patient and his prospective therapist should be introduced to each other ahead of time to see if they are compatible. If either immediately dislikes the other, a different doctor should be found. Shared decision making is vital."

"Come on, Thomas, give me a break. Things don't work that way in the real world. I had only a short time to get rid of my patients, and begin to devote full time to my administrative duties."

"You said 'get rid of your patients.' That suggests lack of concern right there."

"Thomas, you have to judge me by my complete, long record here at the clinic, and not by recent transfers that our director told me to get on with. And don't judge me by a slip of the tongue. At one time or another, we all say things we don't mean."

"You're right, Margret. I apologize. You didn't deserve that wise crack. It's just that I'm worried sick about our patients, Barry in particular.

"The literature says that a patient with schizophrenia will feel abandoned when a transfer is mismanaged. The patient might grieve as much as if the therapist had died. I wish you had required Thein to report back to you periodically and get your opinion before making any changes in Barry's medication."

Margret asked, "Why? What's Dr. Thein done? His credentials are excellent."

"I think you will agree that with all the changes that went on in transferring Barry it wasn't the time to also change his medication."

"Yes. I agree. I hope that Dr. Thein didn't immediately adjust medications, and if he did, that the changes were small."

Thomas said, "Your Dr. Thein increased the doses of all three medications on the very first office visit. He raised the doses of Zyprexa, Paxil, and Cogentin. And the first visit lasted only twelve minutes according to what Thein wrote on the medical chart. How could this guy from Burma have made a sound judgment of someone from a completely different culture in only twelve minutes?

"Medical literature says there is rarely a good reason to change medications in the midst of a transfer of the patient from one doctor to another.

"But that's not all. During the second office visit, Thein raised the dose of Paxil to sixty milligrams. Any dose of this antidepressant above twenty milligrams has no therapeutic benefit, but the toxicity continues to rise. He also kept Zyprexa at a high dose and added Abilify at a high dose. During the third visit, he added Gabicon at a very high level. When he eventually reduced Zyprexa, he didn't taper the dose but withdrew the drug completely in one step."

"Oh my god. Thomas. I had no idea. Did Right Pharmacy catch these sudden huge changes? They had filled prescriptions for Barry for six years."

"You know the answer without me telling you. Right Drugs gets paid according to how many drugs they dispense, not how many patients they protect.

"Thein's medical charts indicate that he just kept prescribing more and more drugs to Barry. If Right Drugs raised the issue, it was never reflected in Thein's prescribing habits. And the pharmacist I talked with was defensive and close-mouthed."

"I'm going to report this to Dr. Conway."

"Good. But I'm beginning to wonder if Conway himself is profiting financially from overmedicating patients. That would explain a lot of what goes on around here."

"I can't imagine that Richard would do anything dishonest. I'm going to pretend you never said that."

"I don't care if you tell Conway what I said. A couple of days ago, I saw Alphatron's Neil Kronberger give him a shopping bag full of drug samples. Next time it'll probably be a gunnysack full.

"But back to Thein's wonderful credentials that impress you so much. They're excellent all right. In fact, they're too good to be true."

Margret said, "What do you mean?"

"I think Thein's credentials are fraudulent. I overheard Newkirk and Crenshaw talking, and they've arrived at the same conclusion. How did Conway and you fall for this guy's line of bull?"

"I didn't have anything to do with hiring Dr. Thein. And in fact, Richard didn't either. Our state office hired him and said 'Here's the replacement for Dr. Graves.' Richard had no say in the matter. So if someone was deceived by Dr. Thein or someone speaking for him—well, that deception occurred at a high level within the state hierarchy."

"Well I'm glad that neither of you had anything to do with hiring the doctor from Burma. Did you know that Burma's central government has been at war with its ethnic minorities since 1948? This is one of the longest-running civil wars in world history. This war-torn, corrupt country isn't exactly a leader in medical training and care.

"Ne Win, the dictator from 1962 to 1988, destroyed Burma's educational and medical systems. He closed universities including medical schools for years at a time. It would have been nearly impossible for Thein to get a decent medical education. Whoever hired

David Thein—whose original name is Maunt Thein—should have thought about those facts.

"Sooner or later this guy will kill someone with prescription drugs. I've gone over his medical charts and prescription records. He prescribes twice as many drugs as Newkirk, and I can't think of a worst statistic. And the doses are too high. I think he's taking bribes from Alphatron Pharmaceutical."

Margret said, "That's a shocking accusation."

"A few weeks ago, Dr. Shelia Marsh said that Laura Nielsen, an Alphatron drug rep, is living with the good doctor Thein. That puts Ms. Nielsen in an especially good position to persuade him to prescribe Alphatron drugs.

"As an aside, after telling on Nielsen and Thein, it turns out that Dr. Marsh has moved in with Alphatron's Neil Kronberger. Neil seems to be taking a cue from Laura. This clinic looks like Peyton Place, and Conway seems oblivious to the whole scene.

"Besides that, I think that Thein was not only poorly trained in Burma, but that while there he also was corrupted—that he took bribes."

Margret said, "Well, I know you don't have proof of that."

"You're right. But there is circumstantial evidence. Transparency International ranks countries according to a corruption index. Burma is consistently one of the most corrupt countries listed year after year. Most years it's at the bottom of the list, and other times it's barely above Somalia or Bangladesh."

Margret said, "That's not evidence. That's supposition."

"You're right again. I'm guessing based on my knowledge of how rampant bribery was and is in Burma, renamed Myanmar in 1989."

Margaret said, "And I bet you don't have any better basis for questioning Dr. Thein's motives here at this clinic."

"Suspicion is raised by the medicine he is prescribing irrationally. It's ridiculous. I know that higher-ups will say that he's a learned intermediary and that doctors can legally prescribe drugs off-label. But wait until some of his patients die. Then the powers that be might recognize that repeatedly prescribing off-label is risky.

"I have evidence of polypharmacy in the form of Thein's medical charts and prescription records here at this clinic. With his very first patient he began to prescribe too much medicine. Maybe he couldn't believe how available medications are in America as compared to Burma."

"I'm going to elevate your concerns to Dr. Conway. You better have your facts straight because his patience with you is wearing thin."

"Thanks. The sooner we can meet with Conway the better. And there is another reason why I came to you."

"And what is that?"

"You treated Barry Vincent with outstanding results. But you transferred him to a very dangerous person. And you've been so involved with your new duties that you've lost interest in Barry and your other former patients. When you were treating Barry, did he ever fail to keep an office appointment?"

"Not that I recall."

"Was he ever late for an appointment?"

"Not that I recall."

"Did Barry ever fail to take medications as you prescribed? Did he ever fail to participate in group discussions or to do anything else that you wanted?"

Margret said, "No. That's why you and I and his whole treatment team thought he was the perfect patient. He really wanted good mental health, and we helped him achieve that."

"He has missed three consecutive appointments with Thein."

"That's not like Barry," Margret said. "Do you know how he's doing now?"

"No. But I'm going to find out."

Chapter 33

A New Onset Seizure

Disgrace to [people with mental illness] is so high that even their caregivers face the spillover effects.

—Dipika Neupane, et al.
Caregivers' Attitude towards People with Mental Illness and Perceived Stigma (2016)

The ambulance arrived at Saint Rita's emergency department. Joan signed papers for Barry's treatment. She acknowledged that a seizure was the proximate reason for him to be brought to the hospital.

But she quickly went on to describe the day's events that had caused her son to overexert himself in hot weather. She explained that this was not a straightforward matter of a simple heat stroke. She pointed to the contributing factors of psychiatric medications and a county doctor failing to treat a mental health crisis.

In filling out the intake form, the male nurse reduced Joan's detailed narrative to, "Walked home in hot weather."

Although Saint Rita's emergency doctors and nurses were working hard, many patients had been waiting for hours for treatment. Barry joined their ranks. Word spread among the medical workers that a new patient had schizophrenia.

Roberto did not want to be Barry's nurse. He hid in a storage room, figuring that eventually the attending physician would assign a different nurse to Barry. Then Roberto would reappear. In the meantime he would think of an excuse for his absence.

Barry had broken his collarbone when he fell against the patio pillar at home. The pain in his shoulder added to the emotions that were overwhelming him. He feared another seizure. Paranoia was saying that his health had taken an irreversible turn for the worst. And the severe inner restlessness that had tormented him for days was raging. His anxiety was intense, but he was strapped to a gurney so he could not walk about to ease his agitation.

"Mom, get Security! Something is hiding under the bed. I want Security."

"Hold on Barry. I'll get help for you."

Joan stopped a female doctor who was hurrying past.

"Please help us. My son is in great pain and is hallucinating."

Dr. Janice Donnelly said, "Don't tell me. I'm not his nurse. Tell his nurse."

"He has a nurse? How do I find this person?"

"Go back to your son. I think I know where Roberto is."

Dr. Donnelly had seen Roberto enter a storage room. She had thought he was getting supplies, but since Mrs. Vincent had not seen him, it was worth checking to see if he was still in the supply room.

Dr. Donnelly opened the door. The room was dark. A scuffling sound. She turned the lights on.

"Roberto?"

Silence.

"Roberto, this is Dr. Donnelly. A patient needs your help. Either help the patient or tell the attending physician why you won't. It's irrational to hide like this."

Silence.

"Roberto, come out right now or I'm calling Security. You'll be in big trouble if the hospital cops have to drag you out."

Another scuffling sound. Roberto came out from behind a cabinet.

Dr. Donnelly asked, "What's wrong?"

"I won't get near a crazy guy."

"Well, tell Dr. Dirkstein. He'll assign another nurse to help the schizophrenic gentleman."

Roberto said, "That would be refusing an assignment. I could get in trouble."

"But hiding out will land you in worse trouble. Come on, I'll go with you to see Dr. Dirkstein."

"No. Don't take me to Dirkstein. I'll help the nut case. Please don't tell anyone that I was hiding."

"I won't tell anyone if you do your job. If you don't, I'm going to Dr. Dirkstein."

Roberto approached Joan and Barry, but at the last moment veered away. He would ask Dirkstein to let him out of the assignment. But he had come into Joan's field of view, and she blocked his path.

"Are you my son's nurse?"

"Yes."

"Well, please see to his needs. He's hallucinating and his shoulder hurts terribly."

"I'll be there in a minute."

Roberto gave Barry a pain pill and a cup of water. Then he disappeared again.

Barry was afraid he would be attacked. He did not visualize a specific attacker. He was gripped by an all-encompassing fear.

Joan again set out to find help. Again the only medical person she could find who was not attending to a patient was Dr. Donnelly.

"It's you again. I said Roberto is your son's nurse. Don't bother me."

"Roberto disappeared. He doesn't care what happens to Barry. Please help us."

Dr. Donnelly walked briskly to Barry's gurney.

Joan said, "Barry, where does it hurt?"

Dr. Donnelly said, "Don't ask him anything. He doesn't know anything."

Then Donnelly asked Barry, "Where does it hurt?"

"My right shoulder."

Dr. Donnelly stopped a male nurse who was passing by.

"Go find Roberto and tell him to get Radiology to x-ray Mr. Vincent's shoulder. And tell him he better do his job or I'm going to Dirkstein."

Dr. Donnelly turned to walk away, but Joan said, "Wait a minute. Barry, are you hallucinating?"

Janice said, "Don't ask him anything. He doesn't know anything."

She then asked Barry, "Are you hallucinating?"

Barry said, "No."

"A technician will take x-rays. And we'll take blood. A pathologist will examine a full range of constituents, especially electrolytes. The staff will find a bed on the fourth floor, and your son will be assigned a nurse who works on that floor."

The x-ray showed that Barry's collarbone was broken near his right shoulder. A massive bruise had formed.

Dr. Robert Chow was assigned to Barry's case. Initially, he did not examine Barry in person, but only reviewed the x-rays and the blood constituents. He wrote in the medical chart that low levels of sodium and potassium were the cause of the seizure as provoked by dehydration and heat prostration.

He ordered intravenous injections of sodium and potassium. He also prescribed Zyprexa and Paxil.

Joan phoned Jack at home.

"Barry is having a tough time. He's scared of things he can't even describe to me."

"Is he hallucinating?"

"Yes, but his main problem seems to be panic. Maybe caused by the hallucinations. He can't lie still. I can't sort it out."

"Hang in there, Joan. Barry and I need you."

"An emergency room doctor said it was a seizure that caused Barry to pass out. I learned that a seizure is a sudden attack caused by abnormal electrical discharges in the brain. The doctors said Barry's was a new onset seizure because of heat prostration and an electrolyte imbalance. The electrolytes sodium and potassium were too low."

Jack said, "That sounds treatable by itself. But the hallucinations and now the panic…"

"The doctors said Barry broke his collarbone when he fell. They said casts are no longer used for this kind of fracture. The collar bone will heal by itself."

"Is there anything else?"

Joan said, "They're keeping Barry at the hospital, but haven't found a bed for him. He's still on a gurney."

"It's one a.m. You must be exhausted after dealing with the county clinic and Saint Rita's."

"I'm getting sick from all the stress," Joan said. "But someone needs to stay with Barry. Can you come to the hospital?"

"I'll be there in fifteen minutes."

Chapter 34

Hold Still

We all are inclined to judge ourselves by our ideals; others by their acts.

—Harold George Nicolson
(American diplomat and biographer)

Jack drove to the hospital and found Joan and Barry still in the emergency department.

Joan said, "This is the most inhospitable hospital I've ever seen. The doctors and nurses are rude to both Barry and me."

Joan used Jack's car to return home.

Eventually, a hospital bed became available. Jack followed a male nurse—not Roberto—as he transported Barry via gurney to the fourth floor. The nurse positioned the gurney alongside a hospital bed. He and two more nurses carefully maneuvered Barry from the gurney onto the bed.

Hilda Seekins, the head nurse on the night shift, handed Jack a printed questionnaire. He filled in the blanks with Barry's health history. He also wrote how the county's Dr. David Thein had refused to provide crisis intervention that would have prevented Barry's seizure. When she read this, Hilda reacted.

"Mr. Vincent, our questionnaire asks for information about a patient's health. It's not meant to be a means for you to criticize a doctor that's not even associated with this hospital."

"I thought Saint Rita's could do a better job of treating my son if you know the context of how he came to suffer heat stroke."

"Well, you thought wrong."

Jack also had written that along with treating Barry for the seizure, Saint Rita's needed to arrange for proper treatment of his mental condition.

"Mr. Vincent, no one associated with this hospital will take on the added responsibility of treating schizophrenia. Your son was brought here because he was dehydrated and overheated. Our treatment is limited to correcting the electrolyte imbalance that we've identified."

"The physical and mental states are related."

Nurse Seekins said, "Where did you get your medical degree?"

Jack shut up. Better let the nurse simmer down. For Barry's sake.

Hilda did not mention that a doctor had taken charge of Barry's case.

Barry had always enjoyed television, so Jack keyed the TV to a channel that he thought Barry would like. Jack thought Barry was out of danger. His electrolytes were being treated. Barry was exhausted and would sleep soundly. If necessary, a nurse would give his son a sleep aid. And Jack still thought of hospitals as places where doctors and nurses took care of the sick.

Jack's back muscles were cramping and aching. He would go home and sleep, after taking aspirin and a hot shower. Then he would return to the hospital to stay continuously with Barry.

At 3:30 a.m Jack phoned Joan and was surprised that she was still awake. She was having trouble winding down. Joan drove to the hospital, picked up Jack, and the two went home to rest.

Nurse Hilda Seekins was trying to insert an IV needle into Barry's arm.

"Mr. Vincent, hold still. I could hurt you by accident."

"I can't hold still."

THE MIND DOCTOR

Hilda said, "Well, you've got to hold still."

"I can't."

"Hold still."

At last, Hilda penetrated the vein, and then taped the IV line to Barry's arm. She left his room.

Barry could not lie still. He had to be up and moving.

Barry ripped the needle and the IV line from his arm. Bleeding and wearing only a johnny, he bounded from his bed and started down the hallway, looking for a way out of the hospital.

At the fourth-floor nurse's station, Hilda was talking with two security police about Barry when he ran past them.

She said, "There he goes now. He can't go outside half naked."

The two officers caught up with Barry and blocked his path.

One of the policemen looked like Barry's friend, James. This and the composed demeanor of the two cops helped Barry calm down. They led him back to his room. James's lookalike—Corporal Darrel Washington—talked with Barry in his room. The corporal did not make him lie in bed.

"The nurse gave me your name. Would you prefer that I call you Barry or Mr. Vincent?"

This show of respect for his opinion caused Barry to smile.

"You can call me Barry."

Corporal Washington said, "You can't leave the hospital right now. Not until after your doctor sees you. But is there something that I can do for you before I leave? Is there anything you need?"

Barry was standing in place, rocking back and forth from the waist up.

"I have to keep moving. The nurse doesn't understand that."

"Would you like to walk around in the halls? Would you like me to walk with you?"

"Please."

Corporal Washington handed Barry a bathrobe.

The security guard in uniform and the patient in hospital gown and bathrobe walked the hallways that circled the nurses' station.

Chapter 35

A Form for Barry to Sign

Stigma against mental illness is a scourge with many faces, and the medical community wears a number of those faces.

—Elyn R. Saks
The Center Cannot Hold: My Journey Through Madness (2007)

The day shift came on duty early enough for a briefing before the night shift left for home. Hilda gave an oral report to her replacement, Cynthia Marino. They had known each other for years.

"Hilda, what do I need to know to pick up where you're leaving off?"

"I'll describe only one patient because the rest of them are ordinary people with problems that we see all the time. But one patient is a real nutcase. Barry Vincent is in his midthirties, and he's goofy as the day is long."

Nurse Marino said, "Not another one of those."

"I'm afraid so. Mr. Vincent suffered a heat stroke yesterday. Both sodium and potassium were low. The goofy guy walked home from the Riverside County outpatient mental health clinic although he was taking psychotropic medications. He walked several miles in the heat. Goofy got home all right but then passed out, fell, and broke his collarbone.

"That goofy Dr. Chow picked up Barry's case and has been treating him. They deserve each other. Both are goofy."

Cynthia said, "Why don't you throw a few more 'goofies' into your briefing? I'm getting the impression that I'm in for a goofy shift. Please tell me that Barry Vincent is scheduled to go home."

"No such luck. Goofy is still here, but I want him gone when I clock in this evening. The guy won't sit still. He pulled the IV needle out of his arm, and ran down the hall with his night gown just a-flapping. Two Security cops were here when Goofy sailed past. They brought him back to his room, and Corporal Washington stayed with him. Somehow he got Goofy to calm down."

Cynthia said, "Does Barry have family?"

"Yes. I didn't meet his mother, but I had Barry's dad fill out our questionnaire. He's got some big idea of forcing us to do a psychiatric assessment."

"Oh god," Cynthia said. "What did Dr. Chow say about that?"

"Chow read the questionnaire where Jack Vincent asked for a psychiatric assessment for his son, but he didn't see Jack and didn't talk to me about the possibility. You know how Chow is. He shows up, lays a foundation for charging MediCal for lots of procedures, and then he's gone in a flash."

"Yeah, I know. Then we're stuck with carrying out those procedures while Chow is free as a bird."

Cynthia thought a while.

"The Vincents are allowed under the law to ask to transfer their son to a hospital like Arrowhead that has a behavioral health unit."

Hilda said, "Yes, that's right. You can bring that up and then work with Chow and the Vincents in working out a transfer. But Jack Vincent has already asked for a psychiatric evaluation to be done here. We could offer a transfer instead, but he might elevate the issue to a hospital administrator. Or Chow might agree with him. We don't want to be forced to bring in a shrink. First thing you know, we'd be running a nut house. I don't want him here when I report to work this evening."

"He's that bad?"

"He won't sit down or lie down. You have less patience than I do when a patient acts out. If I were you, Cynthia, I'd call up Goofy's dad, and tell him to come and get his son."

"I'm not authorized to discharge patients. I'd have to get Chow's approval."

"Yeah, if you can find him. He hasn't answered several pages I sent. You could send Goofy home, and just write down in the records that he left of his own accord. All you really need his dad and mom for is to transport him home. We can't have him wandering the streets. We could get in trouble for abandonment."

Cynthia said, "I could get Barry to sign himself out, taking the responsibility and releasing the hospital from liability, but there could be a claim of diminished capacity. A lawyer could say we should have taken that into account and kept him in the hospital."

Hilda said, "Well then ask Barry's old man to sign him out. He may or may not have receivership, but if he signs the release form, you'll be covered. Even if none of the three Vincents sign a release form, you can still insist that Barry left against medical advice.

"You need to get rid of this guy. Send him home, and I bet that will be the end of the matter. He clearly wants to go home. And trust me, Chow won't care."

Jack and Joan had slept from 5:30 to 9:00 a.m. and were still tired. Coffee revived them somewhat. The phone rang. Jack answered.

"Hello, Mr. Vincent. This is Cynthia Marino, a registered nurse at Saint Rita's hospital. I am the head nurse on day shift for the fourth-floor ward. Did you tell your son that he can go home?"

"No. I didn't. In fact, his mother and I want him to stay at the hospital until after there can be a mental health evaluation."

"This hospital is treating your son for an electrolyte imbalance only. He experienced heat stroke, and we are quickly resolving that problem."

"We need to discuss our options in detail. My wife and I are trying to get Barry the psychiatric care that he needs. Before we bring him home, we want to be sure he's safe. Mental problems are more of a threat to his life than the electrolyte imbalance."

Nurse Marino said, "The hospital will not treat your son for mental health issues. We will not take on any such responsibility. He said you told him he could come home, and now he's here at the nurses' station in only a hospital gown and is demanding to go home. Here, I'll put him on the phone."

"Dad, I want to go home."

"Barry, please hang on. Your mom and I will be there in a few minutes. We'll talk about it then."

"Please hurry. I don't like this place."

In the car, on the way to Saint Rita's, the subject was how to cope with Nurse Marino.

Jack said, "I doubt Barry is in good enough health to come home just yet."

"That's the way I see it."

Nurse Cynthia Marino met Jack and Joan at the fourth-floor nurses' station. She handed Jack a clipboard.

"Mr. Vincent, sign this form so Barry can go home."

"But I don't want him to come home just yet. He needs psychiatric care, and it's best to make those arrangements while he's still hospitalized. And besides, I don't have receivership over Barry."

"Well, he's been a real problem. He won't stay in bed. He removed an IV line from his arm. And he wants to go home."

Joan said, "We'll sit with him until we can see his doctor. We'll keep him calm."

Jack and Joan sat with Barry in his hospital room. He was calm in their presence although he had to struggle to suppress the urge to walk. He moved his feet back and forth while sitting.

Nurse Marino entered the room, carrying her clipboard.

Joan asked, "Does Barry have a doctor? We would like to see his doctor."

"The doctor doesn't answer his pager. I'm speaking for the hospital. Since you won't sign for Barry's release, I have a form for Barry to sign."

The nurse turned to Barry. "Do you want to go home, Barry?"

A FORM FOR BARRY TO SIGN

"Yes."

"Sign here."

Barry signed the form without reading it. Nurse Marino took it back

Jack said, "What about giving us a prescription for medications for Barry? He should not go home without an after plan."

"Since he signed himself out, we're not going to give him a prescription."

The Vincents did not use the closest elevators. They hurried around a corner and down a hallway to a bank of elevators out of sight of nurse Marino.

The August heat was stifling. Barry and Joan waited in the shade of a building while Jack walked the rest of the way to their car. He started the engine and the air conditioning.

Chapter 36

Now Look What We Have

[Akathisia is] a drug-induced neurological disorder that is known to drive people to suicide and violence and madness.

—Peter R. Breggin
A Dance of Death (a section in) *Medication Madness: The Role of Psychiatric Drugs in Cases of Violence, Suicide, and Crime* (2008)

Barry was glad to be out of the hospital, and showed no outward signs of hallucinations or delusions. But polypharmacy was taking its toll.

Because Barry had stopped seeing Thein, his supply of medications was running low. After taking the last of the pills in each vial, Barry had one-by-one thrown the vials away. Unfortunately, this removed evidence that would have helped inform Jack as to which medications were interacting within Barry's body and brain. Barry was no longer able to understand the medications regimen that Thein had prescribed.

Still believing that underlying schizophrenia was the biggest threat to Barry's life, Jack urged his son to take the medications that remained according to the directions on the vials.

Joan and Jack decided to take Barry back to see the private-practice psychiatrist, Dr. Simon Keener in Redlands, who had treated Barry before referring him to the Riverside County clinic. Joan phoned Dr. Keener's office and made an appointment. In the meantime they would try to prevent Barry from overexerting himself.

The inner restlessness resurged. To keep from worrying his parents, Barry did his endless pacing inside the garage. He was determined to never again see the inside of a hospital.

Handyman Dennis Wilson had made improvements to the Vincent home now and then over the last three years. Today, a Tuesday, he was replacing vinyl flooring in the kitchen. Jack put the family dogs in the garage to keep them out of the way.

Dennis finished his job at 2:30 p.m., discarded some scraps of vinyl, and loaded his equipment into his pickup truck. He was climbing into the driver's seat when he heard a crashing sound in the garage. Dennis hurried back into the house.

"I heard a loud noise in your garage. You better take a look."

Jack said, "The dogs probably knocked something over. I'll have a look."

Jack entered the garage through the side door.

Barry lay unconscious, face up on the floor, his left eye bulging out of its socket. Also sticking out of the eye socket was a knife handle. Barry had driven the blade to the hilt in an effort to reach his brain.

Blood covered Barry's abdomen.

Jack reentered the house and dialed 911 on the kitchen telephone.

"This is Jack Vincent at 1616 Windsor Drive. My son has attempted suicide. I don't know if he's dead. Please get the paramedics here as fast as you can."

The female 911 operator said, "Is a weapon involved?"

"I'll give you all the information that I have, but first, I want to know that medical help is on the way."

"Medical help was alerted as soon as you placed this call. Don't hang up. Stay on the line with me. Did your son use a weapon?"

"No. He used a pocket knife. It's lodged in his eye. I'm going outside so I can make sure the ambulance comes directly to the right house."

"Don't do that. Stay on the line with me."

Joan had gone to the garage and had seen her son lying on the floor.

"I want to help, but I don't know what to do!"

"Joan, answer the operator's questions. I'm going out to the street to make sure the ambulance comes to the right house."

Joan took the phone and answered the operator's questions.

Jack went to the curb, expecting to see an ambulance. Instead, he saw police cars. Riverside City cops, male and female, in uniforms and plain clothes, swarmed onto the lawn.

"My son is lying on the garage floor."

A male cop bellowed, "Stand back, stand back! Get back!"

Jack backed up two paces. A fat, young corporal, holding a pistol with both hands, pivoted into the doorway and pointed his handgun at Barry's still body.

The corporal yelled, "He's down. He's down."

Jack said, "Of course he's down. I told the 911 operator, and I just told you guys too. Where are the paramedics?"

A uniformed cop spoke into his handheld radio as he looked up the street. Jack looked in the same direction and saw an ambulance-fire truck turn off Cactus Drive onto Windsor Street.

The ambulance arrived and paramedics entered the garage.

Addressing all the cops, Jack said, "I called for paramedics and got a God-damned SWAT team."

A tall cop said, "We were just following procedure when a weapon is involved."

"A weapon? A pocketknife stuck in my son's eye? You guys wasted time while my son lay near death. If Barry dies I'll sue you bastards."

Joan said, "When Barry had a seizure, I told the paramedics to take him to Arrowhead Medical Center because they have a behavioral health department, but no, they took him to that God-damned Saint Rita's. Now look what we have."

A paramedic said, "We'll take him to Arrowhead, to their trauma center." The ambulance left.

Jack started toward his car.

A plainclothes cop said, "Before you leave, I want to know what happened regarding your son."

"The county mental health center did not provide crisis intervention for Barry, and then Saint Rita's expelled him instead of treating his mental health issues."

The cop said, "I'm sure there's a long history that preceded what happened today. But what I'm trying to figure out is whether this wound was self-inflicted or if someone did it to Barry. Was anyone in the garage with him just before this happened?"

"Barry was alone. I'm going now. Don't hold me up any longer. I'm already disgusted with you guys for delaying medical care so that Corporal Jones got to point a gun at him. Why didn't you go ahead and shoot him? That's what Riverside cops are known for. Joan, I'll call you as soon as I learn anything."

Jack drove to an Arrowhead parking lot, strode to the emergency department, and waited in line. He thought it would be true to form if the doctors refused to treat Barry because he didn't have an appointment.

He spoke to a man behind a thick-glass pane.

"I'm Jack Vincent. My son, Barry, arrived by ambulance. Is he being treated?"

The admittance official stared at a computer screen then placed a phone call.

"Mr. Vincent, your son is in trauma surgery. You can go to the third floor by taking that elevator over there. You'll be asked to sign in. Someone will come out to give you an update."

Jack began a long wait. Only one other person, a man, was in the small waiting room. Jack mentally reviewed his son's health care from the time he began to be treated at the Riverside County mental health center.

Nothing had gone right for Barry for months. By now Jack was painfully aware that Dr. Gross was no longer his son's psychiatrist.

She had transferred Barry to a psychiatrist who was incompetent or uncaring or both.

Barry, Joan, and Jack had always liked Dr. Gross and the team she led, consisting primarily of psychiatric technician Anna Wong-McDowell and psychologist Thomas Prescott. They had worked wonders for Barry.

If Jack had been closer to Barry perhaps his son would have told him when he was transferred to Thein. If only he had known, he could have asked to meet with Dr. Gross, to ask if Dr. David Thein was right for Barry. Maybe Jack could have persuaded Dr. Gross to take Barry back or to transfer him only after finding the best replacement psychiatrist.

As he sat in the hospital waiting room that day, Jack felt that he should have been much more involved in Barry's treatment. He could have gotten to know his son's doctors although he believed it was best that Barry had taken responsibility for management of his own health care. While under Dr. Gross's care, Barry had, with his treatment team, managed his entire health care regimen. He had been thirty-two years old when he became Dr. Gross's patient and was now thirty-eight. He had been entitled to have made his own decisions without his parents hovering over him.

Still, Jack should have tried to learn more about the methods and attitudes of the center's health care providers. Jack admitted to himself that he had been far from vigilant. He had let his guard down because of Dr. Gross's excellent care and Barry's great relationship with her treatment team. He had been lulled into assuming that the center delivered only quality care, and that Barry would always be in good hands.

Jack regretted that he had failed to gain Barry's trust, to convince him that it was well and good for the young man to confide in his father. Jack had always tried to be approachable. He had tried to be always accessible to both Barry and to his brother, Matt. Still, Jack knew he had fallen down on the job at times. Both his sons were closer to their mother than to him.

Yet he believed that there were things that Barry had not told Joan either. Jack believed that all young men kept things from their parents. And maybe that was the way things should be. But if Barry had told either of his parents just how horrible this Dr. David Thein's therapy was, they would have done something.

Two surgeons, male and female, wearing white gowns blotched with blood, entered the waiting room.

The woman doctor's name tag read, "Mary Vroman."

"Are you Mr. Vincent?"

"Yes."

"Your son is in critical condition. We have done what we can for now. Barry used two pocket knives. One is the knife lodged in his eye. During surgery, we found a second knife in his colon.

"We removed a section of his colon. The danger of blood poisoning makes the intestinal wound the greater threat to Barry's life. Partially digested food—some of it close to feces—was spread throughout the abdominal cavity and made it very difficult to achieve sanitary conditions.

"The knife in Barry's eye somehow missed vital blood vessels and major nerves. It's not causing any bleeding so we left it in place until we can study the x-rays to determine how to safely remove it. To remove the knife is not as urgent as it might seem. More important is to remove it skillfully. We will get the advice of eye doctors."

"Thank you both for quickly helping Barry. Pardon me, I have to sit down."

Jack did not sit in a chair. He wanted to feel anchored. He leaned back against the nearest wall and walked his feet out in front of him so that he sank to the floor.

"You must feel there is some chance or you would not have done the surgery."

Dr. Vroman said, "There is a chance. Barry is young and strong, and that's in his favor. But he's very sick, and much depends on how much he wants to live. Although he attempted suicide, normally in cases like this, the patient's will to live kicks in. If we can prevent infection from the abdominal wound, your son has a fighting chance."

The young male surgeon said nothing. His name tag said, "Robbins."

THE MIND DOCTOR

Jack asked, "What happens now?"

Dr. Vroman answered, while Dr. Robbins listened.

"We have placed Barry in a medically induced coma. This allows him to rest and facilitates healing. We will move him into an intensive care unit where patients recover from surgery. You can visit him there. Do you have more questions?"

Jack said, "Barry's care and treatment must take into account his schizophrenia. Barry, his mother, and I have been crushed by the terrible treatment he recently received from medical people. Barry would not be in this terrible crisis if doctors and nurses had not stigmatized him."

"There will be no stigmatization at this hospital. We will bring in the county's top psychiatrist to advise us how to handle any symptoms of schizophrenia that might complicate his health care."

"Do not let a county psychiatrist named David Thein come near my son. I mean it. He mismanaged Barry's medications and then refused to provide emergency crisis intervention."

Dr. Vroman said, "It will not be business as usual while Barry is here. We will get the best mental health experts to advise us as to whether Barry needs psychiatric medication while in the ICU."

Chapter 37

Grief Sharing

Can I see another's woe,
And not be in sorrow too?
Can I see another's grief,
And not seek for kind relief?

—William Blake
On Another's Sorrow (1789)

It was dark by the time Jack returned home. His dinner was set for him, but he did not eat.

Joan looked expectantly at Jack.

"Barry is alive and has a fighting chance. The knife in his eye did not hit a major blood vessel or nerve. The doctors are figuring out how to remove it so there's no bleeding or nerve damage. But Joan, there was a second knife that we did not see.

"He cut open his large intestine, and the knife was lying in his abdominal cavity."

"Good God! Like hara-kiri?"

"Yes. Maybe not as bad or maybe just as bad. I don't know, but like hara-kiri."

Joan said, "I saw blood on his belly. Why would he cut himself open? I've never heard of schizophrenia causing anyone to do that."

"Probably Thein's medications. We don't know everything he prescribed, but we now know there are almost no checks on what psychiatrists are allowed to do."

"But Dr. Gross cared so much. What's with this Thein, this import from Burma?"

"I don't know, but we'll find out," Jack said. "I hate the man."

"Go on with Barry's condition."

"The surgeons removed a section of Barry's intestine and reconnected the two ends. They also, as best they could, cleaned up the partly digested food. Blood poisoning is the biggest threat to his life."

The next morning Jack phoned the Arrowhead Medical Center. Joan and he could visit their son now. They drove to Arrowhead and went to the post-surgery ICU.

Barry lay on his back in a medically induced coma and with a thick bandage covering his left eye. Attached to him were an intravenous line and various sensors. A feeding tube was taped to his face to keep it from being dislodged. His continually changing vital signs appeared on several screens. If a vital sign registered too high or too low, a nurse or doctor came to assess the situation.

Jack was in a waiting room, biding his time until visiting hours began anew. Across from him sat a woman he estimated to be in her late forties. She appeared to be coping, but he wondered what emotions she was holding in check.

Jack asked, "Do you have a family member in intensive care like I do?"

"Yes. My son is here. How about you?"

"Yes, it's my son that I come to visit," Jack said.

"How's he doing?"

A man in his fifties, looking worried, entered the waiting room and sat down.

"Barry cut himself badly. At present he's stable, but his worst wound was to his abdomen, so the biggest concern is whether he will develop blood poisoning. What happened to your son?"

"Kenny has a broken neck. He's twenty years old. He's always been so healthy that I can't believe this has happened. Was your son healthy until recently?"

Jack said, "Well, he was physically healthy, but several years ago he was diagnosed as having schizophrenia. But he had a wonderful doctor for years and he did very well. Then she transferred him to another psychiatrist who proved to be reckless and uncaring.

"Barry's new doctor came from a foreign country and never understood Southern California culture. Dr. Thein made weird medical decisions. That, I swear, is what led to Barry's suicide attempt. The doctor-patient relationship is all important."

Shirley said, "I agree. And it's impossible to know ahead of time who is a good doctor. I think Kenny has a good doctor right now, but who will he have next, if he survives?"

Jack asked, "How was your son hurt? Was it an accident?"

"Kenny went with friends on a camping trip in Nevada. They went for a swim in the Truckee River. He dived from a high bank without exploring what lay below the water surface.

"What a reckless thing to do. You may appreciate how poor the judgment of a young man can be. It was on a dare that Kenny dived from the river bank. His head struck a rock ledge. His friends saved him from drowning, but doctors say he will be paralyzed from the neck down."

Jack said, "That's terrible. How can you handle this tragedy?"

Shirley said, "Well, I think we have a lot in common because your situation also concerns the future of your son."

The recent arrival said, "My name is Bruce. I'm marveling at the strength of both of you."

Jack and Shirley introduced themselves to Bruce. They were three strangers going through similar tragedies.

Bruce said, "Like both of you, it's my son who brings me here. Brian suffers from a severe burn over 80 percent of his body." Bruce's voice quavered.

Shirley said, "Bruce, I'm so sorry."

Jack said, "I'm sorry for you, too."

"Paramedics brought Brian here from a friend's house. He was at the wrong place at the wrong time. His friend was cooking methamphetamines when the concoction exploded. Brian and two other young men were badly burned. Infection is the biggest concern that the doctors have."

Jack said, "Infection is the biggest threat for Barry too."

The time came when Jack, Shirley, and Bruce could return to Barry, Kenny, and Brian. Each young man's life had been diminished forever. But each had parents who cared deeply for him. And on that day, without the aid of a psychiatrist, psychologist, or minister, two dads and a mom shared their grief.

Chapter 38

Insidious Sepsis Takes Its Toll

Sepsis is the body's extreme response to an infection. The condition occurs when an infection triggers a chain reaction throughout your body. Without timely treatment, sepsis can rapidly lead to tissue damage, organ failure, and death.

—US Centers for Disease Control and Prevention Undated brochure, *Get Ahead of Sepsis*

Barry's health improved. Doctors kept him in a medically induced coma so he could rest as much as possible. A respirator made his lungs work with no effort on his part. After four days, the doctors began to bring Barry out of his coma for an hour at intervals two or three times a day to better assess his condition.

On the ninth day, Joan said, "Barry, squeeze my hand if you can hear me."

Faint pressure. Joan told a nurse, and finally there was cause to smile. Maybe Barry would go home with mom and dad.

Four days later, when Joan and Jack were at home, the phone rang. Joan answered.

"Mrs. Vincent, this is Dr. Nelson Rodriquez from Arrowhead's surgery-recovery unit. I met you a few days ago when I was on duty."

"Yes. I remember."

THE MIND DOCTOR

"There has been a development in Barry's case. He has contracted sepsis."

Joan sat down.

"Oh, no. Is this the infection that the doctors were trying to fend off?"

"I'm afraid so. But please don't despair. Sepsis is something we at Arrowhead work with all the time, and usually the patient comes through just fine."

"Jack and I have read about sepsis. It's also called blood poisoning, right?"

"Yes."

Joan asked, "And does sepsis refer to a septic condition?"

"Yes. But sometimes medical terms are unnecessarily frightening. It's the body's reaction to infection, and we can fight infections."

"Specifically how in Barry's case?"

"We need to open his abdomen again and clean out the contaminated seepage that we expect to find. We need your permission. If you approve this procedure, you can just say so over the phone and your permission will be recorded."

"Hang on. Jack is right here."

Realizing that the incoming phone call was about Barry, Jack had listened to Joan's side of the conversation.

"Stay on the line, Joan. I'll pick up the extension phone."

"This is Jack Vincent. Please start over. What's changed?"

"Certainly. This is Dr. Nelson Rodriquez. I specialize in internal medicine. When Barry cut his colon, it released partially digested food, some of it close to fecal matter, inside his abdominal cavity. In other words, the intestinal tract no longer kept waste material away from the other organs and tissues. Today we detected antibodies in Barry's blood. This indicates infection.

"The doctors think it best to go back inside the abdomen and clean up any waste matter that we find. And we need permission from you and your wife."

Jack said, "Nelson, is the decision whether to clean up the abdominal cavity? And not cleaning up would allow the infection to worsen? Is that right?"

"Yes. Of course we never know what we will find until we open the person up."

Joan said, "Oh, God."

"What are the risks?" Jack asked.

Dr. Rodriquez said, "The surgery is not technically difficult, but Barry is weak, and this procedure will further weaken him."

Jack said, "Oh, God."

"What would you do, Nelson?" Joan asked.

"To reestablish sanitary conditions is Barry's best chance. And increase the amount of antibiotic or maybe administer a different kind."

Jack said, "Joan, I think we should approve the procedure. Otherwise, the infection will worsen."

"Yes, the procedure needs to be done," Joan said.

Jack said, "Nelson, we are giving you permission to do the work. When will the surgery be done?"

"At 6 a.m. tomorrow. Will you be at the hospital or where I can reach you?"

Jack said, "At least one of us will be there at the hospital. We will have our cell phones. You have those numbers."

The next morning, Jack and Joan were at the hospital. Barry had already been taken to the operating room. They told an ICU attendant where they would be, and went to the hospital's cafeteria to have coffee and begin their vigil.

Jack recognized Dr. Phil Robbins, the young surgeon who had assisted Dr. Mary Vroman in operating on Barry.

"Hello, Dr. Robbins. I'm Jack Vincent, Barry's dad. This is my wife, Joan."

Dr. Robbins said, "I recognize you, Jack. Pleased to meet you, Mrs. Vincent. I understand that Barry is scheduled for surgery this morning. I've been involved with his case from time to time, as his doctors consulted with me."

"We learned yesterday that sepsis has developed." Jack said.

"I told the head surgeon that we shouldn't close Barry's abdomen, but I was overruled. If we had left the surgical wound open, we could've detected the infection sooner. Rather than wait for antibodies to form in response to toxins in the blood, we could've seen seepage in the abdomen as soon as it began. Barry's doctors might've detected the sepsis a day earlier. And with sepsis every minute counts, as it can rapidly lead to tissue damage and organ failure.

"From the perspective of the senior surgeon and this hospital, I shouldn't tell you this. And if you file a law suit, I'll lose my job. But I have to live with myself, and I can always get a job hanging wallboard. Patients and their families should know when their professional care givers make mistakes. The senior surgeon was trying to make her work look more complete, more tidy.

"I wish Barry and the two of you all the best."

After Dr. Robbins left, Jack said, "Here's another major mistake in the medical care of our son. Dr. Robbins could get in trouble for what he just told us. I appreciate his honesty."

"I'm amazed at how bullheaded some doctors are," Joan said. "Why didn't the head surgeon listen to Dr. Robbins?"

The surgical team cleaned Barry's abdominal cavity, but the sepsis worsened in the days that followed. Barry grew weaker. One day in the ICU, Jack overheard a doctor talking to a colleague.

"We can't keep putting this young man under the stress of surgery. Each time he's weaker."

That night Jack failed to be at Barry's bedside. He stayed home while Joan and Barry's aunt, Bell Lynn, went to sit by him. A Catholic priest, Father Ed Lopez, came to visit Barry. Upon meeting Joan and Bell Lynn, he tried to comfort them.

"Are either of you Catholic?"

Joan said, "I was raised Catholic but no longer attend church. Bell is an active Catholic. Barry was an altar boy, along with his older brother, Matt. His dad was the lector for the earliest morning mass at Saint Alice, and our two sons were perfect altar boys."

Father Ed said, "The hospital called me and said Barry is gravely ill. Would you like me to administer last rites?"

Joan choked up as she gave permission. Father Ed Lopez performed the ancient ritual.

One of Arrowhead Hospital's social workers, Sarah Ann, phoned Jack at his home at 1:00 a.m.

"You visited Barry many times, and I know you love him very much. But now that the end is near, you stayed away."

"I didn't seem to be doing my son any good, and I couldn't handle any more grief."

"Oh, but you were doing him good. Research indicates that many times even comatose patients know when you are present. They may be able to hear you or in some other way sense your presence. For example, if you hold their hand, they still feel your touch.

"Your wife and Barry's aunt were here this evening. And that was good, but you also need to process your son's death or you might always wish you had."

"I've processed and processed and processed what happened to Barry, especially the medical mistakes that were made. I'm all processed out."

"If you'll come to the hospital, I'll make you a cup of tea. Then we'll sit with Barry. He would like that."

"I'll be there in twenty minutes."

Jack drove to the hospital and met with Sarah Ann. Then they sat by Barry's side and took turns holding his hand.

Chapter 39

The Big Golden Howled

But thinks, admitted to that equal sky,
His faithful dog shall bear him company.

—Alexander Pope
An Essay on Man (1733)

Jack remained at Barry's bedside the rest of the night. At 8:00 a.m., Joan joined her husband and son. Mom and Dad were solemn and silent when at 10:00 a.m. a nurse they knew as Wendy said that Dr. Samuel Wong wanted to see them. They followed Wendy to a small waiting room.

Dr. Wong, forty, was in charge of the surgery recovery ICU. He spoke in somber tones.

"Barry has severe blood poisoning. Toxins have invaded all his organs. When he cut open his colon he set up perfect conditions for infection. Sepsis set in, weakening him terribly.

"You did the right thing by authorizing us to clean his abdominal cavity. Without that procedure, he would have immediately died of septicemia. After the first reentry, we left the surgical wound open, but our best efforts could not keep him from growing weaker. Now he is simply too weak to survive without life-support systems.

"It is the professional opinion of Barry's doctors that he cannot survive on his own.

"As his parents, you have some options, limited as they are. The question is whether to keep your son on life support systems and pray for a miracle or to exercise what we call comfort and compassion. I'll describe comfort and compassion in a moment. But first let me explain the basis for our medical opinion.

"This is not my opinion alone. It is the opinion of all the doctors on Barry's ICU team. Unfortunately they have seen many patients in grave situations like Barry's. There is no dissenting opinion within the team.

"Sepsis is a severe medical condition because it is systemic. Toxin in the blood spreads to every organ except the brain, which is protected by the blood-brain barrier. And the toxin can weaken the patient gravely so they no longer can marshal their defenses. You cared for your son the best that any parents could. But now to keep him on life support systems simply postpones the inevitable.

"This decision is yours, but our medical advice is to remove life support systems and allow your son to pass on."

Jack looked at Joan and said, "We have talked about this possibility and I think we can give you our decision this morning. But we don't want to make a mistake. Tell us about your comfort and compassion procedures."

Dr. Wong said, "In comfort and compassion, we continue to provide pain medicine. We have no restriction on visitation so you can stay by Barry's side. We disconnect all life support systems except the respirator. We continue to supply saline solution so that he does not dehydrate, and we monitor his vital signs."

Jack said, "Joan, I think you know I would rather let Barry pass on than to keep him alive artificially in a condition that the doctors say is hopeless."

"I feel the same. Barry has suffered enough. I want you and Dr. Wong to know that Barry was the best son any mother ever had."

Jack said, "Dr. Wong, there are many stupid notions about persons with schizophrenia that are simply untrue. Barry was more caring than anyone else I ever knew. And he was intelligent, too. He could look at a complex, beautiful landscape and then, never seeing it again, weeks later could reproduce it in exact detail on a canvas."

THE MIND DOCTOR

Dr. Wong said, "People with schizophrenia have improved the world through their creativity. Whether this was because of, or in spite of, the disorder can be debated, but either way, they deserve our respect. John Nash is a great mathematician who was jointly awarded the 1994 Nobel prize for economics. Antonin Artaud founded a revolutionary way of presenting theater. William Minor contributed about ten thousand exacting definitions to help create the massive Oxford English Dictionary. Others also saw the world in original and novel ways."

"It means a lot to hear you say this," Joan said. "Jack and I will work to dispel myths about schizophrenia, in Barry's name."

Jack said, "Barry believed in organ donation. Joan and I have talked about what Barry would want to do, and we would like for some part of our son to go on living in someone else. We are giving permission for Barry's heart or other organs to be donated to help someone else. He has no estate, nothing else to give."

Dr. Wong said, "I am sorry, but sepsis, being systemic, has poisoned all of Barry's organs. This could cause a transplanted organ to fail or to transmit an infection to the recipient. There is research that suggests in some cases select organs like the corneas can be suitable for transplanting despite the sepsis. But our policy at this hospital at this stage of our medical knowledge is to not transplant any organ that could have been tainted by sepsis. With regret, we have to decline your offer."

Joan said, "Barry had so little, but would have given anything he ever had to help people. It's sad that his last offer has to be denied."

"I'm sorry," Dr. Wong said.

After a long silence, Jack said, "We give you our permission to remove the life support systems from our son and to exercise comfort and compassion to the best of your ability."

Wendy disconnected the life-support systems at 10:40 a.m. With Jack and Joan at his bedside, Barry Vincent passed away at 3:30 p.m. that same day.

Five days later, on Friday, Barry's dad and mom, his brother, his aunt, and James attended Barry's funeral. Owing to a good mortician, the young man looked like he was sleeping, showing no sign of the traumas he had suffered. Father Ed Lopez officiated.

Jack's eulogy described a kind and gentle young man whose life ended too soon. Although the youngest in a family of four, he was the first to die. He was born on a Sunday and died on a Sunday. That he was afflicted by schizophrenia was not a mark against him. Instead, Barry's exemplary kindness while coping with this disorder was a badge of courage.

From the funeral, Jack and Joan went home, and in their back garden said another goodbye to their son. Sadie took part in the special farewell.

In the upper terrace that they had shaped, Barry and Jack, using only hand tools, had dug a large garden pond, twenty-five feet across and six feet deep in the center, siting it near two large, live-oak trees. Soon after filling their pond, the Vincents introduced water lilies, arrowhead, and water-loving irises, while rushes, sedges, and cattails came in on their own.

Barry had loved to wade in, swim in, or paint pictures of water, whether streams, rivers, lakes, or ponds. So Jack and Joan dedicated the garden pond to their son. While Barry had passed on, his pond made life possible for a number of aquatic and semiaquatic species in this small piece of the hot, dry Mohave Desert. Carp, frogs, and water snails had come in as eggs on the legs of wading birds such as the little cattle egret and the great blue heron.

On this commemoration day, iridescent dragon flies darted about, and a little higher in the sky, violet-green swallows swooped down here and there.

Barry's mom and dad stood facing the pond. Sadie sat between them. At 3:30 p.m., the big golden retriever pointed her muzzle toward the sky and howled. She eased into the water, swam one lap, climbed out of the pond, and returned to her place between Jack and Joan.

Chapter 40

In Pursuit of Justice

Greedy folks have long arms.

—Scottish Proverb

Jack began trying to force the state to improve the care delivered by its community mental health centers. Jack and Joan would eventually take legal action against Dr. David Thein, but at the moment he wanted to give a county official a piece of his mind regarding the local mental health center.

Allen Gibson, director of the Riverside County Public Health Department, refused to meet with Jack. Any of various staff persons spoke for him when Jack placed a phone call or went to his office. Director Gibson either was not in the office or was in a crucial meeting and could not be disturbed. One staff person or another always apologized on behalf of the director who regretted being unable to meet with Mr. Vincent.

Jack did not want to be rude to the director's gatekeepers who were simply doing their jobs. But today he spoke frankly to Margarita del Reno, the receptionist who usually was the one to say that Director Gibson was unavailable. He had driven to the health department, hoping to catch Gibson offguard, and had been told that the director was out of town.

"Miss del Reno, you're just doing your job. But don't you ever get tired of having to lie for your boss? My son died because a county doctor overmedicated him. Director Gibson is in charge of the county agency most responsible for public health policy, and as such he should listen to the county's citizens.

"You would have liked my son. He was an honest, compassionate human being. I deserve a meeting with Director Gibson."

"County officials think you're about to file a wrongful death lawsuit, and they don't want to slip and say anything you can use as evidence. They don't want their bosses and coworkers to think they helped you. Smoot and Lamberti, the law firm under contract with the county, advised Director Gibson to not meet with you."

"That attitude is what drives people to file lawsuits because then and only then will the county be forced to meet with them. Help me out. Where is Director Gibson today?"

"Don't tell anyone that I said this. I'll deny that I did. But I'm sorry about your son. And Gibson hopes to avoid you until you give up. I'm sick of lying for him.

"He's picking up County Commissioner Jose Sanchez, and they're going to a buffet dinner at 1121 Centennial Parkway. Cook up a story that you learned this from someone other than me."

"Don't worry. I'll keep this a secret. Thank you."

Jack drove home and picked up Joan. They arrived at the Centennial Parkway building at 11:50 a.m. The parking lot was full, and people were filing into the building.

Joan said, "I wonder what the occasion is. Is some dignitary in town?"

"I have no idea."

Joan said, "Look at that sign. It says, 'Riverside County Public Health Administration.' This is a county facility."

They entered the building. Their first task was to find out the purpose of the function. A handsome man wearing black slacks, white shirt, and a maroon blazer approached them. His name tag said, "Neil" and "Alphatron Pharmaceuticals."

Neil said, "Attendance is by invitation only. What is your affiliation?"

Jack said, "We're Mr. and Mrs. Brownlee, guests of County Commissioner Sanchez."

"Oh, very good." Neil stepped out of the couple's way.

Joan picked up two copies of the program. Alphatron was training county doctors in the use of Gabicon.

Clusters of well-dressed men and women were standing about, enjoying drinks and conversation. Jack had seen pictures of director Gibson and County Commissioner Sanchez, so he recognized them among the smiling, laughing people.

Jack said, "There's Gibson and Sanchez, and it looks like they're enjoying cocktails before lunch. I guess they can do that on county time, but I don't like it."

Dr. David Thein walked from the buffet line, carrying a lunch tray heaped with prime rib, mashed potatoes, gravy, salads, and desserts. He sat at a table with other doctors from the county mental health center.

Jack was clenching his jaws.

"Jack, stay cool. Don't do anything you'll regret. This is great information that we're gathering. It will bolster our complaint that the county is too cozy with pharmaceutical companies."

"I'm steady as a rock. I don't think anyone has recognized us. They're preoccupied with all the food. Look at them. Pigs at a trough. The county's finest doctors."

The Vincents avoided Thein's field of vision. Neil was squeezing between people, working his way to Commissioner Sanchez.

Joan said, "Looks like we're about to be thrown out. We better leave."

Jack and Joan were about to leave the auditorium when Jack thought better of it.

"Wait, Joan. Our son died because pharmaceutical companies and Riverside County's psychiatrists are in bed together. They work together to overmedicate the county's most vulnerable citizens. Let's make them throw us out. This could add to the story we want to tell."

"Good enough. Lead the way."

The Vincents headed for seats in the auditorium. Neil intercepted them.

"Please hold up a minute. I checked with Director Gibson and Commissioner Sanchez. Neither invited you. And they said your name is Vincent, not Brownlee. I'm asking you to leave."

"As county citizens, we have a right to be here," Jack said. "You obviously are ignorant of the California public meetings law. Get out of our way while we get seated."

"This is not a public meeting. It's continuing education for county medical care givers, put on by Alphatron Pharmaceuticals. Leave now."

Jack said, "You're wrong about the public meeting law. This gathering qualifies as a public meeting."

Two county sheriff's deputies appeared. The bigger one said, "Leave this minute, or we'll arrest you."

"We're not leaving." Jack said

The deputies handcuffed the Vincents.

As soon as they were outside the building, the bigger deputy said, "Mr. and Mrs. Vincent, the county doesn't want us to book you into jail. Commissioner Sanchez said they just want you to leave the premises. If you'll go away and stay away, we'll release you right now."

Jack said, "Why can't we stay? What are they afraid of?"

"Commissioner Sanchez didn't say. We can lock you up, but whatever your grievance is, this isn't the best way to assert it."

Joan said, "Jack, let's bring the best wrongful death case that we can. We'll be a lot better prepared for a legal contest. A trespass charge will complicate matters."

"O.K.," Jack said. "We'll leave if nothing goes on our records."

The dominant deputy said, "Nothing will appear on your records. Just get out of here, and don't come back."

"So in this instance you two are simply glorified bouncers."

"You might say that. Go home."

The Vincents had never filed a lawsuit, and were reluctant to start down that path. Many stories told of the pitfalls of filing a wrongful death claim in California. In almost all cases, the courts found in favor of the defendants: the doctors, hospitals, pharmacists, and pharmaceutical companies.

Jack and Joan decided to first pursue other possibilities for getting a measure of justice for Barry. If regulatory agencies would do their job, perhaps there would be no need to file a lawsuit. First, they sought help from the state agencies.

But the state regulatory agencies like the Medical Board and the Pharmacy Board showed no interest in the evidence that Jack presented. If an agency provided the Vincents with a document under the California Public Records Act, it was unintelligible because so many words had been blacked out. The staffs of the various agencies were polite and eventually returned phone calls and answered correspondence. But sooner or later they all declared that Dr. Thein and Alphatron Pharmaceuticals had done nothing wrong.

Next, the Vincents tried to get the federal government to take action of some kind. But none of the federal agencies they contacted expressed interest in the misdeeds that Jack reported. Jack obtained Medicaid records for the care that Barry had received while he was in Saint Rita's and in Arrowhead Regional Medical Center.

The costs of ambulance services, medications, doctors' fees, hospital fees, bandages, and more all added up to almost five-hundred thousand dollars. The nineteen days that Barry was in Arrowhead's ICU had been especially expensive. Jack argued that all these expenses were the result of polypharmacy practiced by Thein and the county clinic. He wrote to Medicaid that overmedication had caused Barry to complete suicide, and that this led to the reimbursement claims filed by the two hospitals. But for the malfeasance, there would have been no medical expenses to begin with. Medicaid officials rejected Jack's reasoning and ignored the evidence he offered.

The US Attorney for the Pennsylvania District along with the FDA had recently sued Alphatron in federal civil court. The main charge was 'misbranding,' which was shorthand for illegal off-label promotion of prescription medications. Alphatron lost the case, and a judge ordered the company to reimburse Medicare $325 million for wrongfully billing the agency under the federal False Claims Act. But neither the FDA nor the United States Attorney showed any interest in Barry's case, saying they were done litigating against Alphatron.

Jack and Joan came to realize that the only way to get information much less to punish Thein was to file a wrongful death lawsuit.

Almost never would an attorney in California take a wrongful death case on contingency because of a 1975 statute, the Medical Injury Compensation Reform Act. Under MICRA, pain and injury damages could not exceed two hundred fifty thousand dollars. MICRA also capped the attorney fees as a percentage of any damage award, or roughly one hundred thousand dollars at most. The expense of investigating a case, taking depositions, and paying expert witnesses could easily exceed any funds that the attorney might realize if he won the case. Although two parents survived Barry, MICRA allowed only one wrongful death claim.

The Vincents also decided to file two claims for unintentional infliction of emotional distress, although the proof required was even more rigorous than for wrongful death.

Jack checked with various personal injury attorneys concerning the merits of Joan's and his case. None would take the case on contingency. All of course were willing to represent the Vincents on condition that they pay a big retainer and keep the account current. The Vincents accepted this reality. This would be the only way they could get a lawyer to take their case. But since they would pay upfront with hard cash, they would have a wider choice of attorneys.

The Vincents just wanted to win their case, and did not aspire to collect any financial damages. They wanted to stop Thein from practicing psychiatry and Alphatron from promoting medications off-label.

Before hiring an attorney, the Vincents wanted to speak with someone who had brought a medical malpractice lawsuit and who had experience with personal injury lawyers—someone who might know an attorney and an expert witness dedicated enough to do a good job in court.

Chapter 41

I Have the Same Motivation

Bribery [by the pharmaceutical industry] is routine and involves large amounts of money. Almost every type of person who can affect the interests of the industry has been bribed: doctors, hospital administrators, cabinet ministers, health inspectors, customs officers, tax assessors, drug registration officials, factory inspectors, pricing officials, and political parties.

—Peter C. Gotzsche
Deadly Medicines and Organized Crime: How Big Pharma has Corrupted Healthcare (2013)

To let his head clear, late one afternoon Jack took Proton and Sadie for a walk in the foothills near their home. He hiked a route that Barry had often taken. It seemed as though his son were walking with him. Jack believed the dogs missed Barry. Sadie in particular seemed forlorn.

Barry had always walked his dogs on a looping path consisting of dirt roads and trails. One of the roads was atop a long levy intended to keep a Santa Ana River tributary from flooding residential areas. "Barry's loop" allowed Jack to always move forward instead of returning home by retracing his steps. Barry had told his dad the loop made for a more emotionally satisfying walk. Sometimes Barry had walked the loop in one direction and sometimes the other, but he never took any trail that required retracing his steps.

Twilight settled on the foothills. Jack, Proton, and Sadie extended their hike by taking a side trail that went off through the chaparral but eventually rejoined the main trail. Darkness fell.

Jack worried that he might not stand up under the emotional and financial strains of the legal battles that lay ahead. Would he lose his nerve part way through, and only succeed in causing Joan and himself a lot more pain by having to re-live the events that took Barry from them? Where could he find the courage to contend with the combined power of the county and Alphatron?

He remembered an Indian song, called Unbroken, that his Cherokee mother had taught him when he was a boy. She knew there would come this moment when Jack would need to call upon it. He began to chant:

>Hiiiiii Yiiiiii Yiiiiii

>Is my steadfast cry.
>Come what may,
>My courage will stay.

>Fate has spoken
>My spirit will remain
>Forever unbroken.

>I hold my head high
>As I cry

>Hiiiiiii Yiiiiiii Yiiiiiii

Between the walking, the chanting, and some play-acting, Jack felt better when he and the dogs finally got back home.

Joan said, "Tom Prescott called. He's at odds with his coworkers and supervisors, and is heartsick about what happened to Barry."

"Barry respected Dr. Prescott. Aside from offering condolences, did Thomas want anything else?"

"He wants to meet with us about some ideas he has. He wants you to call him. Here's his home phone number."

Jack and Thomas arranged to meet at a cafe next to the Loma Linda Food Market on Sunday at noon. Thomas thought that the cafe was out of the way enough that his coworkers from the county mental health center were unlikely to happen by and see him meeting with the Vincents. To further reduce the possibility of a chance encounter, he chose a table tucked away in a quiet nook.

Thomas said, "I chose this place for our meeting in honor of your son who was a vegetarian. He shared that fact with me during a talk therapy session."

Joan said, "On his own, when he was only seven, Barry decided that animals should not have to die just to satisfy a human's taste buds. He became a vegan so he wouldn't contribute to the market demand for meat and dairy products. While just a boy, Barry prompted Jack and me to think about the morality of eating animals when it isn't necessary for our survival. That's how we came to be vegans."

"For a boy of seven to come to that conclusion was remarkable," Thomas said.

Joan said, "When he was eight, Barry wrote a short poem entitled *Why I Am a Vegan*. Would you like to hear it, Thomas?

"I sure would."

Why I Am a Vegan

When about to die,
Cows cringe and cry
More than celery.

Barry Vincent

Thomas said, "Those few words say so much. I wonder how he developed such compassion while so young."

Jack said, "We've given up trying to work with the county. We intend to file a wrongful death lawsuit against Thein. We also will file two claims for infliction of emotional distress, one for Joan and one for me. But we first need to talk with someone who has been the plaintiff in such lawsuits. We need advice from an ordinary citizen like ourselves."

"That's why I wanted to meet with you," Thomas said. "I wondered if you had decided to file a lawsuit. I didn't want to influence your decision but now that you intend to file, I can be of help."

Jack said, "We'll appreciate any help you can provide. What are you thinking?"

"Sharing information about what goes on inside the mental health center."

"That would be risky for you," Jack said. "You're jeopardizing your career by simply meeting with us today."

Thomas said, "Some things are worth risking a career for. And I'm not the only one who is risking a lot. If you file a wrongful death lawsuit and see it through, your lives will never be the same. To get the case to court will take years. In fact, that's how the county wins most of the suits filed against it—the county court just drags things out. There is always one more legal paper for the plaintiff to file or another series of questions to answer. This goes on and on until the plaintiff gives up. And if you get to have a trial, you'll find that medical defendants have many advantages over the lowly complainant."

Joan said, "Jack and I are prepared to travel a long, bumpy road. He has even opted to retire to have more time to devote to studying medical and legal issues, and to working with the attorney we hire. That's how determined we are."

Jack said, "It's clear why Joan and I are going to sue the county and Thein. They took our son from us. But I don't understand why you're risking your career. Your concern exceeds what I would expect from the most conscientious psychologist."

"Nineteen years ago, my younger brother, Louis, completed suicide when overmedicated by a psychiatrist. His case was similar to Barry's. I still seek revenge for Louis. And I try to prevent similar tragedies. Helping you would help me achieve my goals. You want to prevent Thein from harming others. I have the same motivation—to stop premature deaths caused by pharmaceutical companies and psychiatrists."

"We're sorry about your loss," Joan said. "We had no idea. Was Louis's death why you went into psychology?"

"Yes. I was there the day that Louis ended his life. Every day I relive the horror. Using an office chair as a battering ram, Louis crashed through a window on the fifteenth floor of the Westlake Building and fell to his death."

Joan said, "Oh my god."

"The renowned psychiatrist, Byron Westlake, prescribed an antidepressant, an antipsychotic, and an anticholinergic at high dosages. My parents filed a wrongful death lawsuit and eventually there was a jury trial. Dad and Mom lost the case.

"About a year later the judge went to prison for taking bribes from pharmaceutical companies to rig wrongful death trials. Despite strong evidence that the judge, Jacob Barker, did the same thing in Louis's case, my parents were unable to get a new trial.

"County court is a dirty institution. If you decide to not file for wrongful death after hearing me out, I won't blame you. But my intent is not to sway you to file or not to file. My intent is to help you as much as you want me to, whether or not you file."

Jack said, "We're beyond that decision point. We will file a lawsuit. And yes, we want your help. We've been looking for someone who lived through a wrongful death suit. Your parents were the plaintiffs, but you were old enough to understand the proceedings. We're lucky you're willing to help us. You said Louis's case was similar to Barry's. How so?"

Thomas said, "Louis was seventeen when he was diagnosed with schizophrenia and he died within a few weeks. Barry was thirty-eight when he died, and he had lived with schizophrenia for at least six years, but other than those differences, their cases are similar.

"Both Louis and Barry were diagnosed with schizophrenia and both subsequently developed a psychomotor movement disorder. Each had a psychiatrist who was a firm believer in psychiatric drugs. I've studied how these guys think. And I had good opportunities to do those studies. Remember, Thein is one of my coworkers. As the county center's only psychologist, I see all his patients. In fact, my job includes advising all of the center's psychiatrists as to psychological matters. In addition to studying Westlake and Thein as individuals, I have studied the methods of many other polypharmacists who got sued and many who harmed people but didn't happen to get sued.

"These doctors are not worthy of the name. They believe in magic. They engage in magical thinking, harming or even killing patients as a result."

"What do you mean by magical thinking?" Joan asked.

Thomas said, "Medical history—especially psychiatric history—is filled with examples of what someone considered marvelous cures but which turned out to be no more than magical thinking."

Joan asked, "What are some examples?"

"Trepanning is one. Have you heard of trepanning?"

"No, I've never heard of it," Joan said.

"What about you, Jack? Have you heard of trepanning?"

"No."

Thomas said, "Trepanning was a form of psychosurgery. It was believed that evil spirits caused mental illness, so holes were drilled in the patients' heads to let the spirits escape. Many people died from infection.

"Another example of a magical cure and of psychosurgery was frontal lobotomy. This was the severing of the white matter that connects the frontal lobes with the rest of the brain. Practiced as late as the 1950s in America. Rosemary Kennedy, President Kennedy's younger sister, was seventeen in 1941. Her father was ashamed of her because she had a very mild mental problem, so he arranged for her to undergo a lobotomy. After the operation, she was institutionalized and lived an isolated existence into her eighties. She went from being a beautiful young lady to being a broken, unfortunate woman because of a lobotomy by zealous doctors."

Jack said, "I hope trepanning and lobotomy are now thoroughly discredited."

Thomas said, "Modern Western medicine abhors them, but countries like Haiti and parts of Africa still practice both forms of treatment. And I bet Thein learned to do lobotomies in Burma.

"For years, insulin shock was widely used. Inject lots of insulin to put a patient in a coma. Leave the person comatose for a few days and then bring him out of it and see what you have. Do this repeatedly because one coma by itself was judged inadequate."

Jack said, "I didn't know of the barbaric treatments that were used over the centuries."

"There were hundreds," Thomas said. "I bet historians don't know them all. Immersion in iced water was an early treatment.

"Dr. Benjamin Rush was a contemporary of George Washington and Benjamin Franklin. The American Psychiatric Association regards him as the father of American psychiatry. He had some really goofy ideas of what constituted good psychiatry. He continued to bleed patients long after most doctors turned away from it. Yeah, Dr. Rush bled people to cure mental illness.

"He fed his patients mercurous chloride, also called calomel. This was a powerful laxative so Dr. Rush was trying to purge mental illness from the body. He put people in a chair suspended from the ceiling and spun them around and around.

"In 1851, an American physician by name of Samuel Cartwright described a mental illness called drapetomania that afflicted black slaves. Of all things, this illness made them want to run away. He said if the slaves were sullen and dissatisfied, the owner should whip the devil out of them. That was the preventive measure. To cure the disease and make running physically impossible, he removed both big toes.

"Eventually, electroconvulsive therapy came along. ECT was widely used in many countries for decades. In 1961, as a result of ECT, Earnest Hemingway lost much of his memory and knew his writing career had ended. The literary genius completed suicide in 1961 at age sixty-two after a series of ECT sessions at the Mayo Clinic. ECT is still used today and has many advocates, and possibly certain adaptations are helpful in treating certain kinds of mental problems. But since the 1930s when the technology came into wide use, it has been abused many times.

"Hitler's death camp doctors experimented with giving the mentally ill malaria. The idea was that high fever would cook the bacteria that caused syphilis. In its third stage, if untreated, syphilis can cause general paresis and mental illness.

"There were many goofy ways to treat mental disorders and they all had their advocates. Nowadays, doctors scoff at these methods. But they adhere to use of psychotropic drugs, often in massive amounts. Someday doctors will look back at this medication era and wonder how psychiatrists could have been so wrong and so cruel.

"As you prepare for your wrongful death trial, you'll learn just how flimsy the science is that supposedly justifies the use of these powerful drugs. You'll be appalled for example at the outlandish hypothesis called the chemical imbalance in the brain. This is not really a scientific hypothesis, but is a clever pharmaceutical marketing strategy."

Jack said, "Is it magical thinking that causes psychiatrists like Thein to prescribe too much medicine?"

"That's one of the factors," Thomas said. "But there are several reasons why Thein prescribes so much medication. For example, I'll bet he's taking bribes from pharmaceutical companies."

Jack said, "Do you have evidence that Thein takes bribes?"

"Not direct evidence of major bribes, but lots of evidence of small gifts. Think about it. Joan told me over the phone that the two of you witnessed a huge free meal complete with alcohol that Alphatron set out for county medical officials. You can bet that wasn't the only treat that the pharmaceutical company provided during the three-day symposium. Regardless, that extravagant dinner was one form of bribery.

"The most common form of bribery is the free drug samples that the pharmaceutical companies give to the county psychiatrists. Thein gets so many free samples that he has two large cabinets in his office bulging with them.

"Again, what I'm about to say doesn't prove bribery, but it proves a conflict of interest and says conditions are ripe for bribery. One of Alphratron's attractive female drug reps recently moved in with Thein in his new mansion. This living arrangement is conducive to bribes. And the fact that Thein can afford a fine home and three luxury cars raises questions.

"Also, Thein has been absent from the clinic a lot lately. He's been going to Alphatron continuing education training sessions. I have reprints of two articles that appeared in medical journals that bear his name. I don't see how he could have found time to write those articles, and he doesn't have the necessary knowledge either. Placing a doctor's name on a prestigious medical paper is a form of bribery because authorship bolsters his professional credentials."

The Vincents sat in silence, vowing to pursue the issue of bribery.

Thomas said, "As hard as it may be, let's leave the issue of possible bribery for another session when we can go into it in depth and when I will be better prepared.

"Let me get back to my list of reasons for Thein and quacks like him to prescribe so much medicine.

"First, one reason for administering so much medicine is that it's so easy to do. It doesn't take any effort to write a prescription and you don't need any skill. You don't have to scrub up, put on an operating gown, and have good hand-eye coordination. You only need to scrawl a few words on a pad.

"And, yes, magical thinking is a great big reason why Thein and his kind practice polypharmacy. Are you up to hearing how that works?"

Joan said, "Yes. We'll need this kind of information if we are to give Thein and the county what for."

"Thein believes in magic. The pharmaceutical companies and his flawed medical training have taught him that for every disorder there is a drug or a combination of drugs that will control the problem, and that all he needs to do is to keep trying one medication after another until he hits on a combination that works.

"The magical thinking is that if he just keeps adding another drug to the mix he'll hit on just the right combination."

Jack said, "Doesn't he know anything about side effects? Each drug has unwanted consequences. Moreover, as you add drugs you increase the chances that some will interact badly."

"You're right. But so far Thein has only been rewarded by the drugmakers, and has never been punished for his recklessness.

"I know how these psychiatrists think. I've heard them talking in the lunch room and their offices. They know that if they get sued, the county will defend them free of charge. First, California law sets the civil damage awards so low that it's unlikely a psychiatrist will be sued. And second, as I said, if they are sued, the county will defend them free of charge."

Jack said, "It looks like over the decades an unholy alliance has formed, and it's made up of the pharmaceutical companies, the pharmacists, and the doctors."

"You're right," Thomas said, "and the FDA is part of this unholy alliance. The FDA is a regulatory agency in name only. It's actually a corruption-facilitator. People who have worked for pharmaceutical companies now work for FDA and vice versa. And the National Institute of Mental Health does the same thing, with its bureaucrats becoming pharmaceutical employees and the pharmaceutical crowd becoming staff and executives of the NIMH. Round and round goes the revolving door.

"And Medicaid is part of what you called the unholy alliance. Medicaid automatically pays anyone who files a claim for reimbursement and rarely seeks to recover damages when it is defrauded. It is unscientific and corrupt for the government to pay for excessive use of these drugs, which are neither safe nor effective, over long use. A few of the better drugs are helpful if used at the lowest effective dose for the shortest time necessary. That's the best any scientist can honestly say for any of these drugs. Many doctors and researchers have written books, saying exactly that. *Mad in America*, *Overdosed America*, *Our Daily Meds*, and *On the Take* are just four of the dozens of books that provide evidence of fraud and duplicity in government, medicine, and pharmacology.

"The whole system is corrupt. That's what caused the death of both Louis and Barry and countless others."

Chapter 42

The County Pays My Salary

A jury consists of twelve persons chosen to decide who has the better lawyer.

—Robert Frost
(poet laureate)

Jack and Joan met Thomas for a second time at the cafe next to the Loma Linda Market.

Jack said, "Tight budget. That's the biggest problem we have. We can't afford a lawyer with a national reputation. The same goes for the expert witness that we'll need. The most acclaimed witnesses come from places like New York state or even Wales, so high travel costs are added to witness fees.

"Can you recommend a local attorney or an expert witness? Who did your parents use? Their wrongful death trial was a long time ago, so maybe neither the lawyer nor the witness is still practicing."

Thomas said, "Dad and Mom believed their attorney and expert witness did as well as anyone could have, given the fact that Judge Barker was jailed for accepting bribes in other wrongful death trials very similar to their own. My folks died believing that Barker violated the law in their case and that they deserved a new trial. Anyway, their attorney was Raymond Ferris, and their expert witness was Dr. Michelle Stanton."

Joan asked, "Would you recommend them?"

"Yes. Good researchers. Good listeners. I can introduce them to you. After the wrongful death lawsuit for Louis, I studied what makes a good medicolegal team. Many things can go wrong. The attorney is the weakest link on most teams. Lawyers often don't learn enough about the medical aspects of a case. They seem to think they don't need to know anything about the scientific issues as long as their expert witness is knowledgeable.

"An attorney can't ask good questions if he doesn't understand the fallacy of the chemical-imbalance hypothesis. He can't evaluate the responses from the other side if he doesn't understand polypharmacy, side effects, and drug-drug interactions.

"Your lawyer will need to understand what's called a prescribing cascade, which is a common error that psychiatrists make. A doctor prescribes the wrong medication, causes a bad reaction, blames the patient's original disorder of, say, schizophrenia or bipolar disorder, and therefore increases the dose or even adds more kinds of medication. When the condition worsens again, the doctor prescribes still more drugs.

"The cascade part of the name refers to the psychiatrist making one mistake, misinterpreting the cause of that mistake, and then making the same mistake again. If your attorney doesn't understand the prescribing cascade, he could lose the case.

"I spent days analyzing Thein's records regarding Barry. They are strong evidence that he caused Barry to contract akathisia by prescribing too much Paxil. He upped the dose of Paxil to sixty milligrams per day when no prudent psychiatrist would have prescribed more than twenty.

"Then Thein mistook the akathisia he had caused for schizoaffective disorder, so he changed Barry's diagnosis and added Gabicon, which was never FDA approved for treating any mental illness.

"And he completely mismanaged his attempt to replace one antipsychotic with another that he thought would be less likely to cause obesity and diabetes. He claimed that he was tapering Zyprexa downward while gradually ramping up Abilify. This is called a cross taper, but the tapering got stalled when Thein forgot what he was

THE MIND DOCTOR

doing. So for weeks he prescribed very high levels of both Zyprexa and Abilify.

"He also increased the dose of Cogentin, which is notorious for inducing heat stroke. It keeps the body from perspiring.

"If your lawyer doesn't understand this sort of flawed reasoning and misuse of science, he not only will lose your case, but he won't be able to help you get the information that you seek. He must understand not only the law but also the mistakes that doctors commonly make, the cognitive errors."

"I just read an interesting book," Joan said. "*How Doctors Think* was written by an oncologist so he knew something about the subject. He also had a serious problem with his right hand, which a series of orthopedic surgeons misdiagnosed. The problem turned out to be a lax ligament that over the years had allowed cysts to form in the bones of the wrist.

"The author also described other cases of flawed thinking by doctors, including a woman who over fifteen years saw more than thirty doctors until one correctly diagnosed celiac disease. Doctors just kept making the same cognitive mistakes.

"One of the most common mistakes was to make snap judgments based on the cases they had most often seen in their practices. For example, a misdiagnosis was likely if the doctor routinely treated substance abuse cases but then had a patient with an essential tremor. He was likely to mistake the condition for delirium tremens caused by alcohol withdrawal. Most seemed mentally unable to consider any other possible cause of the medical condition."

Thomas said, "Great examples. Your trial lawyer will need to be aware of the cognitive errors that doctors make. Many lawyers just don't study the medical issues. They're lazy and expect their expert witness to magically raise and expound on every important medical issue. But the lawyer must set these issues before the testifying expert."

Joan said, "And you think that Raymond Ferris is the kind of attorney who can act as master of ceremonies?"

"Yes. But let me tell you another way that lawyers screw things up. Some fear being reprimanded by the judge. They're so afraid of the judge that they don't execute their case properly.

"For example, there's a principle that the plaintiff should not influence the expert witness because this can be interpreted as compromising the independence of the witness' review. Therefore scaredy-cat attorneys don't let the plaintiff and the expert witness even meet before the trial takes place. The only time they see each other is in the courtroom. The attorney prohibits communication between plaintiff and witness. So the plaintiff can only inform the attorney of the key issues and hope he will pass the information along to the expert witness.

"I understand the attorney's need to prevent the plaintiff from unduly influencing the expert witness, but he could let them meet in his presence where he could control the interaction.

"Important facts should not be kept from the expert witness just because a lawyer fears being suspected of allowing collusion between the witness and the plaintiff. Most lawyers just provide the expert witness with the written pleadings in the case. This can result in the witness not recognizing key issues. But the attorney for the defendant drugmaker and psychiatrist might not feel bound by any such ethical constraints. The defense attorney might train their expert witness in how to answer every conceivable question. That is what seems to have happened in Louis' wrongful death trial."

Joan said, "It sounds like we're doomed to lose our wrongful death lawsuit."

"The system is rigged against you. To stay with a case to the end, you must be sustained by more than the hope that you'll win. Here's one of the ways your case is already rigged. Who are you planning to sue?"

Jack said, "Psychiatrist David Thein, Alphatron Pharmaceuticals, and Riverside County."

"Who is the last party that you just named?"

"Riverside County."

Thomas said, "What court has jurisdiction?"

"Riverside County Superior Court."

"So you're suing a county employee in a county court," Thomas said. "The judge is a county official. Don't think for a second that judges are independent. Oh, they have fancy words and fancy legal maneuvers to give the impression of independence, but county government has ways of biasing the judge. The presiding judge for county court gives the trial judge his or her annual performance rating.

"Here's another way that the trial is rigged against you. Suppose you opt for a jury trial to try to offset a judge you believe to be biased. You're thinking that there's a better chance of the jurors not being prejudiced against you. But the pool of potential jurors of course are county residents, and one of the biggest employers in the county is the county itself. No matter how your attorney tries to get an unbiased jury—most don't try hard enough—you probably will wind up with at least four of the twelve jurors being county employees. In Louis' trial, seven of the jurors were county functionaries of one kind or another, clerks or highway maintenance workers. And most county employees will be biased in favor of the county.

"The last time we met, you recited a poem that Barry wrote. Would you like to see one that I wrote regarding the wrongful death legal system?"

The Vincents said yes. Thomas handed them each a copy of his poem.

MEDICOLEGAL SECRETS
(ADMITTED TO ONESELF IN PRIVATE)

County Administrator
I keep my job comfortable.
Although Dr. Thein is culpable,
I pay no heed
To his prescribing for greed.
Dr. Thein's Supervisor
Yearly, I appraise Dr. Thein's performance,
But on one topic I maintain silence.
One doctor must not mention wrongs of another,
Despite his corruption, I treat him like a brother.
State Medical Board
We pretend to protect people from doctors' wrongs.

> Instead we protect doctors from victims' sad songs.
> We reject reports that Dr. Thein prescribes
> Drugs that net pharmaceutical bribes.
> *Dr. Thein's Attorney*
> Dr. Thein's drugs did the patient in,
> But the county pays me to save his skin.
> I do what it takes, putting honesty aside,
> For there are facts that I must hide.
> *Dr. Thein's Expert Witness*
> Have gun, will travel is my motto.
> Principles do not matter.
> I am a psychiatrist I say.
> Telling lies in court earns my pay.
> *County Judge*
> That judges are independent is a fallacy,
> The county pays my salary.

Jack said, "Thomas, this is great. When did you write it?"

"Since we last met."

Thomas resumed his narrative.

"So again, you better have some reason for suing other than the idea you could win. The best reason for you to sue is to get medical and legal evidence that will help you understand how Thein caused Barry's death. Then you can warn other parents what to watch out for. Maybe you can organize a movement or give lectures or write a book.

"The old saying that knowledge is power has to be your guide. With knowledge of how pharmaceutical companies corrupt the practice of medicine with vast sums of money, and how doctors are on the take might help you save lives. I would look at the trial as an intermediate step rather than an end in itself.

"Plan to get valuable information in the run-up to the trial and during the trial. And then figure out an innovative way to get some measure of justice that doesn't depend on the rigged court system."

Chapter 43

He Sounds Well Qualified

In nearly all matters the human mind has a strong tendency to judge in the light of its own experience, knowledge, and prejudice rather than on the evidence provided.

—W.I.B. Beveridge
The Art of Scientific Investigation (1957)

Jack and Joan Vincent filed a wrongful death lawsuit against Alphatron Pharmaceuticals, Riverside County, and psychiatrist David Thein. It took almost five years for the case to come to trial, and in the interim Thein continued to practice medicine for the county.

Thein was represented by the law firm of Smoot and Lamberti, which was under contract with the county. Douglas Smoot, the firm's senior partner, had served in the US Army as a member of the Judge Advocate General Corps and was now a colonel in the army reserves.

The wrongful death lawsuit worried Thein, but did not cost him financially. Riverside County paid the legal fees, expert witness fees, court costs, and related expenses.

Thein had to give depositions, and to prepare a written declaration. He also had to help Attorney Smoot answer the plaintiff's many interrogatories and to understand medical aspects of the claims against him and the county. A successful defense would require sustained close coordination between Smoot and Thein.

As director of the county mental health center, Richard Conway desperately wanted Thein and the county to win the wrongful death trial, thinking this would prevent the regulatory scrutiny that could result from a loss. If medical malpractice were to be proved, regulatory agencies might review all of the clinic's policies and practices. So Conway exercised his influence as director of the clinic to persuade Thein's fellow psychiatrists to help Thein with his caseload of patients so he had more time to prepare for trial. Doctors Newkirk and Crenshaw readily took some of Thein's patients for several months, enabling him to work with Smoot during regular office hours.

For hours on end Thein practiced answering questions under Smoot's tutelage. The lawyer drilled his client on how to answer every question that Raymond Ferris might ask. Smoot and Thein ate lunches at Molly's Family Restaurant and passed the expense along to the county.

Defendant Alphatron had far more money than the county to spend in preparing for the wrongful death trial. Three lawyers and their assistants worked on the case, and their per diem allowance dwarfed Smoot's. Alphatron had a huge budget allotted for expert witness fees.

On a Tuesday morning, Smoot and Thein were engrossed in trial preparation when Alphatron's lead trial lawyer, Leonard Grimes, invited them to lunch. Grimes drove the three of them across town to a French cuisine restaurant.

Attorney Grimes led the discussion about the forthcoming trial.

"Douglas, you better select your expert witness as soon as possible. Your expert will need time to get acquainted with your case. And you will need time to critique his or her draft testimony."

Smoot said, "Understood. It's the county's fault. The head honchoes desperately want me to win the case, but refuse to pay more than three hundred bucks an hour for an expert. For that miserly sum, I can't find anyone artful enough to contend with the plaintiff's expert."

"Are you afraid of Dr. Michelle Stanton?" Grimes asked.

"I don't underestimate her. She's both a psychiatrist and a neurologist, and has testified many times. She has never married so she can devote full time to her career. Dr. Stanton might wake up one day and realize that life has passed her by, but so far she's willing to be a spinster who studies and writes and makes life miserable for guys like us."

Grimes said, "I've been going over her professional resume, thinking about how to deal with her in court. Her qualifications are the main reason I'm telling you to get your own expert as soon as possible. Your witness will need time to review Stanton's declaration and figure out how to counter her main points."

Smoot said, "I repeat—the county's tight-fisted policy has me hamstrung. I can repeat my request for more money, but I doubt it will do any good."

Grimes said, "I thought that might be the problem, so I have a solution for you. But first, I'd like to recommend a specific person for you to consider hiring as a witness. He's Dr. Christopher Rice, an assistant director of the behavioral health department of the Veterans Administration Hospital in Long Beach."

"Why would a VA administrator be an expert on prescribing drugs for mentally ill patients? I'd like to get a research professor from the psychiatry department of a major university. A key opinion leader like Alphatron hires to speak at the continuing medical education seminars."

"It comes down to individuals," Grimes said. "And a great expert witness is like gold—he's where you find him. Dr. Rice is following this Barry Vincent case and wants to testify. And as far as drugs for the mentally ill, he oversees psychiatrists who prescribe tons of medications to veterans with post-traumatic stress disorder, traumatic brain injuries, depression, and high anxiety.

"But here's the main reason why I recommend Rice. He's the best liar—er, I mean expert witness—that I ever met." Grimes laughed at his own joke.

"He sounds well qualified," Thein said.

Smoot said, "I'm more than willing to review Dr. Rice's professional resume. But how can I afford him? What's his witness fee?"

"Now don't go bananas when I say the figure. He charges thirteen hundred dollars per hour. But he'll go out on a limb for Dr. Thein and say whatever is necessary. He enjoys deceiving people."

"Forget it," Smoot said. "The county would never pay that much."

Grimes said, "Alphatron has already hired our expert witness. And I'm sure we'll successfully defend ourselves. But it's also important to Alphatron for Dr. Thein and the county to win your cases. Otherwise you might taint our company or maybe you'd be barred from prescribing our drugs. Alphatron is willing to pay the biggest part of Dr. Rice's fee."

Smoot said, "County regulations don't allow for copay arrangements."

"To hell with county rules. Alphatron will pay one thousand dollars per hour direct to Dr. Rice, under the table. We'll keep this fact to ourselves. Rice will bill the county for only three hundred dollars per hour. Alphatron also will pay most of his per diem expenses so his vouchers will show minimum costs to the county. How does that sound, Counselor?"

"Great."

Grimes said, "And I differ with you about who makes the best expert witness. You said you favor a key opinion leader such as the head of a university psychiatry department. Well, such a person is great for influencing psychiatrists to prescribe medications that just happen to be under patent protection and happen therefore to be very expensive. A university professor may have done research and written textbooks on disorders and medications, but you're looking for something different in an expert witness in a wrongful death trial.

"The issue is whether Dr. Thein behaved like other psychiatrists whose methods are accepted in the medical community. The best witness you can get is another practicing psychiatrist who prescribes medications to patients similar to Barry Vincent. So your best witness will be someone in a position similar to Dr. Thein's, and it's best if he or she practices in Southern California."

Thein asked, "Has Alphatron obtained that kind of witness?"

"Yes we have. He's one of the highest prescribers of psychotropic drugs in California. And he knows your situation very well, having been sued for wrongful death himself. He won each time. Owns a practice right here in Riverside. Name's Byron Westlake."

Chapter 44

How this Game is Played

Tell me with whom you travel and I will tell you who you are.

—Alfred Victor Vigny
(French writer)

When Attorney Ferris learned that Alphatron's expert witness would be Byron Westlake, he held a phone conference with Thomas Prescott and Michelle Stanton.

"Michelle and Thomas, I just received Alphatron's witness list, and you'll be shocked at who their expert is."

Michelle asked, "Is it someone we know?"

"You both know him well."

"That would make him Byron Westlake," Thomas said.

"You're right."

"I'll take vacation time so I can be in court every day."

In preparing for the trial, both the plaintiffs and the defendants retained lawyers and expert witnesses, presented written interrogatories, deposed fact witnesses, filed written declarations, listed their proposed exhibits, and disclosed who their expert witnesses would be.

The defendants filed a joint motion for summary judgment, claiming the Vincents did not have enough evidence to require the county to hold a trial. Judge Janet Fillmore threw out the Vincents' claims that Dr. David Thein negligently caused them emotional distress, but she let stand their claim for wrongful death. A trial would determine whether the doctor had met the standard of care when treating Barry and what part Alphatron and the county might have played in causing his suicide.

Dr. Christopher Rice was rich. He had not inherited wealth, but acquired it by working hard, investing shrewdly, and devising ways to bill two or three parties for the same hour of work. Soon after completing his psychiatric residency, he had obtained a federal civil service position at the Long Beach Veterans Administration Hospital. At first, he worked hard and advanced rapidly through the general salary grade levels, becoming Assistant Chief of the Behavioral Health Department.

Then he began moonlighting as an expert witness on mental illness. For two years, he kept his trial-oriented activities separate from his government job. He did VA work when he was at the hospital, and he did trial preparation at home. Some of his moonlighting took place in law offices where he gave depositions and in courthouses where he took the stand and testified.

Dr. Rice was provided a large office and a secretary at the VA hospital, and it became easy to maintain privacy. He began preparing expert witness declarations and responses to interrogatories at his government office during duty hours. He studied medical records and plaintiff complaints, and prepared his testimony while being paid to do the VA's work.

Dr. Rice still did government work, but only the minimum necessary to make it appear he was dutiful. He set priorities so that he always accomplished the VA duties that were of most importance to higher-ups. He worked only on those tasks whose neglect could get him in trouble. He divided his work into high-priority and low-priority categories not based on their importance to veterans, but instead on whether the work product was likely to be noticed by his superiors. If the VA's executives were apt to blame some other manager for an incomplete or sloppy job, he never gave the task another thought. He mastered the art of delegating work so that his subordinates did the tasks that other division chiefs at his grade level did themselves.

Having freed up an enormous amount of time, Dr. Rice used that time to prepare his testimony for upcoming civil and criminal trials unrelated to the VA. This enabled him to bring in money from two sources at the same time. He drew his GS-16 salary while he sat in his government office and billed various pharmaceutical companies and physicians for time spent studying the cases against them.

At first, Dr. Rice was nervous about doing his expert witness work while on government time. But as the months went by, and as his secretary acted as gatekeeper and guardian of his privacy, no one questioned how he was spending his time. Every day, upon arriving at his VA office, he immediately decided what had to be done for him to stay out of trouble, and then assigned his subordinates to do those things.

He went to the highest-profile meetings with his bosses, calling this "face time." He neglected all other VA work so that he could charge the psychopharmaceutical industry for time spent helping them avoid legal penalties. While he was at it, he padded the number of hours he claimed for assessing courtroom issues. If he worked on Alphatron matters for four hours during the day, he billed for eight. The pharmaceutical companies did not object to the excessive charges because of his great skill as an expert witness.

Christopher believed that the best expert medical witness was more actor than doctor. He had been fascinated with the art of acting since elementary school. Throughout his student days from grade school through medical school, he had performed in plays, and even now acted in local stage productions. In any given trial, his job was to persuade twelve individuals whom he saw as too dim-witted to evade jury duty. So he connected with them on an emotional level more than a cognitive one. And his strategy worked. He was worth the fees he charged.

Dr. Rice's biggest client, Alphatron Pharmaceuticals, owed both its record profits and constant legal troubles to its aggressive marketing of off-label drugs.

Christopher was friends with Paul Warren, Alphatron's regional manager. He also knew midlevel and first-line managers Myron Mulroy and Neil Kronberger. But he worked most of all with Alphatron's office of counsel and in particular Leonard Grimes, the company's chief trial lawyer.

At Attorney Smoot's request, the county mental health center contracted for Dr. Rice to serve as the expert witness for both Riverside County and Dr. David Thein. Rice was at his VA office one November morning, preparing for the trial which was scheduled to begin in January. He was studying Thein's medical records pertaining to decedent Barry Vincent.

Dr. Thein's notes were sometimes illegible. But worse, they often failed to connect his thoughts. For each office visit, he would list the diagnoses he had made, and in a separate list would name the drugs he had prescribed. But he did not correlate the lists. He never specified which drugs were intended for which disorders. To Rice, this lack of connectivity suggested muddled thinking.

Thein kept even worse records regarding informed consent. The county clinic used a standard form intended to show that a patient had been informed of possible benefits and risks of the prescribed medications, and had knowingly consented to comply with the doctor's wishes. To give informed consent, a patient first had to be informed and to understand the significance of the information. Thein never recorded having told the patient the exact side effects that a drug might cause, never that Zyprexa could cause obesity or that Gabicon could cause seizures. Time after time, consent form after consent form, he wrote only "Meds benefit/ risk explained."

To Rice, it seemed unlikely that any of Thein's patients ever gave consent that was truly informed.

Rice phoned Alphatron's, Leonard Grimes.
"Hello, Lyn, this is Christopher Rice."
"Good morning, Chris."

"I'm reading the medical records that Dr. David Thein maintained for Barry Vincent."

"Chris, you should work directly with Attorney Douglas Smoot. My manager asked me to get you on board with Smoot and the county, and naturally there will a lot of overlap with Alphatron, but your day-to-day work should be with Doug since he's under contract with the county."

"I understand. But I'm calling you because this isn't business as usual. Dr. Thein has put you guys in a bad way. I'll serve as his expert witness and do all I can to set things right. But first I need to talk frankly with Smoot and you."

"It's that bad?"

"Yes, I've never seen a case where the level of medication was raised so much during the first office visit. It's also clear that Thein misdiagnosed Mr. Vincent's disorder and committed the prescribing cascade. The mess he has created is not one I can resolve on my own. I want to meet with Smoot and you so we can figure out how we might navigate these troubled waters."

"OK. Give my secretary some dates when you're available, and she will set up a meeting here in my office. Should I have Smoot invite Dr. Thein?"

"No. I'll meet with Thein as many times as it takes, but I don't want him at this first meeting because I'll be very critical of his medical practices. I don't want to argue with him just yet. I want to first educate you and Smoot. I don't want to make Thein mad at me as we will need a good working relationship."

"Sounds serious."

"It is."

The next day, Rice and Smoot met with Grimes in Alphatron's Long Beach office building. Rice took charge of the meeting.

"Leonard and Doug, I appreciate this opportunity to discuss Dr. Thein's care of Barry Vincent."

Smoot said, "Knock off the courtly manner. Did my client screw up so bad that the plaintiffs might win?"

"That's our predicament," Rice said. "Look, none of us has a lot of time, and the trial is fast approaching. I use artful terms when

I'm testifying, but I'm going to be blunt with you two. David Thein either hated Barry Vincent or he was bribed to prescribe massive amounts of medication. Well, there's a third possibility—that Thein's an idiot.

Smoot said, "Better that we know now than to have surprises in court."

Rice said, "You both know what a prescribing cascade is."

"Of course we know," Grimes said. "We're experienced trial lawyers. That's where a doctor misdiagnoses a condition he has caused by prescribing the wrong drug or too much of it. The medication has provoked a serious reaction, but the doctor erroneously blames the person's original disorder. For example, the doctor mistakenly thinks schizophrenia caused the problem when the true cause was Zyprexa."

Rice said, "Added medication worsens the problem that was caused by medication. This may prompt the stupid doctor to again add more drug. The poor patient just keeps getting worse. And the more he complies with the doctor's orders, the worse he gets."

Smoot said, "Well, that would take a pretty stupid doctor. Are you saying Dr. Thein is that dumb?"

Rice said, "He's either that dumb or there's something else wrong with him. There's a phenomenon called magical thinking that might account for how Thein treated Mr. Vincent. That's the belief that for every medical condition, there's a medication or a combination of medications that will cure the problem. It's possible that Thein coming from Burma where there were few medications to prescribe is simply overcome by all the options he has here in California. Of course if Alphatron is providing incentives for him to prescribe medications, well, that just adds to the likelihood that Thein will overprescribe again and again."

Smoot asked, "Leonard, is this guy for or against us? Rice, whose side are you on?"

"I'm on your side, of course. If anyone can turn these issues back against the plaintiff's expert witness, I'm the guy who can do it. And this conversation will enable you to help me make the plaintiffs look foolish. You'll know just what I'm doing when I pursue an issue in court."

"I was just joking," Smoot said. "Go ahead and tell us how Dr. Thein fouled up."

Rice said, "On Barry's first office visit, Thein prescribed too many drugs at doses that were too high. On the second visit, he continued to overprescribe. The third office visit was when Thein misdiagnosed schizoaffective disorder in Barry. This was a version of the prescribing cascade except instead of blaming schizophrenia specifically, he decided that schizophrenia had morphed into schizoaffective disorder which accounted for the excessive energy that Mr. Vincent was reporting. So Thein changed the young man's diagnosis and prescribed the anticonvulsant, Gabicon, off-label."

Smoot said, "Wait. I don't get it. Again, why did he change the diagnosis from schizophrenia to schizoaffective disorder?"

Rice said, "Thein's medical records tell me exactly why he changed the diagnosis, and it was classic prescribing cascade. Thein had caused Barry to contract akathisia.

"Barry told Thein he had too much energy. Instead of suspecting that medications caused akathisia, Thein decided that schizoaffective disorder had cropped up. Thein thought that the increased energy was caused by the manic phase of new onset bipolar disorder. Bipolar is a mood disorder so he thought this justified the schizoaffective diagnosis. In other words, he jumped to the conclusion that now Barry had symptoms of both schizophrenia and clinical depression. But even with this stupid mistake, he could have selected a less-harmful medication than the disastrous Gabicon. I'm afraid that Alphatron had a lot to do with that reckless decision. Lyn, your employer overpromoted Gabicon, an anticonvulsant, to treat mental illnesses off-label."

"I understand," Grimes said.

Rice said, "So far, I've talked about the prescribing cascade, Thein's misdiagnosis, and his incentive to just keep on adding more drugs even though he should have seen he was poisoning his patient. And now he has the gall to say that Barry caused the problem by not taking his medications as prescribed. I expect the young man is dead precisely because he followed doctor's orders.

"But I know how this game is played. Being your hired gun, I'll help you put forth the hoax that Barry was at fault."

"Now you've gone too far," Grimes said. You've gone from straight talk to accusing us of crimes."

"I'm risking my reputation every time I take a case like this. If the law was worthy of its name, I'd be in prison for committing perjury. My salvation is that it's customary for expert witnesses to lie in court. It's accepted as the norm. You better be glad that I can see what Thein did wrong. Otherwise, I couldn't cover for him half as well. But I don't want either of you operating under the delusion that your boy was wrongfully accused."

Grimes said, "OK. We get the picture and we appreciate your talents. But it isn't as though you're under paid."

The three men laughed.

Grimes said, "Continue with your lecture, but don't take too long. You're making me sick."

Rice said, "Well, we covered the prescribing cascade, the misdiagnosis of schizoaffective disorder, and the off-label use of Gabicon, which might as well have been arsenic. Thein's errors caused akathisia, and it was the akathisia that caused the young man to kill himself."

"How can you be so sure akathisia was the cause?" Smoot asked.

Rice said, "Why does the pharmaceutical industry almost never utter the word, akathisia? Why do you call it irritability, agitation, or restlessness when the condition shows up in a clinical trial? Why do you use the term jittery in your package inserts? It's because medical literature links akathisia to suicide. The pharmaceutical industry knows that if the public learned of the lethality of akathisia and its prevalence, there would be a hue and cry that would decimate psychotropic drug sales.

"Akathisia gives caregivers like Barry's dad and mom almost no chance of saving the victim. Suicidal ideation typical of a depressed person gives more warning signs and more time to take preventive action. With akathisia, the patient doesn't even know what's happening to him. The impulse to kill oneself or someone else is sudden and strong. The afflicted person is highly motivated and highly energized.

"Many times depressed people go on living just because they don't have the energy to kill themselves. This sounds humorous but it's true. They just can't get around to buying a rope and fashioning a noose, for example. And then they have to climb up on a stool. It's too much to bother with, feeling as low as they do.

"But the person afflicted with akathisia has so much energy that he absolutely must do something with it. And the incentive to do something dramatic comes from the psychosis inherent in akathisia.

"I'm going to get on the witness stand and make Barry's mom and dad look culpable for not taking him to the Arrowhead Regional Medical Center after a nurse expelled him from Saint Rita's. But they had no clue as to what was going on with Barry. I'm surprised he lived as long as he did.

"Yeah, you're paying me a lot of money, but I'm one of the few people in the country who can save your bacon."

Chapter 45

Create a Disease for Profit

Once lying entirely outside the domain of psychiatrists, ordinary behaviors like shyness began to enter their reference manual as mental disorders that affected growing numbers of the population.

—Christopher Lane
Shyness: How Normal Behavior Became a Sickness (2007)

The courtroom was designed to intimidate the legal contestants and to lend power to the chief intimidator, Judge Janet Fillmore. Her elegant, elevated desk emphasized that she was in charge.

All participants in the wrongful death trial had their own defined space from which they had better not stray without the judge's permission. Plaintiffs Jack and Joan Vincent and their attorney, Raymond Ferris, were assigned to a table of their own. At a second table sat Dr. David Thein, along with a Riverside County administrator, and their counsel, Douglas Smoot. At the third table sat Myron Mulroy who was authorized by Alphatron to make routine management decisions for the company, but who was also under orders to immediately contact the regional headquarters if a major issue arose. Sitting next to Mulroy was Leonard Grimes, the most experienced legal mind in the courtroom.

At an adjacent table were two attorney assistants to Grimes and a senior legal secretary, Clifford Noyes. His job was to produce an immediate record of select parts of the trial. He was not to duplicate the court reporter's transcript but was to focus on major issues that could affect the trial outcome. This instant excerpt was intended to help Alphatron executive Paul Warren make tactical decisions from his office in Long Beach.

The configuration of the room and the arrangement of the furniture made clear that this was a place where legal battles were fought.

A section of the courtroom contained thirty seats, which were occupied by citizens who had been summoned for jury duty. Jurors would be selected from thirty eligibles, and the citizens not selected would be free to go their way. The goal was to select twelve jurors and four alternates. Only four jurors were approved from the first batch of draftees. A second group of thirty people was brought in and from them five more jurors were selected. After interviewing the third and fourth groups of citizens, the opposing attorneys finally settled on the full panel of twelve jurors and four alternates.

The opposing counsels made their opening arguments, then Attorney Ferris called Dr. Michelle Stanton to testify regarding the medicolegal claims the plaintiff was making. Next came the opportunity for the defense attorneys to begin trying to discredit the plaintiff's case.

Defense attorney Douglas Smoot called the plaintiff's expert witness, Dr. Stanton.

Attorney Smoot said, "Your professional resume says you have education and training as both a neurologist and a psychiatrist. Please describe the difference between neurology and psychiatry."

"Both are branches of medicine but they take different approaches to diagnosing and treating health problems. Neurology focuses on the physical brain and nervous systems while psychiatry focuses on the unseen mind and mental disorders.

"Neurology uses laboratory tests while psychiatry relies on the *Diagnostic and Statistical Manual of Mental Disorders*, a document that describes mental illnesses and their symptoms. The manual is a classification system. It classifies mental disorders according to their symptoms. The current edition of the manual, *DSM-IV-TR*, is 943 pages long and lists 365 mental disorders. The illnesses are determined by psychiatrists reaching consensus. Experts vote on whether a cluster of symptoms amounts to a mental disorder and what name to give it."

Smoot said, "Give us examples of laboratory tests that neurologists order."

"Lumbar puncture. This is the taking of cerebrospinal fluid from the lower back through a needle, usually for diagnosis.

"CAT scan. CAT is short for computed axial tomography. Tomography is a technique for displaying a cross section through the human body using x-rays or ultrasound.

"Neurologists also order ultrasound exams of major blood vessels in the head and neck. And the procedures for some genetic tests have been standardized so they now are done on a routine basis.

"Psychiatry, on the other hand, seldom has the benefit of laboratory tests. Mental disorders cannot, at this stage of our knowledge, be diagnosed by blood tests, urine tests, x-rays, or any other physical exam. There is nothing akin to a tuberculin test, for example.

"Psychiatrists use structured clinical interviews to obtain information from their patients. Each interview is carried out according to a standard operating procedure, with the questions published in manuals sold by the American Psychiatric Association. The interview questions are prepared by committees of mental heath care professionals which the APA selects for their expertise with regard to the various mental disorders. The questions are to be asked in a specific sequence, although the format allows some flexibility to modify the questioning as it proceeds, based on the patient's responses. Using the answers to those questions, and the therapist's observations of the patient, he or she decides if the patient has a mental illness and which illness according to the way *DSM* groups the symptoms."

Smoot said, "For purposes of determining whether Dr. David Thein met the standard of care in treating Barry Vincent, is it true that only what psychiatrists do is relevant while what neurologists do has no bearing on this case?"

"I grant you that the legal standard for Dr. Thein's medical practices regarding Barry Vincent is what other psychiatrists, and not neurologists, would do under similar circumstances. But the best doctors, whether psychiatrists or neurologists, know a lot about—"

Smoot said, "For purposes of this trial, we don't care about the best doctors. We're here to help the jury decide if Dr. Thein acted in accord with what other careful psychiatrists would typically do under similar circumstances."

Stanton said nothing.

"Dr. Stanton, do you agree with my last statement?"

"Repeat the statement."

"The Vincent medical and legal team, and Dr. Thein's medical and legal team, are here to help the jury decide whether Dr. Thein followed medical procedures similar to the procedures that other careful psychiatrists would have followed. Some call this accepted community practice. California law calls it standard of care."

Witness Stanton said, "I agree with that statement. And I intend to show that the doctor didn't meet that standard. He didn't measure up to what a careful psychiatrist would have done."

Smoot's face turned red.

"Your Honor, the witness made an unsolicited, conclusory statement."

Judge Fillmore said, "Dr. Stanton, do not say anything that goes beyond what is necessary to answer the question. Do you understand?'

"Yes, Your Honor. I apologize."

Attorney Smoot said, "Dr. Stanton, your written declaration and your answers to deposition questions make it clear that you have a low regard for psychiatric medications, especially Gabicon. Please tell us what you think was wrong with Dr. Thein prescribing Gabicon for Barry Vincent."

"The US Food and Drug Administration never approved Gabicon for treating any mental illness—"

Smoot cut in, raising his voice.

"FDA approval was not needed for Dr. Thein to legally prescribe Gabicon for treating agitation and mood swings. He is a learned intermediary between the pharmacist and the patient, with wide latitude in what he prescribes."

Attorney Ferris stood up.

"Objection. Counsel cut my witness off in midsentence. She was composing an answer, providing context for her response. How can she present her argument if Attorney Smoot won't let her finish a sentence?"

Judge Fillmore said, "Attorney Smoot, when you ask a question, you must give the witness time to answer. If you are not interested in the answer, don't ask the question."

"Yes, Your Honor. I apologize. Dr. Stanton, please tell the jury what you believe was wrong with Dr. Thein prescribing Gabicon for Mr. Vincent's condition."

The witness said, "I realize that once FDA approves a drug for any disorder, a psychiatrist then can legally prescribe that drug for some other purpose. This kind of prescribing is called off-label because it is not approved in the medication's label required by FDA.

"And that is where the defense would like to leave the matter—with a conclusion that off-label prescribing is legal. But there is more to the matter in this instance. Often, it is bad practice to prescribe off-label because the drug probably was never tested by anyone for the mental illness involved. The testing of Gabicon for FDA approval was for adjunct use in treating partial complex epilepsy, not for treating agitation and mood swings, which is what Dr. Thein prescribed it for.

"I realize that a Dr. Norman Thurber published papers that say Gabicon is safe and effective for treating agitation and mood swings. But his tests involved very few individuals. Each time, only about five volunteers were tested, and several researchers have challenged the results.

"So Dr. Thein might have been legal in prescribing Gabicon off-label if that were as far as the matter went. But setting aside Thurber's suspect work, for which Alphatron Pharmaceuticals paid him handsomely—"

"Objection," Attorney Grimes said. "Whether Alphatron paid Dr. Thurber anything is not relevant to the question that Attorney

Smoot asked. That wisecrack was designed to prejudice the jury against Alphatron."

"Sustained. Dr. Stanton, this segment of the trial is devoted to the plaintiffs' allegations regarding Dr. David Thein. Of course, Alphatron Pharmaceuticals is involved, but the company's practices are not our focus right now. We will get around to your criticisms of Alphatron, but we are not there yet. I am warning you to not snipe at Alphatron.

"The jury will disregard the witness's unsolicited remark. Counsel Ferris, during the break, instruct your witness on courtroom decorum."

"I will do that, Your Honor."

The judge said, "Attorney Smoot may continue to examine the witness."

Smoot said, "Dr. Stanton, please finish explaining what you found objectionable about Dr. Thein prescribing Gabicon for his patient, Barry Vincent."

"First, I repeat that Dr. Norman Thurber's studies of Gabicon were widely criticized by well-known psychiatrists. And I am prepared to explain in detail what was wrong with those studies, if you would like me to."

Smoot glanced at Grimes who shook his head.

Smoot said, "Continue with your answer, Dr. Stanton."

"My position is that Gabicon was totally untested for Barry's alleged condition. I say 'alleged condition' because I don't believe that Barry ever had the schizoaffetive disorder that Dr. Thein diagnosed on their third office visit.

"On top of that, FDA sent warning letters to all the doctors in the nation. Those letters said that doctors should not prescribe Gabicon for anyone who had not been diagnosed with epilepsy and was not already taking epilepsy drugs like phenobarbital and carbamazepine. Such drugs, according to FDA, cause the patient to develop enzymes that reduce the potency of Gabicon. The enzymes do this by shortening the elimination half-life. The clearance of Gabicon from the body in induced patients is about sixty percent greater than in persons not taking the enzyme-inducing drugs. This results in lower concentrations of Gabicon in the plasma.

"The recommended dosages of Gabicon were established through FDA-required clinical trials on patients who were taking enzyme-producing drugs. And that starting dose for such patients was eight milligrams per day. For anyone else with epilepsy, but who was not taking phenobarbital or other enzyme-producing drugs, the recommended starting dose was four milligrams per day.

"The FDA did not recommend a dose level for treating a mental illness because the agency never approved Gabicon for that purpose. As far as I could find out, no one has done clinical trials or other truly scientific tests to explore whether Gabicon can be used to treat mental illnesses safely and effectively. Thus far in these legal proceedings Dr. Thein has offered no evidence that he checked with other physicians who may have prescribed Gabicon for mental illnesses as to what their experiences might have been. Therefore, he seems to have had no guidelines to go by.

"To recap, there was no testing of Gabicon for mental illnesses for FDA purposes, no other scientific body tested the drug for such illnesses, Dr. Thurber's research is not credible, and it appears that Dr. Thein did not check with other clinicians who may have prescribed Gabicon for psychiatric illnesses. In other words, he had no good reason to either prescribe Gabicon or select an appropriate dose.

"What did Dr. Thein do? He guessed. He prescribed a starting dose of sixteen milligrams per day for Barry. And one month later he increased the dose to twenty milligrams. And Barry did not have epilepsy and was not taking phenobarbital. He had no protective enzymes.

"The FDA warning letter said that if Gabicon were prescribed for a nonepileptic patient, it could cause seizures. Under these conditions, instead of warding off seizures, Gabicon was more apt to cause them. And indeed it was a seizure that hospitalized Barry. In my professional opinion, it was the reckless use of Gabicon and the resultant seizure that caused him to cut himself and to die in Arrowhead Medical Center some nineteen days later.

"Those are the reasons I find fault with Dr. Thein's prescribing of Gabicon off-label."

To emphasize key points, attorney Ferris asked witness Stanton follow-up questions about the testimony she had just given.

"Dr. Stanton, you just testified that you are trained and experienced as both a psychiatrist and a neurologist."

"Yes."

"Why did you seek medical degrees in both psychiatry and neurology?"

"My mother was a psychiatrist and my father was a neurologist."

Laughter filled the courtroom

Attorney Ferris said, "OK, now tell us why you took all the coursework and fulfilled residency requirements for degrees in both medical fields."

"What I said was my real reason. My mother wanted me to become a psychiatrist, and my father wanted me to become a neurologist. I wanted to honor them both.

"As I studied both subject areas, I wanted to resolve in my own mind why there were two separate fields and not just one. I got drawn into the problems that people with neurological disorders have as well as the problems endured by people with psychiatric disorders. I enjoyed academic challenges, and I had ample time because I didn't have a husband and children who would have needed my attention."

Attorney Ferris said, "It is unusual for a person to remain unmarried and to be so dedicated to medicine and the care of people."

"Unusual, but not unheard of," Stanton said. "Florence Nightingale, the widely respected British nurse of the early twentieth century, never married. Mother Teresa, who took care of the most downtrodden people, never married. Those are two persons that I chose to emulate."

"Were you a university professor for a time?"

"Yes, I am an assistant professor of psychiatry at Stanford University. I still teach there on occasion."

"But for a few years, you were at Stanford full time. Is that correct?"

"Yes, for four years."

"During that time, did you participate in activities of the American Psychiatric Association?"

"Yes."

Attorney Ferris asked, "Did you serve on a panel that prepared a section of the *Diagnostic and Statistical Manual of Mental Disorders, Edition IV,* published in 1994?"

"Yes. I was on the panel that prepared the section on schizophrenia and other psychotic disorders."

"Describe your experiences while on that panel."

"I saw firsthand that the *DSM* was based on very little science. I served on the panel for psychotic illnesses, and I talked with colleagues who served on several of the other panels such as those dealing with mood disorders and severe traumas.

"Science had little to do with what the various panels declared to be mental disorders. The panelists literally voted on whether a cluster of signs and symptoms constituted a mental disorder. That process may be democratic, but it is not scientific.

"Since serving on the APA's panel, I have read the opinions of other professionals and I talked with many of them. These critical thinkers believe that psychiatry has become almost entirely a forum for marketing disorders and drugs."

Attorney Ferris said, "I can understand how your colleagues could have decided that psychiatry is a way of marketing drugs. But how in the world could psychiatry market disorders? And who would buy a disorder? That doesn't sound very lucrative."

"Well, to be clear, the actual sales are of the drugs that the pharmaceutical companies manufacture and that the psychiatrists prescribe. The disorders obviously are not sold, but they are a key part of the broad marketing strategy because they are the reason that people buy the drugs. So the disorders are promoted first and then the drugs to treat them are promoted next. I call this disease mongering. The market for drugs increases whenever psychiatry can get away with claiming that it has discovered a new disorder or found that an existing disorder is more common than previously believed. This enables a psychiatrist to tell a patient 'You need to take antidepressant A or antipsychotic B.'"

"Are you saying that psychiatry groups symptoms into clusters and then names each cluster a separate disorder, and that this results in people buying more medications?"

"That's what I'm saying. Psychiatry doesn't do this by itself. Psychiatry works hand-in-hand with the pharmaceutical industry. Once upon a time, pharmaceutical companies created medications to fight diseases. That still happens, but it is a smaller percentage of what pharmaceutical companies do these days. Increasingly, a drugmaker works with psychiatry to create new imaginary disorders, or to redefine and rename existing disorders."

Attorney Grimes said, "Objection. Lack of foundation. Pure supposition."

Judge Fillmore said, "Dr. Stanton, you better lay a foundation for your beliefs about psychiatry redefining and renaming disorders, or else I will order the jury to disregard that part of your testimony."

"Yes, Your Honor. I will elaborate on the motive and will give examples."

Attorney Ferris said, "Please lay a foundation for your beliefs that drugs are marketed by persuading people that they have disorders they didn't suspect."

"Redefining and renaming disorders is a way to cause more people to believe they have a given condition. This in turn causes them to want to take psychiatric drugs for that condition. This enables pharmaceutical companies to sell the drugs that they already have in their inventory because they just happen—according to the drugmaker—to have the right chemical constituents for treating this newly discovered mental problem. In other words, the drugmaker wants to sell more of a given drug that it has a patent for, and the way to do that is to reward psychiatry for creating new disorders or for redefining existing ones so that it appears more people are afflicted. This broadens the market for the company's drugs and is done by listing supposed new disorders in the next edition of the *DSM*."

Attorney Smoot said, "Objection. What was just said is conclusory, not foundational."

Judge Fillmore said, "Dr. Stanton, break this down for us. What you're saying seems a little too weird. A little too conspiratorial. Does the American Psychiatric Association and the pharmaceutical industry really rig a system to induce the American public to buy and consume drugs they don't need?"

"They do. They use the fact that people exhibit a wide range of variation to life's difficulties. Psychiatrists make the more extreme of those variable responses look like symptoms. They medicalize normal responses. This expands the diagnostic boundaries of existing disorders.

"It's psychiatry that votes a disease into existence. And then they list that disease in their best-selling *DSM*. Here's how the overall process works.

"The pharmaceutical industry, which many refer to as Big Pharma, has great influence over psychiatry through various means of rewarding the individual doctors. Most of the psychiatrists on the *DSM* panels receive grant money from the pharmaceutical industry. And many APA members work for the pharmaceutical industry. There's lots of cross pollination. Some call it incest."

Both Smoot and Grimes rose and said "Objection." Smoot sat down.

Grimes said, "We object to the derisive term 'incest.'"

Judge Fillmore asked, "In what sense did you use the term 'incest?'"

Witness Stanton said, "One definition of incest is 'excessively close and resistant to outside influence.' That is the sense in which I used the term."

The judge said, "Were you implying sexual relations between psychiatrists and drugmakers?"

"I would never do that."

"Objection overruled. Attorney Ferris, you can resume your examination."

Ferris said, "Please finish describing how the boundaries of so-called mental disorders are expanded to create new markets for psychotropic drugs."

Dr. Stanton said, "To bolster the sale of drugs, in the last three decades, psychiatrists began creating mental disorders. As I said, they take advantage of human variability in responding to various stressors. They made extreme but normal individual variations into disorders.

"Here are some examples of normal human qualities that the American Psychiatric Association and Big Pharma have turned into disorders that call for drug treatment. In the *DSM*, shyness, an ordinary human condition, is now social anxiety disorder. And GlaxoSmithKline advertises that Paxil is the best treatment. How many of our jurors were shy as kids or may still be shy? I wouldn't recommend that they take powerful Paxil but if they went to a psychiatrist, they probably would walk out of the office with a prescription for that drug.

"Let's consider the healthy person who is aging and sometimes forgetful. That describes a lot of people. Does the *DSM* call this condition forgetfulness? No. *DSM-IV* calls it minor neurocognitive impairment. And drugmakers promote medication to treat this condition.

"Overeating became binge eating disorder. The *DSM* authors have vivid imaginations.

"A few decades ago, psychiatrists decided the name manic-depressive disorder lacked appeal. So they renamed the malady bipolar disorder, thinking that more people would be willing to admit they have the condition. Bipolar sounds more socially acceptable than manic-depressive disorder. So sometimes names are changed to make problems sound worse and sometimes to make them less stigmatizing. The name chosen depends on what will boost drug sales.

"In the past, doctors didn't think that infants and children suffered from manic-depressive disorder. Well, psychiatry now asserts that childhood bipolar disorder is common and thus children as young as two years are treated with antidepressants like Prozac and mood stabilizers like Depakote.

"How could any psychiatrist determine that a two-year old still learning to talk has the grandiose ideas and euphoria of mania? Depression would be hard to detect with any level of medical certainty, while mania would be impossible."

Attorney Ferris said, "So your testimony is that the pharmaceutical industry tells the psychiatric industry that it could sell more drugs if disorders are invented or if the definitions of existing disorders are broadened to fit more people."

"That's what I'm saying. The *DSM* has become a best seller for the APA, so it's a major source of funds. All the courts must buy the new edition so they can decide what sentence to give a convicted person. Whether a person was insane when a crime was committed depends largely on the language of the current issue of the *DSM*. It's amazing that psychiatrists casting votes for or against supposed diseases can influence the fates of millions of US citizens for years to come.

"Police departments buy the newest edition, as do insurance carriers because they use the *DSM* in deciding which so-called disorders they should cover. Some critics say the *DSM* should be titled, *How to Bill an Insurance Company*. So it is in the APA's interest to invent new disorders, to prepare new *DSM* editions, and to sell lots of books. *DSM-IV-TR (Text Revision)*, issued in the year 2000, describes 365 mental disorders, up from the 106 disorders that existed in 1952 when *DSM-I* was published. Did scientists the likes of Louis Pasteur really discover 259 bona fide disorders in those forty-eight years? No, instead the APA cooked the books to maximize profits.

"Back to my examples. The current *DSM* says the diagnosis of major depressive disorder is generally not given unless bereavement symptoms are still present two months after the loss. Imagine that. After only two months, if the survivor is still sad, psychiatrists may diagnose him or her as clinically depressed.

"But that isn't good enough for the enterprising American Psychiatric Association, the owner of the *DSM* series. A new panel of experts is developing rationale for shortening the time that the next *DSM* will claim is the normal grieving period. A shorter period will greatly increase the market for antidepressants. This raises the question: Is the panel's assignment to honestly try to sort out what might be bereavement from what might be depression? Or is the actual assignment to increase the number of potential consumers of psychiatric drugs?"

Chapter 46

Juror Number Nine

While teaching, I also worked undercover in the lower courts by saying I was a young law teacher wanting experience in criminal law. The judges were happy to assist me but what I learned was how corrupt the lower courts were. Judges were accepting money right in the courtroom.

—Samuel Dash
(Chief Counsel for the Watergate Committee)

Back in his Long Beach office, Grimes pushed a button on his desktop phone and asked Paul Warren's secretary for an audience with the regional vice president. Thirty minutes later he entered Warren's office.

Before Grimes could speak, Warren asked, "How's the Vincent trial going?"

"Pretty well, but Stanton scored points with the jury."

"Janet will rein her in."

"The Judge gave Stanton too much leeway. Paul, I'm asking you to talk with her over the weekend."

Warren asked, "Did Clifford document what happened?"

"Here's what Clifford took down."

THE MIND DOCTOR

Grimes passed the mini-transcript to his superior, excused himself, and left. The Noyes record revealed a lapse in the judge's vigilance.

Warren used a cell phone having prepaid minutes. He would dispose of the phone after using it a few times. He placed a call and spoke with Judge Fillmore. Then he called a hotel in San Diego and reserved a room.

It was 117 miles from Alphatron's Regional Headquarters in Long Beach to the Manchester Grand Hyatt in San Diego. For short trips, Warren preferred a limousine over a helicopter or lear jet. He had used the same chauffer for years.

They checked into the hotel. Paul made himself at home in a suite with a view of San Diego Bay. He lounged in his pajamas and smoking jacket, sipping a mixed drink.

The doorbell rang. Warren opened the door to a smiling Janet Fillmore. Her casual clothes suggested she was enjoying her weekend.

"Hello, Vice President Warren. We meet again."

"Come in, Your Honor."

Paul fixed a martini for his guest.

"Janet, Grimes felt that you allowed Stanton too much discretion yesterday. She raised tough issues for our expert witnesses. It might be better to prevent some of these issues from coming up rather than count on Rice and Westlake for damage control."

"The jury will get suspicious if I constrain Stanton too much. I know what I'm doing."

Paul said, "I'm sure you do, but we would rather coast to a comfortable win than for you to have to do something heroic in the last phases of the trial."

"What specifically is Grimes worried about?"

Paul handed Janet a copy of Clifford Noyes' unofficial transcript.

"Leonard is concerned that you gave Stanton too much leeway in raising issues that our forensic witnesses might be unable to refute. All those *DSM* examples of new or redefined psychiatric disorders really made pharmaceutical companies and psychiatry seem crooked and in cahoots."

"That was just background noise," Janet said. "Stanton didn't say that Thein created psychiatric disorders to increase sales of Alphatron's drugs. She merely said that unnamed industry leaders do such things."

"I know, but nonetheless some jurors could get a low opinion of the accused, lumping all drugmakers and psychiatrists together. Stanton knew what she was doing."

Janet said, "Michelle Stanton is an effective witness. The jury wouldn't like it if I muzzled her in an obvious way. I have to be careful or my partiality could be grounds for the plaintiffs to win an appeal."

"You have a tough job, but we're worried."

"As a judge in open court, I must give the impression that I'm objective. But you can count on me."

"I know we can. I just thought we ought to examine our options."

"Did Alphatron bribe juror number nine like I recommended? He's desperate since he's unemployed and has a wife and kids. Once deliberations begin, of course, there are no longer any legal restraints against advocacy. He can sway the other jurors by immediately taking a position while they're still trying to make up their minds."

"One of my people arranged for a private detective to offer Number Nine a bribe. He jumped at the offer. He'll argue for Thein, Alphatron, and the county."

Janet said, "I can't see why you're worried. Does Smoot or Grimes know about the bribed juror?"

"I saw no reason to tell them."

"Good. Stop worrying. Let's diddle and then watch the TV movie, *Mind Control, My Mother, The CIA, and LSD*."

Chapter 47

The Judge Seeks Advice

The Golden Rule. The one with the gold rules.

—American saying

Attorney Ferris called Dr. Thein to the witness box.

"Please state your name and occupation for the record."

"My name is David Thein, T-h-e-i-n. 'Thein' rhymes with 'gain.' I am a board-certified psychiatrist employed by the Riverside County Community Mental Health Center."

"Are you a United States citizen?"

"Yes."

"Have you always been a US citizen?"

"No. I was born in Burma, which the government renamed Myanmar in 1989. I was a citizen there."

"What was your date of birth?"

"February 3, 1965."

Attorney Ferris asked, "What was your name in Burma?"

"Maunt Thein."

"When did you come to the United States?"

"August 1988."

"Why did you relocate to this country?"

"Most of my life I wanted to live in the United States. In August 1988, there was great civil unrest in Burma, which the government suppressed with violence, killing many people, most of them by gunfire. It was a good time to leave."

Muffled laughter came from the spectators and a few of the jurors.

"Thousands of other citizens also left the country, both before and after me."

"Did you go to medical school in Burma?"

"Yes."

"Please describe that training."

"I received comprehensive training at the Institute of Medicine Number 1, Rangoon. I served a year of supervised medical work at the Rangoon Psychiatric Hospital. And for four years I was a psychiatrist in a remote part of Burma near the border with Thailand. The nearest village of any size, Mae Sot, is actually in Thailand. I cared for the mentally ill in refugee camps. I also fulfilled a three-year residency at the psychiatric department of the biggest general hospital in Mandalay."

"You said you received comprehensive training at the Institute of Medicine Number 1 in Rangoon. Was your training disrupted by civil uprisings and repeated closure of the university? I understand that Ne Win, then the dictator of Burma, severely limited the budget for education, including medical education."

"Prime Minister Ne Win favored medical and engineering schools, and allowed them to operate. My training was not compromised by government closures or lack of funding."

Ferris said, "What did your father do for a living?"

Smoot objected.

"It is immaterial what Dr. Thein's father did for a living. That kind of question might have been appropriate in a deposition, but we have to narrow our focus in this trial. We need to examine what took place in Riverside County during the six months that Barry Vincent was Dr. Thein's patient."

Judge Fillmore said, "Objection sustained. Counsel Ferris, this is not the time to go on a fishing expedition. We do not care what Dr. Thein's father did in Burma or Myanmar as it is now called. Confine yourself to the issues at hand.

"You've worn me out. Time for lunch."

At lunch, Jack Vincent asked, "Raymond, why were you interested in Thein's father?"

"In preparing for this case, I read extensively about the Burma that existed when Maunt Thein lived there. I put together an interesting if vague scenario. There are no family last names in Burma, but sometimes people choose similar names if they want to show kinship. We know that our doctor's name in Burma was Maunt Thein and that his father's name is Maunt Saw. The records that I was able to access describe a Maunt Saw who was an assassin working for the dictator, Ne Win. I found these records only recently, and didn't have time to confirm that Thein's father is the same Maunt Saw who worked for Ne Win, but I think he is.

"I would like to link Thein with Saw, and insinuate that the son could have learned some criminal practices from his dad. But the Judge was right. I was on a fishing expedition, and Smoot was quick to pull me up short. I don't mind. Even if I had linked the two Burmese men, it wouldn't have been evidence that Thein overmedicated Barry. I would have been smearing Thein's reputation on account of his father's misdeeds. Not the sort of thing I should engage in."

"Smoot's quick reaction to your question," Jack said, "suggests that Thein's father could be the notorious assassin. I can see why the defense attorneys would want to keep that information from the jury."

After lunch, Attorney Ferris said, "Dr. Thein, you still are under oath, sworn to tell the truth."

"I always tell the truth. My father was very strict about truth telling. He set a wonderful example, and brought me up to always tell the truth. Even though we lived in Burma, one of my father's heroes was the American President Abraham Lincoln. He urged me to model myself after Honest Abe."

Ferris said, "The Judge told me to not discuss your father so I won't ask about the example he set for you. We need to discuss the administration of medications to your deceased patient, Barry Vincent."

THE JUDGE SEEKS ADVICE

"I understand."

"I am handing you some papers. Please look them over and tell me what they are."

Taking his time, Thein examined each word.

"These are copies of the medical records that I wrote during each of Barry Vincent's office visits."

"From my reading of your medical charts for Barry, I believe you saw him over a period of six months and that during that time you saw him seven times. Do those numbers sound right?"

"Yes."

"During Barry's first office visit, you increased the dosage of the Zyprexa, Paxil, and Cogentin that Dr. Margaret Gross had prescribed for him. Is that correct?"

"Yes. I reported that information on these medical charts."

"How much did you increase the dosages?"

"I increased them substantially because Dr. Gross had prescribed doses so low that the medications could not possibly have helped Mr. Vincent."

"Yet Barry did very well under her care for six years. How do you explain that?"

Thein said, "Maybe he didn't do as well as she claimed."

"Come on, his parents also said he did real well during that time and worsened after he became your patient."

"Maybe they are not being truthful."

Attorney Ferris said, "Specifically, how much did you increase the dosages? Give me some numbers. Did you double the doses? Triple them?"

"I increased the dosages substantially because they were so ridiculously low."

"According to my arithmetic, you increased the dose of each medication six fold. Is that correct?"

Thein asked the court attendant for a calculator. He then checked the Ferris' statement against the figures in Barry's medical charts.

After a few minutes, he said, "Yes. I happened to raise each dose six fold."

Attorney Ferris said, "That sounds like a very arbitrary thing to do. How could raising the dosages of three different medications by a factor of six have been precisely the right thing to do pharmacologically? Each drug was designed to act on the central nervous system in a different way, by different neurological pathways."

"I studied how much to raise each drug. It just happened to be six fold for each of them. That was just coincidence. You messed around with the numbers, looking for anything that you could claim was a problem."

Ferris said, "Then what method did you use to determine how much to raise each drug?"

"I read the package inserts and medical literature."

"Was raising all the dosages at the same time a safe thing to do on Barry's first office visit? Couldn't those increases have been a terrible shock to his neurological systems?"

"Not when the doses were so low to begin with. It was like he was not on any medication at all."

"Could that have been evidence that good mental health doesn't always depend on medication, that there are other factors involved such as a good doctor-patient relationship?"

Thein said, "The main determinant is the medications the patient is taking."

"But raising the doses sixfold resulted in large amounts. And since you elevated them from a very low level, Barry might not have built up any tolerance to the drugs before you upped the doses. If he had acquired no tolerance and was suddenly taking large doses, perhaps you loaded him with more than he could handle."

Thein said, "I did not hear a question."

"Is it your standard practice to prescribe medications for your patients on the first office visit?"

"If the patient appears to be in psychiatric distress, I prescribe medications on the first visit. And other staff psychiatrists at the county mental health center do the same."

"But isn't a six-fold increase of three central nervous system medications an unusually large increase?"

THE JUDGE SEEKS ADVICE

"You do not know anything about psychotropic medications. Your questions are naive."

Attorney Smoot said, "Objection. Your Honor, Counselor is both testifying and arguing with the witness."

Judge Fillmore said, "It's time to move along, Attorney Ferris. You can continue to pursue the amounts of medications at issue, but you need to move on from this specific issue of what happened on the first office visit regarding increased doses."

"Yes, Your Honor," Ferris said. "Dr. Thein, have you read the medical charts that Dr. Gross maintained regarding Barry's treatment over the six-year period before she transferred him to you?"

"I read Dr. Gross's records before I ever saw Mr. Vincent for the first time."

"Oh? Or did you read them more recently, in preparation for this trial?"

"I read them before I ever saw Mr. Vincent in person."

"OK. Do you recall the last medical chart that Dr. Gross completed for Barry? The one that she wrote out the last time she saw him?"

"I read it. Without the records in front of me, I do not remember which record said what."

"I am handing you what I believe to be a true copy of the last medical chart that Dr. Gross filled out for Barry Vincent. Is this a valid copy of what you read?"

"Yes. This appears to be one of Dr. Gross's records."

"Please read aloud this summary section regarding Barry Vincent."

Thein read, "As required by California regulations, I have thoroughly examined the health of my patient, Barry Vincent, to ensure that he can be safely transferred to another professional care provider. This summarizes Barry's condition. He is in good spirits today. He talked about his birthday which is coming in two days. He said he will celebrate.

"He says he is doing well. Compliant with medications. Denies anxiety. Denies paranoia. Denies depression. Denies suicide ideation.

Denies homicide ideation. Sleeping ten hours per night. Appetite has remained good. Tardive dyskinesia is absent. Denies side effects."

Attorney Ferris said, "Does that sound like someone who needed more medications?"

"Mr. Vincent was very sick when he came to me. He was suffering psychosis—hallucinations and delusions. He wore a baseball cap and dark glasses during our get-acquainted session. He believed someone had replaced his brain with someone else's. He was not eating or sleeping well. He was so sleep deprived that it impaired his decision-making ability."

"Are you familiar with medical literature regarding transferring of patients from one psychiatrist to another?"

Thein said, "No, I have not read on that particular topic."

"Did you talk with Dr. Gross about Barry before she transferred him to you?"

"I did not."

"When Barry came to his first appointment with you, and you allege that he was very sick, did you consider recommending that Dr. Gross keep him as her patient until he was doing better?"

"No. I felt it was my responsibility to restore his health."

Ferris asked, "Are you aware that it is against state regulations to transfer a patient within the community health system from one psychiatrist to another if that patient's symptoms are flaring?"

"It was Dr. Margret Gross who transferred Mr. Vincent to me. She is my supervisor. I did not think I should object, but should help him as much as I could."

"How do you reconcile Dr. Gross's description of Barry as doing exceedingly well and your description of a very sick man?"

"Either Mr. Vincent misled Dr. Gross, or else he got very ill between the time she last saw him and the time I first saw him roughly thirty days later."

"I am handing you a copy of the medical record that you prepared regarding your interactions with Barry on his second office visit with you. Do you believe this document is in fact that record?"

"Yes. This appears to be a copy of my record for Mr. Vincent's second office visit."

THE JUDGE SEEKS ADVICE

"Please read this record to yourself and then tell us any adjustments in medications that you may have made during Barry's second visit."

"I increased the doses of Zyprexa, Paxil, and Cogentin. And I added Abilify and Luvox."

"Is Zyprexa an antipsychotic?"

"Yes."

"Is Abilify an antipsychotic?"

"Yes, Abilify is an antipsychotic. So what?"

Ferris said, "Well, Zyprexa is an antipsychotic and you raised its dose during the first and second office visits. Why did you not wait to see if the increased dose relieved Barry's symptoms before adding a second antipsychotic?"

"Mr. Vincent was a very sick man. The United States Food and Drug Administration approved Abilify as an adjunct antipsychotic to be used with other antipsychotics that the patient is already taking."

Ferris said, "OK, Abilify is an adjunct medication. But if the increased dose of Zyprexa had worked, Abilify would not have been needed. Was it wise to increase the dose of Zyprexa and to add Abilify at the same time?"

"I wanted to make Mr. Vincent well as soon as possible."

"You alleged that Barry was suffering psychosis. If his symptoms had improved, how would you have assessed whether the improvement was due to the Zyprexa or the Abilify?"

Thein said, "I would have figured it did not matter. If he was doing better, I would be happy that my medications and I were responsible."

"What if Barry's condition had immediately worsened? You would not have known whether Zyprexa or Abilify was at fault."

"I would not have suspected either medication caused the problem. The problem is always the underlying mental disorder."

"Nevertheless, a basic rule in experimentation is to change only one variable at a time. If you change more than one at a time, you can't be sure which change brought about the results."

Thein said, "I was not experimenting. I was treating Mr. Barry Vincent for mental illnesses."

"You were experimenting when you added one drug after another and increased dosages as well."

Smoot, red-faced, rose and said, "Objection. Counsel is testifying and arguing with the witness."

Judge Fillmore said, "Attorney Ferris, after you make your point, don't belabor it. Just move on to the next point that you hope to make."

Ferris said, "Yes, Your Honor. That's what I will do.

"Dr. Thein, you just now testified that you increased the dose of Paxil and added a new drug, Luvox. Are both Paxil and Luvox antidepressants in the same class of selective serotonin reuptake inhibitors?"

"Yes, both medications are what we in the medical profession call SSRIs."

"Why did you add Luvox before you found out if the increased dose of Paxil would relieve the clinical depression that you claim Barry was experiencing?"

"Mr. Vincent was very sick and I wanted to get him relief as soon as possible."

Ferris said, "But can't these drugs have adverse interactions that you should have tried to avoid?"

"At every office visit, I asked Mr. Vincent if he was experiencing side effects."

"Is that an adequate way to detect side effects or adverse interactions? You were simply going by what the patient said on the spur of the moment."

"That is exactly the way the other psychiatrists at the county clinic determine if there are problems caused by medications. They go by what the patient says and by their keen observations of his behavior. And that is what I did."

"You said you asked Barry Vincent at each office visit if he was experiencing side effects. What did he say?"

Thein said, "Mr. Vincent was a man of few words. During the first two office visits he said he was not experiencing side effects. In the third office visit he said he was highly energized. That is when I changed his diagnosis to schizoaffective disorder."

THE JUDGE SEEKS ADVICE

"At the time of the first office visit, Barry had not yet taken your prescribed medications so I can understand why he would not have suffered side effects. Could Barry's muted response to your questions during the second office visits have been because he was numb from being overmedicated? Did you consider that possibility?"

Smoot rose and said, "Objection. Testifying. Argumentative."

Judge Fillmore said, "Move on, Attorney Ferris."

Raymond said, "OK. Moving right along. Your third office visit with Barry was even more eventful than your first two sessions. This chart records that at the beginning of the third office visit, you were instructing Barry to take Zyprexa, Paxil, Cogentin, Abilify, and Luvox. Is that correct?"

"That's correct."

"The record that you hold says that on the third office visit you increased the dosages of each of those five drugs and added the anticonvulsant Gabicon. Is that correct?"

"Yes. So what? Many patients at the county mental health center are taking more than six medications and at doses higher than the ones shown on this chart."

Ferris said, "I don't doubt it. I have come to believe we should not use the other psychiatrists at the county center as our standard of care. The entire center is overdiagnosing and overtreating the patients. In the last five years, twelve of the center's patients completed suicide, and there are rumors that many more attempted to end their lives. We should compare your actions only with those of psychiatrists who have not been tainted by the county's pro-drug philosophy.

"The center's psychiatrists have been corrupted by pharmaceutical companies. Hell, Dr. Thein, an Alphatron drug rep is essentially your common law wife. Is she on assignment from corporate headquarters?"

Judge Fillmore stood up. "Attorney Ferris, sit down and shut up. Not another word.

"Ladies and gentlemen of the jury, I am releasing you for the rest of the day. Return here not later than eight-thirty tomorrow

THE MIND DOCTOR

morning. Court will begin at nine o'clock sharp. At that time I will tell you how we will proceed.

"The attorneys for the plaintiff and for the defendants will report to my chamber at once,"

The judge's chamber was much less formal than the courtroom. Judge Fillmore hung up her gown and put on a blue blazer. The lawyers loosened their neckties. The attorneys for the defendants struggled to suppress smirks.

Once everyone was seated, Judge Fillmore established eye contact with the plaintiff's attorney.

"Counselor Ferris, you blundered big time."

"Yes, Your Honor. I screwed up."

"I'm not going to waste time admonishing you. As big a blunder as it was, it doesn't necessarily mean the defendants have won their case. It means that I could declare a mistrial if the jurors' neutrality was damaged. That is the question at bay. I have to decide if a mistrial would be in the interest of justice."

Grimes asked, "What effect do you think Attorney Ferris' remarks had on the jurors?"

Fillmore said, "The answer to that question will determine my course of action. I ordered you counselors to meet with me primarily to inform you of how I will assess this issue. What steps I will take."

Smoot said, "Your Honor, do you intend to make up your mind by the time the jury reassembles tomorrow morning?"

"I think the thing for me to do is to ask each juror in private how Attorney Ferris' remarks affected him or her. If anyone is affected to a major extent I will ask if they can set aside any doubts that might have been raised and still make a fair decision. I could replace up to four jurors with alternates if the alternates have not been prejudiced.

"I will see you all in court in the morning."

The attorneys left the judge's chamber.

Janet turned on a compact stereo player to a Mozart symphony. She took a disposable cell phone from her purse, and used it to call Paul Warren's own disposable phone.

"Hi, Janet."

THE JUDGE SEEKS ADVICE

The judge whispered, "Hi, Paul. I need to tell you what happened in court just thirty minutes ago, and to ask what you want me to do about it. It may be a good thing for us."

"Go ahead and give me the lowdown."

"Right in front of the jury, Ferris said the standard of care that Dr. Thein has to meet has been corrupted by pharmaceutical companies, especially Alphatron. He the same as said that your company sent a woman to live with Dr. Thein and seduce him into prescribing Alphatron medications. He said that Alphatron has a cozy relationship with the county and that this results in county doctors prescribing harmful kinds and amounts of medications. He said that they do this for financial gain. And even worse, Ferris basically said the county clinic-Alphatron relationship caused twelve suicides and numerous suicide attempts in the last five years."

"He spewed this out in open court?"

"Yes. These remarks are grounds for me to declare a mistrial if I can get a few jurors to say their deliberative abilities were compromised. On the other hand, we could continue with this trial, and I could use Ferris' bias to make him look like a fanatic nutcase."

Paul said, "If you declare a mistrial what would the Vincents do? Would they call it a day and leave us alone?"

"That is a key question. I believe they would insist on a new trial. They seem as determined as any plaintiff I have ever presided over."

"And what are the chances we will win the case you are now trying? Do you think juror number nine will perform for us?"

"Yes, I think he will. The other evening you said that he gets the final payment only if the jury renders a decision favorable to the defendants. That's a powerful incentive."

Paul said, "Let's take this trial all the way to a verdict. Use Ferris's stupid remarks against him."

"Wilco. Thanks, Paul."

The next morning, Judge Fillmore addressed a packed courtroom.

"Yesterday, the plaintiff's attorney recklessly criticized the standard of care that prevails at the Riverside County Community Mental Health Center.

"What he said was not based on any findings of this court, and simply calls into question his state of mind.

What he said was not based on any findings of this court, and simply calls into question his state of mind. I am now ordering the jury to disregard Attorney Ferris' remarks regarding the medical standard of care. You are to disregard those remarks in both deliberation and decisionmaking.

"The trial will resume where we left off yesterday."

Chapter 48

The Twilight Zone

Those who suffer from serious psychoses make up one of the few segments of our societies whose life expectancy has declined over the past quarter of a century—one telling measure of the gap between psychiatry's pretensions and its performance.

—Andrew Scull
Madness in Civilization (2015)

Ferris called for Thein to return to the witness box.

"Dr. Thein, we are resuming our examination where we left off yesterday. You still are under oath. During the third office visit, you changed Barry's diagnosis from schizophrenia to schizoaffective disorder. How does schizoaffective disorder differ from schizophrenia?"

"Schizoaffective disorder has symptoms of schizophrenia plus symptoms of a mood disorder such as major depressive disorder or bipolar disorder."

"Which is generally the worse disease? Schizophrenia or schizoaffective disorder?"

Thein said, "When generalizing, one must be careful. Both disorders range from mild to severe, so a severe case of schizophrenia could be worse than a mild case of schizoaffective disorder. But in most instances, schizoaffective disorder is more serious because it is more complicated."

"Why did you change Barry's diagnosis from schizophrenia to schizoaffective disorder?"

"During his third office visit. Mr. Vincent said he had too much energy. I recognized that energy to be a symptom of the manic phase of bipolar disorder, and of course bipolar disorder is a serious mood abnormality. Since he already had a diagnosis of schizophrenia, he now had symptoms of both schizophrenia and a mood disorder."

Ferris asked, "Did you consider that Barry might have been suffering from akathisia, which is extreme restlessness almost always caused by medications?"

"No. I did not. That is a ridiculous notion. My fellow county doctors think the risk of akathisia is low."

"As of the date of your third office visit with Barry, had you read medical literature about akathisia?"

Thein said, "Certainly. I read enough to learn that the pharmaceutical industry does not consider akathisia a serious problem for patients like Mr. Vincent."

"Do drug companies refer to akathisia in the labels of their products?"

Thein said, "The label for a prescription medication includes far more than what is said on the little sticker on the medicine vial. The label includes all the background information that a drugmaker generates during clinical testing of a drug proposed for market. The Food and Drug Administration requires pharmaceutical companies to turn over all the data from all the clinical trials, and any correspondence regarding the drug. All of that information constitutes the label.

"You can read the label for drugs like Paxil, Zyprexa, and Gabicon, and you will rarely find mention of akathisia as a possible side effect."

"Did you conclude that the scant mention of the word 'akathisia' means it is a rare condition?"

"Yes. It must be rare. Otherwise I would have found more mention of it in the labels that I read."

"Could there have been some other reason for drugmakers to not use the word 'akathisia?'"

"I cannot think of any other reason."

Ferris asked, "Is it possible that pharmaceutical companies rarely mention akathisia because medical literature links the condition to homicide and suicide? Is it possible the companies censor their warning labels so the pubic won't associate their drugs with akathisia, a term synonymous with violent acts?"

"I do not see how that would be possible. Firstly, pharmaceutical companies are very open, very honest. Secondly, if akathisia were common, there would be no way to hide that fact."

"When you read the labels of the drugs you prescribed for Barry, did you come across terms like agitated, jittery, nervous, jumpy, anxious, and restless?"

"Such terms are used in the labels. So what?"

Ferris asked, "Could such terms be euphemisms for akathisia?"

"Euphemisms? What are euphemisms?"

"A euphemism is a word that makes something seem less severe. It is often a bad idea to use euphemisms. Most of the time we should call a spade a spade."

"What does a spade have to do with akathisia? First you say akathisia is a euphemism then you say it is a spade. You seem confused. You should have your head examined."

The jury and spectators laughed. Judge Fillmore covered her mouth.

"Your medical chart for Barry's third office visit says that after you diagnosed schizoaffective disorder, you prescribed Gabicon. But your notes are cryptic and your handwriting is hard to read. Did you specifically intend to treat schizoaffective disorder with this anticonvulsant?"

"Yes."

Attorney Ferris asked, "Were you aware that the FDA had approved Gabicon only for treating partial complex seizures?"

"Yes. I was aware of that. But as a medical doctor I can prescribe medications off-label. We have established that fact several times during this trial."

"Except that in this case the FDA sent you and many other US doctors letters saying that unless the patient was already taking other epilepsy drugs that lower Gabicon's potency, this medication could cause seizures instead of preventing them."

Judge Fillmore said, "You've brought up that point before. Move along, Attorney Ferris."

"Dr. Thein, you have testified that increasing dosages and adding new drugs was justified because Barry Vincent was very ill. Tell us exactly how ill he was."

"He was sleep deprived. He was losing weight. He showed signs of thought blocking, hallucinations, delusions, agitation, and mood swings. He thought aliens had replaced his brain with one of their citizen's. He was very, very sick and did not make sense when he talked to me."

"Did he give informed consent for you to raise dosages and add drugs?"

"Of course he did. His records include signed consent forms."

"With Barry being so sick, how could he have had the capacity to give informed consent, the capacity to understand the possible consequences of the medications you were prescribing?"

"From the beginning of my treatment, Mr. Vincent always was remarkably clear on the fact that my medications were helping him live in the community."

"Let me see if I understand your testimony. You said Barry was very sick. That he was sleep deprived. That he was hallucinating and suffering delusions. That he believed he possessed the brain of a space alien, that he spoke gibberish to you. Is that your testimony?"

"Yes. He desperately needed medication."

Ferris said, "But you also testified that Barry was able to give informed consent. Is that correct?"

"Yes. Mr. Vincent gave informed consent. And the medical records include consent forms signed by him. He signed a consent form at every office visit."

"So Barry was so sick that you felt compelled to raise dosages and add new drugs. But he wasn't too sick to understand the consequences of those drugs, and therefore gave informed consent."

"Mr. Vincent was very sick, but he understood the medication changes I prescribed and he signed a consent form during every office visit. Those signed forms are in his medical records."

"Dr. Thein, have you seen the television show, *The Twilight Zone*?"

"I have seen it. It has nothing to do with what we are talking about."

"Your honor, I would like your permission to read a dictionary definition of *twilight zone*."

Attorney Ferris handed the dictionary to Judge Fillmore who asked the court reporter to record the reference information. The judge looked at the definition and gave the defense attorneys opportunity to read it. She then asked that the dictionary be returned to Ferris.

"Permission granted."

"Dr. Thein, I'm going to read a dictionary definition of twilight zone. One sense of the term is *the lowest level of the ocean to which light can penetrate*. That is a meaning relative to the physical world. But we're interested in the psychological sense, which is *a conceptual area that is undefined, uncertain, or intermediate*."

Thein said, "Your questioning is stupid, The television show's make-believe zone does not even exist."

"But you placed your patient, Barry Vincent, in just such a nonexistent zone. In your assessment, he was so sick that you had to medicate him excessively, but at the same time he was clearheaded enough to give you informed consent so you could medicate him even more. You claim that he was in a terrible fog, actually deranged, but at the same time coherent enough to understand exactly the risks that your drugs posed. You're trying to have it both ways. Sounds like The Twilight Zone to me."

"You twisted my words."

"No further questions."

Chapter 49

Neuroleptics or Antipsychotics?

From 1955 to 1963, neuroleptics were recast in the minds of doctors and the public from agents that could help stabilize people suffering a psychotic episode into safe, effective antischizophrenic pills.

—Robert Whitaker
Mad in America: Bad Science, Bad Medicine, and Enduring Mistreatment of the Mentally Ill (2002)

Ferris called Alphatron's expert witness to testify. Thomas Prescott watched from the gallery as psychiatrist Byron Westlake made his way to the witness box. He had gained weight and looked much older than when Thomas had last spotted him two years earlier at an upscale restaurant in Riverside. His three-piece suit was tailored to accommodate his expansive midsection.

Thomas wished that Westlake's lavish life style would net him a heart attack. Then he regretted harboring such thoughts.

Thomas was trying hard to rise above Westlake's level. He was trying to follow the advice of nineteenth-century philosopher Friedrich Nietzsche to not become the monster you are fighting. Thomas decided to comply with Nietzsche's edict by wishing merely that Westlake would blunder in his testimony and fail to protect Alphatron's corrupt business enterprise.

NEUROLEPTICS OR ANTIPSYCHOTICS?

After the drugmaker's expert was sworn in, Ferris asked, "Dr. Westlake, is it possible to prescribe too much of a neuroleptic drug like Thorazine, Haldol, or Zyprexa?"

"Of course it's possible. But don't call them neuroleptics. That's an obsolete term that we psychiatrists no longer use. Thorazine, Haldol, and Zyprexa are antipsychotic medications."

"When you say 'we psychiatrists,' do you mean all psychiatrists everywhere regardless of whether they are in practice, academia, or government? Regardless of where they got their medical training and who they associate with?"

Westlake said, "Well, no. But I am speaking of the vast majority of psychiatrists, especially those who actually treat patients and prescribe medications."

"So prescribers call them antipsychotics while some other medical professionals call them neuroleptics. Is that correct?"

"That's right, except that the psychiatrists who call the medications antipsychotics far outnumber those who insist on using the misnomer neuroleptics."

"Why do you and like-minded psychiatrists refer to the drugs as antipsychotics instead of neuroleptics?"

"Because we are enlightened and understand pharmacology and that these miracle drugs reduce psychosis in mentally ill patients."

"Which term came first—'neuroleptic' or 'antipsychotic?'"

"Neuroleptic," Westlake said. "And 'tranquilizer' or 'major tranquilizer' was another term that was used then but is little used today."

"When did the term 'neuroleptic' come into use?"

"About 1955. A couple of French psychiatrists gave that name to chlorpromazine and some other chemically related drugs."

Ferris asked, "When did psychiatrists with your perspective start to refer to the drugs as antipsychotics instead of neuroleptics?"

"About 1964. The National Institute of Mental Health published an influential report about schizophrenics in nine hospitals who were treated with these medications. The benefits to the patients were marvelous, so NIMH said the medications were truly antischizophrenic agents. From that point on, 'antipsychotic' began to replace 'neuroleptic' and 'tranquillizer.'"

"Why do some psyciatrists cling to the term 'neuroleptic?'"

Westlake said, "In my opinion, they are uninformed or misinformed."

"But what reasons do they give?"

"That the medications are either ineffective or unsafe."

"So some doctors and researchers say drugs like Thorazine, Haldol, and Zyprexa have dangerous side effects?"

"Well, yes, they say that. And there are some adverse side effects if the patient doesn't follow the doctor's directions. But those who persist in using the term 'neuroleptic' overstate the risks and understate the benefits."

"What does 'neuroleptic' mean?"

"The word comes from the Ancient Greek language. It means to seize the nervous system, but this is not at all what happens. There's no seizing of anything. What's your hang up with this subject anyway? Whether we say 'antipsychotic' or 'neuroleptic' or 'tranquilizer' has nothing to do with why Barry Vincent committed suicide."

"I'll ask the questions. Alphatron Pharmaceuticals put you forth as an expert on psychiatric medications, and these questions are in that realm."

Attorney Ferris checked his notes.

"I have only a couple more questions in this line. What happened between about 1955 when the French psychiatrists coined the term 'neuroleptic' and about 1964 when that term began to be replaced by 'antipsychotic'?"

"I told you. The evidence kept coming in that these medications were safe and effective. The most influential study was the one that I just referred to which was funded by the National Institute of Mental Health, and which was conducted in 1963 and was published in 1964."

Ferris said, "Yes, you told me. I should have constructed a better question. Here's what I should have asked: From the mid 1950s to the mid 1960s, did the pharmaceutical industry aggressively promote chlorpromazine, also known as Thorazine?"

"Sure. It was the industry's right to advertise. This is America, you know."

"Was chlorpromazine the first drug in this class for the FDA to approve for marketing in the United States?"

"Yes. The FDA approved chlorpromazine in March 1954, and two months later Smith, Kline & French introduced it onto the US market under the trade name Thorazine."

Ferris asked, "Was Thorazine initially approved as a treatment for psychosis?"

"No. At first it was approved as an antivomiting agent."

"Why not for treating hallucinations and delusions?"

"The pharmaceutical company was in a hurry to get it on the market, and it had not been adequately tested for treating disorders like schizophrenia."

"So how much time passed after it appeared on the market before Thorazine was used to treat psychosis?"

"Oh, there was no delay," Westlake said. "There was a huge need for an antipsychotic, and so doctors immediately prescribed it for that purpose, especially in the mental asylums."

"But how did it happen that Thorazine was immediately used to treat mental illnesses when the FDA had approved it for use as an anti-emetic only?"

"I don't know," Westlake said.

"But at that time, early 1954, when Thorazine was approved for the U.S. market, it was not referred to as an antipsychotic."

"You're right."

"At that time Thorazine and other phenothiazines were called neuroleptics. Is that right?"

"Almost. As I said a minute ago, it was in 1955 that two French psychiatrists coined the term neuroleptics for chlorpromazine and its chemical cousins. So in 1954, in the United States, chlorpromazine or Thorazine was referred to as a major tranquilizer."

"How much did Smith, Kline & French advertise and promote Thorazine in the early years after its introduction?"

"The company promoted it assertively and successfully in every state."

"Is it possible," Ferris asked, "that Smith, Kline & French promotions had a significant impact on how physicians and the pub-

THE MIND DOCTOR

lic viewed Thorazine? That the company caused the view to change over the years from neuroleptic to antipsychotic? Remember, you are under oath."

"The company wanted its medication to be seen in a positive light, and its advertising campaign was assertive. So yes, the advertising and promoting helped doctors and the public to see more innovative ways that Thorazine could be used."

"So would you admit that Smith, Kline and other pharmaceutical companies promoted long and hard for Thorazine and other new drugs to be referred to as antipsychotics rather than neuroleptics? I have with me several medical journal advertisements that say this very thing."

"I concede the point, but I don't see what that has to be with any connection between Alphatron and Barry Vincent."

"Just answer my questions and don't worry about my end of this business. I am now turning from the pharmaceutical advertising that helped cause practitioners and the public to automatically think of the new drugs as antipsychotics instead of neuroleptics. We will discuss how the pharmaceutical industry during the fifties, sixties, and seventies affected the content of both the news media like the *New York Times* and the medical literature such as the *Journal of Clinical Psychiatry* to help transform problematic neuroleptics into miraculous antipsychotics."

Grimes said, "Objection. Attorney Ferris has been on a fishing expedition for the last hour. Now he wants to launch a whole new flotilla including cannery ships."

"The attorneys are to come forward for a sidebar," Judge Fillmore said.

The attorneys huddled around the judge's desk as she switched off her microphone.

"Counselor Ferris, what do you hope to show with this new line of questioning that you so clumsily announced?"

"I want to demonstrate that drugs like Thorazine, Haldol, Zyprexa, and more truly are not antipsychotics but are neuroleptics. I want to show that there have not been scientific advancements but simply propaganda and misinformation designed to make these dangerous drugs look miraculous like penicillin or insulin. The transformation was through massive advertising and misrepresentation, not science and technology. And I want to show that pharmaceutical companies did this by using their vast wealth to the detriment of the public. Having provided that context, I then will show that Alphatron has done the same kind of deceptive promotion, especially regarding Gabicon."

Grimes said, "What he proposes is too far afield. It's not specific to the claims he made in his core complaint."

"Objection sustained. Attorney Ferris, choose a more specific line of inquiry or withdraw your complaint."

Chapter 50

The Chemical Imbalance Hypothesis

It may surprise you to learn that there is no convincing evidence that most mental patients have any chemical imbalance... The theories have changed very little over the years despite much evidence that they cannot possibly be correct.

—Elliot S. Valenstein
Blaming the Brain (1998)

After court recessed for the day, Thomas reached Attorney Ferris by phone.

"Ray, Westlake caused my brother to take his own life by persuading my parents that Louis needed heavy doses of psychiatric drugs. Westlake was persuasive primarily because he told and retold the myth that mental illness results from chemical imbalances in the brain. He sold Mom and Dad on the fallacy before they ever heard any counter arguments. They started to question the chemical-imbalance hypothesis soon after Louis died, but didn't learn just how unscientific it is until the wrongful death trial in which you represented them.

"Now, all these years later, Alphatron is still using this counterfeit hypothesis as a ploy to sell drugs. Since Westlake is scheduled to testify again tomorrow, you might have an opportunity to expose the dishonesty of this marketing strategy."

"That's my intent," Ferris said. "First, I'll need to get Thein to say under oath that in prescribing medication for Barry, he was guided by the chemical imbalance hypothesis. I am confident I can do that. Then maybe I can discredit the concept by outsmarting Westlake. But it won't be easy. He has peddled this imbalance notion for a lot of years. He wants the jury to believe the hypothesis is good science.

"I'll have Michelle testify just before and after Westlake. I hope the contrast between his overly simplistic, reductionist sales tactic and her scientific analysis will cause the jury to reject the chemical imbalance hypothesis. Michelle will bring in context and confounding factors that any scientific hypothesis must take into account."

"That's all anyone can do. Thanks, Ray."

Ferris called his own expert witness to the stand to help him set the stage for the questions he would ask Alphatron's expert.

"Good morning, Dr. Stanton. You are still under oath. I will ask you a few questions about the anatomy and functioning of part of the human nervous system. We will focus on only the network of neurons or nerve cells that we all have in our brains. This is not an overview of the entire nervous system, but just the specific part of it that the psychopharmaceutical industry says is key to understanding what causes mental illnesses such as schizophrenia and clinical depression.

"In other words, we will examine neurons, the spaces between neurons which are called synapses, and neurotransmitters which are chemical substances within the synapses."

"I understand."

Ferris said, "Your Honor, I have a large diagram that depicts two interacting nerve cells. This drawing is listed as one of the exhibits that I intended to use in court therefore defense counsels were duly notified. I would like to have an exhibit number assigned and permission to post the chart where the jurors can see it."

The judge approved the exhibit. The court attendant provided an easle, and showed Ferris where to set the diagram.

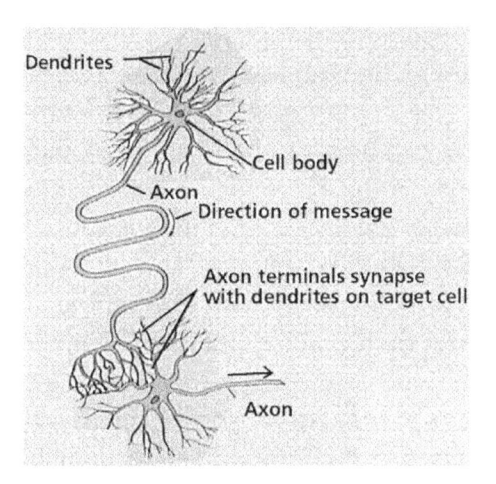

Ferris said, "Dr. Stanton, "Please help us interpret this chart."

"The neuron is the fundamental functional unit of nervous tissue. This drawing is of two typical neurons in the brain and the connection between them. The picture is stylized to represent a generic situation. Neurons do not all look exactly like this, but this is a fair representation of most neurons in the brain.

"A neuron has four main parts: the cell body, branching structures called dendrites, a projecting surface called an axon, and the tag end of the axon called the nerve terminals. Let's consider these parts one at a time.

"Part one is the cell body. Nerve impulses can both enter and exit the cell body.

"Part two is a set of dendrites. Dendrite means branching like a tree, so we see on the chart that the dendrites indeed look like tree branches. This branching out helps the nerve cell to soak up a neurotransmitter such as dopamine or serotonin. Neurotransmitters are chemical substances that facilitate the transfer of nerve messages between neurons. Whatever neurotransmitter is involved in an individual case enters the cell body by means of the dendrites.

"Part three is called the axon. It is a long cell projection that typically carries impulses away from the cell body. Each neuron connects with many synapses.

"The neuron's fourth major part is the nerve endings, and these tiny fibers are where impulses leave the axon and enter the tiny synaptic gaps. The synapses or synaptic gaps are the minute fluid-filled spaces between the endings of one neuron and the dendrites of the next neuron."

Dr. Stanton paused and established eye contact with the jurors who would look in her direction.

"The human brain is immensely complex. An adult human brain weighs about three pounds and isn't all that impressive to gaze upon. Since it has the consistency of jello, if you remove the brain from the cranium, it expands a little outside its container. A fresh brain before being preserved looks like a gray blob with pink lines running all through it. But looks are deceiving.

"Scientists consider the human brain the most high-powered computer in the world. Its complexity strains the imagination. It has billions of neural circuits and even more synapses and nerve cells. And since the brain is so infinitely complex, it stands to reason that mental illnesses also are exceedingly complex. And yet the psychopharmacological industry—which is the unofficial merger of psychiatry and pharmacology—has reduced the complexity of mental disorders like schizophrenia and clinical depression down to too much dopamine or too little serotonin in the brain's synapses. This is simple for people to understand and also suggests that families did not cause the disorder. Simple to understand and guilt free. This is a wonderful sales gimmick, but scientifically it's all wrong, and it's a dangerous, even deadly concept.

"How did psychopharmacology cook up this chemical imbalance hypothesis anyway? The idea arose in the mid-1950s after it was found that Thorazine, the first widely used neuroleptic, lowered the dopamine level in the brain. This caused Smith, Kline, & French chemists to assert that psychosis was caused by too much dopamine. The chemical imbalance notion became far more broadly accepted after Prozac, then a new kind of antidepressant, came on the market in 1987. Prozac's inventor, Eli Lilly Company, observed that the drug increased serotonin levels in the synapses of rat brains. So, company chemists postulated that low levels of serotonin cause depression. This broad acceptance by doctors, the media, and the public was the result of historically massive promotions by the drugmaker."

Judge Fillmore had repeatedly ordered the jurors to not discuss the trial until they entered the deliberations phase. Usually everyone obeyed her instructions, but occasionally, a topic was just too enticing for jurors to resist. Ellen Scaletti and Kenneth LaMont had been classmates in high school some twenty years earlier. Today, in the courthouse cafeteria, they got carried away, and failed to notice Clifford Noyes sitting alone two tables away pretending to read legal papers.

Kenneth asked, "What do you think of Dr. Stanton's nerve cell exhibit?"

"It makes a lot of sense. She's saying that drugmakers and doctors have drastically oversimplified the cause of mental illnesses by claiming the problem is nothing but the amounts of chemical substances in the synaptic gaps."

"The diagram makes it much easier for me to understand the hoax that Big Pharma has perpetrated on the public. For the first time, I see how they have oversimplified what causes schizophrenia and depression. They place all the blame on the amounts of dopamine and serotonin."

"Ken, you sound like a pharmacologist."

"I guess I picked up some expert witness jargon. But I keep thinking of my nephew, my sister's nineteen-year-old son, Robbie. During jury selection, I forgot to mention what happened to him. Well, I guess I chose to keep quiet because the matter is so hurtful."

Ellen asked, "Did what happened to your nephew have to do with prescription drugs?"

"Yes. He committed suicide. Robbie was a great kid."

"I can see that it still bothers you."

"It's okay," Ken said. "I mention Robbie because Stanton's exhibit helps me see the role that his psychiatrist played."

"How so?"

"The psychiatrist used the exact ploy that Stanton is describing. He told Robbie's mom and dad that their son had a chemical imbalance in the brain. Then he prescribed drugs supposedly to restore the balance. Robbie got sicker and ended up hanging himself."

Ellen said, "So this subject is personal to you."

"Yes. And I never suspected the chemical imbalance notion might be wrong. Of course, my sister and her husband bought into it too. I'm trying to decide whether to tell them what I've learned here. It might just make them feel worse, to feel like they were duped, which I think they were."

"Yeah, I never thought much about it, but I guess I thought of the chemical imbalance story as profound science. Now Stanton is telling us it's just a ploy to sell more drugs."

"Did you notice how other jurors reacted to the nerve cell exhibit and what Stanton was saying?"

Ellen said, "No. But I never had a family member harmed by psychotropic drugs. Maybe you noticed because you wanted to see if anyone else was affected the way you are."

"Some jurors seemed startled when Stanton began explaining the exhibit."

Clifford was careful to appear unaware of Ellen and Kenneth as he gathered his papers and slowly walked away. Once outside the cafeteria, he speeded up, heading for the courtyard where the Alphatron medicolegal team was gathering prior to reentering the courthouse.

Clifford told his supervisor, one of the assistant attorneys, that he needed to talk to Chief Counsel Grimes before court resumed. His supervisor relayed the message to Grimes who stepped over to Clifford. Smoot and the other team members looked on.

"Sir, I just learned something that you might want to remedy. I just overheard a conversation between two jurors."

"I hope you didn't get caught."

"No, I was discrete," Clifford said. "They were talking in the cafeteria and didn't even know I was around."

"Good. What did you hear?"

"I don't know their juror numbers, but it was a man and woman that I can point out to you."

"Okay," Grimes said. "What did you hear?"

"They were talking about Stanton's nerve cell exhibit and what effect it had on the man and probably other jurors."

"So?"

Clifford said, "The exhibit and what Stanton is saying about it is having a powerful effect on some of the jurors. The man said that seeing the diagram caused him to believe that the chemical imbalance hypothesis led to his nephew's suicide. He thinks other jurors are having similar suspicions about deceased relatives."

Smoot said, "Stanton probably practiced her delivery for hours in front of that chart."

"Did these two jurors say whether it was the exhibit or Stanton's words that had the biggest impact?" Grimes asked.

Clifford said, "It was the combination of the diagram and how Stanton interpreted it. But the diagram seemed to be what impressed them the most, especially the man. The visual impact. He said this is the first time he ever suspected that the chemical imbalance theory played a role in the suicide of his nephew."

Grimes said, "We should have objected to the graphic back when Ferris included it on his list of exhibits."

"I didn't know what grounds to cite," Smoot said. "What do you think, Leonard? Do we try to make Ferris take it down? And what would be our objection?"

"Yeah, we have to get the thing out of sight of the jurors and hope they forget it. We can't let Stanton keep using it to denigrate a perfectly good scientific theory."

Smoot said, "The afternoon session is about to start, and Stanton is first up."

"As soon as we get inside, I'll ask for a meeting in the judge's chamber. Doug, think up some legal reason why we oppose the exhibit."

The attendant called the court to order. Judge Fillmore asked if anything needed her attention before testimony resumed.

THE CHEMICAL IMBALANCE HYPOTHESIS

Grimes said, "Your Honor, I request a meeting in your chamber before we hear any more testimony."

"Can't we put it off until our afternoon break? The jury's time is precious."

"The jury's time is indeed precious. But this concerns the proceedings immediately at hand."

"Very well," the judge said. "The jury can go back out in the hall or to the breakroom. The attendant will come for you as soon as we conclude this unscheduled meeting."

In the judge's chamber, Fillmore said, "Counselor Grimes, you know that I don't like to keep the jury waiting. This better be important."

"It is, Your Honor. Attorney Smoot and I have come to realize that Attorney Ferris is bringing in a completely irrelevant issue by harping on the chemical imbalance hypothesis. And it is the large courtroom exhibit that we object to in particular. It creates a false impression in the minds of the jury. The exhibit is worse than immaterial to the issues at bay. It is a red herring, a diversionary trick."

Ferris said, "I listed the diagram of two interacting nerve cells in my list of proposed exhibits weeks before the trial began. I met a standard requirement of your court, Your Honor. I complied with procedures, and neither Attorney Smoot nor Attorney Grimes raised an issue, and neither did you."

"We acknowledge the lapse in vigilance and apologize for the oversight," Grimes said. "But just because we fell down on the job once does not mean we have no right to object now."

Ferris said, "I disagree. The fact that you did not object at the time means that you can't object now. Court procedural rules will bear me out on this."

"But the judge can always correct an oversight," Fillmore said. "That is what it means to be a judge, Counselor Ferris.

"Why do you call the exhibit a red herring, Chief Counsel?"

"Because the exhibit is nothing but a fallacious attempt to discredit the chemical imbalance theory of mental illness which has served psychopharmacology for decades," Grimes said.

Fillmore said, "That's for the jury to decide. I don't understand your concern. Where's the red herring?"

Grimes said, "The red herring is that Barry Vincent's medical records show no sign that Dr. Thein ever told him that his mental illness was caused by a chemical imbalance. The plaintiff has no basis for bringing up the subject of a chemical imbalance. Even if Attorney Ferris could find fault with the theory, the whole subject is immaterial to this case."

Ferris said, "I bet I can find places in Barry's medical records where Dr. Thein told Barry he had a chemical imbalance."

"Not so," Grimes said. "The written record for this patient doesn't include any reference to a chemical imbalance. And Attorney Ferris was not present in any of the office visits. He cannot provide evidence that the chemical imbalance hypothesis played any part in the patient's diagnosis or treatment."

Ferris said, "It's a virtual certainty that drug reps, including Alphatron reps, used the chemical imbalance argument to persuade Dr. Thein to prescribe certain drugs to Barry."

Grimes said, "Now you're really reaching. You cannot produce any document that says drug reps referred to the chemical imbalance theory when meeting with Dr. Thein."

"Why not let the jury settle this issue?" Ferris asked. "What's with this backroom skullduggery?"

Judge Fillmore said, "Watch your mouth, Counselor. I thought you learned your lesson."

"I apologize, Your Honor. But I can't put on a case at all if I can't mention the chemical imbalance issue."

The judge said, "I am ordering you to take down the nerve cell exhibit on the ground that it is an outrageous display designed to upset the order of the court."

"You can't do that," Ferris said.

"I am the judge. I can do what I want. File an appeal if you don't like my ruling."

"I will do just that. And I'm walking out of this courtroom right now and taking my expert witness with me. You can jail me for contempt, but there are news reporters out there right now who will give me extensive coverage. You will be tainted by this I assure you."

The judge said, "Now calm down. Here's what we can do. You take down the exhibit, and I will let you argue the chemical imbalance issue without it. You just won't be able to use the exhibit or refer to my order for you to take it down."

"And if I don't agree?"

"I will have the court attendant remove the exhibit and I will jail you for contempt of court."

"You win, but I will appeal."

Chapter 51

The Harold Shipman Standard of Care

It is quite likely that some of the deaths Shipman caused resulted from experimentation with drugs. I think he was fascinated by drugs.

—Dame Janet Smith (2003)
Said by High Court Judge Smith after she led a two-year inquiry into all the deaths Shipman had certified.

Judge Fillmore had told the jury she estimated the trial would take a month. Today was the beginning of the sixth week, and the jurors were restless. They resented especially the plaintiffs' team because they were the ones who kept raising issues and demanding detailed answers.

The conscripted jurors were not accustomed to processing complex issues. They just wanted to get back to their regular lives.

Judge Fillmore reminded the jurors to not discuss the case until they were in the deliberation phase of the trial. Jurors Kenneth LaMont and Ellen Scaletti were recalling memories of high school during an afternoon break when Ken changed the subject.

"Ellen, will this case ever end?"

"I can't tell you how glad I'll be when that time comes. This ordeal has upended my whole life."

Ken asked, "Which side do you think will win?"

"I can't say who will win, but I know how I'm going to vote."

"You've already decided?"

"I'm disgusted with the whole process," Ellen said. "How are we to understand all these medical terms? I don't get it. I don't know much about mental disorders or medications. It's all I can do to keep track of my own family's medical needs. The state should figure out a better way to decide these complicated issues."

Ken said, "I'm sick of all the well-dressed experts and their medical and legal terms. It's condescending. It's like they're saying they're better than us lowly jurors. How will you vote?"

"It's obvious that the doctor and the drugmaker are crooks. But it makes my blood boil to have to spend so much time here. The plaintiffs are the ones who keep raising issues. They're the ones who keep this process going and going. Why can't they just shut up? I'm voting against the plaintiffs for upsetting my life. I would vote against the judge if I could. Jury duty is a form of imprisonment and I'm lodging a protest vote."

Dr. Stanton explained in detail that akathisia is severe inner restlessness.

"It is a motor disorder and a psychological disorder rolled into one. The afflicted person not only cannot sit still but also is in emotional agony. Akathisia is closely linked to suicide, often by jumping from a great height or by cutting open one's abdomen."

Michelle provided scientific hypotheses and statistics to support her arguments. The jurors grew weary and wished she were not so thorough. They wanted to return to their daily routines.

The expert witness for Thein and the county gave testimony that was briefer and more colorful than Dr. Stanton's.

Dr. Christopher Rice tracked Dr. Thein's declarations almost word-for-word. Whatever Thein did was correct and the best of medical care. Whatever Dr. Stanton said was wrong. Barry Vincent's parents caused his death by not getting him the emergency medical care he needed. They helped Barry leave Saint Rita's Hospital against medical advice. And if they felt that Saint Rita's had failed Barry, they should have taken him to a hospital like Arrowhead Regional which has a behavioral health center.

Rice sat in the witness chair and grinned.

"Akathisia is nothing more than a mild case of restless leg syndrome."

He sat in a relaxed position and crossed his right leg over his left. Smiling, he uncrossed his legs and casually tapped his feet on the floor. Taking his time, he crossed his left leg over his right.

Then he let both feet rest flat on the floor for a few moments and crossed his legs again. He continued to grin.

Judge Fillmore adjourned court for the day. The plaintiffs, their attorney, and expert witness along with unofficial advisor Prescott met at the Vincents' home to discuss their legal case.

Michelle said, "Of the severe psychiatric illnesses, schizoaffective disorder is misdiagnosed the most often. Over time, researchers and committees appointed by the American Psychiatric Association have studied this problem. Using *DSM IV* criteria, psychiatrists disagreed on the diagnosis more often than not, coming up with wildly different conclusions. And get this.

"The studies show that the disorder is highly overdiagnosed. Exactly what Thein did to Barry. The APA has known about this grave problem for more than eight years but has never changed the *DSM* criteria. Imagine how many patients have been harmed during those years. Finally, the APA has recently assembled a panel to recommend revisions to the manual's diagnostic criteria for schizoaffective disorder."

"Prepare an argument that Thein misdiagnosed schizoaffective disorder and that he should have diagnosed akathisia. He might have purposefully assigned schizoaffective disorder to hide the fact that he had caused akathisia. I will put you back on the stand."

Michelle said, "Good. But do you know what our biggest problem is?"

"I know exactly what it is," Joan said. "We've been trying to show that Thein failed to meet the standard of care, but that's impossible because the standard is so low. I wonder just how low the standard of care is at the county community mental health center."

THE HAROLD SHIPMAN STANDARD OF CARE

Michelle said, "Harold Shipman would have exceeded the standard."

"Who is Harold Shipman?" Jack asked.

Thomas said, "Shipman was a British general practitioner who was apprehended in 1998. Killed many of his patients. One of the most prolific serial killers in recorded history. In January 2000, a jury found Shipman guilty of fifteen murders, but a later inquiry confirmed he was responsible for at least two hundred eighteen. Most were elderly women whom he killed at their homes during house calls. Overmedication was his forte. He changed the wills of most of them so that he inherited a lot of money."

Jack asked, "What came of him?"

"Hanged himself in 2004 in his cell in England's Wakefield Prison," Thomas said.

Joan said, "There is no way we can show that Thein fell short of California's regressive standard of care. Most psychiatrists believe drugs will solve all mental health problems. If they don't hold this belief, they may undervalue the lives of their patients. What they value more are cushy, well-paying jobs. Like Shipman, their prime motivator is money."

"You're right," Raymond said. "Doctors and drugmakers seem to believe that there is a technological fix for each of life's problems. The standard of care should be on trial. Accepted community practice is corruption galore. But unfortunately, that's the standard we're stuck with."

Thomas said, "From this day forth, California's mental health care criteria shall be known as *The Harold Shipman Standard of Care.*"

The group cheered.

Thein was back in the witness chair. Ferris was questioning him.

"Please tell the jury again how you came to decide that your earlier diagnosis of schizophrenia needed to be changed to schizoaffective disorder. First, remind us what the difference is between the two disorders and then describe your method of making the new diagnosis."

Thein said, "Schizophrenia is a disorder of perception. The afflicted person often cannot tell whether what he is perceiving is real or illusory. In schizoaffective disorder, the patient has symptoms of schizophrenia and symptoms of a mood disorder like bipolar disorder or major depressive disorder. When Barry Vincent suddenly had excessive energy, I knew this was the mania of bipolar disorder."

"Did you get a second opinion? Did you ask another doctor what he or she thought the problem might be?"

"No. The standard of care does not require a second opinion."

Ferris said, "I agree. But looking back, do you think a second opinion would have been a good idea?"

"No. I have made many diagnoses, have never sought a second opinion, and have never been proved wrong."

Ferris said, "You heard Dr. Stanton testify that she believes you caused akathisia in Barry by wrongheaded medications, and that you then misdiagnosed the akathisia as schizoaffective disorder."

"Miss Stanton has a vivid imagination."

"Medical experts define akathisia as a psychomotor disorder. Do you believe that this malady and other forms of psychosis can be brought on or worsened by psychiatric medications such as antidepressants, stimulants, and sleep aids?"

Thein said. "Not nearly as often as the detractors of psychiatry would have the public believe."

"But you agree that prescription drugs can precipitate or worsen psychotic symptoms at least sometimes."

"I would say rarely rather than sometimes. And then it is because the patient disobeys the physician's orders."

"But you realize that you are sitting in this courtroom and answering my questions today precisely because Barry's parents have made a preliminary showing that you may have misprescribed psychiatric medications?"

"I realize that. So what?"

"Do you realize that whether psychiatric drugs are misprescribed in a serious issue? You seem cavalier, even flippant about it."

Attorney Smoot stood up.

"Objection. The defense stipulates that prescribing psychiatric medications is a serious matter. I want the plaintiff's attorney to stop browbeating Dr. Thein and get to the technical issues."

Judge Fillmore said, "Counselor Ferris, stop trying to make Dr. Thein grovel. Get to your next legal or medical issue."

"I will do that, Your Honor. Dr. Thein, please define diagnosis by exclusion."

"Diagnosis by exclusion is the elimination, one by one, of the various possible causes of a disorder to aid in identifying the true cause. Only after eliminating certain possibilities can a doctor arrive at an accurate differential diagnosis."

"Did you take any steps to exclude or eliminate other possible causes before deciding that Barry Vincent's schizophrenia had morphed into schizoaffective disorder?"

"I expect that you have an example in mind."

"You're right," Ferris said. "Did you order any blood screening tests to rule out the possibility that any of your antipsychotics or antidepressants had reached toxic levels in Barry's serum?"

"No, I did not."

"Why not?"

"To save the Riverside County Community Mental Health Center from having to bear an unnecessary expense."

"Why did you consider blood screening to be an unnecessary expense?"

"Because I was the doctor who had prescribed the medications, and I knew I had not prescribed too much. Also, I was sure that if Mr. Vincent deviated from my medication schedule it would have been to take less medicine rather than more. I was not worried about toxic levels of psychotropic medications."

Jurors sat up straight. Grimes looked at Smoot, who slowly shook his head.

Ferris paused, allowing the jurors to absorb what Thein had just revealed. Then he asked, "Dr. Thein, by way of diagnosis by exclusion, did you order a spinal tap to obtain cerebrospinal fluid so it could be examined for metabolites of the psychoactive drugs that you prescribed for Barry Vincent? This might have enabled you to rule out psychiatric drugs as a cause of the excessive energy he was feeling."

"No."

"Why?"

"Firstly, I did not think Mr. Vincent would consent to undergo the somewhat painful procedure. He was afraid of the slightest pain. Secondly, I never considered that my medications could be even remotely involved with him being energized."

"By way of diagnosis of exclusion, did you order any urine screening tests for prescription drugs before concluding that Barry had contracted schizoaffective disorder?"

"No."

"Were your reasons the same as for not ordering screening tests of blood or cerebrospinal fluid?"

"Yes. I wanted to save the county from paying for unnecessary medical screening."

Ferris said, "I understand there are some dietary supplements that do not show up in blood or urine screening. Is that your understanding?"

"Yes, that is correct."

"Again, to rule out substances that could have caused Barry's problem of boundless energy, did you ask him or his family members if he was taking various supplements such as vitamins?"

"No."

Ferris said, "Now that we know some things you did not do, what methods did you use to arrive at the diagnosis of schizoaffective disorder?"

"I read the descriptions of psychotic disorders contained in the *Diagnostic and Statistical Manual of Mental Disorders* published by the American Psychiatric Association. I used the version known as *DSM-IV*."

Attorney Ferris said, "Is this a copy of *DSM-IV*?"

Thein said yes, and the judge accepted the document into evidence.

"So you followed the methods set forth in the *DSM*. What are those methods?"

Thein said, "To be precise, there are several handbooks and guidance documents published by the American Psychiatric Association that tell psychiatrists how to apply the wonderful ideas the *DSM* embodies. The methods that I used are set forth in that supplemental guidance as well as in the *DSM* itself.

"Thank you for the clarification. As guided by the *DSM* and by APA supplemental guidance, what are the methods that you used?"

"I conducted a structured interview, following exactly the American Psychiatric Association's manual, *Structured Clinical Interview for DSM-IV*. I did not ask just any old questions. I asked specific questions in an exact sequence. I evaluated Mr. Vincent's answers and observed his behavior as he answered them."

"That's it? Those were your methods?"

"That's the standard of care."

"By way of background and since you relied on the *DSM*, please tell the jury how the American Psychiatric Association decides what constitutes a mental disorder that should be included in the *DSM*."

Thein hesitated. He froze in place. He could not speak.

Smoot stood and said, "Objection. It does not matter how the APA decides what to include in the *DSM*. For purposes of this trial, it matters only whether it is standard practice for psychiatrists to rely on the manual when making diagnoses, and whether that is what Dr. Thein did."

Ferris said, "The jury is entitled to some context. Psychiatrists hotly debate the classification of schizoaffective disorder and whether it is even a legitimate mental illness. How does the American Psychiatric Association decide whether to include a condition in its diagnostic manual? I simply want Dr. Thein to describe his understanding of this process. This will provide the jury insight into whether he should have embraced it as a disorder that many psychiatrists totally reject."

Judge Fillmore said, "I will not allow the question. It is time to conclude this trial. Jury instructions will be next, right after the break."

Chapter 52

Unfair Standards

The law in its majesty equality forbids the rich as well as the poor to sleep under bridges, to beg in the streets, and to steal bread.

—Anatole France
The Red Illy (1894)

The Vincents lost their wrongful death lawsuit. The jury voted unanimously in favor of the defendants who responded by returning to their customary ways of practicing psychiatry and pharmacology. The trial had reopened the Vincents' emotional wounds, how the medical system had failed Barry, and how much he had suffered. It took months for the pain to subside.

For Jack, grieving felt like a place, a zone of pain. He was enclosed in a cloud of gloom that moved with him. The mobile prison that engulfed him seemed designed to keep Jack not only depressed but mystified. Why had Barry been made to suffer so much? Why were Jack, Joan, and Matt being made to go on suffering? Jack who had never been superstitious could not help but wonder if Maunt Thein had somehow cast a spell over the Vincent family.

The agony would never end because it was a place, a zone, not a time period. It was always there, and Jack was always stuck in the middle of it. He wished he were living through a stage of grief because that concept embodied the hope that the emotional pain, after going through successive stages, would eventually diminish. Instead, he lived in a place of emotional pain and flashbacks.

Sometimes he felt as though Barry were with him, particularly when he was walking Proton and Sadie. The illusion comforted Jack until he tried to hug Barry, and found that his son was not there.

Jack needed tactile contact with something substantial, something permanent or at least long-lasting. He embraced the big, rugged trees in Riverside's suburbs. He literally became a tree-hugger, clasping plane trees, eucalyptus trees, and California peppers. Sometimes he flung himself facedown on his lawn, lay there, and pretended that the soil and grass beneath him were the only things that existed in the entire world. He buried his face in the grass, extended his arms outward and gripped the turf with both hands, holding on with all his might. He held fast to the earth. He momentarily felt safe. He could not fall off the ground.

When he hiked with his dogs along the desert wash, he sometimes fell to his knees and held tight to the boulders. Those rocks had withstood eons of erosion, and would withstand countless more if only man would not turn them into gravel, ballast for a roadbed or parking lot. And that is what Jack needed—contact with something rugged, sturdy, and durable. He felt better when he was hugging or trying to get his arms around the big trees or big boulders. Tactile. Contact. Something to cling to.

Jack knew the only way he could get emotional relief would be to renew his efforts to get a measure of justice for Barry. The adverse wrongful death verdict would not keep him from reaching his goal. Jack recalled Philippians 3:13 because it captured his mindset exactly:

> This one thing I do,
> forgetting those things
> which are behind,
> and reaching forth
> unto those things that are before,
> I press toward the mark.

And the mark that he would press for was a measure of justice for Barry. The quest for justice afterall was what had been driving him from the day he and Joan had allowed their son's life-support systems to be shut down.

Joan was in her backyard, sitting on a boulder that Barry and Jack had half-burried to make it appear it had been there for centuries. She was gazing at Barry's pond and its busy water striders. Proton and Sadie were sleeping nearby.

Joan thought of how two legal standards institutionalized by powerful people had eliminated any chance that she and Jack could have gotten justice for their son. Those two standards had undervalued Barry's life. First, the Medical Injury Compensation Reform Act enacted in 1975 had set wrongful death damages so low that grieving relatives could secure a lawyer only by paying fees upfront, compromising the rigor of the legal case they could mount.

The second standard was just as unfair. The medical standard of care was so low that it had allowed Thein to put his self-interest above Barry's. The Harold Shipman Standard of Care had become law just as much as any common law that had come from Great Britain over the centuries. But the standard of care was counterfeit, not a valid standard.

Most judges and juries seemed to believe that doctors would leave the profession if held to a high standard. A doctor shortage could mean jurors might not receive needed medical care. Better to find for the doctor, and a low standard of care provided the necessary rationale. Uncaring actions had been incorporated into the standard of care solely because over the years doctors had done such things. "Tyranny of the precedent" was the phrase that came to Joan.

In her jury instructions, Judge Janet Fillmore had rigidly defined the standard of care, admonishing the jurors that they were not to ask themselves whether Dr. Thein had achieved excellence in medicine but to ask only if he had done what a reasonably careful psychiatrist would have done under similar circumstances.

Joan recalled the judge's exact words: "As California jurors, the standard of care you are to use is the level of skill, knowledge, and care in diagnosis and treatment that other reasonably careful practitioners would use in the same or similar circumstances. You are to rely on the testimony you have heard from the expert witnesses to understand what reasonably careful practitioners would have done if they had been in Dr. Thein's position."

In her jury instructions, Judge Fillmore did not mention Thein's counterparts at the Riverside County community mental heath center, but she also did not discourage the jurors from doing the natural human thing of comparing Thein's behavior to that of his coworkers.

The judge told the jurors that their role was restricted to fact finding. They were not to ponder whether the standard of care were just. That was a judicial decision. She alone was authorized to apply the law to the Vincent wrongful death case.

An idea was forming in Jack's mind. Maybe he could make legal procedures more fair by making people aware of a legal doctrine—jury nullification. He had learned of this legal principle during his wide reading in the years that it took for Barry's wrongful death case to come to trial. Jury nullification was an ancient right expressed in the Magna Carta and Greek and Roman scrolls. Maybe Jack could engage in a public education campaign to make potential jurors aware that use of the nullification doctrine could upgrade the standard of care. Maybe jury nullification could put an end to the suffering wrought by an unfair medicolegal system. Jack was sure that over time millions of patients had suffered because of low medical standards. Maybe citizens could exert a grass roots effort to oppose the powerful psychopharmaceutical industry.

A 1670 case in London involving the juror Edward Bushell came to Jack's mind as he groped for a means of reforming the Harold Shipman Standard of Care. The case that Bushell sat on was that of two Quakers, William Penn and William Mead, and the law they had violated was the Conventicle Act, which made the Church of England the only legal church. They were charged with preaching an unlawful religion to an unlawful assembly. They had preached a Quaker sermon.

The jury acquitted Penn and Mead against the judge's instructions, nullifying the unjust Conventicle Act. The enraged judge fined the jurors and jailed them, intending to keep them locked up until they paid their fines.

Mr. Bushell and three other jurors refused to pay up. They were imprisoned for nine weeks, during which Bushell filed a writ of habeas corpus. Surprisingly, he prevailed in the Court of Common Pleas. Chief Justice Sir John Vaughan delivered the opinion of the court which established the right of juries to give their verdict according to their conviction and abolished the practice of punishing juries for verdicts which offended the courts. Besides reestablishing the right of jury nullification, this ruling in favor of William Penn established freedom of religion, freedom of speech, and the right to peacefully assemble. These rights became part of the English Bill of Rights, and later, part of the First Amendment to the United States Constitution.

But Jack began to doubt that his idea would help stop unfair court decisions like those rendered in Louis's and Barry's wrongful death trials. Jury nullification was a way for common people to offset unjust laws prone to unfairly convict a person. Nullification worked because an acquittal could not be overturned thanks to the double jeopardy clause of the Constitution.

But Jack wanted just the opposite. Instead of preventing a good guy from being unfairly punished, Jack wanted to prevent a lax standard from protecting an offending doctor, a threat to public health. He wanted the likes of David Thein to be held accountable, and there was no legal doctrine that would keep a biased judge like Janet Fillmore from overturning a jury nullification decision. There was no counterpart to double jeopardy that could be invoked. Jury nullification could go against a corrupt standard, but the judge could overrule the jurors, having warned them to not interpret or apply the law. Or the decision could be appealed because there was no legal doctrine to prevent a refiling of such a case.

However, maybe just maybe, the medicolegal community could be forced to develop a more just standard if jurors time after time nullified unfair jury instructions that favored the Harold Shipman Standard of Care, and if those same jurors knew of a more rigorous and fair standard that they could insist on. Jack realized that if Joan and he were to undo the Shipman standard, they would need to propose an alternative criterion and to educate the populace. To attract people to their cause, they needed to come up with an option that would make sense to the many California families who had been or could be harmed by psychiatric drugs. They would need an easy-to-explain, easy-to-understand medicolegal standard.

In his research, Jack came across strict liability, which seemed the ideal legal doctrine to replace the standard he hated so.

The concept of strict liability seemed to address exactly the balky, corrupt standard of care that strongly favored practitioners like David Thein, clinics like Riverside County's, and pharmaceutical companies like Alphatron.

Strict liability makes a person legally responsible for the damage caused by his acts or omissions regardless of culpability. It is not necessary for a plaintiff to prove fault, negligence, or intention, but only that a wrongful act occurred and that the defendant was responsible.

Strict liability applies only to situations that a law defines as inherently dangerous. The concept is that stringent criteria will reduce the harm to the public by discouraging reckless liability through forcing potential defendants to take every precaution. Jack was certain that the prescribing of psychotropic drugs met, even exceeded, this dangerousness criterion. Lawmakers and courts had not honestly assessed the hazards inherent in these chemical substances. Any honest risk assessment would have concluded long ago that when it came to psychotropic drugs, strict liability must replace the lax, virtually unenforceable community standard of care.

Documented harm to patients included akathisia, dyskinesia, dystonia, neuroleptic malignant syndrome, serotonin syndrome, seizures, obesity, high blood pressure, diabetes, suicidality, and premature death. Documented harm to family members and the public included maiming or death as when the drugs drove patients to homicidal acts.

The potential harms to the patients and the public, considered with the vast and increasing supplies of medications available made it clear that prescribing them is fraught with danger.

Jack reasoned that strict liability would partly compensate for the great harm caused by the regressive 1975 Medical Injury Compensation Reform Act. MICRA had eliminated the courts as a means for any but the richest citizens to gain justice for a wrongful death caused by medical malpractice.

As he thought through the steps necessary to replace the Shipman standard, Jack realized that it would not be enough for juries to frustrate the California court system. Jury nullification would be essential but insufficient by itself. Repeated nullifications would need to be coupled with pressure on the legislature to enact a statute that mandated the use of strict liability. Jack broadened his plans.

He began to think up approaches that included jury nullification, legislation replacing the Shipman standard with strict liability, and a vigorous campaign to educate the public on the harm caused by the psychopharmacology industry.

Chapter 53

The Lessons Learned Meeting

Say what you know, what you don't know, and what you believe — and label each accordingly.

—Father Richard Polakowski
As quoted by Otis Webb Brawley
In *How We Do Harm* (2011)

The Vincents needed to analyze the information they had gathered during the pretrial activities and during the trial itself. They also needed to reflect on the information they had come by outside of court. People with mentally ill family members had thanked the Vincents for trying to reform the Riverside County mental health system. The well-wishers sometimes provided useful information when they described how they too had lost loved ones to reckless healthcare professionals.

Many times during the run-up to and during the trial, the Vincents or their lawyer or expert witness had to quickly analyze fragmntary data and hurriedly make decisions. But now the Vincents were entering a new phase in their reform efforts. Their analysis must be comprehensive. They needed to examine all the information they now possessed. They needed to analyze and interpret that information and then decide what actions they would take. Whatever actions they were to choose would consume much of their time and energy for years to come.

At home one day, Jack asked his wife, "What do we do with all this information? We have medical charts that Thein filled out during office visits with Barry. We have transcripts of depositions, we have written declarations, and in-court testimony as well as our own notes. How can we process and interpret it all?"

"First, we have to dedicate ourselves to the task," Joan said. "We have to believe that contained in this mass of information are facts that we can use to prevent psychiatrists like Thein from harming patients like Barry. Pharmaceutical companies are still marketing dangerous drugs, and psychiatrists are still accepting bribes for prescribing them."

"When we filed the lawsuit we knew the time would come when we would have to analyze this information. We didn't realize there would be so much of it."

Joan said, "We need advice so that we don't waste time on leads that look good but end up in blind alleys."

The Vincents decided to bring together the medicolegal allies who had helped them press their wrongful death claim. They would meet with expert witness Michelle Stanton, attorney Raymond Ferris, and secret adviser psychologist Thomas Prescott. The Vincents asked them to bring information and insights to a meeting at their home.

They wanted in-depth discussions.

Thomas was the first to arrive. He knew the emotional pain that gripped Jack and Joan. Every day, Thomas recalled the death of his brother, Louis. He yearned to prevent similar fates from befalling others, and knew the Vincents felt the same.

Thomas believed Jack and Joan wanted to live the rest of their lives trying to find meaning in Barry's short life and tragic death. He understood that they needed a reason for living. Thomas had contemplated suicide many times after losing the brother he was so close to. And he sensed that Jack was dealing with the same recurring impulse. Thomas appreciated the importance of this meeting far more than either Ferris or Stanton ever could.

THE LESSONS LEARNED MEETING

Raymond and Michelle arrived at the same time, and the meeting began.

Jack said, "For Joan and me, the verdict for the defendants was a sad outcome. The trial forced us to relive what happened to Barry from the time he became Thein's patient until we permitted his life support systems to be shut down. Not only was the verdict in Thein's favor, but his expert witness was allowed to say that Joan and I were to blame. The state's medicolegal systems are deeply flawed, and anyone who says otherwise...."

Joan said, "Jack is hurting, and so am I. We asked the three of you to meet with us regarding a few vital matters. I'll ask a few questions and then we would like your views.

"First, we aren't asking if it was worth bringing the lawsuit. An answer to that question wouldn't tell us where to go from here, which is what we want to determine. Here are the questions.

"First question—what are the lessons learned? We want to examine every significant fact in the mass of information that we now possess.

"Jack and I want to prevent anyone else from suffering like Barry did. Thomas understands what I'm saying because he's devoted his life to ensuring that his brother, Louis, did not die in vain. Thomas inspires us. At our age, neither Jack nor I will become a medical professional like Thomas, but we can do something to reduce corruption in the psychopharmaceutical industry.

"Here's our second question. Did Thein accept bribes from pharmaceutical companies, especially Alphatron, to prescribe drugs, especially Gabicon?

"Here's the third question—how did this so-called doctor get the medical training that his resume claims? During the years he trained in Burma, there was severe civil strife. The dictator Ne Win reacted by closing many universities, some for years. It had to have been almost impossible for Thein to get good medical training.

"In Burma, the state pays for medical education, and Ne Win budgeted little funding for that purpose. I doubt Thein's education and experience come anywhere near the claims made in his resume. The California Medical Board is supposed to ensure that foreign medical graduates coming here to practice medicine attended legitimate schools in their home country. It's clear the board did not investigate Thein's education in Burma.

"Another question we want to explore is, why don't state or federal agencies do something to stop the rampant polypharmacy? The FDA, the National Institute of Mental Health, the California Medical Board, the Board of Pharmacy, and MediCal—not one of them seems to care.

"Do any of you three have answers?"

Raymond said, "This lessons-learned meeting is a good idea, and I'll contribute to the best of my ability. But first I propose a ground rule of nonattribution. I'm asking that none of us tells anyone outside of this meeting who said what. Please don't say 'Attorney Raymond Ferris told me such and such.'

"We need to share information about Riverside County's and Alphatron's mismanagement of psychopharmacology and the company's control over psychiatrists like Thein. But our remarks could be misunderstood by anyone who is not in this meeting. Michelle, Thomas, and I all have professional reputations to protect."

"Nonattribution is vital," Michelle said. "I pledge to not divulge anything that is said in this meeting."

"As an insider at the county mental health center, naturally I'm for nonattribution," Thomas said.

Jack said, "Joan and I acknowledge the risk that the three of you are taking by coming here and sharing ideas with us. We assure you that we will say nothing that would draw attention to you."

Joan said, "So we agree that nonattribution is our main ground rule. Information will come up that must be kept confidential. So let's proceed on that basis because it's also important that we speak freely tonight. Jack and I are in desperate need of anything that could guide us from now on because we've lost our moorings."

Thomas said, "I can tell you, Jack and Joan, that your lawsuit affected the county more than the political hacks will ever admit. They act like they're pure, but they're in bed with every pharmaceutical company that operates in this county, and your suit scared hell out of them."

THE LESSONS LEARNED MEETING

"Will they change their behavior?" Jack asked.

Thomas said, "They'll continue in their corrupt ways and just do a better job of covering up. Nonetheless the fact that you scared them badly should make you feel better. I overheard some of the county managers talking, and their voices quavered when certain topics arose. They're trying to figure out how to keep Jack from informing the public that drug reps enjoy unlimited access to the county's psychiatrists. And especially that these sales persons come bearing hundreds of free drug samples."

Silence.

Finally, Thomas said, "I have a question for Ray regarding the matter of the drug reps meeting so often with the county psychiatrists."

"Fire away," Ferris said.

Thomas said, "Jack was on the right track when he asked the mental health center for the sign in/sign out records of drug reps visiting the psychiatrists. Jack cited the California Public Records Act and asked for the records for the last five years. Those records are maintained by a private security firm that the mental health center contracts with.

"Ray, why didn't you ask for those records as part of the court's discovery process? Jack said you wouldn't make that request. Your refusal left him having to make the query on his own as a private citizen. County mental health bosses stalled as long as possible and then wrote Jack a letter saying they couldn't find any records of drug rep visits. That was a lie because the county's own rules require it to maintain those records.

"Every working day, I see drug reps sign in and out. The sign-in forms are in a ledger at the front counter. The mental health center must have believed Jack would be unable to do anything about the lie in the short time that remained before the wrongful death trial was to begin. To lie in writing like they did, the county superiors must have wanted desperately to keep Jack from seeing those records.

"I wish the jury could have seen the sign-in/sign-out records of hundreds of visits by Alphatron's drug reps. Pharmaceutical companies buy prescription records from private companies and from the American Medical Association. You could have bought the same kind of information. Then you could have correlated, for example, the number of Alphatron visits to Thein with how many times he prescribed Gabicon. If you had done that for all the drug reps who visited Thein, you would have assembled some very incriminating information. It looks like you failed the Vincents by not using the discovery process to reveal how much access drug reps have to the county psychiatrists."

Ferris said, "Jack identified information that could have suggested that Thein is in Alphatron's back pocket, and that could have made the jury suspect that he prescribed Gabicon for financial reasons and not for Barry's benefit.

"But I couldn't seek that information under discovery rules. The wrongful death claim was limited to the issue of whether Thein wrongfully caused Barry's demise. Even if he was visited every day by Alphatron reps, it doesn't necessarily follow that this led to Barry's premature death.

"If I had asked for the records of drug rep visitations, Smoot and Grimes would have objected and argued that they were not material, not relevant."

"Those records were material," Thomas said. "Of the things that scared the county administrators the most it was Jack seeking those sign-in/sign-out records."

Jack said, "But the purpose of this meeting is not to pile on you, Ray. We need you to help us analyze the case and how we might change laws to make them less hostile to the mentally ill."

Raymond said, "As an attorney, I've developed a thick skin. If you have more concerns, let me know."

Joan said, "I would like Michelle's opinion of Dr. Christopher Rice."

Michelle said, "This meeting is about lessons learned, so I guess this question concerns what I learned from an opposing expert witness. I didn't learn much from Rice that I can use because most of what he said were lies. I won't resort to telling lies."

THE LESSONS LEARNED MEETING

"What about his play acting for the audience?" Joan asked. "He sat in a chair, grinned, and made akathisia seem like a mild case of restless leg syndrome. Do you admit his play acting was effective?"

"His play acting was very effective," Michelle said. "He sat there grinning, occasionally crossing and uncrossing his legs, and jiggling his feet a little. This misrepresented akathisia, but I admit his act influenced the jury."

Joan said, "You could've portrayed a true picture of the disorder. You would've been portraying the truth. You could've asked the judge's permission and then paced up and down, back and forth. You could've sat down and immediately jumped back up and started pacing again. You could've pretended to be frantic, acting like a patient trying to survive the inner restlessness and psychosis that is akathisia."

Michelle said, "I could've done my own pantomime, and because akathisia is a movement disorder and an emotional disorder rolled into one, I could've dramatically paced back and forth, sat down, got up, and paced some more, grimacing all the while. The thought just never occurred to me.

"OK, lesson learned. If I testify in another case involving akathisia, I'll develop a skit that shows it's pure hell."

Jack said, "Michelle, I thought you were going to make the point that the very manner of suicide that Barry suffered was indicative of akathisia. The defense's argument was that Thein's medication did not cause Barry to contract akathisia, that he didn't suffer that dreaded disorder. I thought you were going to make the case that to cut into one's abdomen is a statistically strong indicator of akathisia. The very method that Barry used was strong evidence that he had akathisia."

Raymond said, "I can answer that question. Attorney Douglas Smoot is a smooth operator. After Michelle answered several of Smoot's questions, he casually asked if she had anything more to add. That sounded like an innocent question. It sounded like Smoot was simply making sure that Michelle was being afforded ample opportunity to put her message before the jury.

"But it wasn't an innocent question. When Michelle said she had nothing further to add she was thinking only that she had no immediate follow-on remark on that particular subject. But her 'no' made it possible for Judge Fillmore to rule that our expert witness had said all she intended to say and was done testifying. So the judge—being biased in favor of the county—barred Michelle from testifying any further. The court has hundreds of rules and many of them pertain to running an efficient trial. Fillmore denied Michelle the chance to point out that some akathisia sufferers cut their abdomens open to release the horrible inner stress. The judge barred Michelle from pointing out that no other medical condition, including schizophrenia and schizoaffective disorder, causes a patient to commit the equivalent of hari-kari. Our team didn't get to make an important point."

Jack said, "That was a dirty trick that Smoot and the judge pulled off. The trial was supposed to get to the truth. Judge Fillmore didn't have any idea of what Michelle wanted to add to her testimony, so she couldn't have assessed its importance. The judge didn't care. She didn't care about justice."

"You're right," Raymond said. "The judge should have let Michelle, as an expert witness, provide the information. Fillmore should have ignored Smoot's old trial lawyer's trick. At the least, the judge could have had a sidebar with the lawyers, learned the importance of the issue, and then decided whether to let the jury hear from Michelle."

Thomas said, "But why? Why did the judge take such an unfair position? Attorney Smoot provided Fillmore the opportunity, but she still had the option of letting Michelle testify."

Raymond said, "Throughout the trial, the county judge favored the county psychiatrist and the pharmaceutical company at every opportunity. This was just one example.

"Anyone who believes judges are independent is dead wrong. Fillmore is a county judge whose salary is paid by the county and whose performance ratings are assigned by a presiding county judge. Fillmore pretended to be fair while protecting the county in any stealthy way she could."

Jack said, "That explains why she didn't let Michelle finish testifying. It also suggests why she was so rude to you. She cut you off

THE LESSONS LEARNED MEETING

almost every time you opened your mouth. That showed the jury that she felt contempt not only for you but of course for our case as well. Maybe we should appeal on that basis."

Raymond said, "Jack, you still don't get it. These courts do whatever they want. Unless you're O. J. Simpson, have loads of money, and a jury strongly biased in your favor, the court is going to violate your rights with impunity. Thomas warned you that you would lose your wrongful death claim."

"You're right," Jack said. "I've got to stop looking for fairness. County court is about power and influence, not fairness.

"So in keeping with our 'lessons learned' theme, was there anything we could've done to prevent Judge Fillmore from gagging Michelle?"

Raymond said, "I should have warned Michelle about the trick that Smoot pulled off. When he asked 'Is that all?' she should have said, 'I reserve the right to provide more testimony as issues arise. Also, I might think of something more that the jury needs to know.' That is a way to keep the court from cutting off your testimony. The witness should always say she is likely to provide more testimony even if she doesn't have anything more to add right at the moment."

Chapter 54

Individual Differences

Centuries ago, sensitive clinicians intuitively knew the role of individual differences in vulnerability to disease. Two individuals could get the same disease, yet the courses of their illnesses could be quite different...

—Robert M. Sapolsky
Why Zebras Don't Get Ulcers (2004)

The five friends talked far into the night. They honored two good, young men who died before their time.

Thomas said, "Westlake and Thein are next of kin to the ancient alchemists who believed they could change lead into gold if they found the right combination of ingredients.

"As I watched Westlake testify, one notion came to me over and over. I just kept thinking how wonderful it would be if we could make all the psychiatrists like him take the medications they so recklessly prescribe. Wouldn't it be wonderful if they had to consume psychotropic drugs before they were allowed to prescribe them? Imagine Westlake and Thein swallowing Paxil, Zyprexa, Luvox, Cogentin, Abilify, Valium, lithium, and Gabicon."

The group laughed.

Jack said, "I'd like to see how well Thein would comply with orders to take Paxil, Luvox, Abilify, and Cogentin in the morning, Gabicon both morning and evening, and Zyprexa in the evening. First, I doubt he could keep track of such a complicated regimen. And second, he'd be sick to his stomach and out of his head at the same time."

As the hours passed, the feeling of kinship grew. The group drifted into discussing philosophical and eventually supernatural topics. Jack wished he could divine life to make sense. Why was there such a thing as mental illness? And why did some people feel they had the right to maximize profits when they treated persons with mental disorders?

Michelle said, "My grandparents said that before the days of television, friends often swapped stories all night long."

Thomas said, "I read a story about Mary Shelley, the author of *Frankenstein's Monster*. She and her husband, Percy Shelley, the poet, and their author friends used to sit up all night telling ghost stories, seeing who could spin the scariest yarn. Long, night-time visits were the norm. Technology like artificial lighting, radio, television, computers, and movies have taken an important custom from us—that of oral storytelling. Oh, we have movies and TV and other high-tech ways of telling stories, but in the past, everyone was a storyteller. And old-fashioned imagination created all the special effects that were needed."

Joan regretted breaking up the escapism that the group was enjoying, but foremost in her mind was doing something to lessen the hold that the psychopharmaceutical industry had on the populace.

"I want to raise a broader topic than Thein's malfeasance. I'd like your opinions as to how well the community mental health centers are serving their mentally ill outpatients. I have personal experience with only the Riverside County center, but I've heard stories about other community centers failing their patients. And I've done a lot of reading lately about the centers nationwide. I don't like what I read.

"What's your take on this issue? Ray?"

"I'm biased because in my legal practice I represent patients and their families. So I work only with those who claim they've been wronged. I don't see the people who may have had better experiences."

"On the other hand," Thomas said, "Some of the patients whom you don't see might have had bad experiences but are not complaining for one reason or another. I expect your caseload represents a very small percentage of the patients who have been severely harmed by community mental health centers."

Raymond said, "I'm sure there are many patients who either lack the capacity to make formal complaints, or are intimidated from trying. Or they may not have family who can speak for them."

"Many homeless people have mental illnesses," Michelle said, "and I know from working with them that a high percentage endure hardships and never complain to the authorities. How much the community mental health system is failing the public is vastly under reported."

Joan said, "It sounds like it's hard to even measure the quality of the job the community centers are doing."

"That's right," Michelle said. "One reason is that county psychiatrists don't let family members sit in when they diagnose patients or prescribe medications for them. They exclude significant others even though county regulations call for doctors to invite the primary caregivers into their meetings with the patients. For example, county psychiatrists are supposed to try to include the patient's family or friends in developing an individualized treatment plan for the patient.

"The patient and his family should not have to search through the medical charts for the elements of an individualized plan. The plan should be an entirely separate, stand-alone document, just as specified by state regulations. But the psychiatrists almost never prepare one for their patients, and county bossess never hold a psychiatrist responsible for failing to make a plan. Thein disregarded the plan that Dr. Gross had prepared for Barry, and did not develop a new one. Such a plan might have saved Barry's life by causing Thein to think more carefully about his treatment, and having other medical staff review the document and offer advice for improvement.

"Under privacy laws, the doctor has to get the patient's permission to include others in the office visits or to share the patient's medical information. I think a good share of the patients would gladly give permission for their parents to participate but they don't know they have that right.

"Most psychiatrists don't want family members in the patient consultations. They strongly discourage participation. They like having the power to intimidate the mentally ill patient. Having a family member sit in could equalize the balance of power. The psychiatrists hide behind confidentiality rules, but those rules are intended for the patient's benefit, and he or she has the legal right to give permission for family members to join their treatment team."

Thomas said, "Even though inclusion of family members would greatly improve treatment outcome, this is almost never done because the patient's well-being is not the main concern of these shrinks.

"Their main concern is having a comfortable, uncomplicated career position. Adding a family member to a consultation risks that person asking if a given medication is really needed. What exactly is that medication intended to do for the patient? Is there a life style change that could negate the need for the medication? Is this medication known to interact badly with other medications?

"The psychiatrists that I work with don't want to be bothered with such issues. They want to have a private meeting with the patient, coerce him or her into signing a consent form, write out a prescription, and do the same thing with the next patient."

Raymond said, "Regulations specify how the county is to comply with legislation that authorized the implementation of the community mental health centers in California. If the therapists followed the regulations, they would do a much better job.

"But the psychiatrists don't follow the regulations. Most have never read them. In Thein's written declaration for the trial, he unwittingly revealed that he ignored the regulations. He wrote that Barry was alone in the meetings with him and that Barry's parents were not privy to the information exchanged. He was making a virtue out of excluding Jack and Joan when county regulations say he should have included you two if Barry were willing."

Joan said, "Part of the answer to my question is that the centers are failing the patients by not following regulations. And Thein's outright violations of rules cost Barry his life."

Michelle said, "Thein's biggest transgression might have been failing to treat Barry as a whole person, an individual, and not just a bundle of symptoms. Thein should have asked Barry if he wanted Jack and Joan to participate in the office visits. Shared decision making and true informed consent could have saved Barry's life. The *DSM* does not consider context, what is going on in the patient's entire life. It says if these symptoms are present, the patient has this disorder."

"Ray, can you expand your answer to my question?," Joan asked. "Are the community mental health centers doing more harm than good?"

Raymond said, "The centers fail their patients in large part because the facilities are terribly underfunded and understaffed. Community mental health centers have almost entirely replaced the large psychiatric hospitals that mostly warehoused the patients. For most of America's history, those who were perceived to be mentally ill were locked up in state-funded and state-managed hospitals.

"By the 1960s this pattern was rapidly changing. In 1965, amendments to Medicare provided federal funding so the states no longer had to bear the major costs of treating mental illness. So Medicare helped give rise to the community mental health centers and smaller, decentralized places like board-and-care homes where patients could live and be treated. Medicare paid for patient care in localized facilities like nursing homes, but not for care given in the psychiatric hospitals. Naturally the states moved people out of the hospitals and into private or community facilities.

"Chlorpromazine, marketed as Thorazine, came on the market in the mid-1950s. Haloperidol came along a few years after Thorazine. Other drugs like lithium carbonate arrived at about the same time. This development gave lawmakers the idea that patients with mental illness could be treated at decentralized locations within their own communities Doctors, the public, and elected officials believed these new drugs were wonderfully safe and effective. This mindset led to the Medicare provisions for funding localized mental health treatment.

"President John Kennedy signed the Community Mental Health Centers Act in October 1963, the last piece of legislation that he approved before he was assassinated.

"Community mental centers are a colossal failure in large part because lawmakers have refused to adequately fund them. Congress refuses to recognize how prevalent mental illness is.

"The community mental health centers lack facilities, equipment, and staff. They have been assigned a vital mission but denied the funding to carry it out."

Michelle said, "Congress's refusal to adequately fund the nation's community mental health centers is one of America's greatest medical tragedies. It results in many grave problems."

"And many of those problems," Thomas said, "stem from the very reason that lawmakers thought community centers were a good idea in the first place. Remember, it was the advent of drugs like Thorazine, Haldol, and lithium carbonate that caused lawmakers to believe that mental illnesses did not have to be managed in hospitals. The idea was that new drugs could convert inpatients into outpatients. They could live at home and receive medications in their communities. The idea of the centers was based on drugs, drugs, and more drugs."

Michelle said, "The community mental health centers are based on using drugs so people don't have to live in hospitals. The problem is that the drugs cause many problems. The centers are not only based on a drug culture, but they promote that culture.

"In recent years, mass shootings in public places, particularly schools and workplaces, have been rampant. Never in American history has there been so many mass killings. These massacres correspond in time with establishment of the community mental health centers. The correlation is strong.

"I have found in my research that almost all of those shooters were taking psychotropic drugs or were suffering withdrawal effects. In 1989, Joseph Wesbecker, an ex-employee of a printing plant in Louisville, Kentucky, used an AK-47 to kill eight of his former coworkers, and to wound twelve more before turning the gun on himself. He was taking Prozac. In 1999, Erick Harris and Dylan Klebold killed thirteen and injured twenty-nine others at Columbine High School in Littleton, Colorado. Eric was taking Luvox. Because of privacy laws, we don't know what medication Dylan might have been taking.

"Recently, there was a tragedy in northern Minnesota on the Red Lake Indian Reservation. Jeff Weise, sixteen years old, was taking Prozac. He shot and killed his grandparents then went to his school where he shot and killed five students, a security guard, and a teacher, and wounded seven before killing himself. These are just three of dozens of examples.

"Prozac first came on the American market in 1988, and that's when these kinds of shootings increased dramatically. Paxil was approved in 1992. A number of pharmaceutical companies won FDA approval for their own versions of antidepressants and antipsychotics in the early 1990s, and that is when these mass murders began to skyrocket."

As the group talked through the night, Joan continued to raise questions. Her friends were experts on California's policies on treatment of mental illnesses. Prescott, Stanton, and Ferris had years of experience in dealing with medicolegal issues, and in recent years Jack had read widely on the subject. Joan was determined to make the most of this opportunity for intelligent discourse on why the medical treatment of the mentally ill was so flawed.

Joan said, "Mahatma Gandhi once said the greatness of a civilization can be measured by how it treats its most vulnerable citizens. To Gandhi, vulnerable citizens included the poor, the sick, and even animals. It would be wonderful if Gandhi's compassion could be infused into psychiatry."

"Some psychiatrists may be compassionate," Raymond said. "but their concern for the suffering of others is overtaken by their fear of repercussions if a patient commits a crime or completes suicide. Would the doctor be blamed? So they overdiagnose and overtreat the patient, thinking they're doing the right thing, when in fact they're making matters worse. They overestimate the danger and then proceed with their medications to create real problems to replace the ones they had imagined."

Michelle said, "The propensity for psychiatrists to overdiagnose is beautifully illustrated by the Rosenhan experiment. How many of you know that story?"

Thomas raised his hand. "It's a story worth telling."

Michelle said, "In 1973, the journal *Science* published a report titled *On Being Sane in Insane Places*. David Rosenhan, a psychology professor at Stanford University had designed an experiment to test the reliability of psychiatric diagnoses.

"There were two parts to Rosenhan's study. In the first part, three women and five men faked auditory hallucinations to gain admittance to psychiatric hospitals in five states. Their single complaint was that they heard voices. They said they couldn't understand the voices except that they heard the words *empty*, *hollow*, and *thud*. All were diagnosed with a psychiatric disorder and hospitalized.

"After admission, the pseudo patients acted normally and told the staff that they felt fine and no longer heard voices. All were forced to admit to having a mental illness. They were not released until they agreed to take antipsychotic drugs. The hospital stays ranged from seven to fifty-two days and averaged nineteen.

"The second part of Rosenhan's study involved a challenge issued by a reputable hospital. It was agreed that Rosenhan would send one or more pseudo patients to its facility. The hospital administrators said their staff would detect the impostors. In the following weeks, out of one hundred ninety-three new patients, the staff identified forty-one as pseudo patients. In fact, Rosenhan had sent no one to the hospital.

"Rosenhan concluded, 'It is clear that we cannot distinguish the sane from the insane in psychiatric hospitals.' Thus, the diagnostic process was not reliable. He also pointed out the dehumanization and labeling that his pseudo patient volunteers had endured."

"Someone should do a similar study of community mental health centers today," Jack said. "The pseudo patients might not be hospitalized since the centers specialize in outpatient treatment, but I bet they would be diagnosed as mentally ill, and would be prescribed powerful medications. And I bet the community centers would never declare them recovered."

Thomas said, "Rosenhan's report provoked controversy. Of course psychiatry vigorously defended its practices. Rosenhan's experiment is famous, but he wasn't the first to test psychiatric diagnosis by faking illness. We will never know the first such impostor, but in 1887 journalist Nellie Bly feigned illness to gain admittance to what folks in those days called a lunatic asylum.

"She was admitted and described horrid conditions in her report *Ten Days in a Mad-House*."

Chapter 55

Some Saw It Differently

I shall be telling this with a sigh
Somewhere ages and ages hence:
Two roads diverged in a wood, and I—
I took the one less traveled by,
And that has made all the difference.

—Robert Frost
This is the last stanza of *The Road Not Taken*
In the collection titled *Mountain Interval* (1916)

Joan's conscience nagged her. Jack and she had been delving into only the worst conduct of medical men and women. For years, they had focused on combating wrongful medical activities. And again tonight during this lessons-learned meeting, they had focused on corrupt doctors and drugmakers. This perspective was necessary if the Vincents were to bring reform to psychophamacology. But Joan regretted that they were ignoring the medical contributions that had been made over the ages by compassionate doctors, nurses, and researchers.

To her confidants, Joan said, "All night long, I've urged you to tell us about wrongful acts that have been done in the name of medicine. That of course has to be the focus of a lessons-learned session. But just so Jack and I don't become totally embittered, it would be good if we could talk a while about doctors, nurses, and researchers who did the opposite of the Theins and Westlakes of this world."

Thomas said, "Fortunately, there are more examples of altruism than you can count. What kinds of things are you thinking about?"

"Anything that's contrary to the ways that Thein and Westlake treated their patients. They treated Barry and Louis like guinea pigs, recklessly prescribing drugs without regard to toxicity, side effects, and bad drug-drug interactions. They were willing to take chances with our loved ones' lives as long as profit was in the air. And that horrid Alphatron would do anything, however immoral, in pursuit of the dollar."

Thomas said, "Are you interested in doctors who took risks themselves rather than put their patients in danger? By doing things like experimenting on themselves?"

"That would pick me up. I imagine that many doctors have put themselves in harm's way for the sake of their patients or public health. To hear about any truly selfless act would help restore my faith at least in some doctors."

Michelle said, "I take it that you're thinking of more than hard work. Most doctors work hard to help people."

"Thomas used the word 'altruism' a minute ago," Joan said. "Altruistic acts are the exact opposite of the things that Alphatron, Thein, and Westlake did. That's what I want to hear about."

Michelle said, "You're talking about a vast number of people throughout history. We don't have time enough to mention one percent of the ones who made the greatest contributions. I can offer a few names that immediately come to mind. In particular, I'm thinking of doctors and researchers who took great risks, and in some cases, suffered injury or death in the process of advancing medicine."

"In this case, an anecdote or two would be the perfect antidote—a remedy for what ails me," Joan said.

Michelle said, "Pierre and Marie Curie were a resourceful married couple who did historic research in France in the late 1800s and early 1900s. But I'm sure you know about them."

"I know they did pioneering research in radioactivity, but when I learned of them in school, I wasn't as interested as I am now."

Raymond said, "Michelle, remind us of the things that Pierre and Marie did. It's a remarkable story of physics and chemistry. Some of their discoveries had important medical applications."

"Yes," Michelle said. "And they had many barriers in that day and age, especially the prejudice directed at Marie simply for being a woman scientist. She grew up in Poland so she retained citizenship there, but she got most of her university training and did her research in France. After marrying Pierre, she had French citizenship as well as Polish. Over the years, she went back and forth in deciding where to live and work. Scientists and medical institutions in both countries were strongly biased against women entering the male-dominated professions of physics, chemistry, and medicine.

"It's impossible to discuss the Curies' achievements without also discussing the grim circumstances that they endured."

"From my reading," Thomas said, "it's sometimes hard to sort out which achievements to credit to Pierre, which to Marie, and which to their combined efforts."

Michelle said, "That's true. Pierre was eight years older than Marie so he had a head start in science, but she lived twenty years longer than he did and was highly productive during that whole time except for when she was gravely ill with radiation sickness.

"Pierre was a physicist while Marie became both a physicist and a chemist, but university degrees and longevity are only part of the picture. They were married in 1895, and by mid-1898, Pierre was so intrigued by Marie's work that he dropped his study of crystals and joined her.

"Here are some of the things that Pierre and Marie accomplished together. In 1898, they published a joint paper announcing the existence of an element that they named 'polonium,' in honor of her native Poland. In December of that same year, the Curies announced the existence of a second element, which they named 'radium.' In the course of their research, Marie coined the word 'radioactivity.'

"Between 1898 and 1902, the Curies published, jointly or separately, over thirty scientific papers, including one that said that, when exposed to radium, diseased, tumor-forming cells were destroyed faster than healthy cells.

THE MIND DOCTOR

"In 1903, Pierre and Marie together with Henri Bequerel were awarded the Nobel Prize in physics for research on radiation. Bequerel was a university professor whose early work with uranium had led Marie to select radiation for her PhD thesis at the University of Paris.

"Pierre died suddenly in 1906 so of course, any accomplishments after that time were Marie's alone. But from the beginning of their teamwork, it was Marie who led the way on matters involving radioactivity. In 1910, Marie succeeded in isolating radium. She also defined an international standard for radioactive emissions that was eventually named for her and Pierre, the curie.

"In 1911, Marie was awarded a second Nobel Prize, this one for her advancement of chemistry by discovering radium and polonium, by isolating radium, and especially by revealing the nature of radioactivity.

"Marie is remembered mainly for discovering and isolating radium. But her greatest discovery was that radioactivity is a property of the atom. This led scientists to study the atom and opened the door to twentieth century investigations. Before her discovery, scientists thought of the atom as a solid ball, the smallest particle that existed.

"During World War I, Marie learned that many wounded soldiers, who might have survived, were dying because it took too long to get them medical help. She also learned that battlefield surgeons were maiming soldiers by hacking off limbs and probing for bullets and shrapnel. She believed both of these problems could be reduced by establishing radiological centers near the front lines.

"And so, she developed mobile radiography units. This was a huge achievement. She did a quick study of radiology, anatomy, and automotive mechanics, and then procured x-ray equipment, vehicles, and auxiliary generators. She also trained other women as aides. Many men lived or were less disabled because of Marie and her daughter assistant, seventeen-year-old Irène."

Thomas said, "I can't even imagine what Marie would have accomplished if she had not been stigmatized for being a woman scientist. Stigma reared its ugly head much like it does against those having a diagnosis of a mental illness or happening to be of a different race. Or hell, being different in any way. Marie was a pioneer in how to cope with stigma."

Jack asked, "Why did Pierre die so much earlier than Marie?"

Michelle said, "Pierre was killed in 1906 when he was walking across a busy street in Paris during a rainstorm. He was hit by a horse-drawn wagon and fell under the wheels where his skull was fractured. He was forty-six. Some historians theorize that he was weak from radiation sickness, and that this made him more likely to fall.

"Marie was sixty-six when she died in 1934 in a sanitorium in Southeast France. The cause of death was aplastic anemia. The Curies experienced radium burns, both accidentally and voluntarily, and were exposed to extensive doses of radiation while conducting their research. They experienced chronic radiation sickness and clearly that is what took her life.

"Had Pierre not been killed as he was, it's likely he would have eventually died of the effects of radiation, as did not only Marie, but also their daughter, Irène, and Irène's husband.

"The damaging effects of ionizing radiation were not known at the time of their work, which had been carried out without the safety measures later developed. Marie had carried test tubes containing radioactive isotopes in her pocket, and she stored them in her desk drawer, remarking on the faint light that the substances gave off in the dark. Marie was also exposed to x-rays from unshielded equipment while serving in the field hospitals during World War I. Although she suffered chronic illnesses, including near-blindness, and ultimately death, she never really acknowledged the health risks of radiation exposure.

"A radium medical industry sprouted up soon after Marie isolated the element. But she refused to patent the radium-isolation process so that the scientific community could do research unhindered."

Raymond said, "Jonas Salk is another medical researcher who refused to seek a patent that could have made him a fortune. In the early 1950s, he developed a breakthrough polio vaccine, but never sought financial compensation.

"When newscaster Edward R. Murrow asked Dr. Salk, who owned the patent on the vaccine, he said, 'Well, the people, I would say. There is no patent. Could you patent the sun?'"

Thomas said, "I have a story for you, Joan. And this one fits in with your desire for doctors to find ways to reduce their use of dangerous chemicals. In 1921, Dr. Evan O'Neill Kane in a rural hospital in Pennsylvania removed his own appendix. Of course, doing the surgery himself, he couldn't use general anesthesia, and this suited him just fine because he wanted to make the point that local anesthetic was safer.

"Ether was the general anesthetic most often used at that time. Dr. Kane had data showing it was much more dangerous than local anesthetics. For his self-surgery, Kane used novocaine, a recent replacement for the more dangerous cocaine. Kane did the operation with the aid of mirrors that enabled him to see the work area. The operation was much more major than today, as the incision to remove an appendix was much larger than that needed for modern keyhole surgery techniques.

"Dr. Kane said that showing that the operation could be done without the use of a general anesthetic would save many individuals who had heart or other serious health problems. A local was safer than 'going under.' He felt that patients would feel they could surely tolerate the operation if a surgeon could do the job on himself. Quite the showman, Kane had doctors, nurses, and news reporters present while he cut into his abdomen and closed off the blood vessels as he went along. He pulled up the end of the infected appendix, snipped it off, and bent the stump under. He let an assistant close the surgical wound as he would have with a regular patient.

"Kane's operation was a sensation at the time and for years to come."

Jack said, "I've read of doctors operating on themselves when they had a crisis in a remote area where there was no one to help. But I never heard of anyone doing an appendectomy on himself solely to teach doctors and the public. What a history lesson."

Thomas asked, "Do I get credit for spinning a good yarn?"

"Yes," Michelle said. "But I can top it. I have a story about another doctor who also performed a procedure on himself. Like Dr. Kane, this physician also had an altruistic motive.

"Today, if you go to a hospital with a suspected cardiac problem, it's likely that a catheter will be inserted into your heart for diagnostic purposes. And if you indeed have a heart problem, the catheter then could enable any of several treatments such as delivery of medication. But use of a catheter in human cardiology is a surprisingly recent development. In the mid-1800s, two French scientists inserted catheters into horses' hearts for research purposes. And French physiologist Claude Bernard published a book in 1879 that showed he catheterized horses on a clinical basis. But there seems to be no verifiable record of anyone inserting a tube into a human heart until a young German doctor named Werner Forssman did that very thing in 1929 in a small hospital in Eberswalde, a town near Berlin."

Raymond said, "In all those centuries since Hippocrates no one had placed a tube in a human heart?"

Michelle said, "Well someone might have. But there is no verifiable record. For example, a doctor named Johann Dieffenbach claimed that in 1831 he put a catheter into the heart of a human patient dying of cholera to drain away excess blood. But x-rays would not be discovered until 1895, so naturally, he did not have a picture to show the catheter in the person's heart. Also Dieffenbach apparently failed to persuade other doctors of the validity of his claim. On the other hand, Forssman made sure he got an x-ray picture that showed the catheter in his heart, and he had witnesses who saw him threading the tube into a vein in his arm and also saw the x-ray picture being taken."

"But what about all those centuries since Hippocrates? Had no one inserted a tube into a human heart?" Raymond persisted.

Michelle said, "Ancient Romans prohibited dissection of humans because they vacillated about what body parts would be necessary for a person to possess to get by in the afterlife. So to be safe, they prohibited dissections of humans. Now, Galen did see some living hearts because he was a doctor for gladiators who often got sliced open. And later on, he became a traveling doctor and showman who did dissections in the public square, but he was unusual in having a huge ego and being an extreme extrovert. Almost no one else in Roman times knew much of anything about the heart.

"Leonardo da Vinci in the 1400s and 1500s made many realistic medical drawings, but he focused on the skeletal-muscular system, the exteriors of bodies. I'm not saying the heart was simply overlooked. To the contrary, it was regarded as very special. In fact, this special status is a big part of why doctors left it alone, would not operate on it. In other words, there were religious prohibitions, superstition playing its part.

"For thousands of years, the heart was viewed philosophically as untouchable. Many cultures viewed the heart as the soul or as the source of emotion. Doctors often imbued the organ with magical powers holding the essence of life. And most doctors stigmatized any colleague who might even consider intervening in the ways of the heart.

"So taboos discouraged doctors from intervening in whatever the heart was doing. But the technical problems were even greater deterrents. The heart is literally a moving target. It beats, sometimes vigorously. Any operation would have had to be done in time with the beating. And since heart-lung machines did not exist, any operation had to be done very quickly. After three minutes without oxygen, a patient would either die or suffer brain damage. These problems were not well understood. So, because of superstition, stigma, ignorance, and performance anxiety, there is no historic record that anyone except possibly Deiffenbach preceded Forssmann in catheterizing the human heart."

Joan said, "Okay, so what did Dr. Forssmann do and why do you think it was altruism?"

"Werner's pioneering action led the way to development of a range of cardiology research techniques and clinical procedures. Once the catheter is in place, procedures can be either diagnostic or therapeutic. An example of a diagnostic procedure is coronary angiography, which enables the doctor to visualize the coronary vessels. A therapeutic procedure is installation of mechanical stents to increase blood flow in previously blocked vessels. Catheterization can be used to help heal the heart and blood vessels that otherwise would be impossible.

"The only catheter available to Werner was the kind used to drain urine from the bladder, and it was huge. Forcing this large-diameter tube up the vein in his upper arm all the way to his heart could have proved fatal. He could have torn the vein wide open. His motive for choosing to insert the big tube into his own heart was to avoid harming anyone else. There's no doubt that what he did was courageous and altruistic.

"Werner and his supervisor, immediately published a scientific paper describing the technique. Two doctors in the United States read the report and used the idea in their clinic, modifying and improving the technique. But years went by before Werner learned of their work. And how did he find out? He was informed when he was told that he and the two US doctors were to be awarded the 1956 Nobel Prize for physiology or medicine. The prize itself is evidence of altruism."

Raymond said, "Now it's my turn to provide a little medical history. I'll tell two stories of heroism. Each story is about a young man who allowed himself to be infected with a deadly disease to gain knowledge that saved many lives. The two men were Daniel Alcides Carrión and Jesse Lazear. I'll begin with Daniel since he came first in time.

"In 1875, a mysterious epidemic in Peru delayed construction of a critical rail line from the coastal city of Callao to the mining town of La Oroya in the Andean Plateau. This disease, marked by severe fever and hemolytic anemia, killed hundreds of rail line workers and became known as Oroya fever. It was a national priority to bring it under control.

"Several medical experts suspected that Oroya fever was linked to a peculiar skin disease, whose medical name was verruga peruana and common name was purple warts. But the symptoms of the chronic verruga were different from those of the acute Oroya fever, causing many doctors to believe they were two entirely separate diseases. People were dying while the doctors debated.

"A few years after the outbreak at La Oroya, Daniel Carrión became a medical student and chose Oroya fever as the subject of his thesis. Daniel had a plan for solving whether there was one disease or two. He begged his supervisors at a hospital in Lima to allow him to be injected with tissue from the lesions of a patient with the chronic form of the disease. The answer was no, the risk was too great. So Daniel in Peru in 1885 did what Werner Forssmann in Germany would do forty some years later. He took matters into his own hands.

"Using a lancelet, Daniel scraped some material from around a wart on a a patient who was hospitalized with the chronic symptoms of verruga peruana. At his request, a friend, a young doctor named Evaristo Chavez, took the lancelet from Daniel and inoculated him twice in each arm. Within three weeks Daniel was very sick and had to be hospitalized. He kept meticulous records as his condition changed. When he got too ill to take notes, his friends took over the task even as they helped see to his medical needs.

"The only infection that Daniel had been exposed to was the chronic form of the disease, and yet he developed classic symptoms of the acute form. This demonstrated conclusively that there was only one disease, helping researchers to focus their efforts. Subsequent investigations demonstrated that the disease is caused by a genus of bacteria, which are transmitted by sand flies.

"Daniel was only twenty-eight when he died on October 5, 1885. Dr. Chavez was charged with murder, but the charge was dismissed because of overwhelming public sentiment. A Peruvian law later declared Daniel a national hero. Oroya fever became known as Carrión's disease. The Peruvian government recognizes October 5 as the day of Peruvian Medicine."

Joan said, "What Daniel did is remarkable but tragic that it cost him his life. This was altruism by a young, idealistic medical worker."

"Here's my second story," Raymond said. "Jesse Lazear was another young medical man who took a risk to save others, and like Daniel paid with his life. In 1895, Jesse was a physician at the Johns Hopkins Hospital in Baltimore where he studied malaria and yellow fever. In 1900, he reported for duty in the US Army as an assistant surgeon at Camp Columbia in Quemados, Cuba. Yellow fever was ravaging the camps of US soldiers in that country.

"At Quemados, Jesse served under Major Walter Reed, who today is honored not only for his achievements in fighting infectious diseases but also for his early advocacy of informed consent. Along with two other army officers, and under Reed's leadership, Jesse participated in what was called the Yellow Fever Board.

"The board focused on figuring out the particular route by which the disease was transmitted. This approach brought them to the work of Carlos Finlay, an epidemiologist who lived in Cuba. The board members visited him at his home and discussed his theories on yellow fever transmission by female mosquitoes. The men decided to repeat Finlay's experimental trials but with stricter laboratory controls.

"The experiments to test Finlay's theories involved having mosquitoes feed on volunteers. The intent was to get controlled proof of a patient coming down with yellow fever via a mosquito bite.

"Jesse hatched mosquitoes from eggs to use for these experiments. To feed them daily, he took the mosquitoes to the yellow fever ward of the hospital and allowed them to feed on sick patients. Each individual mosquito was kept in a test tube. Records were kept on which patient each mosquito fed on and what stage of the illness the patient was in.

"More convincing evidence was needed to persuade skeptics that mosquitos carried the disease, so Jesse allowed an infected mosquito to bite him. He contracted yellow fever, became ill on September 18, and his illness progressed quickly. On September 25, 1900, Jesse Lazear died at age thirty-four.

"Along with his colleagues on the Yellow Fever Board, Jesse's research at Camp Colombia confirmed the 1881 hypothesis of Carlos Finlay that mosquitoes transmitted this deadly disease. This resulted in the US Army taking immediate measures to control mosquito populations and consequently the disease."

Joan said, "Ray, you were right in saying there is great similarity in the actions taken by the two young men. Jesse's story, like Daniel's, is both uplifting and depressing at the same time."

Suddenly Joan felt that for the time being she could not handle any more information about diseases and dreariness.

"Let's change the subject. I'd like the rest of this meeting to put us all in a better mood."

"I'll play some uplifting music," Jack said. "We can listen to Barbara Streisand sing *Happy Days Are Here Again* and Louis Armstrong croon *What a Wonderful World.*"

Thomas said, "After spending hours telling each other how screwed up the world is, it's only right to let Louis have the last word."

After Michelle, Raymond, and Thomas left, Jack stood on his front porch, watching the sun rise. He thought of Hemingway's first novel, *The Sun Also Rises*, first published in 1926. That was thirty-five years before the literary genius died of suicide brought on by a psychiatrist's reckless use of electroconvulsive therapy. The treatments caused Hemingway to lose much of his memory, and he knew that his writing days had ended.

Chapter 56

No Say in the Matter

Patients lose credibility and autonomy to the extent that psychiatrists view them as deviants and incompetents. Thus their experience of illness and side effects are of little concern to providers.

—Phil Brown and Steven C. Funk
Tardive Dyskinesia Barriers to the Professional Recognition of an Iatrogenic Disease (1986)

Dr. Thein had practiced psychiatry in Riverside County for more than five years. For the first three years he had focused on his county practice. But as time went on, he shifted much of his attention to his private practice of seeing elderly patients in hospices and assisted living facilities. Most suffered from depression or dementia.

Some of Thein's geriatric patients were taking as many as twenty-five medications. Other doctors may prescribed up to eighteen or nineteen medications for various perceived physical problems, and Thein did not hesitate to add seven or eight psychotrophic drugs to the mix. The number of drugs increased the longer a patient was in a care facility. Once prescriptions were written, few doctors, including Thein, ever reevaluated whether there was a continuing need for any given drug.

Regulatory oversight of Thein's private practice was even more lax than that of his county practice. Old people die, so the medical and legal authorities did not make much of it when a large percentage of Thein's geriatric patients passed away. They occupied many different hospices, rest homes, and assisted living facilities, therefore it was rare for more than two or three of his patients to die at any one location within a month. Authorities rationalized that Dr. Thein had done nothing wrong because most of his patients suffered from multiple conditions.

Two brothers in their thirties forced the California Medical Board to ask Dr. Thein about one of his elderly patients, Bertrand Garrett. Mr. Garrett, 83, had beaten himself until his face was black and blue and his eyes were swollen shut. He died after beating himself for the third time.

Mr. Garrett's grandsons, Nick and Ted, alleged that Thein's medications was a major cause of death, but the medical board concluded that old age was entirely to blame. It was legal for Thein to prescribe Zyprexa, Abilify, Geodon, Gabicon, and Valium for Alzheimer's disease. This was well within the standard of care that had been established in hospices in Southern California in recent years.

Many board-and-care facilities for persons with mental illness were operating in Riverside County. Licensed by the California Department of Health Care Services, these were nonmedical facilities that provided safe places to live.

The Social Security Act required states to annually certify to the US Department of Health and Human Services that they had established standards for every board-and-care home that housed Supplemental Security Income recipients.

Some of the board-and-care facilities had been old mansions. After the original owners parted with their properties, some of the new proprietors converted the elegant old homes to housing for mentally ill patients. Construction contractors installed interior walls and added plumbing and electrical wiring to create separate, small apartments. They also added outside entrances and separate heating-and-cooling systems for the individual units. Small investors sometimes were the ones to modify an old home and then they lived in and managed the property.

These private owners then leased the board-and-care homes to the state for occupancy by mental health patients who were trying to recover enough to live independently. The state deducted the rent payments from the monthly Supplemental Security Income that the residents received. In this way, the owner-operator of the home received reliable, on-time lease payments. And since Riverside County screened the patients, the tenants almost always were well behaved and cooperative.

Some of the tenants had come from Patton State Hospital in San Bernardino, having served their sentences or having improved mentally, or both. Others had found it too difficult to continue living with their families. Still others came from homelessness, having been unable to hold a job and earn rent money. For patients to be accepted as tenants, they had to be nonviolent, shun street drugs, and take medications as prescribed. The owners and operators of the board-and-care homes were not trained in medicine, but nonetheless were responsible for making sure their renters took medications as prescribed. From time-to-time, a nurse or technician from California Health Care Services visited each board-and-care home to ensure that medications were being properly administered. In some of the homes, the owners fixed meals while in others the tenants prepared the food themselves.

Alan and Darlene Pruitt bought a large, old residence on the outskirts of Riverside, and turned it into a board-and-care facility. Five young men, all mental patients, lived there, along with Alan and Darlene, who were in their midsixties. Alan maintained the house, the detached garage, and the grounds. Darlene did the cooking and supervised the house cleaning, which was done mostly by the tenants.

The Pruitts owned the property free and clear and each had a Social Security pension. With this financial foundation, the monthly rental income made them financially secure as long as their health remained good enough for them to do the necessary chores.

THE MIND DOCTOR

Alan and Darlene felt that their small business helped not only their tenants but society as well. They found qualities to admire in each young man, and experienced cooperation and only minor problems. Neighbors never complained about noise or anything else.

Randy Cole, Miquel Sanchez, Marvin O'Malley, Ralph Reynolds, and Sammy Conklin rarely quarreled, and mostly kept each to himself. None had lingering legal problems.

Two years earlier, Randy Cole had been diagnosed as having schizophrenia. His psychiatrist was Frederick McDevitt, an elderly man in private practice. Dr. McDevitt helped Randy adopt a healthy life style, and even took long walks with the young man. The doctor pointed out the health benefits of proper nutrition and ample rest. They looked forward to the day when Randy could hold down a job. He was on his way to recovery.

One September day while doing yard work at his home, Dr. McDevitt suffered a heart attack, laid down on the lawn, and died. Despite his sorrow, Randy could not help but feel abandoned.

No one took over Dr. McDevitt's psychiatric practice, and his patients ended up divided among various other psychiatrists, except that no one from the county contacted Randy. Since he depended solely on Supplemental Security Income, he doubted he could afford the services of another private-practice psychiatrist. Who would settle for the small fee that Dr. McDevitt had charged?

For three weeks after Dr. McDevitt's death, Randy did not seek a replacement doctor. But the state's main requirement for Randy to live at the Pruitt board-and-care home was to take medications as prescribed.

One evening after dinner, Alan said, "Randy, that's the last of the medications that Dr. McDevitt prescribed for you. That's all you had on hand."

"Can I go without taking any medicine for a few months?"

"No, Randy. We need to get you a new psychiatrist and a new prescription."

"I don't want to see another doctor," Randy said. "What if he dies too?"

"That's not likely to happen. And it would be dangerous for you to go off medications. The state of California says you must take medications if you live here unless a doctor says you don't need any. We need to go to the county mental health center and ask for a new doctor."

"I used to go to that clinic before I found Dr. McDevitt. I hate to go back."

Alan asked, "How long has it been since you were a patient there?"

"About two years."

"Randy, things could have changed a lot during that time. Maybe it's a better clinic now. Anyway, we don't have a choice. Darlene and I like having you as a resident, and we don't want the state to bar you from living here."

"That's the problem. I never have any say in the matter. If we go to the county clinic, I bet I won't be able to pick my doctor. They'll assign me one, and that person will never be as good to me as Dr. McDevitt was."

"Maybe after you're there for a while, you'll be able to ask for a new doctor if you don't like your first one."

"Mr. Pruitt, you don't know how they manipulate a person. They would blame me if I don't like my new doctor."

"Dr. McDevitt was a caring person. You and he had a great doctor-patient relationship that you may be unable to duplicate, but you're out of medication, so we have to find you a new doctor."

"I like living here. I don't want to get kicked out. I'll catch a bus to the county clinic."

"After you get a doctor, you can ride the bus to keep your appointments. But let me drive you this one time."

"OK. That's nice of you."

Alan said, "Let's leave here at eight thirty tomorrow morning."

Randy dreaded going through the front door. It had been two years since he had been treated at the Riverside County community mental health center. Mr. Pruitt had said that maybe things had changed at the center, but Randy felt sick to his stomach when he recognized Julie at the counter, behind a thick glass pane.

Julie looked at Randy, said nothing, and waited for him to speak.

"My private-practice psychiatrist passed away. I'm on SSI. So I'm here to see if I can get a county doctor."

"Were you a patient here before? You look familiar."

"I came here for about a year. The last time was about two years ago."

"Who was your doctor?"

"Dr. Loren Bridges."

"He's no longer with this clinic. So we'll find you another doctor. Here are some forms for you to fill out. You can sit down over there."

Randy explained on the forms that Dr. McDevitt had changed his diagnosis from what Dr. Bridges had made. Dr. Bridges had diagnosed Randy as having schizoaffective disorder, but Dr. McDevitt changed it to schizophrenia.

Randy turned in his forms. Julie took them to Dr. Margret Gross, who was responsible for matching each new patient, based on their particular medical needs, with the most appropriate psychiatrist, based on his or her medical aptitude.

Dr. Gross had come to believe there is great therapeutic value in the doctor and patient being of the same ethnicity. Research findings and clinical experience indicated this was true. A common culture was important for a good doctor-patient relationship and for clear communications. Moreover, being more attuned to the social context of the patient's disorder, the doctor was less likely to attribute a mental illness to a biological cause. He or she was more likely to understand the situations that made life difficult in the patient's culture.

If the doctor and the patient were both Northern Europeans or both Asians or both Mexicans, the likelihood was that the doctor believed the patient had become ill from suffering repeated setbacks and traumas. The doctor knew enough about the patient's customs and living conditions that he or she understood the trials and tribulations that the patient met with.

Dr. Gross had come to believe that Barry's death was due in part to Dr. Thein not understanding Southern California culture. So subsequently she had tried to assign only Asians to him.

But she had transferred fifteen Caucasian patients from Thein to the clinic's other doctors who then complained of heavy workloads. Randy Cole's intake form showed that he was a Caucasian, yet Dr. Gross did not think that in good conscience she could assign him to any of the psychiatrists with heavier workloads. She had to even out the number of cases among the staff psychiatrists.

Dr. Gross walked to the lobby to get a look at Randy. She would not interview him but wanted to see who she was assigning to Dr. Thein. She remembered the mistake she had made by transferring Barry Vincent to him and not requiring Thein to report back to her as treatment went along. She would instruct Thein to report to her every month as to how he and Randy were getting along and what medications he was prescribing.

Randy appeared well nourished and aware of his surroundings. Reluctantly, Dr. Gross asked Julie to schedule Randy an appointment with the doctor whose attitude and abilities she had come to distrust.

Julie called Randy to the counter.

"You're in luck. I'm making you an appointment with Dr. David Thein. You'll like him."

Chapter 57

More Medications and New Neighbors

It is somewhat of a disaster to have a bad neighbor.

—Plautus
Mercator (about 206 BC)
Quoted as an ancient saying

It was Randy's first office visit.

Dr. Thein said, "Dr. Loren Bridges, formerly of this clinic, diagnosed you as having schizoaffective disorder. Later, a private practice doctor changed the diagnosis to schizophrenia. Do you know why Dr. Frederick McDevitt made that change?"

"Dr. McDevitt said I didn't show signs of serious depression or bipolar disorder. So he said the mood aspect of schizoaffective disorder wasn't present."

"You never have a change of mood?"

Randy said, "No major changes. Just a few ups and downs, like most everyone."

"That sounds like a mood disorder. Have you run out of medication since your doctor died?"

"I ran out of meds a week ago."

Dr. Thein said, "You have been without medication for a week?"

"Six days to be exact."

MORE MEDICATIONS AND NEW NEIGHBORS

"I am changing your diagnosis back to schizoaffective disorder, and I am increasing your medications. There is a wonderful new drug called Gabicon that will help you. Plus I am prescribing Paxil, an antidepressant; Luvox, another antidepressant; Zyprexa, an antipsychotic; Abilify, another antipsychotic; and Cogentin. Cogentin is an anticholinergic that will prevent movement disorders. And since you might be in the manic phase of bipolar disorder, I am prescribing lithium carbonate, a mood stabilizer."

"Dr. McDevitt prescribed only Resperdal, and I did fine."

"Are you questioning my judgement?"

"No Sir, but this seems like a lot more medicine than I need."

"I will be the judge of that. Fill these prescriptions this morning and begin taking your new medications no later than this evening. Follow the directions on the vials because some of the medications must be taken in the morning, some in the evening, and some twice a day. Some you will take with food and others on an empty stomach. Make an appointment to be back here in two weeks."

Caught up in her new duties, Dr. Gross did not check on Dr. Thein's prescriptions for Randy. While hastily dispensing medications, a Right Drug pharmacist did not notice that Randy's medication regimen was being increased from one drug at a low dose to seven at high doses.

Alan and Darlene Pruitt were shocked when they learned the large number of medications and the high doses that Randy's new doctor had ordered. At first, they did not see the need for the increased medication because Randy had been doing very well. He was calm and polite, and got along well with the other four young men that he lived with.

But as Alan and Darlene talked, it occurred to them that maybe Dr. Thein was going beyond simply helping Randy hold his own against mental illness. Maybe Dr. Thein was trying to cure Randy. The Pruitts agreed that, yes, that must be the explanation. The mix of drugs at high doses must be intended to cure Randy. This Dr. Thein was probably a genius, and was bold enough to go beyond what Randy's previous doctors had been content with, which was a suppression of symptoms.

Randy did not want to take all the medications. He hit on a strategy. He would have all of Dr. Thein's prescriptions filled so that no one could accuse him of not following doctor's orders. And to prevent the Pruitts from reporting him, he would act like he was taking the medications but would cheek them and spit them out later. Randy's strategy did not always work because sometimes one of the Pruitts or a visiting nurse was especially watchful when the patients took their medications.

Also, Dr. Thein had ordered too many pills for Randy to cheek them all. He swallowed many even while trying to hold them in his mouth until, undetected, he could spit them out. It was not always possible to quickly get outside or to a sink or commode.

A large family moved next-door to the Pruitt group home. Alfred Copeland was a big, gruff, impatient man, while his wife, Francine, accepted life's tribulations as God's will.

The Copelands' newly-acquired three-story house was huge, which enabled an adult son, Bill, and his wife, Gloria, to move in with his parents. The young couple would save money by paying below-market rent, and at the same time they would financially assist Alfred and Francine. Bill copied his father's gruff manner of dealing with people.

The Copelands also had a seventeen-year-old son still in high school, along with a nineteen-year-old son and a twenty-year-old daughter who had not yet left home and were attending the University of California at Riverside.

Alan Pruitt noticed that the big house had sold. The new family included enough young men that Alan did not need to help them move in. He would introduce himself as soon as his new neighbors got settled.

In the meantime, he had a tree stump to remove from his front yard. He remembered when instead of the stump, there was a fine tree that in addition to shade, provided olives that he and Darlene had pickled each fall. It had been three years since a disease killed the tree and the day that Alan reluctantly cut it down. Having caught up with his other grounds-keeping chores, Alan set out to remove the stump.

He liked doing things by hand. He would dig all the way around the stump and chop off any roots he could expose. Then he would wrap a log chain around the stump and use his Ford cargo van to pull it out of the ground.

Juan Villalobos walked across Magnolia Street to meet his new neighbors. He lived alone and loved to visit. Juan saw two large men coming down the front steps of the home's expansive front porch. He had seen them earlier with a load of furniture.

"Welcome to the neighborhood. I'm Juan Villalobos."

"I'm Alfred Copeland. This is my son, Bill."

Juan asked, "Bill, are you a body builder or weight lifter?"

"I played sports in high school and try to stay in shape."

"Well, you're doing a good job of it. It's getting hot and I've got cold beer in my refrigerator. Would you two like to sit on my porch and drink a cold one?"

Alfred said, "No, we better be on our way to pick up our appliances. What can you tell me about the neighborhood?"

"It's a great place to live. My wife and I moved here thirteen years ago. She passed away three years ago, but I stayed on because I had made so many friends."

"You sound like a good neighbor," Alfred said. "I can't imagine you having wild parties or that kind of thing."

"No, my partying days ended even before I moved here. I'm getting along in years."

Alfred said, "So I guess the only noteworthy thing about the neighborhood is that it's peaceful and has big shade trees."

"You're right. People take good care of their property. Your neighbors on this side here are Alan and Darlene Pruitt. They keep their place in good shape, and you'd never know that it's a group home."

Alfred said, "Group home? This is the first I heard of a group home. What kind of group are we talking about?"

"Oh, it's just of a group of five men, not much more than kids, who have mental illnesses."

Alfred said, "Mental illnesses? We have a nuthouse next-door?"

"I wouldn't call it that. They're the nicest young guys you'll ever meet. The county let all the neighbors know that the Pruitts had applied for a license to have what I call a halfway house. The county calls it a board-and-care home."

"Well, I don't like the idea of living next to people who might come unhinged at any moment."

"Sounds like your real estate agent failed to mention the group home. Probably forgot, I suppose."

"I'll object to the agent and his broker, but I won't stop there."

Juan said, "I hope that doesn't mean you're going to move out."

"I won't move out. I like this place. It was hard to find just the right house for my family. And I've sold the place where Francine and I lived. Bill and his wife ended the lease where they lived. Maybe I'll make the group home shut down."

"I've lived across the street from the Pruitts for years and have never had a problem. I bet you won't either. Come with me, and I'll introduce you to Alan Pruitt. You'll like him."

"No. I've got appliances to move. It's getting hot, and what you said has put me in a bad mood. I'll see Pruitt later on."

Juan watched Alfred and Bill drive away in their pickup. Trouble was coming to his quiet neighborhood. He walked back across Magnolia Street and sat on his porch, gathering his thoughts.

Juan decided to warn Alan Pruitt that their new neighbor might stir up trouble. He crossed the street again. Earlier that morning, Juan had seen Alan digging out a tree stump. He was still at the job, sweating profusely and muttering under his breath.

"Hello, Alan. Looks like you have your work cut out for you."

"Hello, Juan. Did you come to lend a hand?"

"I could work for an hour or so."

"I'm kidding. I've got the rest of my life to remove this stump."

"OK, you talked me out of it. But hold up and rest. I'm going back to the house to get you a cold lemonade."

"Sounds good."

Juan always had a pitcher of lemonade in his refrigerator in the summer time. He was back within minutes. The two men sat on the lawn near the stubborn stump and sipped lemonade.

"Juan, I saw you talking with our new neighbor. I'll welcome them aboard soon as I finish removing this old stump."

"Alan, that's what I came to talk to you about—our new neighbor."

"Oh?"

"Yeah, the papa is an odd one. I mentioned that you have a small group home here, and he went bananas. Maybe he had a bad experience sometime in his past, but he doesn't like anyone with a mental illness. Seems afraid he'll contract a disease."

Alan said, "Maybe he'll relax after he lives here a while and sees there's no trouble."

"In fact, it's trouble that I smell. The guy's aggressive."

"Juan, I appreciate the warning. I'll tell Darlene so she won't be caught off-guard."

That evening Alan and Darlene talked about the possibility of their new neighbor causing trouble. They made a plan for getting on the good side of Alfred Copeland.

Chapter 58

A Caged Tiger

These drugs...attack from so deep inside you, you cannot locate the source of the pain... You ache with restlessness, so you feel you have to walk, to pace. And then as soon as you start pacing, the opposite occurs to you, you must sit and rest. Back and forth, up and down you go in pain you cannot locate...

—Jack Henry Abbott
(regarding akathisia)
In the Belly of the Beast (1991)

The four young men who lived with Randy saw the change come over him. It happened quickly. He paced endlessly and did not speak unless forced to.

Sammy Conklin asked, "Randy, what's happening? You haven't said three words in the last two days."

"I'm OK."

"You're so restless. I'm not messing in your business. We have to watch out for each other."

Randy said, "I've got to go."

"I'm worried about you. Please tell Mr. Pruitt."

"I will."

A CAGED TIGER

Randy pushed past Sammy in the hallway, and quickly went down the stairs to the outdoors. Sammy looked out a window and watched Randy march up and down the sidewalk.

Sammy found Alan at work digging out the olive tree stump.

"Mr. Pruitt, we've got to do something. Randy marches around all the time. It might be the meds."

"He didn't say anything to me this morning when I gave him his medications. How long has he been doing this?"

"Two days. He's like a caged tiger."

Alan said, "I'll take him to the county clinic this afternoon. First, Mrs. Pruitt and I are going to deliver a welcome basket to our new neighbors."

Alan was careful to store his axes, shovels, and rakes under lock and key. But today he was distracted by Alfred's hostility and Randy's worsened medical condition. He stopped digging for the day so he could head off the potential problem with his new neighbor and then take Randy to the county clinic. Alan overlooked a spade when he put his tools away.

Alan entered the kitchen. Darlene placed lids on two large bowls. Beside the bowls on the table sat two huge apple pies.

"Darlene, the food smells good. Maybe we should eat it ourselves.'"

"We better take it next door before we change our minds."

With Darlene beside him, Alan rang the Copelands' doorbell. He carried the two large bowls while Darlene carried the pies. They heard a woman call out that someone was at the door.

Scowling, Alfred Copeland opened the door. His expression changed to one of puzzlement.

Alan said, "Welcome to the neighborhood. We're the Pruitts from next-door."

Alfred said nothing, but his expression softened. Francine appeared beside him.

Darlene said, "We brought you dinner and two pies. I know how hard it is to cook when you're just moving in."

Francine said, "We would invite you in, but our house is a mess. Alfred, have one of the boys bring some chairs."

A young man appeared with a chair then brought out three more, setting them all on the porch.

Alan offered his hand. Alfred shook hands without hesitating.

Darlene began telling Francine what was in each dish.

Alan said, "You're wearing a Marine Corps ring."

"I did four years right after high school. Went in when I was eighteen. Never regretted it."

Alan said, "I was nineteen when I enlisted."

"You were a marine?"

"I sure was," Alan said. "Makes a man out of you, doesn't it?"

"That's for sure. When I went in, I had no idea of what responsibility was, but I damned well learned. Where were you stationed?"

"Okinawa."

Alfred said, "That's where I was. What years were you in the Corps? And before I forget it, thanks for the dinner. I was about to go buy fried chicken and rolls. Your wife's cooking will beat that all to hell, I bet."

"Darlene's a great cook. I was in the Marines from August 1960 to August 1964."

The Pruitts and the Copelands visited for twenty minutes. The Pruitts excused themselves, saying they knew their new neighbors had a lot of work to do to get settled in.

Back home, Darlene said, "The Copelands seem like nice people. Did Alfred complain to you about our group home?"

"No. He invited me over for a game of horseshoes tomorrow evening. I've got to see how Randy's doing. I'm going to take him to the county clinic to see Dr. Thein. We've got to get his medications reduced."

Alan went to Randy's room but couldn't find him. He went outside but still couldn't find him. None of Randy's housemates knew where he was.

Alan said to Darlene, "I can't find Randy. If he keeps marching around in this hot weather, with all his medications, he could get heat stroke."

Alan got in his car and began searching a wider area.

Randy had intended to permanently leave the group house. He did not know where he would go, but he would not take any more medicine. He walked toward city center.

After two hours, heat and hunger changed his mind set. He turned around and started back. When he finally arrived at the group home he was exhausted, but still could not stop marching.

Sammy told Darlene that Randy was back. She called Alan on his cell phone.

"Alan, Randy is home, but won't stop marching."

Alan said, "I'll be there right away. Make him sit down and drink some lemonade. He's probably dehydrated."

At 25, Bill was Alfred and Francine's oldest child. He and his wife, Gloria, were hauling their belongings to their section of the big house. Bill had lost his job a few months earlier, and had found only part-time work. Neither Bill nor Gloria was happy about having to move in with his parents. They were grateful that Alfred and Francine would welcome them in, but they nevertheless were disappointed about having to leave their apartment.

When they arrived at Alfred and Francine's home that afternoon, Bill backed the rented trailer into the driveway. He and Gloria began carrying belongings into the big house. It was hot. Bill was hungry.

Randy marched up and down the sidewalk. Bill ignored him.

Randy marched past Bill again. Randy's movements were mechanical and jerky.

Sammy asked Randy to sit in a lawn chair that he had placed in the shade of a live oak tree.

"Sammy, I can't stop moving. I can't explain it."

Randy sat in the lawn chair next to Sammy, but only for a minute before beginning to march again.

Bill carried in some chairs by himself. Where were his brothers? They had promised to help him move his stuff into the house. Bill was hungry.

Randy marched past Bill again, still not saying anything. Bill watched Randy march to the end of the block, turn around, and come back past him. This time Bill stopped work while he watched Randy march to the other end of the block. Randy made another about face and marched toward Bill again.

"If you're trying to get my goat, you've succeeded. If you don't stop marching, I'll knock hell out of you."

Randy said nothing.

Bill said, "You better apologize."

Gloria returned from taking a load into the house.

"Bill, leave him alone. He can't control his movements. I saw him marching earlier today."

"I'll leave him alone if he'll get out of my sight."

Sammy touched his friend's shoulder.

"Come on, Randy, let's go in the house."

As Sammy and Randy turned toward the Pruitt house, Randy spotted a spade lying on the lawn. He picked it up and headed for Bill whose back was turned as he bent over and reached for a box in the trailer.

Gloria screamed. Randy swung the spade. The blade wracked Bill across the shoulders and neck. He landed facedown on the driveway. He tried to turn over and get up to face the crazy guy, but he could not move.

Randy restrained himself from swinging the spade again although he had a vision of the blade connecting with Bill's face. In a flash he was the old Randy, and he knelt beside Bill, wishing he could undo what he had just done.

On the porch, Francine phoned 911.

Randy asked, "Are you hurt?"

"I didn't think you had the grit to stand up for yourself."

Randy said, "You scared me bad. I'm sorry I hit you."

Bill was still lying face down on the driveway when Alfred arrived.

"How bad are you hurt?"

"No pain… Can't move… Dizzy…"

A Riverside City police car pulled up to the curb. Then two more. Cops approached the persons in the front yard of the Copeland home.

"What happened?"

Alfred said, "This guy from the group home smacked my son with that shovel over there."

Randy began marching away, headed for the city.

One of the cops said, "Stop right there."

Randy kept marching. A second officer ran up behind him, placed a stun gun against Randy's back, just over his right kidney, and zapped him with a bolt of electricity. Randy fell onto the sidewalk, twitching.

"Stop twitching or I'll zap you again."

Randy twitched. The cop zapped him again.

Randy twitched.

"Stop twitching."

The cop pressed the Taser against Randy's forehead and fired it again. Randy twitched then lay still.

The cop said, "There. That's more like it."

Another cop said, "Larry, I think he's dead."

Larry knelt and felt for Randy's pulse. No pulse.

A cop on the lawn said, "I've called the paramedics."

Two ambulances arrived. A paramedic checked for Randy's pulse. There was none.

Two of the paramedics left in an ambulance with Randy. At Saint Rita's Hospital he was pronounced dead.

The paramedics with the second ambulance took Bill to Arrowhead Regional Medical Center. He was paralyzed from the neck down.

Randy's only living relative was his uncle Herman who lived in nearby Redlands. Herman filed complaints against Dr. David Thein for overmedicating his nephew.

The Riverside County Health Department defended Dr. Thein, as did the California Medical Board. The two agencies' letters used almost identical wording. Both missives said, "Mr. Randolph Cole's demise was his own fault because he should have sought immediate medical care when symptoms first appeared. Furthermore, Dr. David Thein could not have foreseen that Alan Pruitt, Cole's landlord, would be so careless as to leave a virtual weapon, a spade, within decedent's reach."

Herman also complained to the California Board of Pharmacy for dispensing such massive amounts of medications. The Pharmacy Board's response was similar to those of the county health department and the medical board.

Herman did not file a wrongful death lawsuit because no lawyer would take the case on contingency.

Chapter 59

A Clique Begins to Form

Similarity is the mother of friendship.

—Euripides
Ancient Greek Dramatist

Harriet Shetler and Beverly Young of Madison, Wisconsin had sons who were diagnosed with schizophrenia. Believing their sons deserved better treatment and more respect, in 1979, they founded an organization now known as the National Alliance on Mental Illness. Pleased with the big turnout for the first meeting, they could not have known that eventually there would be more than one thousand NAMI chapters in the United States.

A local chapter held a monthly meeting in Riverside. Most of the members were relatives or partners of individuals diagnosed as having mental illness. Persons with diagnoses were referred to as consumers, and they made up from ten to fifteen percent of the membership, as numbers fluctuated over time.

Some people joined NAMI after the death of a mentally ill friend or family member. This was why Jack and Joan Vincent, Alan and Darlene Pruitt, Nick and Ted Garrett, and Thomas Prescott had joined this grassroots organization. Other meeting participants had not suffered as severe a trauma but benefitted from the exchange of views with other persons in similar circumstances. Coping skills were a staple of every meeting.

The evening meetings of the Riverside NAMI started with a Care and Share session. Consumers and their primary caregivers told of their experiences, good and bad. While Care and Share was an important part of each meeting, some people came only for the second part of the program to hear a guest speaker or a panel discussion.

Care and Share usually ran for an hour and the subsequent guest presentation lasted slightly longer. After the meeting, some attendees lingered and visited, talking mostly about what had come up during the meeting.

By 10:00 p.m., most of the folks had gone home, but a few did not have their fill of visiting or advocating. By custom they went from the NAMI meeting to Molly's Family Restaurant.

The Vincents and seven fellow NAMI members reconvened at Molly's one April evening. Besides Jack and Joan, there were Alan and Darlene Pruitt, Thomas Prescott, Betty Lockhart, Arnold Fletcher, and the Garrett brothers, Nick and Ted.

The group rearranged two tables so they all could sit together, placed their orders, and began to visit. Sometimes two or three conversations ran at the same time. At other times, interesting remarks would draw everyone into one conversation, and that happened when Jack brought up the name of a psychiatrist.

"Have you noticed how often Dr. David Thein's name comes up when misdiagnosis and overmedication are discussed?"

The eight others all began speaking at the same time.

Jack asked, "Did I strike a nerve?"

Nick, the older of the Garrett brothers, said, "You struck a nerve with Ted and me. Thein was the psychiatrist who treated our grandfather during the last weeks of his life. Bertrand was eighty-three years old, but he was doing well in an assisted-living center. Tough old guy. Had been a logger, a miner, even a bronc buster in his day.

"Thein loaded Bertrand with drugs. One was an anticonvulsant called Gabicon. He gave him other drugs like Zyprexa that's used to treat schizophrenia. Grand Dad didn't have seizures or schizophrenia, and had only mild dementia. Of course Thein didn't give Bertrand a medication that FDA approved for treating dementia. That would have been too logical.

"For most of his life Grand Dad avoided medications. But Thein told assisted living to make him take several drugs. All the medication—in my opinion—made him go downhill fast. They moved Bertrand from assisted living to a hospice.

"He started beating himself in the face. Imagine beating your own face black and blue. Made his eyes swell shut. The nurses strapped his hands to the bed frame.

"Ted and I were in Alaska at the time. Ted was commercial fishing, and I was working in a fish cannery. Long hours. Hard work. We didn't keep track of the care that our grandfather was receiving.

"When we got back home we went to see Bertrand. He didn't know us. Face was puffy and bruised. Died four days later. One of the nurses, without telling her bosses, took pictures of our grandfather after he beat himself. She gave Ted and me the pictures with dates written on the back.

"Assisted living and then hospice never did stop giving him all those drugs. Ted and I were slow to figure out that Grand Dad was being overmedicated. Thein avoided us. We were able to see him for only a few minutes. He insisted that Bertrand's decline was entirely because of dementia. I guess the nursing staff saw their responsibility as making sure the old man complied with doctor's orders. In my way of thinking, Thein poisoned Grandfather and made the nurses complicit in the crime. Ted and I complained to the California Medical Board, but the board didn't do a thing.

"Yeah, Ted and I hate Dr. David Thein, and we hate the regulatory systems that let him practice."

It was getting late, but Molly's was a 24-hour café, and the night owls recognized a rare opportunity to share stories with people who understood the pain they lived with.

Thomas told of how similar in attitude Thein was to the psychiatrist who years earlier had overmedicated his younger brother, Louis.

"His name is Byron Westlake, You may know of him, as he's still practicing."

Jack and Joan alternated in telling how Thein caused the wrongful death of their son, Barry. Thomas then explained that both Louis and Barry had suffered akathisia.

"A lot of people have this mistaken idea that suicide always fits a classic pattern. That everyone who completes suicide is depressed, deliberates for weeks, leaves a note, then takes the fatal step.

"Akathisia doesn't work that way. It's inner restlessness of the worst kind. It's both a movement disorder and severe emotional pain—terror in fact. Endless pacing is so obvious that doctors consider akathisia to be a movement disorder. But the psychotic component is worse, just not visible.

"Akathisia in Greek means without sitting. Most of the sufferers can't sit still long enough to write a suicide note. If they survive a suicide attempt and recover they explain that the feeling was unbelievably terrifying. Their inability to describe the agony during the ordeal is one reason why doctors misdiagnose the problem. The afflicted can't identify the source of the terror because it's so generalized and overwhelming. Some say they wanted to jump out of their skin, and some do jump from heights.

"Others complain of inner turmoil—something inside them clawing to get out. Some complete suicide by cutting their abdomens open and slicing into their stomach and intestines. Much like harakari, which is a Japanese ritualistic suicide, done for honor's sake. But there's nothing honorable about akathisia. Suicide is done to end the terror.

"Some who contemplated or survived a suicide attempt said they had seen death as welcoming and comforting. I'm sorry, Joan and Jack, but that's what Thein did to your son."

Alan asked, "Can akathisia cause other forms of violence like assault or homicide?"

Thomas said, "Absolutely. It erases impulse control. The sufferer might be unaware or barely aware of what he's doing. He just reacts. Akathisia has caused many assaults and homicides.

"The cause of akathisia is almost always prescription drugs. The main culprits are antipsychotics and antidepressants."

Alan said, "This sounds like what happened to Randy Cole, one of our board-and-care residents. He did great under the care of psychiatrist Fred McDevitt who emphasized a healthful life style. Fred was in his eighties and was semiretired so he had lots of time for Randy. Unfortunately Dr. Fred died, and the county mental health center transferred Randy to David Thein.

"From your description, Thomas, I bet Randy contracted akathisia because he marched endlessly. Randy hit a neighbor man with a shovel after the guy provoked him. A city cop used a Taser gun to kill Randy.

"Randy's uncle filed complaints, but county and state regulators wouldn't do a thing."

There was silence while it sank in that evidence indicated Dr. Thein had caused both Barry and Randy to contract akathisia, and that Dr. Westlake had caused the same disorder in Louis Prescott. Three young men died because of a disorder most people had never heard of.

Ted Garrett said, "I wonder if it was akathisia that afflicted our grandfather. He must have had inner restlessness. He was bedridden and unable to pace and that might have been why he beat himself. Instead of marching around, he hit himself."

"That would be my guess," Thomas said. "Psychiatrists don't want the public to know about akathisia. It's so lethal. If people knew of akathisia, sales of psychotropic drugs would plummet."

Again there was silence. After a minute, Darlene asked, "Betty, would you care to share with us whether you ever encountered Dr. Thein? I heard you groan when Jack brought up his name."

"My husband, Clarence, went to Dr. Thein because of depression. The first medicine he prescribed was Paxil. The doctor didn't give the drug time enough to work. He had Clarence coming to the county clinic every two weeks, so two weeks later he added that antiseizure medicine called Gabicon that Nick mentioned. Two weeks later Thein doubled the dose of both Paxil and Gabicon, and added Zyprexa.

"Clarence got worse instead of better. He was more depressed than ever, and he couldn't remember anything. In Alzheimer's disease, the patient loses short-term memory but might retain long-term memory. Well, my husband lost every kind of memory there is.

"I took Clarence to the county mental health center and asked for a different psychiatrist. The authorities there said we were to stay with Dr. Thein for an additional six months and if we were still dissatisfied, they would see if they could assign a replacement doctor.

"I found a private general practitioner for my husband. I took him a shopping bag full of Clarence's medications. Dr. Hernandez took one look at the medications and began doing what he called deprescribing, tapering down the dosages one-by-one over time and then removing one drug after another.

"Clarence is alive—he's home right now probably sound asleep. His memory returned. At first, recovery was gradual and we didn't know if he would fully recover, but all at once his memory was as good as ever. The only medicine he takes now is a vitamin supplement."

The group laughed and cheered.

Thomas said, "Arnold, I hope you can give the group another report of recovery."

"After hearing your stories, I'm sheepish about airing my complaint—it's so minor. But I'll go ahead and tell you of my experience. I've gone to the county clinic for the last two years. I have a diagnosis of bipolar disorder.

"I was seeing Dr. Ralph Newkirk. It didn't matter how long other patients and I had been waiting, he always took the drug reps first. I didn't even know who these people were the first couple of times he took them ahead of us patients. They look like movie stars, and that's how Newkirk treated them."

"Were they well-dressed and energetic?" Thomas asked.

Arnold said, "You bet. The third time they got in ahead of me, I asked the other patients who these guys and gals are. Most of the patients didn't know, but one guy said they were drug reps.

"I'd never heard of drug reps, but I've learned that they want the doctors to prescribe their company's drugs. I wouldn't mind them going first once in a while, but every time they breezed in, Newkirk welcomed them right in."*

Thomas asked, "How long did he keep the patients waiting?"

"Usually twenty or thirty minutes, but once almost an hour."

"Did Newkirk ever apologize for making the patients wait?" Jack asked.

"Not once."

Thomas asked, "Did you complain?"

"Yes," Arnold said. "I complained to Newkirk's assistant and the next time to Newkirk himself."

"What happened?"

"Nothing. The doctor said he had to keep current with advances in medications and that it was patients like me who benefited from what he learned from the pharmaceutical representatives, as he called them."

Thomas said, "Arnold, there's nothing trivial about your having to wait longer time after time for your doctor's appointment. That can be aggravating especially when it happens repeatedly. It suggests that the other patients and you are not the doctor's main concern. This is a mild form of the collusion that takes place between drug reps and psychiatrists. I composed a poem about a bigger problem when drug reps and doctors collude."

Arnold said, "Well, Thomas, don't keep us in suspense. You want to recite it. Otherwise you wouldn't have brought it up."

Thomas said, "OK. Because of popular demand, I give you the poem, 'Dr. Henry's Price.'"

Dr. Henry's Price

A pharmaceutical representative said to Dr. Henry,
"This new drug treats mental illness, and is remedy
For anxiety, mood swings, and depression. It really
Matters not that FDA approved it only for epilepsy."

Dr. Henry said, "What's in it for me?" Privately,
The drug rep said, "Samples you can give freely
To keep patients coming back. And your family
Can take them at no cost so they stay healthy."

Dr. Henry said, "What more?" Again, privately,
And with a wink, the drug rep said, "Would a fee
For consulting make you happy?" "Whoopee!"
Said Dr. Henry.

Dr. Henry asked again, "What more?" Wealthy
Was the rep's drug company, and so he willingly
Said, "How about a training session in Hawaii?"

Said Dr. Henry, "Have you one beginning in January?"

The group laughed.

Ted said, "These stories make me think someone should give Thein a dose of his own medicine. Someone ought to make him take psychotropic medications and suffer akathisia."

The group cheered.

Alan said, "Ted, I'll hold him down while you force medicine down his throat."

Nick said, "I'll bring a funnel."

The hour was late. The group broke up, and the budding allies went their separate ways.

Chapter 60

A Plan Begins to Form

Unjust laws exist: shall we be content to obey them, or shall we endeavor to amend them, and obey them until we have succeeded, or shall we transgress them at once?

—Henry David Thoreau
Civil Disobedience (1849)

After the next meeting of the NAMI Riverside Chapter, the same nine night owls adjourned to Molly's to discuss corruption in the state's mental health system.

Jack asked, "Is there anything that we can do to reduce the overuse of drugs by the county clinic? Is there any direct action that we can take ourselves? I've lost faith in regulatory agencies and elected officials. The pharmaceutical industry seems to have bought every last one of them."

Thomas said, "I presume you're thinking of something more likely to pay off than a complaint letter or a lawsuit."

"Yes," Jack said, "I'm sick of asking for consideration from the county, the California Medical Board, the FDA, MediCal, the Nursing Board, the Pharmacy Board, and all the other worthless agencies.

"I've contacted *The Los Angeles Times*, but couldn't get the paper interested in writing an expose. Doctors drugging people until they're

THE MIND DOCTOR

homicidal or suicidal doesn't seem newsworthy. I've also contacted *Pro Publica* and Ralph Nader's Public Citizen. Both are overextended.

"Last time we met here at Molly's, some of you said you didn't have any better luck in getting regulatory agencies to act. Or getting a nonprofit to take up our cause. I don't know what can be done."

Arnold said, "Jack, don't give up. I was inspired by what you said last month. I've thought a lot about all of you since our meeting."

Alan said, "Henry David Thoreau's essay, *Civil Disobedience*, says that sometimes the only thing a citizen can do is to disobey the law—to take matters into his own hands."

Betty said, "Some things are worth breaking the law for. Especially when authorities won't act."

"Few people are willing to fight for those with mental illness," Ted said. "Maybe we should set an example for other care givers. I wonder if Thein is taking bribes from pharmaceutical companies. Maybe we could get him in trouble on those grounds."

"There are different levels of bribery," Thomas said. "I see Alphatron and other pharmaceutical companies continually bribing psychiatrists with gifts like free drug samples. But the law considers these to be harmless gifts, and lots of justification is put forth by the drugmakers, the American Psychiatric Association, and the doctors themselves. Our objections probably could never do more than slightly reduce this garden variety bribery.

"We could focus on the levels of bribery that we might hope would result in criminal charges. I'm thinking of things like cash payments for prescribing certain drugs. But as long as the pharmaceutical companies are happy paying the bribes, and the psychiatrists are happy receiving them, it's unlikely we could get a law enforcement agency to investigate, much less file charges.

"Huge volumes of drugs, high dosages, prescribing drugs against FDA warnings—all of this goes to say Thein was not prescribing to help his patients but to enrich himself. It's a shame we seem unable to do anything about it."

Jack said, "Joan and I saw Thein at a lavish lunch sponsored by Alphatron. We've learned that he put his name on technical papers written by the drug company. He took part in continuing medical education where the training was held in exotic locations like the French Riviera.

"One of Alphatron's high-volume drug reps, a lovely young lady, has moved in with Thein. She's lived with him for six months. Does that sound like a conflict of interest? The California Medical Board didn't see anything wrong with this living arrangement but it might be a form of bribery, considering the vast amounts of her company's Gabicon that he prescribes. By living with him, she's in a perfect position to bribe him.

"Thein arrived in Riverside with little money, judging from his former lifestyle. Now he has one of the grandest homes in the county and three luxury automobiles."

Darlene said, "We talk in circles. We lament that we can't do anything about Alphatron bribing Thein. Then we lapse back into listing indicators of bribery. We see wrongs, but can't do a thing about them."

Alan said, "After what he did to Randy, I hate that David Thein. I saw Randy disintegrate right before my eyes. A fine young man made violent by Thein and then Tasered to death by a city cop.

"That's something else we haven't talked about—the poor training of police in California. They don't seem to be trained in how to de-escalate issues that arise when dealing with persons with mental illness. I'm judging from stories in the *Los Angeles Times* and the *Press Enterprise* and others on television. The cops usually escalate the confrontations and end up shooting or Tasering the individual to death.

"I recall a lady in Los Angeles. She had a PhD in literature and held a professional job until she fell ill to schizophrenia. One day two cops saw her pushing a shopping cart on the sidewalk. She wasn't supposed to have the cart, but she was living out of it. All her belongings were in it.

"The cops ordered her to dump her belongings on the sidewalk and return the cart to a supermarket. They approached her. She pulled out a screwdriver. A little old lady with a screwdriver. Two big burly cops. Could have simply stayed at a distance. Instead, they shot her dead and claimed they were scared for their lives.

"Authorities didn't care about what led up to the shooting. They looked only at whether the cops could have thought their lives were threatened. Since anyone can think anything, the authorities decided the cops were scared right out of their minds. So the shooting was ruled justified."

Arnold said, "If any of you cook up a plan where we take matters into our own hands, I'll help carry it out."

"Let's let this ride until we meet next month," Joan said. "In the meantime we can gather more information. This could be a cooling-off period. Or we could decide to take Thoreau's advice."

Darlene said, "I want to do something tonight, right now, this minute. But Joan is right. We need to pause."

She added, "If we take action, it must be directed at the worst offender that we have identified—David Thein."

Nick said, "Last month Ted said that someone should give Thein a dose of his own medicine. We joked about holding him down and forcing pills down his throat. That would be direct action by citizens. And it would be poetic justice. Thoreau would approve."

Thomas said, "I know of an ancient cabin high in the San Bernardino Mountains. Back among rim rock. It's in the San Bernardino National Forest. My great-grandfather, Percy Prescott, didn't own the land but in 1860 that didn't stop him and his brother James from building the cabin. For generations the Prescott clan has regarded it as our own. It's not only remote from any town, but it's hidden among rimrock. Recessed under a rock ledge.

"As for amenities, it doesn't have any. It's like the Unabomber cabin. No electricity. Water from a hand pump. Closest community is Big Bear Lake, over five miles away. From my house in Riverside, I get on State Route 38 at Redlands. Takes half an hour to get to where I pull onto a dirt road that goes back into the woods. Then it's a two-mile hike uphill. I see us taking Thein there and drugging him with his own medicine."

Arnold said, "Except that we'd probably go to prison, that's actually a good plan. It's direct, filled with irony, and action-packed like an old western movie. Fires up the imagination."

"I love the notion," Thomas said, "but it would be foolhardy. At least it made us laugh."

Jack said, "It's a crazy idea but the very thought of it makes me feel better. Joan and I are leaving now. We'll see you desperadoes next month at NAMI."

Chapter 61

A Hideout and Seven Outlaws

*My object all sublime
I shall achieve in time—
To make the punishment fit the crime.*

—William Schwenck Gilbert
The Mikado (1885)

Betty Lockhart invited Joan Vincent and Darlene Pruitt to coffee at Molly's.

Betty said, "Thanks for coming. I wanted to talk with you both about the wisdom of doing something drastic to stop Dr. David Thein from overmedicating people. I'm worried that the Garrett bothers might do something that could get someone killed. They scare me."

Darlene said, "Do you want out, Betty? Your husband, Clarence, was harmed by Dr. Thein but with your help he recovered. I saw one of my tenants—a young man I felt responsible for—killed by a cop with a Taser gun, and Joan's son was driven to take his own life. Thomas Prescott's brother suffered the same fate although because of a different psychiatrist. The Garrett brothers' grandfather beat himself to death under the spell of psychiatric drugs prescribed by David Thein.

"In our group of nine, the trauma for Arnold Fletcher and you was far less than for the other seven of us."

Betty said, "I don't want out unless the group decides to do something foolhardy. I just don't want to be pressured by anyone prone to violence. I want to do something bold, something gutsy, but not reckless. It won't do any good for us to serve prison time."

Joan said, "I see where you're coming from. You favor taking action but want to avoid recklessness. Forcing Dr. Thein to take his own medicine doesn't seem like the right project to you."

"That's it exactly," Betty said. "This started in an offhand way when one of the Garretts said Dr. Thein should have to take his own medicine. For a time, the men treated it as a joke. But I could see them warming up to the idea, including holding Thein in a remote cabin. The plan itself is like a hypnotic drug. It's a spellbinder."

"I agree with Darlene," Joan said. "Neither you nor Arnold has suffered enough to make you as desperate as the rest of us. If your son dies because of a self-serving doctor, and you try for years without success to get regulatory authorities to do something—anything—well, you finally get to the point of taking risks.

"Darlene is just saying that our perspective is different from yours, and that we might be willing to go to prison if we can strike a blow against drug-dealing doctors."

Darlene said, "We appreciate you greatly, Betty, but we can't expect you to see this problem the way we do. I never lost a blood relative like Joan has. But I saw a young man in my care get killed only a few steps from our board-and-care home. That kind of horror changes your view of the world forever."

"I see what you mean," Betty said. "I'll talk to Arnold because the harm he experienced was that Dr. Newkirk kept seeing drug reps ahead of him. That doesn't compare to a loved one being induced to complete suicide. After the next NAMI monthly meeting, Arnold and I will let you know what we decide."

After the next NAMI meeting, the same group of nine went to Molly's for coffee and decision making. Betty and Arnold said that since they had not suffered nearly as much as their seven friends, they did not feel as strongly about the need to punish Dr. David Thein. They had decided to withdraw from the group. They would keep secret that there had been discussion of civil disobedience. They wished the seven good luck, and went to a different part of the restaurant.

Nick asked, "Will Betty and Arnold keep our secret?"

"They did the honorable thing," Thomas said. "Didn't want to learn our specific plans."

Darlene said, "Almost a month ago Betty told Joan and me that she and Arnold might pull out. So we've known about this possibility. It's better that they got out now."

Jack said, "The rest of us must confront the same question of whether to stay in the group. Because after tonight you'll know more than you need to—or want to, for that matter—if you decide you want out."

Thomas said, "That's the way I see it. Jack and I have a plan to propose. It's basically to do what we joked about. If anyone is squeamish, I ask you to get out now before you hear the details of the plan."

"Let's have a round robin," Jack said. "We'll go around the table, and each of us will either bow out or will commit to keeping our plans secret and seeing this thing to its conclusion. The going will be rough, even dangerous. We might all serve prison time.

"If you're faint of heart or don't hate Dr. Thein enough to do something illegal, you should get out now. I'll start the round robin. I'm in for the duration, however long that might be."

Joan said, "I feel as strongly as Jack does. I want revenge for Barry. I'm in."

"I'm in," Thomas said. "I'm willing to die. I want to put Thein out of business. This will be revenge for my little brother, Louis, who died too young because of Westlake. Maybe I'll propose that we punish him next."

"I want to kidnap Thein," Alan said, "and pretend to be his psychiatrist."

"I'm in," Darlene said. "I can see Randy smiling."

Ted said, "Grandfather didn't believe in revenge, but he would want us to stop this money-hungry, so-called doctor from harming more people. I'm in."

Nick said, "For Bertrand's sake, I'm in."

Jack said, "So we're all in this for wherever our scheme leads us. Thomas and I have sketched out a plan. We'll describe the rough outline. There'll be a lot more planning of the details that we can do later on. Thomas, tell the group what we've come up with."

Thomas asked, "What is the remark that we hear most often from caregivers who have lost loved ones because of overmedication?"

Nick said, "Every psychiatrist should be forced to take psychotropic drugs before being allowed to prescribe them."

Thomas said, "Exactly. And to appreciate all the side effects, each doctor should take the same combination of drugs that he proposes to prescribe, and for long enough to feel their full impacts."

Alan said, "So your plan is to somehow make Dr. Thein take all the medications that he recklessly prescribed."

Ted said, "But, Jack and Thomas, do you think Thein will take psychotropic drugs just because you ask him to?"

"No," Thomas said. "He'll resist with all his might."

Ted said, "Then how is your plan feasible?"

Then Ted laughed. "You really do intend to kidnap him!"

Thomas said, "To kidnap him and keep him in Percy's remote cabin and make him take the drugs that our loved ones left behind when they died. Drugs are everywhere. If we need more, we can get them from other so-called noncompliant patients."

"I'm proud to be part of such a gutsy group," Nick said. "I say we call ourselves the Serious Seven. This name is like *Magnificent Seven* which was a fictional band of good guys. They fought bad guys who exploited poor villagers in Mexico in the 1800s. That's what we're doing because the psychopharmaceutical industry is exploiting our most vulnerable citizens."

Thomas said, "A name gives us an identity. Is Nick's suggestion OK with all of you? Is the Serious Seven our name or does someone have a better suggestion?"

Ted said, "I like the Seven Desperadoes, but that handle could work against us if the legal beagles got wind on it."

Thomas called for another round robin. Each member agreed that the Serious Seven was a good name for the group.

Thomas said, "Good. I've warned up to the name with Nick's description of how he thought it up. Now we need to get back to planning. Does anyone other than Jack and I have a plan? I'd love for us to evaluate more than one plan for how to stop David Thein."

No one offered an alternative plan.

Thomas said, "We've crossed the Rubicon. There's no turning back now. We can modify the plan as we work out the details, but the broad strokes are in place. We're going to kidnap Thein and hold him in Percy's mountain cabin. We'll force him to take psychotropic medication. And maybe to squeal on pharmaceutical companies.

"We need to meet at least once a week. I propose that we meet at my house at seven every Wednesday evening."

Everyone thought of personal schedules and commitments. The group decided to meet on Thursday evenings at seven thirty at Thomas's house.

"The sooner we act on a plan the less chance there will be that anyone else will find out what we're up to. I live at 8875 East Lugo Street. See you all on Thursday."

Chapter 62

A Rube Goldberg Scheme?

We do not what we ought
What we ought not, we do,
And lean upon the thought
That chance will bring us through.

—Matthew Arnold
Empedocles on Etna (1852)

All six of Thomas' guests were on time for the first meeting at his home. The mood was jubilant.

Jack said, "Please tell us if you have a recording device. I hope no one will make a record of our planning. None of us will search you. We have to trust each other. I pledge to not make any records of what we're doing."

The other six took the same pledge.

Thomas said, "There are seven of us. That's a lot to keep a secret, but a whole team is required to hold the Mind Doctor prisoner because we'll have to take turns guarding and medicating him.

"So far the plan is loose knit. We'll nab Thein, trying to not hurt him initially. We want to hurt him all right, but we want to do it biochemically over time. When we nab him we'll bind his hands and feet and tape his mouth shut. We'll take him to Percy's cabin."

Ted said, "Tom, at our last meeting you said this cabin is remote and secluded. I have questions about the place because our plan depends on the authorities not finding it."

"What are you concerned about?"

Ted said, "Well, remote sounds good as far as making the cabin less likely to be found by the cops. But if it's too distant, some of us won't be able to go there except maybe on weekends."

Thomas said, "Remoteness is a plus in that not many people will just happen to be in the vicinity. But you're right that it's also a problem. The older members of our group will find it hard to hike there. Yet I think any of us can get there in four hours from downtown Riverside. But distance is a problem so maybe one of us should stay for several days at a time. That's one way to cut down on the number of trips to and from the cabin. Also, the less we come and go the better our chances of not being detected."

Ted said, "You said that the cabin is on Forest Service land. Since you don't hold title, how are you going to ensure that someone else isn't squatting there? Some recluse or rock climber?"

"Good question," Thomas said. "I go there from time to time because I might be one of those crazy reclusive types. People have squatted there in the past, and I carried out the trash they left behind. But I've been going there for decades, and during all that time I found signs that only twice had anyone ever stayed there. You'd have to see the place to understand why it's so hard to find. It's built into a recess back under a huge rock overhang. You can't see the place from the trail. You round some huge boulders and have to almost double back as you weave in and out among the big rocks. If you didn't know the cabin was there, you would've walked right past it."

Nick asked, "Why did Percy and his brother build in such a remote and secluded area? Were they prospectors?"

"No, they were bank robbers."

Joan said, "Well, come on, Thomas. You've made us curious about this colorful cabin we plan to use. Fill us in on the rest of the story. We're about to become outlaws following in the footsteps of your ancestor."

Thomas said, "I haven't told this story but twice before to my nieces and nephews. And I passed along to them the map that Percy drew of how to find the cabin.

"Percy, his wife, Claire, and his brother, James, were living near Conestoga, Pennsylvania in 1858. They were Amish but they didn't have a dairy farm like the church members who were better off. Percy and James were dirt-poor, and were employed in building Conestoga wagons, big, specially designed, heavy-duty covered wagons.

"A lot of people came through the Conestoga Valley on their way west. Some bought Conestoga wagons for their journey, and all loaded up with provisions. Percy, Claire, and James dreamed of going west themselves maybe to join a gold rush or a land rush. Their plans weren't well defined, you might say. Well, somehow they wound up in Salt Lake City. They were jealous of the Mormons who were prospering. By now the trio was even more desperate than before.

"So one day, without telling Claire, so the story goes, Percy and James held up the Zion State Bank there in Salt Lake City. James had an old cap-and-ball revolver, and Percy had a big, old double barreled shotgun but he had only one shotgun shell. Apparently the shotgun was an effective theatrical prop because the bankers turned over some two hundred dollars to the Prescotts, an absolute fortune in those days. Percy and James escaped on foot and blended in with the crowds of bustling Salt Lake City. This most likely was just dumb luck.

"Anyway, the two brothers got home, didn't tell Claire what they'd done, and the next morning all three left for California. They had two rugged workhorses named Sally and Jenks. They had a wagon, but it wasn't an elegant Conestoga model, not much more than a cart. This is all oral history passed down within the Prescott family."

Alan asked, "How did they wind up in the San Bernardino Mountains?"

"Percy figured that mountains were the best places to hide from the law. They just picked a range that was a long way from Salt Lake City.

A RUBE GOLDBERG SCHEME?

"It took them almost a year to build the cabin because they picked a site that was so hard to get to. They fell lodgepole pine, but Sally and Jenks couldn't drag the logs all the way to the site because it was back in among the rocks. The horses could drag them only as far as the nearby forest opening. From there the two brothers had to lift or roll the logs into place. They used axes, ropes, pulleys, and pry bars. They notched the logs and fitted them together. They also built a shed—it wasn't big enough for me to call it a barn—for the horses."

Alan said, "They must have had to come out of the mountains to get provisions."

"Yes, they did, but only about twice a year. James eventually left the cabin and got work in the citrus industry that was taking hold in the Riverside area. That's the history of the cabin that I'll show you soon."

Nick said, "Tom let's get back to the biochemistry damage that you said we could inflict on Thein."

"We'll explain to Thein what we're going to do," Thomas said. "Then we'll medicate him and watch him contract akathisia. I hope you all will go along with causing akathisia because that's what destroyed Louis, Barry, Randy, and probably Bertrand. There's another psychomotor disorder that we might cause Thein to contract. It's called dyskinesia, and there's an acute form and a delayed onset form. Dyskinesia is very disabling."

Nick said, "Akathisia and dyskinesia are great ideas. Appropriate. Ironic. Poetic justice. Couldn't happen to a nicer guy. But I keep wondering about the end game. Are we going to let him recover by tapering his doses? Are we going to just stop the drugs abruptly and see if he can handle the withdrawal symptoms?

"Are we going to induce suicide and make it easy for him to jump from a high place? Or maybe provide him with a knife? What's the end game? Is there a plan to keep us out of prison?"

Thomas said, "Those are good questions. I don't have answers. I suggest that we plan carefully how to capture Thein, how to drug him, and how to keep him captive. But from there on let's play it by ear. That sounds half-baked, so we could call the tactic by a different name. Instead of 'playing it by ear,' we could call it 'making midcourse corrections.' Those lofty words make it sound like we know what we're doing.

"The guy might force us to change our plans by having a heart attack. Let's just concentrate on getting Thein to Percy's cabin and keeping him drugged for several weeks. Then we can decide what to do with him. In other words, we can make a midcourse correction at that time.

"To keep secret what we're doing is the best way to keep our options open. If we can keep the authorities from knowing what we're doing, we'll buy time to figure out how we might avoid prison sentences. We have to keep our mouths shut. Don't tell even your dearest friend what we're doing."

Nick said, "We should build in some measures to prevent Thein from reporting us to the authorities."

Alan said, "I agree that we must try to keep Thein from getting us in trouble with the cops."

"That sounds ominous," Darlene said.

Jack said, "If we're overwrought about being punished by the law, we should cancel our kidnap scheme. We have to be willing to stand trial because there's a good chance that we'll be caught regardless of whether we silence Thein.

"If we just wanted to punish Thein or to stop him from prescribing drugs, there are simpler ways than what we're planning. We could just shoot him or run him down with a car. So our kidnapping him, holding him captive, and drugging him might seem unduly complex and therefore unnecessarily risky.

"But ours really isn't a Rube Goldberg scheme because we want to do more than just eliminate the quack. We want him to suffer mentally the way he made our loved ones suffer. We want to watch his symptoms develop and worsen. This is what requires a more complicated plan and thus increases our risk.

"We need to resolve to not regret this adventure even if we get caught and punished. We should be defiant and proud that we will have punished an evil person, and maybe caused other psychiatrists to reform, that is if they learn what happened to their colleague."

A RUBE GOLDBERG SCHEME?

Alan said, "A trial and news coverage would inform the psycho-pharmaceutical people that there are citizens who object strongly to overmedicating patients."

Thomas said, "Enough gloom and doom. We all recognize the risks we're taking. Let's work out the details of how to capture this fiend. The first step of our plan concerns where we apprehend Thein. At his home? At the county mental health center? At a hospice? On his way to work in the morning?"

"We need to avoid security cameras," Nick said. "So let's rule out the county mental health center. Let's also rule out stopping a moving car. It's too dangerous. But we might grab him just as he gets into or out of his car."

Ted said, "I like the idea of taking him when he's getting into his car. And if we seize him in the evening, it might take longer for someone to notice that he's missing. You know what I mean? If we grab him in the morning just before work, his bosses will immediately wonder where he is.

"But nowadays there are security cameras at the hospices and most everywhere. Someone should follow Thein for a few days and see if he routinely stops some place where there are no cameras."

Jack said, "Joan and I will follow Thein's car for a few days. Although he knows us, he doesn't know our car. The rest of you have to work for a living and don't have the time to follow the devil."

"Thein will fight back," Thomas said. "Ted and Nick are the biggest, strongest, and youngest of us all. To carry hod for a construction project takes a strong man. Ted and Nick, are you two willing to apprehend Thein?"

Ted said, "Glad to. But we need a driver, so Nick and I can double up on him."

Alan said, "I'll be happy to drive."

Nick said, "We shouldn't use Thein's car to transport him. Cops would know which vehicle to look for."

Alan said, "I have a cargo van that's perfect for the job."

Chapter 63

This is The Place

'Tis my opinion every man cheats in his way, and he is only honest who is not discovered.

—Susannah Centlivre
The Artifice (1722)

A few days later, at their home, Joan asked her husband, "How do you feel now that we've decided on a plan?"

"I keep asking myself what Barry would say. I never knew him to seek revenge."

"Neither did I. But he would want to prevent Thein from harming anyone else."

"Our plan has two goals. To stop Thein from doing further harm is the noble goal. To punish him by force feeding him drugs is the ignoble goal. Barry would like our first goal but not our second."

Joan said, "I suppose we could imprison Thein without making him take his own medicine, or maybe we could fit him with a straitjacket and ship him back to Burma. But I don't think the Garretts, Thomas, or Alan would like those options."

"I wish we could come up with a plan that Barry would like all parts of. I'd like to make Thein real sick but then allow him to recover. But from what I've read, long-term use or heavy doses of psychotropic drugs may not result in just a temporary altered state of consciousness. More likely the result will be lifelong traumatic brain injury. Tardive dyskinesia for example usually is irreversible."

"It would be good if we could teach him a lesson without making him a permanent basketcase," Joan said. "But these drugs are not the precision tools that Alphatron claims."

Jack said, "I can't deny that revenge is one of my motives, but I have always placed the most importance on preventing Thein from harming others."

"Maybe we can keep the Garretts from being overzealous. Other than that, we may have to just accept that our plan is not perfect. The main elements are to kidnap Thein, take him to Percy's cabin, and feed him the drugs that he prescribed so recklessly. If we like those parts of our plan, we may have to accept some unavoidable collateral damage. I can't believe I'm saying this. I sound like Niccolò Machiavelli."

"We've searched our souls and found some dark places," Jack said. "I just pray that Barry likes our overall intent. Let's move on to planning how we're going to follow Thein."

After taking a couple of deep breaths, Jack continued.

"We're going to follow Thein for three days and report back to our group. We're going to learn his daily routine and when he's most vulnerable to being snatched and shoved into Alan's cargo van."

Joan said, "We'll start out each morning by following Thein from his home. We'll track him until he gets back home at night. That's the only way we can learn the best place for our guys to grab him."

"We'll have to spend a lot of time just waiting and watching. We can come back home or go to a coffee shop when Thein is working at the county clinic, but the rest of the time he'll be coming and going, and we'll have to stay in our car so we can take off the instant he does."

Joan said, "Let's go over our checklist. Cell phone. Binoculars. Sun glasses. Baseball caps. Note pad and pens. Snacks. Reading material. We've got a full tank of gas."

The next morning, the Vincents woke up early. After coffee, Jack said, "Let's go before Thein leaves home for work."

Jack and Joan climbed into their gray Honda Accord, and Jack took the wheel. They parked on Belladonna Drive near Thein's driveway, anticipating which direction he would turn.

A tall wrought iron fence protected Thein's mansion. Just as Jack pulled up to the curb, an electronically operated gate slid open. Thein went the opposite direction of what Jack had guessed. His luxury car swung onto the street and headed in their direction. The Mercedes' headlights lit up the inside of the Honda. Jack and Joan had no time to scrunch down in their seats to try to hide. The lights shined directly on their faces.

Thein continued on his way.

Jack made a quick U-turn. Traffic was light, so he was able to draw near enough to recognize Thein's car. Then he dropped back a short distance.

Jack said, "I'm sure Thein is headed to the county clinic so I'm not worried about losing him, but the idea is for us to observe everything he does for three days. We don't want to take anything for granted. If we do, we might miss something important."

Thein drove to the county mental health center, through the front parking lot, and all the way to the back to a secure garage. The Vincents pictured Thein parking and letting himself into the locked building. It would be another thirty minutes before outpatients would be admitted to the building.

Jack and Joan knew Thein's routine while he was at the county clinic. He would eat lunch at the cafeteria and was unlikely to leave during the day. They went home, and tried to relax while Thein was at work.

By 4:00 p.m. the Vincents were parked in the clinic's front lot. At 5:10 p.m. Thein's Mercedes moved through the lot and onto the street. Jack eased his Honda into the same lane of traffic that Thein was traveling but kept at least one vehicle between his car and the Mercedes.

Thein pulled into the parking lot of the Crescent Commons Assisted Living Center, and parked in a space reserved for physicians. Jack parked on the street. He and Joan waited for Thein to go inside, and then tried to look like visitors while they scanned the area for security cameras.

Joan said, "Most cameras are hidden or are up high to keep people from disabling them. This is not a good place for the Garretts to nab Thein."

Thein had three patients at the Crescent facility, so he was there for thirty-five minutes. He drove several blocks to Inland Senior Living where he had two patients. The Vincents again parked on the street, and again decided this would not be a good place to capture their quarry. So it went until late at night when Thein's electronic gate slid open to let the Mercedes in.

Joan said, "We learned some about Thein's mode of operation, and we eliminated a few places as unsuitable for the kidnapping."

"All we need to do is find one good place to nab the devil. Let's go home and get some sleep.

The next morning, Jack and Joan arrived fifteen minutes earlier than the day before, and parked their car on the opposite side of Belladonna Drive. They pulled their baseball caps down low.

At 7:15 a.m., the black Mercedes pulled out of the driveway and headed in the same direction as of the day before. The Honda followed at a distance.

Thein drove through the county mental health center's front parking lot and into the garage at the back.

Jack said, "I feel guilty that we aren't monitoring this guy at every moment. I feel like we're letting our team down."

"It's a natural feeling," Joan said. "We want to implement our plan as soon as possible, but there are some things we can't rush. Most days, Thein will spend eight hours here at the county clinic. And I bet he'll overdiagnose and overtreat innocent patients, but we can't sit in his office and object. That's what his supervisors should be doing—making sure he practices safe medicine.

"Our contribution to the team effort—at this point at least—is to see what he does when he leaves the clinic. We're just trying to find the best place to set our trap. We can't feel guilty because we spend time at home waiting for him to complete his shift at work."

Jack said, "You're right. I just feel that I must do something at every moment to avenge Barry's death."

"We'll get revenge. Now that we've admitted to ourselves that we're normal humans with a strong desire for payback, we'll get revenge. There are just places in our plan where we have to be patient. There'll be other places where the action will speed up."

Jack and Joan went home. While Joan prepared lunch, Jack went over the team's plan. He did his best thinking when he sat at his desk and doodled. He told himself to not make any sketches that could be used as evidence against the Seven, but he could doodle as long as he destroyed his drawings.

Jack created a cartoon strip like those Barry used to draw. He drew Ted punching Thein so hard that the doctor sailed through the air and landed in Alan's cargo van. In place of Thein's eyes, Jack drew two +s.

Thein was stretched out, unconscious, while Nick duct taped the quack's hands behind his back. Alan drove furiously along a twisting mountain road, then Nick and Ted forced Thein to march through the forest until they arrived at a remote cabin. Ted pushed Thein into the cabin.

Next, the comic strip showed a festive group using a gigantic funnel to pour pills down Thein's throat. The next panel showed them sticking him with a huge hypodermic needle while singing and dancing.

Joan said, "Let's eat."

Jack left the comic strip on his desk, intending to sketch a few more panels and then destroy it.

Jack and Joan were back in place parked alongside the county center's main driveway when Thein left work for the day.

Thein visited two hospices, Nature's Way and Bright Star, and then an assisted living facility, Helping Hand. It was 9:00 p.m. when Thein stopped at a private residence.

Jack said, "I guess the good doctor is making an old-fashioned house call for someone being cared for at home."

"It looks that way. There's no sign saying that the facility is protected by video surveillance. We might've found what we've been looking for."

Jack said, "I'm getting out of the car to see what I can learn. I want to make sure there are no watch dogs or security guards."

Wearing sneakers and dark clothing, Jack surveilled the place on foot: private residence, apparently no security cameras, and no yard lights. The window blinds were drawn and no light came from the house.

After forty-five minutes, the backdoor opened. A faint light from inside the house was enough to illuminate a woman seeing Thein out the door. Then the door closed, and all was dark as he made his way to his Mercedes. The engine started, but the car's highlights stayed off until the vehicle was on the street headed west.

Jack hurried to the Honda. It took him two miles to regain sight of the Mercedes. Jack and Joan wanted to make certain that this was Thein's last stop for the day. The security gate at Thein's home opened, and he drove through.

Joan said, "You could see more than I could, but that last stop didn't seem to be an official call."

"'Unofficial' is a discreet name for it. Thein has a girlfriend in addition to Laura Nielsen."

"Have we found what we've been looking for? Is this where Alan and the Garretts should kidnap Thein?"

Jack turned the Honda in the direction of home.

"As Brigham Young said, 'This is the place.' Tomorrow while Thein is at the county center, we'll inspect the residence more thoroughly. We'll have daylight and plenty of time to make sure that it's a private dwelling and to look for security measures."

The next morning, the Vincents followed Thein again. After he arrived at the county center, they drove to the house that Thein had visited the night before.

Jack said, "This is a quiet street."

"It looks like the best tactic would be for Alan to park his van on the street and for the Garretts to grab Thein after he comes out of the house, but before he gets into his car."

"I agree," Jack said. "If Alan pulled his van into the driveway behind Thein's Mercedes, he might see it and either stay in the house, or run out the back door, or call the police."

"Do you think the Garretts will force-march Thein to the van, or will they carry him and toss him in?"

Jack said, "I guess it'll depend on whether he's conscious at that point."

The Vincents had promised their team they would follow Thein for three days, and this was their third day. The first day, Monday, had been uneventful, but the second day yielded a good site for the kidnapping to take place. On this, the third day, the Vincents wondered if Thein would stop to see his girlfriend again. They got another surprise when, at the end of the day, Thein visited a second girlfriend.

The Vincents were delighted. This was an alternative location where Alan and the Garretts might apprehend Thein. No surveillance cameras or watchdogs were evident.

Joan asked, "What would Brigham say now?"

"He would say, 'This is the second place.' And since Brigham was a polygamist, he would give Thein his blessing."

Chapter 64

Serious Planning by the Serious Seven

Make no little plans; they have no magic to stir men's blood.

—Daniel H. Burnham
(American architect and urban designer)

On Thursday evening, the Serious Seven met at Thomas' house. Jack and Joan described what they had learned about Thein's routine.

Nick said, "So it's up to Alan, Ted, and me to decide which girlfriend's house is the better place to kidnap Thein. I wonder whether he always sees one on Tuesday night and the other always on Wednesday night. We'll check out both places and choose one.

"This might take two weeks. The first week we'll watch to see where he parks his car, how he sneaks into each house, and especially how he leaves the house and gets back in his car. We'll pick the less risky house. The next week we'll stake out that house and trust that Thein keeps to his routine."

Nick, Ted, and Alan discussed techniques for subduing Thein. They decided to not threaten him with a gun because he might not see it in the dark and would not be intimidated. Also, a gun would make it more likely that someone would be injured or killed.

They considered pulling a canvas bag over Thein's head. They thought about bonking him on the head with Ted's five-cell flashlight. Finally, they decided that Nick would distract Thein while Ted slipped up behind him and hit him on the head with a blackjack.

Thomas said, "I want to take you all to Percy's cabin this weekend. Each of us needs to know how to get there. At least one of us will need to be there continuously to prevent Thein from escaping or doing something dumb like burning the place down. Wear sturdy shoes and field clothes. We'll rest a few times during our hike in because it's all uphill.

"We'll stock up on groceries. We can shop at Food Land on our way to the cabin."

Alan said, "Whoa, Thomas. You sound like a Boy Scout leader organizing a hike. If we all go into Food Land at the same time buying picnic goodies, someone might remember us. The store will have security cameras. We'd be smart to each buy our stuff ahead of time from the stores where we regularly shop."

Thomas said, "You're right, Alan. Let's each buy whatever we want before Saturday. If we stop at Food Land, it'll just be for some item we forgot, and only one or two of us will go into the store. Now back to my scout master speech.

"We'll need backpacks because it's a long hike to the cabin from where we'll leave our cars. Carrying anything uphill to the cabin is a real chore, but we need to take water, lemonade, or sports drinks. Stay hydrated and keep our electrolytes up. Remember what happened to Barry.

"I remind you that the cabin is primitive. Percy built it more than a hundred years ago. There's no electricity and no plumbing except for the hand pump. A wood stove heats the cabin and serves as a cook stove too. A latrine is located about twenty yards from the cabin.

"The cabin is nestled in among rock outcroppings. Here and there, water seeping from the hillside supports watercress, moss, and duckweed. Besides the lodgepole and Jeffrey pines, there are huge incense cedars. As soon as you move away from the rimrock, there's a clearing with wildflowers that you'll be drawn to."

North and northeast of San Bernardino, the mountains by the same name predate the city by some eleven million years. They were created by tectonic uplifting and thrusting along the several strands of the San Andreas Fault.

The San Bernardino Mountains run for sixty miles from Cajon Pass in the northwest, which separates them from the San Gabriel Mountains, to San Gorgonio Pass in the southeast, which separates them from the San Jacinto Mountains.

The highest summits of the San Bernardino Mountains occur in the south part of the range, with Mount San Gorgonio being the highest at 11,503 feet. Percy's cabin was nestled inside a granite formation at 9,000 feet on this rugged mountain peak. Many of the surface rocks on Mount San Gorgonio were brought up from deep below by massive upheavals of tectonic forces. Most of these ancient rocks began as either sedimentary materials deposited in a marine environment, or as igneous materials of granitic composition. Whatever their origin, the parent rock was subjected to high temperatures and great stresses that reconfigured the original components into layers of granitic rock.

During the next meeting at Thomas' place, Nick said, "Ted, Alan, and I figure the best place to nab Thein is at his Tuesday night girlfriend's. Ted and I practiced arresting him, and Alan pretended his old van is really a paddy wagon."

Thomas said, "OK, go ahead and arrest Thein next Tuesday. Jack and I will be at the cabin that night. We want to be there when you guys bring him to his new home, or maybe I should say jail cell or hospital room."

"After we grab the guy," Alan said, "we'll enter a whole new phase of our adventure. Meeting here will be too risky."

Thomas said, "You're right, Alan. Let's make this our last meeting here. So we need to figure out how we'll stay in touch with each other."

"One way would be after the NAMI meetings," Joan said. "Since we've been going to Molly's for months, to continue to do so won't arouse suspicion. We'll just have to be careful that we don't sit next to a plainclothes cop or blab too loud."

"That's one good way to share information," Thomas said, "but to meet only once a month will not satisfy all our communication needs. Since we'll rotate as guards at the cabin we can exchange information there. The incoming guard will bring information to the person he or she is replacing, and the guard who was on duty can bring out news as to Thein's condition."

Darlene said, "Those are good ideas, but we'll need to exchange information more frequently. The problem is how to communicate effectively—which might mean quickly—while still keeping our operation secret."

Joan asked, "What do you have in mind?"

Darlene said, "I propose that we use cell phones. If Alan and I are on the mountain and he has a heart attack, I'll want to call 911. Same if Thein attacks me. I might want to call one of you even if I've bonked him on the head.

"I expect transmission and reception will be spotty at best. But maybe by moving around to different locations outside the cabin we could pick up radio waves. At lower elevations, as we hike in and out, we should be able to make contact with a team member in Riverside.

"I read that police can track you by your use of cell phones. I don't know just how to prevent that except that we should keep cell phones turned off most of the time."

Jack said, "Darlene, you make a good point about emergencies. We're going to kidnap a county doctor and imprison him in a mountain cabin. We'd be nuts to think that there won't be any spur-of-the-moment problems. There'll be times when any of us will need to contact another team member real fast. And cell phones seem to be the only answer. I've been thinking about them a lot since Thomas first proposed taking Thein to a remote hideout. At first I thought we better not use them. But then I thought of alternative forms of communication and the risks they involve. Things like sneaking around to see each other, which might enable the cops to follow us.

"So we need to use cell phones, but just be smart about it. I read how to use them without alerting the cops. I went through the same kind of thinking that you are now: leaving the phone turned off much of the time, removing the battery, and so on. But if we do those kinds of things, the phones won't be very useful. And they can be tracked as soon as we resume using them.

"So here's what most techies advise. Use cash and buy a disposable phone. Along with the phone buy some cards with prepaid phone minutes on them. This way you don't have a contract with a service provider so the police have no way to link the phone to you.

"I'll buy a cell phone for each of us to use. I'll buy only one or two at a time by going to different stores over the course of a week or so. I'll give each of you your own phone. Before I hand out the phones, I'll write down the numbers alongside the initials of who gets which phone.

"So I'll give each of you a phone and a list of the phone numbers of your teammates. Guard both the phone and the list with your life. Better yet, memorize the phone numbers and dispose of the list. Some of you know that you can store phone numbers on cell phones to make calling people real easy. So you might be thinking, 'I'll just store the numbers on the cell phone that Jack is going to give me. That way I won't have to worry about remembering them.' Well, that would be a smart thing for a normal citizen to do, but you aren't a normal citizen any more. You'll soon be a kidnapper, and already are guilty of conspiring. So you have to think like a kidnapper. If you store the numbers on the phone's directory, and if the cops seize that phone, well you've not only identified your whole gang, but you've told them how to find us. Keep the list separate from the phone, if you keep the list at all.

Figure out ahead of time an exceptionally good place to hide the phone when you're not using it. Assume cops will search your home, and assume they'll be thorough. Use only this phone to call team members, and never use it to call anyone else unless there's an emergency and there's no other phone available. If we survive this crime we're about to commit, give your phone back to me, and I'll dispose of it."

"These are good ideas," Thomas said. "The more we foresee problems the more I realize that carrying out our plan will be tricky."

Alan said, "Let's prepare a schedule as to when each of us is on guard duty."

Jack said, "I volunteer to be on duty throughout the week because I no longer work for anyone. Joan can accompany me now and then. That leaves weekends and holidays for the rest of you to cover."

"Here's an idea," Nick said. "For the time being, Ted or I will be on guard duty every Saturday and Sunday. We live together so we'll decide between us who guards Thein on any given weekend. You can count on the Garrett brothers to cover every weekend. That'll reduce the number of communications that the cops could intercept."

"Good," Alan said. "This schedule worked out ahead of time will reduce phone calls and spur-of-the-moment meetings. Darlene and I will take guard duty on the holidays."

Thomas said, "No, Alan, you and Darlene will be needed at your board-and-care home to watch over your tenants. I'll cover holidays because I won't have to be at work. I'll just have to be especially careful that the cops don't follow me, as I'll be a prime suspect.

"I appreciate the way you all are offering help. No more meeting here. Jack and Joan will be the guards throughout the week. Ted and Nick will take weekends. I'll guard Thein on holidays."

Thomas paused, then continued, "Since we've decided to not meet here again, this is the last time we'll all be together until after we have Thein locked up in Percy's cabin.

"And we won't be able to get together right away after we capture him. We'll have to lie low. We'll have to see how law enforcement reacts, and we'll have appearances to keep up. We won't want to arouse any further suspicion. So if anything is bothering you that needs the full group's attention, bring it up now."

Darlene said, "Just how will any one or two of us up on that mountain administer the drugs to Thein?"

Thomas said, "There will be two main ways to administer the drugs. Orally and by subcutaneous injection. Don't try to give intravenous injections. It would be too difficult, and Thein would fight like a tiger. You could end up getting stuck by the needle yourself. So either give Thein the drugs by mouth or by subcutaneous injection."

Alan said, "It seems to me that to make Thein swallow pills or capsules would be the most appropriate way if we're trying to duplicate what he did to Barry, Randy, and Bertrand."

Ted said, "Alan, you're mostly right. But in Bertrand's last few weeks of life, he lost the ability to swallow, so Thein told the nurses to inject the medicine."

Nick said, "Swallowing pills can be our main way of making Thein take his favorite drugs, but Ted and I want the right to inject our patient."

Jack stood to ease the pain in his back.

"Nick, where would you get the injectable form of Gabicon that Thein administered to Bertrand? On the other hand, we have an immense supply of pills and capsules that our loved ones left behind."

Nick said, "We might not be able to come up with any injectable. To look for a source could arouse suspicion big time."

Ted said, "I know what we can do, Nick. We can give Thein pills for the toxic effect, and inject salt water so we still get the pleasure of sticking him with a needle. We have a syringe and needle left over from when we gave shots to our dog."

Thomas said, "I don't mind you giving Thein shots to duplicate his treatment of your grandfather, but let me bring you some clean needles. The idea is to punish by polypharmacy, not infection."

Within a few days, Jack purchased the disposable cell phones and handed them out to his team members.

At home, Jack said to Joan, "I wish we didn't have to rely on these things. If the cops find them, our goose is cooked for sure."

"It's going to add complexity to our lives. That's also for sure. How are we going to hide the phones from the cops and yet be able to use them when we need to?"

"We're going to have to find a good hiding place for them and dial the ring volume all the way down to vibrate. We're going to have to leave the phones hidden and take them out at the last minute before we need them. And we've got to be religious about this."

Joan said, "It'll be tricky. I doubt we have the discipline."

"We have to. That's all there is to it."

"I'm with you. I'm just worried. The cops probably will search our house, our cars, and even our persons. How can we hide the phones and still use them when the need suddenly comes up? We're amatures."

"The key is finding exactly the right hiding place."

Jack and Joan spent hours figuring out where to hide the disposable phones. They ruled out hiding them in the house or garage where the cops were most apt to search intensively. Yet the phones had to be protected from the weather. They made a trip to a home improvement store and bought two hard-plastic, waterproof cases.

When they got back home they searched the backyard for hiding places. They examined a brick wall. Jack was intrigued with the idea of removing bricks and replacing them with the cell-phone cases disguised as stonework.

Joan said, "Give it up, Jack. That's an old trick from spy novels. Cops probably are trained to look for loose bricks."

Finally, Jack settled on the pile of firewood in the backyard. He selected two pieces of oak and spent hours working on them with his handheld jigsaw. He cut recesses of just the right size to accommodate the plastic cases. In each chunk of wood he fitted a small piece to cover the cavity he had made.

"Joan, these chunks of firewood look just like the others in the pile. We'll have to be careful to not throw them in the fireplace some cold night."

"This is better than hiding our phones in a brick wall. I think George Smilely would approve."

Chapter 65

Nabbing the Prolific Prescriber

Ideas won't keep. Something must be done with them.

—Alfred Lord Whitehead
Dialogues of Alfred North Whithead (1953)

Ted, Nick, and Alan were waiting in Alan's cargo van, parked on Lime Boulevard, near the home of Thein's Tuesday-night girlfriend.

At 9:00 p.m., Alan said, "Here comes the Mercedes."

Thein pulled off the street and into the driveway of the small Spanish-style house. He got out of his car and walked to the front door. Before he could knock, the door opened, and he stepped inside.

Ted and Nick got out of the van, and hid behind a California pepper tree in the front yard, near the Mercedes. No light was coming from the house. The shades were drawn.

Eventually, the backdoor opened. A faint light from inside the house enabled the Garretts to see Thein's silhouette.

A feminine voice said, "When will I see you again?"

"Tuesday night like always."

Thein walked toward his car, fishing his car keys out of his pants pocket. He came to the driver's door and reached down to open it.

Ted hit Thein across the back of the head with his blackjack.

Nick whispered, "Good job, little brother."

There had been hardly a sound. Ted grabbed Thein under the arms from behind. Nick picked up his feet. They walked to the van whose side door was open. Ted and Nick swung Thein's horizontal body back and forth twice to build up momentum. On the third swing they released their grasps, and the limp body sailed through the air. Like a sack of spuds, it thumped against the far wall of the van and lay still.

The Garrett brothers climbed into the van through the side door. From the outside, Alan slid the side door shut, and hurried around the van to the driver's seat. He started the engine. The kidnappers and their captive were on the way to Percy Prescott's primitive cabin.

They were on State Route 38 halfway to the turnoff for the cabin when the captive groaned and began to stir. He was lying on his back.

Nick grabbed Thein by his hair, raised his head several inches and brought it down hard onto the floor.

"Poison my grandfather and this is what you get."

Thein groaned again. Nick slammed Thein's head on the floor again. Neither Ted nor Alan told him to stop. But he stopped because Thein stopped groaning.

Alan pulled onto a narrow side road that headed deep into the forest. He drove to the end of the road which narrowed even more in the forest's thick vegetation. From that point, they would hike two miles on a winding trail up the side of San Gorgonio Peak.

Ted was the first to carry the unconscious doctor slung across his shoulders. Then it was Nick's turn. The brothers took turns carrying him. Alan shined the flashlight so the Garrett brothers could see the way.

They finally arrived at the cabin. Thomas came out, followed by Jack, carrying a gas lantern.

Ted dropped Thein onto the ground.

Jack asked, "What happened?"

Nick said, "He resisted arrest. I banged his head on the floor of the van."

"Is he alive?" Thomas asked.

Nick said, "He's alive. He's been groaning. I expected you to be wearing a mask. Aren't you afraid of Thein seeing you since he works with you?"

"I doubt Dr. Thein will leave here alive," Thomas said. "I can say that since the women are not present. He'll probably die of akathisia, dyskinesia, or suicide."

"Then why do you care whether he's already dead?" Nick asked.

Thomas said, "I want to experiment on him. See how much medication he can handle before he kills himself. Don't you have an experiment or two that you'd like to do?"

"You're very persuasive," Nick said.

Jack asked Nick, "Where's Thein's cell phone? Is it on him?"

Nick found the phone in one of Thein's jacket pockets. He handed it to Jack who passed it to Alan.

"Alan, there's a chopping block and an ax over there by the porch."

Alan walked over and chopped Thein's phone to pieces.

Thein scrambled on all fours, headed for the woods. Ted hit him on the back of his head with the blackjack.

Ted and Nick grabbed the unconscious man in the same potato-sack carry they had used earlier. Thomas opened the cabin door. The two brothers swung the limp, horizontal body back and forth two times. On the third oscillation they let go of their load and he sailed through the air for the second time that night. He landed with a thump.

Five men laughed.

Jack said, "I expected a bound-and-gagged captive. It's time to tie his hands and feet and to tape his mouth shut. Then we'll celebrate our capture of this murderous quack."

A few minutes later, five men drank California wine and talked. The sixth man said nothing. He was unconscious, and his mouth was taped shut.

The next morning, Wednesday, a tired Thomas Prescott arrived at the Riverside County Mental Health Center at his regular time.

Patients came to see Dr. Thein, but he had neither come to work nor called in. Dr. Gross tried to reach him at his home phone, but connected with voice mail only. Then she called his cell phone, but a recorded message said that either the number had been changed or the caller had reached this number in error. None of the staff knew his whereabouts.

Dr. Gross informed Dr. Conway of David's absence. They distributed his patients among the center's other psychiatrists. Each therapist would see some of his clients.

It was late afternoon, and Thomas had seen his last patient for the day when Dr. Gross came to his office.

"Thomas, do you know why Dr. Thein didn't come to work?"

"No idea."

"The city police found his car at a house on Lime Boulevard. His car keys were laying on the ground. They think someone kidnapped him."

Thomas said, "Sounds like the cops were rather loose with their information."

"They're talking freely because they decided to ask the public's help in finding Dr. Thein."

"I guess the cops have checked his residence," Thomas said.

Margret said, "I don't know."

"I'm sorry. I have no idea where he is."

On Tuesday night, Laura had begun to worry when David did not return home by 11 p.m. He kept long hours, but always was home by 10:30.

She took two Percodan, chased them with vodka, and sat down to read a novel, *The Drug Lord.* Laura fell asleep, awoke at 2:30 a.m., and looked in the master bedroom. No David. She looked in the garage. No Mercedes.

Later that morning, Wednesday, Laura made her rounds of local psychiatrists whom she hoped to entice into prescribing Alphatron medications. She called David's cell phone but reached a recorded message that said the number had ben changed or the caller had reached the number in error. She went home early and found that David had not returned.

At 6:30 p.m., Laura heard the doorbell ring. Two cops, one in uniform and the other in gray slacks and a blue blazer, stood there looking official.

The uniformed officer spoke.

"Hello, mam, I'm Sergeant Oliver Ryan and this is Detective Keith Conners. Is this the home of Dr. David Thein?"

"It is."

Sergeant Ryan said, "May I ask your name?"

"I'm Laura Nielsen."

"Ms. Nielsen, you may be aware that Dr. Thein didn't go to his county office today. Is he at home at present?"

"No. He's not here."

"Have you heard from him?"

"The last time I saw him was yesterday morning when he left for work."

Sergeant Ryan said, "You're saying you saw him yesterday morning, not this morning?"

"That's right. He didn't come home last night."

Ryan asked, "Has this sort of thing happened before? Does Dr. Thein sometimes stay elsewhere overnight?"

"No. This is the only time this has happened."

Detective Connors asked, "May we come in?"

"No, the house is a mess."

"Oh, we don't mind."

"I said no."

The detective said, "Here are business cards for Sergeant Ryan and me. Please call us if you hear from Dr. Thein or get any information about him."

"I'll do that."

The cops left. Laura sat in her favorite easy chair. Where was David? What should she do? She usually felt comforted when she sat in the big, overstuffed chair, but not this evening.

Sergeant Ryan and Detective Connors returned to their cars. Connors asked, "What do you think?"

Ryan said, "If Dr. Thein left of his own free will, he's the stupidest man in California."

"That goes to the heart of the case. It's unlikely that he left on his own unless he has bad eye sight."

Ryan said, "I don't think she had anything to do with the doctor's disappearance. Why is the department on this case so soon? Usually a person has to be missing forty-eight hours before we even fill out a form."

Connors said, "It was the county mental health center who reported the doctor's disappearance. So first of all, this is a government official who's missing. Also, the center's director, Richard Conway, said that people hate Thein for allegedly prescribing excessive amounts of psychotropic drugs. Those folks allege he caused patients to commit suicide.

"Also, a landlady called the station and reported that a car that turned out to be Dr. Thein's was parked in her tenant's driveway. The caller resents her tenant's many boyfriends. One of our officers investigated and found the car along with the doctor's car keys on the ground beside the driver's door. That's strong evidence. A man is missing, and his car keys are on the ground beside the car. If both the man and the car were missing, I could envision him off somewhere having fun."

Sergeant Ryan asked, "What do we do now?"

"Director Conway said his staff psychologist, Thomas Prescott, was the professional who objected the most to Dr. Thein's prescribing practices. And Conway said that a Jack and Joan Vincent lost a wrongful death trial when they sued Dr. Thein over their son's suicide.

"For now, let's just bide our time. We have plenty of other things to do, and I don't have enough evidence to ask for a warrant to surveil any suspects. It's possible that Dr. Thein will come back home from some sordid adventure."

Chapter 66

Playing Doctor

The Devil enters the prompter's box and the play is ready to start.

—Robert W. Service
The Harpy (In *The Spell of the Yukon*, 1907)

The plan was for Jack to guard Thein each week from Sunday evening to Saturday morning. Joan would stay home to give neighbors the impression that life went on as usual at the Vincents'. Jack would hide out in Percy's mountain cabin and medicate the man who in the name of psychiatry had caused Barry's wrongful death.

Today was the first day for "Dr. Jack" to perform his new medical duties. A cabinet tacked to a wall contained three dozen vials of pills and capsules of many colors and hues.

Hands and feet tied, Thein was sitting on a homemade, wooden chair, staring at Jack who was wearing a white lab coat. A toy stethoscope hung from Jack's neck. Although he realized that psychiatrists rarely used stethoscopes, the prop furthered his mockery of their image.

Jack stepped over to Thein and ripped the duct tape from his mouth. Tears came to Thein's eyes, but he did not cry out.

"Do you recognize me?"

"You're Barry Vincent's father."

"Do you know why you're here?"

"Because Barry died and you still blame me even though a jury found that I met the standard of care."

Jack said, "Ah, yes, the notorious Harold Shipman Standard of Care."

"I met the psychiatric community standard of care. What does this Harold Shipman have to do with it?"

"Harold Shipman was a doctor in England who one-by-one killed more than two hundred of his patients. Recently, the American Psychiatric Association renamed the criteria that psychiatry must adhere to. The official name is now The Harold Shipman Standard of Care."

Thein said, "I met the standard of care that was established over many years, and it is what both medicine and the law go by in California."

"You lied on the witness stand. And your medical witness, Christopher Rice, lied too. He's the biggest liar of all the lying psychiatrists that I ever heard. And to think that he works for the VA. Guys like him are why the agency fails to provide the vets with decent health care. Rice knew that akathisia is one hundred times worse than restless leg syndrome, yet he claimed that it was nothing more."

"I beat you in a court of law in your home country."

"The court case was rigged from beginning to end. And you know it. I wish I had Attorney Smoot tied up in a chair right next to you. I might go after that criminal next. Yeah, maybe that's my next project."

Thein said, "You need your head examined."

"That's a stupid thing to say when you're tied up and I have a club."

Jack tapped the palm of his left hand with a heavy dowel that he held in his right.

"You can murder me, but you cannot break me," Thein said.

"You're wrong. I can break you. In fact, that's what this whole thing is about. My friends and I are going to cause you to kill yourself like you did my son."

"The police will find me before that could happen."

"If they show up at the door, I'll bash your head in."

They stared at each other. A minute passed. Thein looked at the floor.

"Do you know what we're going to do to you?"

Thein said nothing. Jack repeated, "Do you know what we're going to do to you?"

"No."

"We're going to give you the same medications that you gave to my son, to Bertrand Garrett, and to Randy Cole. We have leftover medications that you prescribed, and you're going to experience first-hand what they can do to a person."

Thein stared at Jack.

Jack said, "You're going to learn the meaning of the phrase, a dose of your own medicine."

"Please do not do this to me. I am sorry for what happened to Barry. If you release me, I will make certain the police do not arrest you. We will forget all about what you and your gang have done."

"Don't call us a gang. You can call us the Seven Avengers. I'll make you stop pretending that what happened to Barry was not your fault. You'll admit that your drugs and your greed killed my son. You'll admit that Alphatron gave you money and other things."

Jack pulled a small, wooden table up next to Thein. He sat across the table from his enemy, reached into its drawer, and pulled out a printed form.

"Maunt Thein or David Thein or whatever your name is, you are now my patient. I am your doctor—Dr. Jack—and you will do whatever I say. You have a broken brain, and will never recover. I will keep you medicated so that you won't cause trouble.

"This consent form says that you agree to ingest Paxil, Zyprexa, Abilify, Cogentin, and Gabicon today. We'll add more drugs in the days ahead. This form says that you have been advised of the benefits and risks of taking these medications and that you choose of your own free will to take them. It also says that you had opportunity to ask questions."

"This is stupid. I will not sign that form."

"You're not in a position to make that decision. You have a broken brain. Long ago, psychiatrists decided that unlike patients with other disorders, a person with mental illness has no autonomy. So I'll make this decision for you. In other words, I'm playing your role as someone who caused patients to do things that you knew would harm them."

"I did not do that at all. I always put my patients' welfare first."

Jack said, "Yeah, and there really is a Tooth Fairy. Now read the form."

Thein glanced at the form but did not read it.

Jack placed a pen next to the consent form on the table in front of Thein. Then he untied his prisoner's right hand so he could sign his name and take his pills.

"Sign here."

"I will not sign. You cannot make me."

Jack jabbed Thein in the chest with his dowel. Thein grabbed the end of the dowel. Jack punched his enemy in the face and wrenched the dowel away from him. He retied Thein's hand.

"As your psychiatrist, I'm declaring you mentally unfit to make your own decisions. I already decided that you had to be hospitalized against your will, and now I'm deciding that the state must force you to take your medicine. Since I'm acting on behalf of the state, I will now force the medicine on you. Be quiet while I record my decision in triplicate."

Jack wrote down his decision and the basis for it. The sadness that had engulfed him since Barry's death was dissipating for the first time. He was having fun.

Jack rose, walked to the cabinet, and got five vials.

There was a knock at the door. Jack looked out of the cabin's only window, saw Ted Garrett, and opened the door.

"Your timing is perfect. Thein is about to take his first medications, and I was wondering how I could administer them by myself."

Ted said, "When I got off work I couldn't wait to visit our prisoner. I won't do this again when I have to work the next day. This is just too far to hike, and I don't need the exercise.

"How were you going to get him to take the medicine by yourself? I could see how you might do it if you had a gun and threatened to shoot him."

Jack said, "I was going to beat him with my homemade club until he cooperated."

Ted looked Thein in the eye.

"You're lucky that I got here when I did. You could be dead by now. When a mourning father starts beating you with a club… well, there's no way of knowing when he'll stop. What if Jack had remembered the baseball bat in the closet?"

Ted went to the bedroom and returned with a baseball bat.

"Here, Thein, read what that trademark says."

"Louisville Slugger."

"Jack here could use this bat to smash your head like a melon. Are you listening?"

"I am listening. I apologize for causing Barry's death."

Jack said, "That's more like it, Thein. That's the first decent thing I ever heard you say."

Thein said, "May I ask a question?"

"Mr. Arrogance is improving," Ted said. "He asked permission to speak. Yeah, what's your question?"

"I know why Mr. Vincent is upset with me, but I do not even know who you are. Did I do something to you?"

"I'm glad you asked. Great time to tell you just before you take your medicine. You probably don't remember my grandfather, Bertrand Garrett. He was eighty-three years old, but was doing well in assisted living when you began medicating him. You gave him what FDA calls off-label medication.

"You think you're so smart that you can use medicine for purposes not approved by the FDA. You gave Bertrand medicine approved for treating schizophrenia. Bertrand might have had a touch of dementia, but he didn't have schizophrenia. Three or four times he beat himself with his fists. Yeah, hit himself in the face. His eyes swelled shut. You probably thought it was funny. They moved him from assisted living to a hospice where he died."

Ted stared at Thein who looked at the floor.

Ted said, "Do you remember Bertrand?"

"Yes. I liked him."

"Prove you remember him. What assisted living facility was he in and when did he die?"

Thein said, "Bertrand was in Down Home Assisted Living, and he died about two years ago."

"You don't remember him," Ted said. "He was in the Spring Valley facility. Come on, Jack. I'm tired of talking to this devil. We need to develop our medication technique."

Jack said, "Maunt Thein, you can make this easy on yourself or you can make it hard. I'd rather that you take the medicine willingly, but that's up to you.

"I'm laying the pills here on the table so you can see what's coming. Three of Paxil equals sixty milligrams. Three of Zyprexa equals thirty milligrams. Oh, and here's your favorite medication, twenty milligrams of Gabicon. Let's throw in some Cogentin and Abilify. Just as your consent form says."

"Please stop. You do not know what you are doing. You do not know what that combination will do to me."

Ted said, "You didn't know what your combinations were doing to Barry and Bertrand, but that didn't stop you."

Jack said, "We're about to administer medicine, and are experimenting with which technique will work best. I have my homemade billy club, and Ted has his Louisville Slugger. If he smacks you, he could break any bone in your body."

Again, Jack untied Thein's right hand.

"Now, with your free hand, place the pills in your mouth and swallow them. If that doesn't work, we have a funnel. Show him the funnel, Ted."

Ted went to the bedroom and returned with a big, metal funnel with a long tube. It stank of kerosene.

Although he was hobbled, Thein lunged forward. He tried to rise but fell to the floor. Ted grabbed him and shoved him back onto the chair.

Jack grabbed Thein by the hair and jerked his head back. He wedged a kitchen knife between Thein's teeth. He twisted the knife, forcing Thein's mouth open. Ted shoved the funnel's tube down Thein's throat.

Jack dumped pills one at a time into the funnel. Thein gagged and threw up.

Ted slapped Thein on the side of his head.

"This isn't working," Jack said.

Ted reached behind his back and extracted a Glock pistol from his waistband. He chambered a round, and pressed the muzzle against Thein's forehead.

Ted said, "We've had it with you. Take those pills. Now!"

Thein began taking the pills, but was gagging.

"Please, I need water."

Jack brought a cup of water. Thein took his medicine.

Ted said, "Let this be a lesson to you, Jack. A dowel is a poor persuader when you're dealing with this guy. A Glock is more effective. I'm going to leave this pistol here for you to use. This looks to be the only way we can force him to take his medicine, although next time I'll twist his arm just as an experiment.

"Retie his hand. And don't try to medicate him unless you have either a helper or a gun."

A loud *ugh* came from Thein. He was doubled over, retching. Jack darted to a corner of the cabin and grabbed a bucket, but he was too late.

Jack and Ted cleaned the cabin floor, but ignored Thein's discomfort.

Ted said, "You know, Jack, vomiting just might prolong the Thein's life. If he throws up most of the drugs we feed him, he might survive for months. Or maybe he'll die of dehydration instead. We might have to feed him good, digestible food, or dose him less so we can poison him. Ironic, isn't it?"

"As his doctor," Jack said, "I still have a job to do. Should we dose him again this evening?"

"I doubt he could keep anything down. Let's call this a practice run. We learned a lot."

Chapter 67

Join In

A little time for laughter,
A little time to sing…

—Philip Bourke Marston
After (1885), taken from stanza one

On a Monday evening Thomas and Alan met at Subway Sandwiches.

"Alan, please tell team members to keep their cars in the garage when not driving them. This will prevent the cops from attaching electronic tracking devices. Also I want all of you to watch for suspicious vehicles following you. Don't pull off State Route 38 onto the dirt road to the trailhead if you see any vehicles in your rearview mirror. If a car is behind you, drive right past the turnoff. You can turn around and come back when no cars are in sight."

"I'll tell Darlene as soon as I get home. She can phone Joan, and I'll call Ted and Nick."

Thomas said, "After Thein has been missing for a certain critical period, the cops will search intensively for him. They'll get search warrants and come into our homes. It's just a matter of time until some of us are monitored around the clock or are pulled in for questioning."

"Anything else?"

"Yeah, while Darlene and you are making your phone calls, please ask our team members to meet at the cabin next Sunday morning at, say, 11:00. I want everyone to attend."

"Is there anything special on the meeting agenda?"

"I want to make sure that we're all of the same mind. We need to keep acting as a team and everyone needs to feel he or she is appreciated. Some of our group might think we're being too hard on Thein, while others think we're not hard enough."

Sunday morning arrived, and at 11:00 o'clock, the Serious Seven came together at Percy's ancient cabin. None had been arrested or questioned. They left Thein tied up in the hut while they gathered in the clearing.

Thomas said, "It's great that you all could get here today on such short notice. The suspense of when and how the cops will take action against us must be weighing heavily on each of you. I thought we ought to get together, and renew our commitment to hang together.

"It was at the signing of the Declaration of Independence that Benjamin Franklin said, 'We must all hang together, or assuredly we shall all hang separately.' With Ben's recommendation in mind, I thought we ought to renew our commitment to hang together. What we're doing today comes under the heading of team building, or more exactly, team reinforcing.

"The distinguished Nick Garrett has asked that he and his equally distinguished brother, Ted Garrett, lead our program today with a lively musical creation of their own."

Ted broke out a harmonica and Nick a guitar. Ted made background music while Nick introduced their act.

"Ted and I were reminiscing about how much our grandfather enjoyed country and western music. So we wrote a song that celebrates how we're medicating the doctor who medicated Bertrand to death. We have only two verses. You guessed the first one: 'Have fun. Come join in. As we give the Mind Doctor his own medicine.'

"Here's the second verse: 'Whether you're young or old, there's always a shrink to say, 'Do as you're told.'"

THE MIND DOCTOR

"For the tune, we borrow from one of Bertrand's favorite old songs. Pretend that I'm Roy Acuff and sing along to the lively tune of *The Wabash Cannon Ball*."

With that, Nick and Ted showed a side of themselves that the team had never imagined. When the song ended, the little audience laughed and clapped.

Jack said, "There's nothing like a little levity. I love that song. I wrote a poem while I've been sequestered at this wonderful mountain cabin. It's about a drug rep who bribes a doctor to prescribe an off-label drug."

Darlene said, "After hearing a great tune, we're in the mood for a poem. Go for it, Jack."

> The Drug Rep
>
> We know about the neighborhood
> Drug dealer with reputation no good.
> Who when arrested says he is misunderstood.
>
> We know less about his counterpart
> Who deals in drugs more smart,
> Through doctors with a polished art.
>
> The title of pharmaceutical representative
> Against criminal charges is preventative.
> Regulators do not find his dealings reprehensive.
>
> With impunity this dealer plies his trade,
> Telling doctors the best drugs on parade,
> Of course, are the ones his company made.
>
> The drug rep cares not if his products are dangerous,
> Being paid if the doctor finds them meritorious,
> Prescribing them to patients who should be more curious.
>
> The drug rep need only dupe the doctor, or make him

JOIN IN

> Complicit in fooling the patient whose chances are slim.
> When drug rep and doctor team up, the prognosis is grim.
>
> The drug rep gives samples to doctors to entice
> Prescribing drugs with the highest price.

Again, the team laughed and cheered.

Chapter 68

Delusions and Hallucinations

...I need at this point to say something about the word "psychosis." The word has its own problems owing, in part, to the fact that the pejorative label "psycho" is a shortened form for "psychosis" and "psychotic." On the other hand, the word "psychosis" alerts us to the fact that we are concerned with serious or severe mental illnesses in which the personality is seriously disorganized and contact with reality is usually impaired.

—Donald Capps
Understanding Psychosis (2010)

Thein had prescribed a different regimen of psychotropic drugs for each Barry, Bertrand, and Randy although Paxil, Zyprexa, and Gabicon formed the core of each regimen. The exact combination of drugs that Thein was now forced to ingest depended on which of his "doctors" was on duty at the time. Dr. Jack forced Thein to consume the drugs that he had prescribed Barry. When Nick or Ted played psychiatrist, he caused Thein to consume the drugs he had given Bertrand. During each mock office visit, the doctor on duty asked the patient to sign an informed consent form. After a few days, Thein became indifferent and signed any paper set before him. Then severe restlessness and other side effects set in, as the drugs and their metabolites accumulated in Thein's brain and body.

He became constantly delusional, suffering thought blocking and thought insertion. Over a week's time he lost five pounds and babbled continually. At times he hallucinated. In one of his hallucinations, he was under the control of Ne Win and Saw.

> Ne Win said, "Maunt Saw, you are like a wizard, in an important way."
> The Fixer asked, "How is that, Chairman Ne Win?"
> "You make people disappear."
> Maunt Saw smiled.
> The Dictator asked, "How many have you caused to vanish?"
> "I lost track after sixty. I guess I've helped about seventy undesirables move on to their next life."
> Ne Win said, "I have a new assignment for you. I want you to make Than Aung Foy disappear. He's a psychiatrist at Rangoon Psychiatric Hospital, and he's blaming me for causing mental illnesses.
> "He's working with Human Rights Watch, gathering information against me, hoping to bring me before an international tribunal for crimes against humanity. Guess how I learned this."
> "Sir, I have no idea."
> The dictator said, "Your son, Maunt Thein, told my sergeant major. Thein works with Than Aung Foy at the psychiatric hospital."
> The Fixer said, "I'm glad my son served you well, Chairman Ne Win."
> "Actually, I'm unhappy that it took Thein so long to report on his friend. I understand that he knew of Foy's seditious activities for months before coming to my sergeant major."
> "I'll tell Thein to be more prompt in the future."
> Ne Win said, "I have a better idea. Recruit your son to help you make Than Aung Foy disappear."
> "We'll make it a father-and-son project."

By this time Jack had learned a great deal about mental illnesses and was much more than a layman. But Thomas possessed far more knowledge, having suffered the loss of a family member to psychopharmacology years earlier than Jack did. Thomas had studied the dimensions of mental illnesses much longer, and was driven enough to obtain a PhD in abnormal psychology and a minor in pharmacology. All of this was followed by even more learning during his subsequent career. Jack respected Thomas and looked to him for technical information, advice, and leadership.

Jack arranged to meet Thomas on Sunday morning at the cafe next to the Loma Linda Food Market.

Jack asked his friend what to expect as he and others of the Seven continued to force Thein to take psychotropic drugs. What symptoms would Thein be liable to suffer, and how would he act? What behavior might emerge?

Thomas said, "I suppose you're wondering most of all about psychosis, mania, and depression. We're giving Thein a complex mix of drugs with different mechanisms of action, making it hard for me to predict which of various problems will crop up."

"I understand, but give me your best guess. I know you have insight."

"I'll do my best, but my crystal ball is cracked and foggy."

"That's okay. Gaze into your mystical sphere and tell me what you see."

"Well, first of all," Thomas said, "bear in mind that psychotropic drugs are notorious for causing the very mental disorders that their makers claim they prevent or correct. Compare psychotropic drugs to medications of all other classes. None—not cardiac medicine, not asthma medicine, not cancer medicine, and not antibiotics—is so prone to cause the conditions they are claimed to counteract.

"It's vital for doctors, patients, and significant others to understand this irony. Gabicon, a so-called anticonvulsant, is likely to cause seizures. Paxil, said to be an antidepressant, often causes depression. Thorazine, the oldest widely used neuroleptic, causes symptoms of encephalitis lethargica, which is a potent variety of brain inflammation. Its manufacturer claims that Zyprexa prevents suicide, but time after time, civil trials have found that the drug caused the suicide at issue."

Jack said, "So this means that unless Thein dies first, he's almost certain to suffer severe mental illness of some kind owing to our dosing program."

"Of course. He already is suffering psychosis. I just can't predict which long-lasting or permanent disorder will come first or be the most severe. Broadly speaking, he's apt to come down with a psychotic disorder of some kind, a mood disorder of some kind, or a movement disorder like akathisia or dyskinesia. And making matters even more dicey, these possible conditions might combine in various ways. Even when I try to stick with broad categories, there are a variety of possibilities."

"Again, I'm asking for your best guess as to what I'm apt to see Thein do in the next few weeks."

Thomas said, "I expect Thein to suffer tardive dyskinesia. "Tardive" refers to late onset because at standard doses of antipsychotics, TD has a delayed onset. But we're giving huge does. At high doses, TD can come on suddenly and in a short time. That's what I expect will happen to Thein."

"And TD has both a movement component and a psychotic component?"

"Right. The movement dysfunction is usually of the face, things like lateral jaw movements, the tongue darting in and out of the mouth, and eyes blinking. But the impairment also can cause the torso to contort and the limbs to involuntarily make the same motions over and over."

"What about the psychotic part of TD? I believe it was the psychotic component of akathisia that brought down both Louis and Barry."

"Right," Thomas said. "In akathisia, psychosis is more likely to be expressed in violent acts like homicide or suicide. In TD, psychosis is more likely to manifest in weird beliefs. Remember the classic symptoms of psychosis are hallucinations and delusions. The hallucinations are most likely to be auditory with visual ones being in second place although the senses of taste, smell, and touch also can be involved.

"Psychosis in TD is tricky. Some of those afflicted are not even aware of their involuntary body movements. Some people see a person with TD and attribute the unusual movements to a mental disorder but the condition is due entirely to the medications. Often TD symptoms are masked by the drugs and do not manifest until after they are withdrawn.

"If Thein succumbs to TD, he may become delusional, with paranoid delusions being the most likely form. He may think someone is persecuting him. On the other hand, delusions of grandeur are possible. If Thein gets grandiose delusions, he might think he is a great statesman or a spiritual leader. Grandiose delusions can cause the individual real trouble, but suicide is not a possibility since he is so proud of himself.

"When a person has delusions of grandeur, his educational and cultural background influences who he will imagine himself to be. A French man might think he is Napoleon whereas an American will be George Washington."

Chapter 69

Midcourse Correction

It is the advantage and nature of the strong that they can bring crucial issues to the fore and take a clear position regarding them.

—Dietrich Bonhoeffer
(German theologian)

To assess Thein's mental condition, Thomas took Nick's guard duty shift one Saturday. By coincidence, Joan and Darlene also chose that day to monitor Thein's health. Thomas was surprised when he met them in the clearing. They exchanged greetings and spoke of how beautiful the mountains were.

Darlene said, "Thomas, I always marvel at how secluded this cabin is. Your great-grandfather created a real hide-away."

"Percy and James built this cabin to serve as an outlaw hideout. Now that we're illegally holding Thein, the cabin is again more or less serving its original purpose."

Joan asked, "May we see Thein?"

"He's in bed, behaving himself like a good patient. Come on in."

The bedroom stank of medication, vomit, and urine. Thein was dressed in pajamas, his hands were tied above his head to the bedstead.

The women would not have recognized Thein in some other setting. He had lost weight, had a beard, wore a baseball cap pulled down low, and was trembling.

Thein said, "Go away."

Darlene and Joan backed out of the room. Thomas closed the door.

Thomas said, "It'll soon be time for his afternoon medications. You can help me. I always untie one of his hands so he can take the pills. Otherwise, I have to put every pill in his mouth, and sometimes he bites me."

Darlene said, "Help you? What would we do?"

"You can make sure he doesn't cheek any pills, and spit them out later. Or you can aim my pistol at him. He's more cooperative with a gun pointed at his head."

Joan said, "Could we first go outside and look around? On our first trip here you showed us huge cedar trees, wild flowers, and a golden eagle that was circling overhead."

"Yes, look around."

Once beyond earshot, Darlene said, "I'm horrified. Did you see how much he's changed?"

"He looks like death warmed over. Gaunt. Tremors. Baseball cap. Glassy eyes."

Darlene said, "That's Thein. I was referring to Thomas. He's become a monster."

"Thomas always said he hated David Thein along with the psychiatrist who overmedicated his little brother. But Thomas's core personality was kind and decent. He was a gentle and caring psychologist. Now look at him. He scares me. All he wants to do is torture Thein."

"Let's sit a while," Darlene said. "I need to let what we just saw seep into my subconscious. What have we Seven set in motion? What are we doing not only to Thein but to ourselves?"

They sat on a granite outcrop. A breeze ruffled the Jeffrey pines.

Joan said, "My husband has become a monomaniac. All he talks about is torturing Thein. He's thrilled when his so-called patient develops a new symptom. Jack left a baseball cap in Thein's bedroom and was pleased when Thein took to wearing it to block aliens from stealing his thoughts. And he was overjoyed when Thein developed akathisia."

Darlene said, "Alan also is enthralled with what Thein is going through. He says Randy is dancing and singing in heaven."

"The Garrett brothers already were tough customers. I wonder if this experience has hardened them even more."

Darlene and Joan wondered what had happened to the men who were tormenting Thein. It seemed Thein was descending into Hell and taking his captors with him.

Darlene said, "A famous philosopher once said that when you oppose evil, you may become evil yourself. You must resist becoming the monster that you oppose."

"I can give you the exact quote by the German philosopher, Friedrich Nietzsche. 'He who fights monsters should see to it that he himself does not become a monster. And if you gaze for long into an abyss, the abyss gazes also into you.'"

Darlene said, "I guess by 'abyss' the philosopher meant hatred or an overwhelming desire for vengeance, something that could corrupt one's soul."

Joan said, "Whether you call it 'soul' or 'mind,' that's what's at stake for us Seven. At first, I favored teaching Thein a lesson. And I liked it when the guys captured him. But at some point in the last few weeks, the Seven went too far. We crossed a line. Darlene, we can't allow the torture to continue.

"Barry would not approve of what we're doing now. My son's aura of kindness lingers although he is deceased. Barry would say, 'Dad and Mom, don't hurt this man anymore.'"

Darlene said, "What can we do? There's only the two of us. I imagine all five of the men still want to torture Thein."

"We've got to speak up. Thein could die at any time. Some of the men wanted to induce him to commit suicide. I think Thein would gladly jump from a cliff or even slice open his abdomen if given the opportunity."

Darlene said, "We must persuade the men to stop what they're doing. We start by appealing to Thomas right now."

Joan and Darlene returned to the cabin.

Thomas said, "It's time for Thein to take his medicine."

Joan said, "Darlene and I have been thinking about what our team is doing. Thein has learned his lesson. To continue what we're doing will result in his death."

"If we let this guy live, he'll get the cops down on us, and we'll all do prison time. He killed Barry, Bertrand, and Randy just as surely as if he shot each in the head. His life isn't worth our going to prison. We can bury him a mile away, in the forest. He might never be found."

Darlene said, "Maybe we can persuade him to not report us to law enforcement. Or to testify on our behalf. Or maybe even persuade him to inform on Alphatron Pharmaceuticals."

Thomas shook his head.

"You're forgetting how corrupt this guy is. He took bribes from pharmaceutical companies for overmedicating our loved ones. He lived high on the hog while Barry, Bertrand, and Randy suffered and died."

Joan said, "But look at what torturing Thein is doing to you. You're not the same person who offered to help my husband and me after Barry died. You're not the same person at all."

A long, low moan filled the cabin. Thomas entered the bedroom while Joan and Darlene looked in.

"I want to die," Thein said, "Leave the gun with me for a few minutes."

"You'd shoot me."

"Then leave a knife. I cannot take any more medicine."

"Be quiet. You're disturbing our guests."

Thomas came out of the bedroom, and closed the door.

Joan said, "Thomas, you've got to let Thein recover if he can. This whole misadventure has gone too far. You need to call a meeting, and show some leadership."

Thomas said, "We Seven talked about the possibility of a midcourse correction. You two are saying the time has come to figure out how to finish this project. Tomorrow is Sunday. Let's meet here tomorrow at 11:30. I'll depend on you to tell your husbands. Ask

Alan to phone the Garretts. And of course you will need to be here to present your case.

"The Seven will write the final act of our drama."

Late the next morning, the Seven met in the clearing in front of Percy's cabin. The colorful Indian paintbrush and alpine phlox gave the appearance of a festive event, but the Seven were in a somber mood.

Every team member was worried. They had taken revenge against a psychiatrist whose practices had led to the deaths of Barry, Randy, and Bertrand. And now the little band was facing severe legal penalties.

Thomas said, "We came together a few months ago because Louis, Barry, Bertrand, and Randy died too soon. We wanted to stop the wrongful deaths caused by affluent pharmaceutical companies and the greedy psychiatrists whom they bribe. But we had no effective way to battle the overall medicolegal system. So we settled for punishing Thein alone because he was the only bad guy who was vulnerable.

"We kidnapped the shrink with the falsified professional resume. And we overmedicated him with the same psychotropic drugs that he caused our loved ones to take.

"We wanted revenge and we got it. We ruined Thein. He's near death. One question is, was it worth it for the looming prison time? But the more pressing question is, can we lessen the likely legal penalty by cutting back on the medications, and helping Thein recover as much as possible? That would show we are remorseful, and are trying to make amends.

"Yesterday, Darlene and Joan told me they're horrified by what we've done to Thein, and that Barry, Randy, and Bertrand would be appalled. I've thought about it and believe that my little brother, Louis, also would disapprove. Ted and Nick, would your grandfather approve of what we're doing?"

Nick said, "I guess not. Bertrand was a gentle soul."

Ted said, "We came together after the NAMI meetings because we were on fire with anger from being screwed by regulators that protect doctors, drug companies, and pharmacies no matter what. So we did what we could. We picked off a prolific prescriber who happened to be more vulnerable than drug company executives.

"I don't feel sorry for Thein. Thomas urged him to lighten up on the drugs for the sake of all of Thein's patients. But he wouldn't listen. He deserved what we gave him.

"But here's where I agree with you. Thein's paid a high enough price. Even if he recovers fully—which is unlikely—he has suffered plenty. It's like a person who deserves a jail sentence. Once he's served his time you don't have to feel sorry for him but you don't punish him anymore. So let's lay off Thein.

"As far as whether we go to prison for what we did—well, that's a distinct possibility. Maybe it's time to disband and go separate ways."

Alan said, "Are you saying it's every man for himself? You might be able to pack up and leave the state, but it's not an option for Darlene and me. We've got a group home that's both our residence and our livelihood."

Ted said, "We should stick together if it will do any good. But we're likely to be tried separately and to get separate prison sentences even if we remain a team."

Joan said, "I want to explain what motivated Darlene and me to request relief for Thein. Up to a point, we were right to punish him. But we're not the CIA. By going too far we lowered ourselves to Thein's level. Or maybe even as low as that horrid Alphatron drug company. Oh, God, now that's low.

"We were the primary caregivers for our loved ones. That's what we did. We provided the best care we could. That's who we are. We try to allieviate mental illnesses, not cause them. We can't continue to violate our core principles."

Thomas said, "Jack, you haven't weighed in. You've been silent all morning. We can't make this decision without hearing from you. What's going on?"

His team members looked at Jack, and saw tears in his eyes. When he finally answered Thomas, his voice quavered.

"I'm struggling. There's a war inside me."

The group waited. Jack struggled to gain composure.

"Each of you is dealing with emotions, so I don't want to act like I'm anybody special. Maybe I shouldn't help make this decision but just go along with whatever the group decides."

Alan said, "That's not the Jack Vincent that I know. Come on, Jack, we need your counsel. What's going on inside your head?"

"Conflict," Jack said, "that's what's going on. I told you. I'm incredibly proud of Joan and Darlene for having the decency and courage to urge us to change direction. I couldn't respect them more."

Thomas asked, "Then what's wrong?"

"I'm having trouble forgiving Thein, who with Alphatron and the county, killed my son."

Thomas said, "No one's asking you to forgive Thein. Letting him live and nursing him back to health isn't necessarily forgiving him. We stand to benefit by lessening our legal penalties."

"I understand that, but for me with my way of viewing things, I'd have to forgive him. And if he were to show remorse, I could almost forgive him except for one thing. And that thing… It's complicated. To just work toward forgiving Thein, I'd first have to forgive myself. And I can't do that."

Nick said, "It's natural to feel guilt. Maybe you feel like Ted and I did. We felt we failed Grand Dad by not protecting him from Thein."

"That's part of it. But this is more terrible, so terrible that I've never been able to speak of it. Even to Joan."

"Then maybe you should come right out with it now. It might be good for you to tell us," Nick said. "If anyone can understand, it's us right here."

Jack didn't reply. His team members began to think he wouldn't. They began to look at each other, wondering what this terrible thing was that was crippling their friend.

Some thought they knew. At last, Jack spoke haltingly.

"I not only didn't protect Barry, I was complicit in causing his death."

Ted said, "How? I don't believe it."

"I insisted that Barry take the so-called medications that Thein prescribed. I made him take the drugs that remained on hand after he suffered his seizure and had left Saint Rita's Hospital. I urged him to take them all. He was turning away from Thein's drugs, but I talked him into consuming the remaining pills while we were arranging for a new psychiatrist to replace Thein.

"I helped kill my son because he already was suffering from polypharmacy. Thein made me complicit in murdering Barry, and for that I can't forgive him… or me either."

Alan said, "Hold on, Jack. I'm suffering the same emotions regarding Randy. I've hated myself for requiring him to take the drugs that made him unable to control himself."

Thomas said, "See, Jack, you aren't alone in feeling this way. My parents talked about having forced Louis to take Byron Westlake's poisonous pills. It was like Westlake rubbed salt in their wounds. It wasn't enough for him to prescribe poison. He had to make Mom and Dad administer that poison.

"I'm putting on my psychologist hat for the moment. You're suffering because you've learned how crippling and even lethal psychotropic drugs are. You now know what they do to a person. And so you say to yourself 'How could I have made Barry take those drugs?'

"So here's the key to forgiving yourself. You've got to get it through your thick head that you didn't know those things when your son was dealing with the label of schizophrenia and with medical authorities who insisted that their medication was the way to treat mental illness. You've got to drum this message into your head: You didn't know then what you know now. You believed you were warding off schizophrenic psychosis. You were sure of it. That's what psychopharmacology had told you over and over. You did the absolute best you could."

Joan said, "Jack, I felt the same things that you're feeling. And I couldn't talk about them either. About being complicit in harming Barry. Thomas is right. Over and over we must tell ourselves that we didn't know then what we learned later. We were victims of mercenary psychopharmacology as much as Barry was."

Jack said, "I'll try. Whatever the group decides, I'll go along with you."

Darlene said, "Well look you guys, we haven't been arrested or charged just yet although I don't know why. We might have a chance to regain some of our decency and to again live those core principles that Joan referred to.

"I propose that we nurse Thein back to health as best we can. And try to get him to understand the error of his ways. Maybe we can get him on our side, against the pharmaceutical companies.

"He might have an epiphany."

Chapter 70

Thein Repents

A man should never be ashamed to own he has been in the wrong, which is but saying, in other words, that he is wiser today than he was yesterday.

—Jonathan Swift
Thoughts on Various Subjects (1727)

The Serious Seven began trying to reverse the harm done by the psychotropic drugs they had forced Thein to swallow. Which effects could be stopped, and which reversed? Which effects would remain, and which might worsen if drugs were withdrawn too quickly?

If Thein died, they could be charged with murder. What if cops raided the cabin before the Seven could show they were now acting in good faith? Thein would be provided professional health care, true enough, but the Seven preferred to help him themselves. That was the best way to show their good intentions, and to get Thein on their side against Alphatron.

At first, delusions and hallucinations prevented Thein from realizing that his captors now were helping him.

The reborn good Samaritans recognized several risks to Thein. One was dehydration because of diarrhea and vomiting. Another was either of two kinds of drug withdrawal syndromes that could result if they withdrew either antidepressants or antipsychotics too quickly.

They would taper his drugs gradually to low levels, hopefully zero. If symptoms were to flare, they would stop reducing a drug for a time and might even increase the dose for a short period. If he stabilized, they then could resume their tapering.

But with so many drugs involved, how would they know which dose to hold steady or even temporarily increase before tapering again? These were the hazards of polypharmacy. Keeping Thein alive much less helping him recover seemed highly unlikely.

Akathisia threatened his life. Because he had been tied down in bed, he had been unable to pace, so when his hands were untied he beat himself in the face. Physical restraints or strict supervision were necessary to prevent Thein from attempting suicide. One of the Seven's greatest fears was that Thein would contract tardive dyskinesia. If Thein developed dyskinesia, any jury, any court would hold them accountable for severely harming him.

Since most of Thein's day-to-day care fell to Jack and Joan, improvements of setbacks in his health were most likely to occur on their watch. Thomas cautioned the Vincents that TD symptoms often manifested only after the offending medications were withdrawn.

The Vincents made sure that their prisoner-patient ate regularly even when he had no appetite. At first, they had to spoon-feed him foods like broth, oatmeal, and pudding.

Gradually, Thein's health improved, and his caregivers allowed him to get up and move about.

Whenever Thein was out of bed he was pacing in the cabin or in the clearing. At times he felt that his skin was crawling and at other times that insects were burrowing beneath his skin. Snakes squirmed inside his stomach, and electricity streamed through his veins. He could not describe the sheer, generalized terror.

Jack said, "Joan, do you recall the instances when psychiatrists said that symptoms were due solely to mental illness and not to medications?"

"Oh yes, it was never the drugs. To blame schizophrenia or bipolar disorder was standard for defendant psychiatrists."

Jack said, "Well, Thein was strong and healthy when we began dosing him, and look at all the mental symptoms he developed. We have proof right here that prescription drugs alone can make a person behave irrationally."

"I thought about that. The *New England Journal of Medicine* wouldn't publish our study because it doesn't exactly meet scientific standards, but I bet we persuaded Thein that medications can make people crazy."

Thein begged for a firearm, a knife, or a rope. Jack said, "No" even as he was sometimes tempted to give Thein what he wanted.

Akathisia continued. The Good Samaritans did not administer an antidote like propanol. To acquire the drug would arouse suspicion, and they believed that propanol could only provide brief symptom relief at best, and might produce bad side effects of its own

After weeks of drug tapering and nurturing by his captors, Thein gained insight into the emotional pain his former patients must have felt. He began to regret what his prescriptions had done to Barry, Bertrand, Randy, and hundreds of other patients. Eventually there were times when Thein's akathisia subsided for brief periods, and he was able to express himself to Jack and Joan.

"I knew my prescriptions could cause akathisia in my patients, but I never dreamed how horrible, how terrifying it is. No one can imagine the horror until they are themselves afflicted.

"If I recover enough to practice medicine again, I will go into talk therapy, and will never again prescribe psychotropic medications. They do not relieve specific symptoms, as psychiatry claims. Instead they affect the entire brain and body. They are not magic bullets that hit the bullseye. Instead of a rifle bullet they are scattershot."

Several days later, during another lucid period, Thein said, "I have recovered enough that akathisia is absent most of the time. I pray that I continue to recover. When akathisia returns, it is sheer terror.

"Prescribing drugs is not a game I would ever play again. If I live, I will practice only talk therapy. I will emphasize lifestyle changes, things like exercise, dancing, wading or swimming, playing music, and occupational therapy. Meditation. Yoga. Anything but drugs. And I will include the whole family in the therapy. If I live, I will focus on interpersonal relationships. There will be no more of this excluding Mom and Dad."

Thein was silent for a long time. Finally, he said, "Psychiatrists and pharmaceutical marketers twist the English language to make psychotropic drugs seem more effective and safer than they really are. They rarely call the substances drugs. They call them medications to give a favorable impression. 'Side effects' makes it sound like good effects predominate and any undesirable effects are just incidental. The implication is that being forewarned, people can manage the side effects in order to benefit from all the good that a chemical substance has to offer.

"But because the Seven forced me to take these drugs, I now understand what blunt instruments they are. They do not cure anything so they do not have side effects. They have effects—only effects. Now some of these effects might be the temporary disruption of hallucinations and delusions, but if continued they cause hallucinations, delusions, and violence.

"Therefore, these drugs induce diseases, and the appropriate designation is not side effects but disease-inducing effects or DIES."

As time passed, and Thein was weaned off some of the medications, he became lucid more of the time. He asked if he could contact Laura Nielsen. When Jack said no, Thein was saddened but not angered. He understood the risk was too great for the Serious Seven.

One day while they were sitting in the clearing in front of the cabin, Thein said to Joan and Jack, "When I was a boy in Burma, my parents took me to a spirit festival. Actors pretended to bring spirits out of limbo to meet the audience. The play acting, the music, and the crowd's reactions combined to cause me to pass out. When I came to, I was in a trance that lasted off and on for months.

"My father took me to a psychiatrist in Singapore who helped me understand that it was not spirits but my own mind-set that caused me to suffer. This revelation was so powerful that I decided to become a psychiatrist.

"So you see, I entered psychiatry for the right reason—to help relieve suffering caused by mental illnesses. At medical school, when I met Than Aung Foy, the man who would become my best friend, I told him I wanted to be a psychiatrist so I could relieve suffering as did Siddhārtha Gautama, the original Buddha. I wanted to—and again want to—be as much like the Buddha as possible."

One day when akathisia abated, Jack and Thein were sitting in the clearing. Jack knew the names of only a few of the wild flowers, but he marveled at their many colors: purple, yellow, blue, white, red, and many shades in between. The great variety of flowers attracted honey bees, bumble bees, and butterflies also of many colors. The flowers and their pollinators caused Jack to reflect on life and to feel good about the Seven's decision to help Thein to live instead of to die.

Thein also was reflective that warm sunny morning as he examined the small works of nature that surrounded Jack and him.

"Buddha taught that plants and animals have as much right to live as does any human. They might have been human in a past life or on their way to being a human in their next life. And we can learn so much from them. This budding flower symbolizes the cycle of life.

"Here, behold this caterpillar as he crawls along. Do you know what the caterpillar symbolizes better than any other creature?"

"Transformation," Jack said. "The ability to change dramatically. The ability to become a beautiful butterfly."

As if he were troubled by a new thought, Thein abruptly changed the subject.

"I deserve blame for becoming a crooked psychiatrist. But there were bad influences in my life. My father was a military officer who reported directly to the dictator of Burma. Dad carried out sinister, cruel acts that helped keep Ne Win in power. Maunt Saw was called the Fixer. In secrecy he killed people for Ne Win. He was so crafty that rarely were people able to determine what happened to their family and friends. Dad was the worst possible role model.

"The corruption that was ingrained in Burma helped me rationalize that it was morally acceptable to solicit and accept bribes. That is the way medicine was practiced. I deeply regret that I brought my bribery mind-set to America."

"The change in you is profound," Jack said. "Are you really the psychiatrist that Joan and I sued for wrongful death?"

The man from Burma said, "The answer is yes and no. I am now a mixture of the young idealistic, medical student and the corrupt, evil, money-grubbing, disease-mongering doctor who caused your son's death. But I know who I want to be for the rest of my life. I want to be as much like the original Buddha as possible. I want to help the mentally ill—really help them, not just pretend to."

Joan had come out of the cabin in time to hear what Thein had just said. He stood up when he saw her. She hugged him and then immediately regretted it. What was happening to her? This was the man who had caused her son to complete suicide.

Jack stood and shook Thein's hand. Then he wondered if he should have. Better get a grip on himself.

Later the same day, Joan and Jack locked Thein in his bedroom while he was napping. They did not bind his hands or feet.

The couple stood under an incense cedar that reached 120 feet into the clear blue sky.

"Jack, I apologize for hugging the man who took Barry from us. I just felt he is trying to revive what good there might be in him."

"There's no need to apologize. I shook his hand for the same reason. Are you like me? Wondering if he's really changing? Is this a true change of character or is he manipulating us, trying to get us to let our guard down?"

Joan said, "I think he's being truthful. But let's see what the next few weeks bring."

Chapter 71

Do Not Call Me Doctor.

I will suggest that you should study upon yourselves the effects of the most valuable remedies. I well believe that you will never know fully the action of certain remedies, if you have not ascertained on your own person, what effect they produce on the brain, the eye, the ear, the nerves, the muscles, and the principal viscera.

—Charlés-Edouard Brown-Séquard
(nineteenth-century neurologist)

Parts of the San Bernardino mountains, at higher elevations, receive as much as forty inches of precipitation a year. This contrasts with the arid valleys that receive an average of ten inches of rainfall. The differences in climate and plant and animal life between the desert floor and the mountain tops are so dramatic that ecologists call the upper regions a sky island.

At nine thousand feet elevation, where Percy's cabin was situated, it was much cooler, and the air was much cleaner than in Riverside, lifting the spirits of Jack, Joan, and David. The natural beauty of San Gorgonio Peak, especially the rock outcrops, big trees, wild flowers, and pollinators added to the sense of well-being that they were enjoying. Goodwill was growing between Jack and Joan on the one hand and Thein on the other.

All three had come to feel at home in this mountain hideout. They were sitting in the clearing and watching four mule deer work their way along the edge of the forest.

The Vincents were wondering if Thein had changed. Or was he still the crafty psychiatrist, and was trying to deceive them?

As if he read their minds, Thein said, "You are wondering if you can trust me. Let me say that your team has changed me. You have ruined my health, and what you did is neither legal nor honorable. But it is understandable. You felt you could not get justice in any other way. The state's medicolegal systems are rigged in favor of the pharmaceutical industry. Whoever has the most money makes the rules. And the pharmaceutical industry is awash in money. Through various crafty means, companies like Alphatron have bought off the elected and regulatory officials who can either help or harm its business. So you did what you felt you had to."

Jack said, "You can't begin to know how much we hated you. And now you're stirring up a lot of conflicting feelings in us both."

"Do you understand the Buddhist concept of karma?" David asked.

Joan said, "Not as well as Buddhists understand it. But to me, karma is the reward or the punishment that one receives based on the sum total of all the good and bad things that a person has done in this life and all his or her past lives."

David said, "That is a good enough definition. I always admired the original Buddha because he founded his philosophy on reducing suffering. And he said that if one worked to reduce suffering, he would enjoy good karma.

"That is what I now want to do. I want to reduce suffering. I want to make merit and improve my karma score. I can do those things only if I improve the lives of others. You may be shocked to hear me say this. But I am glad that your group overmedicated me. You shattered my health but taught me what is important in life."

Joan asked, "Do you think all psychiatrists should have to take psychotropic medications before being licensed to prescribe them?"

"Absolutely. Only by consuming these so-called medications can one truly understand what they do to a person. If all psychiatry students were required to take psychotropic drugs, only one or two percent of the drugs would ever be prescribed again. They are that terrifying."

Jack said, "Joan, I didn't realize that we were conducting cutting-edge, medical research."

All three laughed.

David said, "When I say medical students should have to take these drugs, I am not blessing your barbaric methods. There would have to be safeguards to protect the students. No more than two drugs at a time. And two drugs would be allowed only so that the students could experience adverse drug interactions. Monitoring vital signs would be necessary. But yes, all doctors should have to take the drugs they prescribe, even doctors in fields other than psychiatry."

Jack said, "When the cops apprehend us, as I'm sure they will, you'll be in a position to testify for or against us. What do you plan to do?"

"I will recommend no punishment. You gave me a dose of my own medicine. It was Buddha's way of telling me to be a good doctor. To persuade you that I am a changed man, I will tell you things you can use against me. I will give you power to get me jailed if you choose."

Joan looked at Jack who was staring at Thein.

The man from Burma said, "Please never again call me Dr. Thein. I did not earn the title of doctor of medicine. The Burma Socialist Programme Party required me to spend a minimum of four years in a medically underserved part of Burma. In fact, I did not spend a minute in such a place. I lied to California's medical accreditation authorities. I also did not do a residency in Mandalay. And in the United States, I was illegally given advance questions for the third part of the medical licensing exam."

Jack asked, "How did you get past all those requirements of Burma, of the United States medical licensing officials, and the State of California?"

Thein said, "You will not believe me when I tell you."

Joan said, "You must have had help in fooling all those authorities."

"I did," Thein said. "You will think I am delusional when I tell you how the deception was accomplished."

Jack said, "We're listening."

"My backers and I gamed the medical accreditation system in several ways. Who was crafty enough to accomplish this? It was none other than the Central Intelligence Agency, your CIA."

Jack said, "Bull."

Joan said, "I don't believe it."

"I am not lying. The spy agency created false documents to make me look far more educated and experienced than I was. The most recent act was that of the CIA bribing the California Medical Board to give me in advance the questions on the medical licensing exam."

Jack stood up. "Why would the CIA deceive medical education authorities for you?"

"To get information from my father. The CIA was worried that Burma's dictator was getting too cozy with Communist China and North Korea. My father was very close to dictator Ne Win, having killed many people for him. Father knew secrets, and was in a position to receive even more information that could affect America's security."

Jack said, "How did the CIA persuade your father to spy for the agency?"

"My father, Maunt Saw, in the 1950s attended Harvard Law School. He stayed in touch with a former classmate, Lester Jordan. So years later, on my behalf, Saw contacted Mr. Jordan and asked for help in bypassing educational requirements for me so that I could become a psychiatrist in America. His friend turned out to be working for the CIA, and the agency was worried about what Ne Win might be up to regarding China and North Korea. Father and his friend negotiated a deal that helped me land a medical residency at UCLA Medical School and eventually a position of psychiatry at the Riverside County Mental Health Center. I said you would not believe me."

Jack said, "You said you were going to give us something that we could use against you. The cops will never believe me if I say the CIA bribed officials so you could become a psychiatrist in California. Are you jerking us around?"

"I am being honest. I want to help you understand why bad things happened to Barry, Randy, and Bertrand. This is part of my effort to make amends before I die. I am not a doctor, and I do not want anyone to call me Dr. Thein."

"What should we call you?" Joan asked.

"Call me either Maunt Thein, which was my name in Burma, or David Thein, which is my name in America. Either name is legitimate. I do not need a title or honorific, but if you feel the need, you can call me Maung Maunt Thein or Maung David Thein. Maung means 'little brother.' Since you are older than me, I would be your little brother."

Jack said, "I can't call you Little Brother after what you did to Barry."

"I understand."

Jack said, "But I do appreciate your telling us that you are not a doctor. And that you deceived educational and medical authorities. That takes courage."

"Two days ago you asked if I was the old corrupt person or a new honest person, and I said I was a mix of the two. That is true, but I hope I am becoming a new person—a Buddhist. I may not live as Maunt Thein much longer so I am trying to make merit and accumulate good karma. The best way to do that is to help the Serious Seven whose loved ones I harmed because of my greed and hard heart."

Joan said, "The best way you can help us is to reveal dishonest things done by the pharmaceutical and psychiatric industries."

David said, "I will expose all the crooked dealings that I took part in or that I have learned about. But I must first warn Laura Nielsen that I will be making disclosures that could implicate her in illegal activities. I will try to get her to join me in exposing corruption because she can strengthen our case and maybe gain legal impunity for herself. She is a good and decent person who was corrupted by

Alphatron Pharmaceuticals. The company took a naive cheerleader and turned her into a crooked drug dealer.

"I must warn Laura of the legal investigations that will come. Then I will provide you details about the corrupt practices that I encountered in the marketing of so-called medications."

The next afternoon, Jack, Joan, and David again were sitting on the ground in the forest opening in front of Percy's cabin. Jeffrey pines surrounded, shaded, and helped hide the cabin, but the clearing was a tiny world with a character all its own. Sunlight made the difference. The dark forest was home to wood rats, tree voles, and the spotted owl. The sunny clearing was where wild flowers and pollinators flourished. And the edge between the forest and the clearing was favored by mule deer and mountain quail.

Sitting on the ground had become a ritual for the trio, a way of feeling close to nature. No floor or chair separated them from the earth. They felt the coolness or the warmth of the earth through their trousers and on their skin. They sat cross-legged like the Buddha, mindful of the nearly pristine surroundings.

Thein said, "Alphatron and other pharmaceutical companies have an unfair share of America's wealth. One must understand this to comprehend what led to the deaths of Barry, Bertrand, and Randy.

"Drugmakers use their riches to corrupt everyone they deal with. They corrupt not only doctors but regulators like the United States Food and Drug Administration and the California Medical Board. They corrupt the clinical trials whereby new drugs are approved.

"They corrupt the medical journals. Editors accept articles they know are ghost written and which misrepresent medications as safe and effective. A scientific journal can be damaged financially if a pharmaceutical company withholds funding for advertising. Full-page, glossy advertisements paid for by opulent corporations are a major source of revenue for technical journals. Realizing this, the Alphatrons of the world dictate the content of the technical reports that are published.

"Pharmaceutical companies bribe university researchers to falsify their findings. And the professors, especially the heads of psychiatry departments, have become pitchmen for the drugmakers. These key opinion leaders, as they are called, are so influential that whatever they say at symposia quickly skews the prescribing of hundreds of psychiatrists.

"Suicide and homicide rates will remain high until pharmaceutical companies are somehow made to stop lying about their drugs. Fines levied against the drugmakers are ineffective deterrents because the companies are so wealthy. The only way to stop the illegal marketing is to put the top executives in prison when they make false claims and misbrand their products."

Jack asked, "Would you join with the Serious Seven to bring reform to the pharmaceutical industry and the psychiatry industry?"

"Yes. I have stories to tell."

Chapter 72

The Transformation

I don't know what will happen now. We've got some difficult days ahead. But it really doesn't matter with me now, because I've been to the mountaintop.

—Martin Luther King, Jr.
Said the evening before he was assassinated in April 1968

Detective Keith Connors assembled a team of both city and county police. They divided into Units A and B so they could simultaneously search the Prescott and the Vincent homes. Sergeant Oliver Ryan was in charge of Unit A while Connors led Unit B.

Thomas was at home, and he allowed the Unit A cops to search his house, the garage, and the grounds. They found nothing incriminating.

At the Vincent home, Joan was preparing to drive to the trailhead to pick up Jack after his five days of both guarding Thein and nursing him back to health. To get her car keys, she went to the desk that she and Jack shared. She took a moment to tidy up the clutter on the desk. What's this? The cartoon strip made her think of Barry. But the sketches were in Jack's hand. She was amused, then frightened. The cartoon showed three men kidnapping a fourth man in violent fashion. My god, this equaled a signed confession. She would take the cartoon with her and stick it in Jack's face while scolding him for being so stupid. And to think that he was the one who lectured against keeping records that could be used against the Seven.

As Joan turned from the desk, her gaze took in the scene in the front yard. A cop car pulled into her driveway, boxing in her Honda, while a second black-and-white pulled up to the curb. She tore the cartoon in half, stuck both halves into her mouth, chewed vigorously, and swallowed hard. Half went down and half remained in her mouth. The first cops were already in the front room. She swallowed again, and managed to not vomit.

Detective Connors showed Joan the search warrant.

"Are you Mrs. Vincent?"

Joan nodded.

"Is anyone else here at your home today?"

She shook her head.

The detective asked, "What's wrong? Are you sick?"

She shook her head.

"You don't look well. Can't you speak?"

Joan said, "No… I mean yes. I can… speak."

She swallowed hard while the detective stared at her. She swallowed again.

"Where's your husband?"

"I'm not sure. He said he was going to run some errands."

Detective Connors said, "How many cars do you and your husband own?"

"Two."

"Then your husband must be running his errands on foot because there are two cars in the driveway."

Joan said, "Oh, maybe he's just walking in the neighborhood."

"But you said he's running errands."

"I don't really know where he is. I wasn't paying much attention when he left. As he went out the door he yelled that he'd be out for a while. I assumed he was running errands. Maybe he's walking the dogs."

"How many dogs do you own?"

"Two"

"There are two dogs in the front yard."

THE TRANSFORMATION

"I guess he's not walking the dogs."

Joan prayed that Jack had not drawn any more cartoons. If he hadn't, they would survive this search for evidence. As the search went on, she could see that Detective Connors was growing frustrated.

"Mrs. Vincent, do you know anything about the disappearance of Dr. David Thein, the psychiatrist that your husband and you sued for the wrongful death of your son?"

"Sorry. I can't help you."

Finally each of Connors' lieutenants reported to him, and he ordered the squad to return to the county police station. The cops left although not as dramatically as they had arrived. The Vincents' belongings were piled wherever drawers had been dumped out and wherever clothes had been snatched from the closets.

Joan fought her instinct to panic. She sat down and breathed slowly. She suspected that some cops might have stayed behind to observe her next move. She waited then went outdoors and walked around the neighborhood. She came back into the house and waited some more.

Finally, Joan went to the woodpile, got her disposable phone, and went up by the garden pond to place her call to Jack.

"This is Jack."

"Jack, something's come up. Where are you?"

"On the trail. Almost to where we meet."

"Stop walking while we sort this out."

"Sort what out?"

"The cops just left. They looked through all our possessions and papers, even our photo albums. They took our desktop computer and my smart phone. Thank God that they didn't find this phone. I'm afraid to come get you. They might follow me. Can you go back to the cabin and stay there until we can figure out what to do?"

"Sure. That's the best thing to do for the moment. Nick relieved me so he's at the cabin. I'll tell him what's happened. Call Thomas. The cops might have already searched his place. But call and warn him just in case."

"I'll call his throwaway phone."

"I'm guessing the cops didn't find anything at our place," Jack said.

"The cops seemed frustrated so I don't think they found anything. But there was an army of them. We're in trouble. I don't see any way out."

"It might be time for Thomas or me to ask Ray to arrange for the Seven to surrender to the cops. But we would need the consent of the full team. If any one of us gives up, all of us will be arrested. I'll go back to the cabin, and we'll talk later."

Joan said, "Don't let Nick make matters worse."

As Jack approached the cabin, he tried to regain his composure, taking a moment to drink in the serenity of the alpine setting. But Joan had delivered bad news that even the mountain could not compensate for.

Jack knocked on the cabin door. Nick looked out the window and opened the door.

"Thein's still asleep."

"Good. Let's go outside to make sure he doesn't hear us talking."

As soon as they were outside, Nick asked, "Why did you come back?"

"Bad news but nothing that we haven't expected all along. Joan called me. An army of cops searched our house. Joan and I are prime suspects in Thein's disappearance, and now the cops are bearing down on us."

Nick said, "I'm asking as a friend, Jack. Are we better off with Thein claiming he'll take our side? Or would we be better off if he was dead and buried?"

"His health has improved. The authorities won't know how near death we pushed him. And he shows remorse for what he did to Bertrand and Barry. I think he'd be a friendly witness, and that's worth a lot."

"Fair enough. I'll take your lead. What do we do?"

"First, we need to inform the rest of our team that the cops have moved into a full-court press. So you should call Ted right away."

"I'll do that."

"Then we need to find out what the team wants to do. I think I'll recommend that we have Raymond Ferris arrange for us to turn ourselves in."

Nick said, "I still think we did the right thing to overmedicate Thein."

"I do too. Maybe we can spin any court trials in our favor. We might be able to use the publicity against the psychopharmaceutical industry."

Nick said, "Let's not panic. I was fixing breakfast. Let's eat before we make our phone calls."

"Good idea. Breakfast would calm me down. I got rattled when Joan called, and I'm still shook up."

"We'll even give Thein a few pancakes," Nick said. "Treat him nice so he'll testify for us."

They walked back to the cabin and went inside. Nick began mixing pancake batter.

Jack opened the bedroom door.

"Come on out, David. Breakfast time. Flapjacks are on the menu."

No answer.

Jack said, "Second call for breakfast."

No answer.

Jack knocked on the bedroom doorjamb and looked in. Thein was sitting on the edge of the bed. He rose and staggered toward Jack and the open doorway. He wobbled and bumped into the doorjamb. With jerky steps, he headed for the cabin's door to the outside.

Jack opened the door and helped his patient off the tiny porch. Thein was having trouble weaving in and out among the boulders that separated the cabin from the rest of the world. He said nothing, staring straight ahead.

Nick said, "What's wrong?"

"Some kind of movement disorder. I'm going to help him get to the clearing where he can move around."

Jack held Thein by one arm and guided him to the meadow, where he then walked without assistance.

Nick followed the pair to the forest opening. He stood next to Jack, and the two of them gave Thein room to stagger about.

Nick said, "Involuntary movement disorder, I guess."

"Yeah, he has to keep moving. Keeps repeating the same movements."

"God, his body is twisting. Does he know he's screwed up?"

Jack said, "Some dyskinesia victims recognize what's happening, but others don't because of the psychosis component."

Jack stopped Thein by stepping in front of him. Nick stood nearby, staring at the man he still blamed for the death of his grandfather.

Jack said, "David, how are you feeling?"

The man said, "David Thein has died. When he will be reborn and in what form is not for me to know."

"Do you know me?"

"You are Jack Vincent, and your friend over there is Nick Garrett."

"Where are we?"

The man's face twisted, and his tongue darted in and out of his mouth like he was catching flies. His jaw continually moved from side-to-side of its own accord.

"We are in the San Bernardino Mountains in Southern California, outside of Percy Prescott's cabin where you held Thein captive."

Jack said, "Tell me about yourself."

"I teach The Middle Way."

"What is The Middle Way?"

"The Middle Way lies between the extremes of hedonism and asceticism. Hedonism is greed and endless cravings like sexual promiscuity and gluttony. Hedonism keeps one immersed in suffering, which is ingrained in the endless cycle of birth, death, and rebirth. I tried asceticism as a way to avoid hedonism but it deprived me of too much and made mindfulness too difficult. It failed me."

Jack asked, "How did asceticism fail to counteract hedonism?"

THE TRANSFORMATION

"There was no clear end to my efforts to deprive myself of worldly things. I ate only one leaf or one nut each day. I got weak and almost drown while bathing in a river."

"How did you recover?"

"Friends helped me to the shore. I lay there and would have died but for a village girl who brought me rice pudding. It was then that I decided there must be a better way for people to live."

Nick asked, "What did you do?"

"I sat under a Bodhi tree. I vowed I would sit there until I awoke as to how people can escape suffering. After forty-nine days I understood that the Middle Way is the best path to take."

"Path to where?" Nick asked.

"Nirvana. Awakening. Enlightenment. Freedom from craving. It is endless craving that causes suffering. When I awakened with this knowledge, I was in Nirvana."

Nick said, "This is too much for me to swallow, David Thein, alias Dr. Thein, alias Maunt Thein."

The strange man said, "Those are all names for the same individual. He died early this morning while it was still dark."

Nick said. "Don't play games. If you're not Thein, who are you?"

"Siddhārtha Gautama."

Nick turned to Jack. "What's he saying? Who does he think he is?"

"Get used to it, Nick. Come to grips with polypharmacy's complicated version of reincarnation. Thein is no more. He's been reborn as the ancient Buddha but with a modern-day psychomotor disorder."

The End

Acknowledgments

Some very bright people lent me their time and talents to make *The Mind Doctor* a good story. Don Hall Rodgers designed the distinctive front cover and provided me with a wealth of technical information on medical and legal issues. Gene Obersinner made the tale more accurate by reviewing it from a psychological standpoint; any errors are due to my own misunderstanding. In reviewing early drafts, Patrick Harrison showed me the value of adhering to proven story-telling conventions. Reviews by Mike Moran and Dana Vion addressed theme, organization, readability, geography, and more.

I thank Alexandria Mongera, Page's Publication Coordinator, for so effectively ushering this book into being. I appreciate also the Page editors and artists. I am indebted to Caroline Morse, Tom Morse, and Wilda Downing for providing much-needed inspiration and moral support.

My wife, Jennifer, and our son, Monty, contributed greatly to *The Mind Doctor* by encouraging me and keeping me mindful that the story would be an effective way to warn vulnerable citizens of the many perils of polypharmacy.

About the Author

Photographed by Chris Mihulka

For twenty-eight years, John Gill served as an environmental regulator for a series of federal agencies, including the Federal Energy Regulatory Commission, the Nuclear Regulatory Commission, the Army Corps of Engineers, and the US Air Force.

John led teams of biologists, botanists, hydrologists, geologists, and civil engineers as they prepared environmental impact statements for the proposed construction and operation of projects such as dams, nuclear power plants, and ballistic missile bases.

CPSIA information can be obtained
at www.ICGtesting.com
Printed in the USA
FSHW010243240819
61272FS